CONSTRAINT
OF
EMPIRE

Contributions in Comparative Colonial Studies
Series Editor, Robin W. Winks

Empires in Collision: Anglo-Burmese Relations in the Mid-Nineteenth Century
Oliver B. Pollak

Social Engineering in the Philippines: The Aims, Execution, and Impact of American Colonial Policy, 1900–1913
Glenn Anthony May

The Politics of Dependency: Urban Reform in Istanbul
Stephen T. Rosenthal

Rhodes, the Tswana, and the British: Colonialism, Collaboration, and Conflict in the Bechuanaland Protectorate, 1885–1889
Paul Maylam

Between Black and White: Race, Politics, and the Free Coloreds in Jamaica, 1792–1865
Gad J. Heuman

British Rule in Malaya: The Malayan Civil Service and Its Predecessors, 1867–1942
Robert Heussler

Economic Control and Colonial Development: Crown Colony Financial Management in the Age of Joseph Chamberlain
Richard M. Kesner

CONSTRAINT OF EMPIRE

The United States and Caribbean Interventions

Whitney T. Perkins

Contributions in Comparative Colonial Studies, Number 8

G
P

Greenwood Press
Westport, Connecticut

Library of Congress Cataloging in Publication Data

Perkins, Whitney T
    Constraint of empire.

    (Contributions in comparative colonial studies;
no. 8 ISSN 0163-3813)
    Bibliography: p.
    Includes index.
    1. Caribbean area—Foreign relations—United
States. 2. United States—Foreign relations—
Caribbean area. 3. Intervention (International
law) I. Title. II. Series.
F2178.U6P47   327.730729   80-27269
ISBN 0-313-22266-5 (lib. bdg.)

Library of Congress Catalog Card Number: 80-27269
ISBN: 0-313-22266-5
ISSN: 0163-3813

First published in 1981

Greenwood Press
A division of Congressional Information Service, Inc.
88 Post Road West
Westport, Connecticut 06881

Printed in the United States of America

10 9 8 7 6 5 4 3 2 1

CONTENTS

Part IV Consequences and Return Engagements

SERIES FOREWORD

Too often "colonial studies" have failed to include the United States as a colonial power, and as a result, the literature on American colonial and imperial history generally lacks a comparative dimension. American historians often chose to refer to "American expansionism," a largely unexamined term, either to suggest that there was no imperial phase in American history or that American imperialism differed from that of other nations so greatly as to require a special vocabulary. Then, in the 1960s, a group of young historians became all too conscious of the idea of an American imperialism, and a new literature, usually called "revisionist" or "the New Left" because of its use of Marxist concepts and terminology, began to grow. In the 1970s yet another phase was reached in the American debate, when scholars no longer felt compelled to fight out the battle over an American imperialism in pro- or anti-Marxist terms. In the 1980s this non-Marxist approach, as it may most accurately be called, began to play a major rôle in the shaping of American historiography.

The American empire was largely informal, without annexation, and traditionally it was to be found primarily in Latin America. The dominant voice in the field of United States-Caribbean relations has been that of Dana G. Munro, though other scholars have made major contributions as well: Gellman, Macaulay, Millett, Tulchin, Bryce Wood. The most recent student of the subject is Whitney T. Perkins, whose present book comprises, in effect, a companion volume to his earlier work, *Denial of Empire: The United States and Its Dependencies*, published in 1962. That volume was an ambitious study of American policy toward formal empire from the Northwest Territory to Okinawa. While readily admitting (when it was still unfashionable to do so) that there was an American empire, Perkins was resolutely non-Marxist in his analysis. Emphasizing the American "mystique of freedom," Professor Perkins explored the dilemma of a democratic people ruling another people undemocratically. His major contribution was interpretive, in a clear-headed point of view toward material already much discussed in the context of a received interpretation so long unexamined as to embody the very notion of a "conventional wisdom." In exploring his new view, Professor Perkins examined in succession Alaska, Hawaii, Puerto Rico, the Virgin Islands, the Philippines, and the lesser Pacific Islands that came formally into American hands.

Whitney Perkins has now carried his argument and his methods into the informal empire. Again his work is largely interpretive, though buttressed by a careful presentation and reassessment of the facts. He concludes that the United States intervened in the Caribbean primarily for idealistic reasons expressed most closely in political terms. Just as formal empire posed contradictions, so too did informal empire, and even if one could assume intelligent administration—and one could not always make such an assumption—intervention was bound to fail. This was so for two major reasons: Americans of many political persuasions found the idea of empire at base repugnant to their perceptions of American ideals, and the United States invariably was drawn so closely into the politics of the countries where the interventions occurred as to lack the free hand and at times even the dominant rôle necessary to an effective imperialism. Thus Perkins draws upon the idea of "the collaborator" as developed by British and other scholars to account for the dynamics of a constrained empire. In this sense his work is both inherently and explicitly comparative, and it is a welcome addition to this series in Comparative Colonial Studies.

INTRODUCTION

This book traces the policies and actions of the United States in relation to four countries of the Caribbean region—Cuba, Nicaragua, the Dominican Republic, and Haiti. These are the countries (apart from Puerto Rico) into which the United States intruded most deeply in trying to implant political practices that would be compatible with its interests and values. The experiences in these areas therefore illuminate the goals, processes, and limitations of American imperialism. The steps and stages are detailed through which the United States entered into each, exerted control (without formal political subordination), and responded to the consequences of its role, eventually being induced to withdraw and to renounce further imposition (although not, it turned out, always with finality).

What most clearly distinguished the approach and experience of the United States from those of other Western imperialists was the central role in its political culture of a commitment to self-government which it considered both exceptional and exemplary. Possessing dominant power and professing liberal values, the United States had to attempt to reconcile a capacity to control with a commitment to liberate. The avowed objective was not political subordination but to promote practices and institutions of self-government that would remove both impetus and opportunity for continuing intervention. This objective gave credence to the idea that intervention would be liberating, but such a claim could not be maintained against opposition which could credibly represent nationalism. Because of its liberal political values, the United States was particularly affected by the political incapacity that makes alien rule unstable. Despite military and economic preponderance, it could not impose compliant political behavior. American policy could succeed only by adaptation to indigenous political response.

An attempt by a dominant power to promote genuine self-government is bound to strain credulity, whether simply because of cynical awareness of the potency of self-interest or because its intrinsic difficulty makes success unlikely. It is a paradox of power that it can rarely muster the strength to relieve itself of burdens of commitment and dilemmas of choice. The significance of the American commitment to self-government is not negated, however, by the inconsistency, insufficiency, or inappropriateness of the methods used and the admixture of other motivations that sometimes prevailed, nor by the paucity of favorable results.

A similar phenomenon, denial of empire, the attempt to make plausible a liberating purpose, was manifest in the government by the United States of formally dependent populations, the subject of an earlier study. (Whitney T. Perkins, *Denial of Empire: The United States and its Dependencies,* Leiden, 1962). Although denial did not change the evident reality of domination, it was not just sham and hypocrisy. It facilitated the attainment of self-government by people of different cultures who came under American sovereignty, particularly those of the Philippines and Puerto Rico.

The bulk of this work deals with epiphenomena in narrative fashion rather than being explicitly shaped by a particular methodological or conceptual approach or entering directly into issues of definition and fundamental explanation. There is, however, a rationale for sequential detail. This derives from a perspective on imperialism which emphasizes its basis in and its implications for politics and a perspective on the role of politics which gives central significance to events, perceptions, and responses rather than stressing postulations of structure.

To be sure, dependency has shaped political structures within and including these countries. Both the immensity of United States power and wealth and the obscurity and penetrability of the smaller countries left them open to the disintegrative effects of self-interested effluvia from the metropole. The corrupting agents of economic interests, oblivious or contemptuous of residues or revivals of indigenous cultural integrity, found clients or *compradores* who would deny and repress, even as they subtly felt and feared, the possibility of effective nationalism.

But explanatory efforts which are content to expound the consequences of structure or economic interest neglect the realm of contingency and adaptation in which politics functions. To attribute that which is produced by political interaction to a systemic quality, whether within the dominant state or in economic relationships, is to impute cause to condition, with politics little more than an ephemeral fizz in a rigid conceptual container. Such an approach tends to foreclose inquiry into process, failing to take into account the vitality and fallibility with which, through politics, possibilities are explored and the understandings and adaptations which provide settings for further choice and change are worked out. Where there is great discrepancy in power, there is latitude in the intensity and means of its exercise and in the purposes for which it is used. Outcomes are not produced by structure; there is scope for the indeterminacy which makes politics possible and necessary, and enables it, within limits, to make a difference.

Politics refers to processes of decision-making regarding public policy that engage a variety of actors and interests under conditions of conflict and uncertainty and which may have significant consequences. When authority and institutions are not well established, uncertainty relates not only to allocations of benefits but to the identities and capacities of actors and the methods of interaction. When conditions and events give rise to conflicts of value and are recalcitrant to the capacities and understandings of institutions and decision makers, outcomes are products neither of choice nor of chance but of the politics which conjoins and complicates them.

In a continuing relationship between separate societies, the political systems through which authority and society respond one to the other are themselves interlinked through decision processes which are activated by issues between them. The intensity and scope as well as the modes of intersocietal politics depend on the relative power of the participants and upon the nature of the issues which must be resolved. International politics, unless the actors are abstractly postulated as fixed, monolithic entities, is the product both of horizontal (between states) and vertical (within states) interaction and adaptation. Insofar as responses on the horizontal plane are governed by concern for "balance of power," pressures for adaptation flow back "around the corner" into the vertical political systems of the participants, reducing tolerance for conflict and compromise in domestic politics. On the other hand, when there is great discrepancy of power between states, particularly in political capacity, norms and practices which are supposed to be reserved to domestic politics are likely to encroach upon the horizontal plane as intervention and imperialism. Unless a dominant state extirpates a weaker and penetrated entity as a functioning society, politics is not extinguished in their relationship. Rather, it flows between domestic and international settings, not just resolving or reshaping particular issues but giving definition to the identities and interests of the participants.

Between societies which have such disparity in power that one may dominate the other, the relationship is inherently imperialist—at the very least in that policies which may mitigate domination have to originate in and be carried out by the stronger state. But in such a relationship there does not cease to be interplay and intermeshing of political systems. Several variables contribute to the character of politics within an inherently—or overtly—imperialist relationship, creating a broad range of interactive modes within which influence may take several different forms. Imbalance of military and economic power may be offset by differing intensities of motivation. Access and susceptibility may not correspond to large and tangible dimensions of power. Capacity and motivation are brought to bear on different issues in different ways. Imposition, insistence, prevention, or co-option on the part of the strong meet variously with obstruction, harassment, denial, or indifference on the part of the weak. The balance of politics may not coincide with the formal allocation of authority. A society which has been deprived of sovereignty may nevertheless retain an important and varied capacity for political assertion. A state which is formally independent may on the other hand be almost entirely lacking in such capacity.

The most impressive intellectual buttressing for an approach to modern imperialism with prime concern for politics is to be found in the works of Ronald E. Robinson and John A. Gallagher [conveniently summarized and discussed in

William Roger Louis, ed., *The Robinson and Gallagher Controversy* (New York, 1976)]. Their particular focus is on the means through which alien power gains the collaborative response that is necessary for effective domination. Impetus and capacity for expansion of power and control derive both from the politics of a metropole and from competitive striving among modernizing states. A critical variable in making control effective is the "excentric" component of "collaboration, noncollaboration, mediation, and resistance" which represents linkage with "indigenous social politics." In a fundamental historical process of adaptation, collaboration gives rise to assertive nationalism.

Extending and applying their approach, one may conceive of the principal divisions of the world of politics as separate and different (although sometimes overlapping) systems, each representing some degree of capacity for authoritative response to issues which give rise to contending interests. By far the most prominent custodians of such capacity are states. Although their domains are lightly overlaid by transnational politics and may be somewhat configured by localized capacities, states are uniquely distinctive. It is their defining function to maintain coherence within a large and complex society while also conducting external relationships. Successful performance of these simultaneous roles is the essential source of the autonomy and authority which set the state apart. The recurring threat that coherence may be lost, as response to demands from one setting prevents continuing adaptation to the other, is countered by a self-strengthening quality of authority that attaches to the state as state until or unless incapacity destroys authority itself.

Political capacity (that is, stability and competence in fulfilling functions of government) is unevenly distributed. Culture and history did much to make it so, and imperialism was both a consequence and a furtherance of this unevenness. Societies exposed to pervasive economic and cultural influences from the modernizing world outside proved incapable of political adaptation. In some places, authority collapsed. Imperialism could take charge of external linkage, but it could not provide authority after traditional institutions had been overwhelmed by new demands. A symbiotic, self-strengthening relationship between authority and political capacity depends on the effectiveness and representative character of political institutions.

In a longer perspective, however, the cultural and economic changes which accompanied imperialism, together with the challenge of alien rule, aroused political assertion and thus helped to provide the legitimacy and effectiveness deriving from participation upon which authority in a modern society is based. A further consequence of political assertion in a dominated society was feedback to the politics which sustained imperialism, touching the sensitive but usually shielded issue of legitimacy in the metropole. Thus, by lowering sluice gates between domestic and international politics, imperialism exposed authority to necessities and vagaries of politics in ways not ordinarily experienced. Because imperialism represented a distribution of political power that did not correspond to the distribution of societal interests but which reflected a transient imbalance of political capacity, it was unstable and of relatively brief duration.

Imperialism is politically inefficient in that it is not subject to the discipline either of institutionalization or of a stable system of competing interests. In relationship to another society that is unable to resist imposition, a government is constrained or guided neither by direct demands which emanate from important sectors of its own society nor by confrontation with a hostile power. Nor is it closely responsive to interests within the weaker society. There is little to prevent issues and interests that pertain to this particular relationship from being subsumed under broader concerns which derive from domestic or international politics. The most effective influences are likely not to be rooted in the interests of either society. Private interests have considerable opportunity to assert themselves, as do bureaucracies. Practices and commitments may, therefore, develop which are inappropriate to the real needs of either side and which do nothing to improve the management of common interests. Improvement of political capacity in the dominated society can alleviate the random and sometimes disruptive effects of spillover and feedback from politics that is not contained and guided by the institutionalized expression of societal interests.

In a basic sense improvement of political capacity is not only a probable consequence of imperialism but represents its intrinsic function. By one means or another, a dominant state tries to provide means of linkage to and within the incapacitous society. In one way or another, imperialism stimulates interests that require response and activates processes of response which represent political capacity. Extraneous imposition gives ground in some fashion to a process of adaptation that takes account of interests within the society that has been imposed upon. The role of the state as arbiter of politics emerges.

This is not to suggest that the issue which did so much to induce imperialism—a distribution of political capacity which did not conform to patterns of activity as they were altered by modernization—has been resolved. It simply demonstrates that the alleviation of this discrepancy through Western imperialism was limited and self-liquidating and has been superseded by other and partial devices which do not directly restrict the functioning of politics on a territorial basis. Whether a stronger supersession, eclipsing or transcending political processes of incremental adaptation, will take place, we do not yet know. That, if it happens, will, as they say, be a different ball game.

The relationship between the United States and the Caribbean countries that are subjects of this study was essentially similar to other manifestations of Western imperialism in that it was more the consequence of contrast in the stability and competence of government than the product of clear design. It was similar also in that control proved to be transitory, eventuating in attempts to escape moral and political dilemmas by formal deference to the presumption of capacity which is represented by the state.

The commitment of the United States to the explicit purpose of promoting virtuous self-government meant that its imperialistic role was never intended to be complete or lasting. Virtual collapse of government in several Caribbean countries coincided with a surge of strength and confidence and a naive sense of mission in the United States. Authority in Cuba became an issue when Spanish control was displaced through war. Requirements of security provided plausible rationale for interventionism. As concern for the costs and risks of political instability increased, a heady mixture of vigor and virtue, self-interest and self-regard, overcame prudence and scruple. Under Taft and Wilson intervention was expanded in a complex sequence of events which these administrations did more to produce than to prevent, but which they did not fully intend or direct.

The dilemmas of interventionism are abundantly illustrated in American Caribbean experience. When the United States undertook to instill political virtue by direct action, it became involved in competitive political maneuvers which it could not control or fully understand and was charged with responsibility for outcomes which it may neither have intended nor desired. Once it had assumed control, it had to look for ways of justifying and tempering its role and eventually of terminating it without handing the country over to dictatorship. When it decided to abstain in the face of repression, it became, in a sense, captive as well as sponsor of a regime which it was not prepared to repudiate or remove from power. Permanent escape from such dilemmas was only possible if these countries should become politically self-sufficient. When they were slow to do so, the United States found only partial shelter behind a reconstituted rule of nonintervention which held that they must be accorded the full formal prerogatives of sovereignty.

This examination of the processes of involvement, imposition, resignation, and limited disengagement should demonstrate that, contrary to current myth, there was never a time when the United States could blithely work its will in countries that it could dominate in military and economic terms. The politics of domination was always complex and frustrating. In part this was because of unrealistic expectations and demands emanating from the political culture of the United States. In part it reflected the expedient adaptation of local figures and forces to a relationship of dependency and irresponsibility. Essentially, however, complexity and frustration characterized the role and function of politics in giving expression to interests and demands which in an imperialistic relationship have no adequate rooting and nourishment in a stable society.

This is terrain which, particularly in recent years, has been well scoured by able scholars. I have drawn heavily on such thorough surveys as those by Dana G. Munro and Bryce Wood, as well as on detailed accounts and analyses relating to individual countries. In addition, I did supplementary research mainly in the Root papers and in Department of State archives. I am acutely aware that others have been more thorough and have developed a deeper comprehension on particular periods and topics. I hope that they will accept the uses I have made of their work as appropriate tribute rather than find it either distorted or exploitive.

What the present work may add to other interpretations lies mainly in a perspective which emphasizes the interaction of American goals and actions with men and issues in the political life of the countries under study. Presumably there is also something to be gained in carrying the story forward within a single frame of reference all the way from early hopeful involvement through the time of formal disengagement and into a period when global confrontation raised the perceived or potential stakes of political contention in Caribbean countries.

Each of the four countries is discussed separately within each of four temporal stages with a view to capturing the continuity of events and responses which in itself constitutes an indispensable component of explanation. There is a brief introduction to each part.

Part I
ESTABLISHING COMMITMENT

INTRODUCTION

The United States became a dominant presence in four Caribbean countries under four different presidents during the two decades following the war with Spain and the occupation of Cuba. Its goals were essentially similar in each country, but the origins and forms of control varied. In Cuba, under William McKinley and Theodore Roosevelt, indigenous government was twice superseded. In Nicaragua, during the William Howard Taft administration, revolution produced a client government which was sustained by marines. In the Dominican Republic, after the breakdown of an attempt, initiated by Roosevelt, to preclude revolution by controlling revenues, the United States Navy took the place of a Dominican government, under the direction of Woodrow Wilson. In Haiti, also under Wilson, disorder precipitated an occupation that swept the constitution aside but left a Haitian president in office.

In no case was the assumption of control a clear act of U.S. policy that eclipsed other goals. It resulted from efforts to resolve or alleviate particular problems by expedient means. Several factors pushed and pulled toward greater involvement, while resisting forces were weak. Under the pressure of events, the belief that surveillance or control by the United States could transform politics overcame scruples and prudence. There had as yet, despite the early Cuban experience, been no telling demonstration of the difficulty either of implanting political capacity or of providing essential order and justice during a prolonged attempt to do so. Complications and contradictions were more likely to accelerate and extend involvement than to lead directly to its reversal. Only gradually did it become evident that control could not be sustained without perpetuating the incapacity and disorder it had been intended to rectify and violating the values it had been expected to promote.

Initial motivations included strategic and economic concerns, but the complexities of involvement set up a dynamic of induced demand and improvised response that tended to supersede broader considerations. It became evident that there was no effective challenge to the strategic and economic superiority of the United States in the region as a whole, while within particular states it was political instability that limited secure access and attracted intermeddling. The belief that improvement of government would serve strategic and economic purposes gave added importance to the task of breaking a cycle of abuse and revolution. Policymakers defined the role of the United States more through day-to-day accommodation in trying to manipulate, grapple with, or evade the often elusive and recalcitrant forces which afforded or obstructed access to particular societies than through formulating and carrying out a consistent plan of action.

The Caribbean ventures of the United States during this period took place within broad parameters set in relation to Cuba. Having gone to war to remove a festering condition of government that offended both strategic and moral sensitivities, the United States renounced annexation while refusing to recognize the Cuban insurgents. The government which it left in place had to concede to the United States a right to assess its adequacy "for the protection of life, property, and individual liberty" and to undertake rectifying intervention. Shortly afterward, Roosevelt's "Corollary" to the Monroe Doctrine extended a similar rationale for intervention to other countries of the region.

It was soon demonstrated that the possibility of intervention acted more to intensify than to moderate political contention. It invited rather than deterred revolution unless it was clear that the government would be supported, but in that case it would not deter an abuse of governmental power, which would stir up revolution. Much as the United States might try to stay out of domestic political games, efforts would be made to induce reaction from it. Or it would find itself deterring some activities and providing shelter to some contenders. Intervention in the Dominican Republic and in Cuba was as much by invitation and contrivance as by the initiative of the United States. Attempts to keep itself politically neutral—by removing customs revenues from the reach of political factions in the Dominican Republic and by sweeping political contenders aside in the "clean intervention" of 1906 in Cuba—brought the United States into more complete control while leaving the dilemma unresolved.

Under Roosevelt and Elihu Root, affirmation of a rationale for intervention was counterbalanced by awareness of costs and risks and a sensitive regard for Latin American reactions. Under Taft and Knox these restraints lost strength, intervention being seen more as an opportunity to promote stable government and less as a burdensome necessity. But a preference for indigenous government remained. The U.S. hoped to give government an interest in stability and the means of maintaining it, not only through economic and military support but also by curbing electoral abuses. "Dollar diplomacy" was not the abdication of public interest to the interests of investors. It was premised, to be sure, on a reciprocal relationship between what dollars could contribute to stability and the economic return which stability might provide through investment and trade. But the administration had other concerns as well—to limit European influence and to keep political involvement within prudent limits. By and large it was the government that took the lead in trying to use dollars in the service of diplomacy. In the resultant mix it became difficult to distinguish between public and private advantage or between indigenous and American interests. But fusion was not complete or permanent as long as there remained, at least incipiently, a capacity for politics in the state which was the object of this activity.

While in Cuba the end of the second occupation left a relationship of limited dependency that did not change much during subsequent administrations, in Nicaragua, the Dominican Republic, and Haiti, under Taft and Wilson, the commitments of the United States were deepened by a complex interplay that resulted in a drastic reduction of political autonomy. That the process of involvement was so prolonged and complex and that it bridged presidencies which differed sharply in avowed policy objectives shows that the American imperialism which it exemplified was more the consequence of interaction than the imposition of a plan. It found support from more than one element in the structure of interests and values which represented American culture and power.

In Nicaragua, during the Taft administration, opposition to what was regarded as a disruptive and disreputable regime led to support for a conservative revolution, which gained power quite unexpectedly and without the political strength to establish its authority. A succession of events, which the State Department neither controlled nor anticipated, led to the dispatch of a contingent of marines in support of a president who sought the protection of a treaty relationship.

In the Dominican Republic Roosevelt and Root had resisted pressures to extend intervention during a governmental breakdown after the takeover of the customshouses and were rewarded by a period of almost unprecedented stability, but the assassination of President Cáceres late in 1911 caused the country to fall apart. During Taft's last year the United States moved toward further intervention. It was averted through the election of a stopgap president who asked for stronger support from the United States and resigned shortly after Wilson took office in Washington.

Woodrow Wilson and his secretary of state, William Jennings Bryan, came into office without previous experience or concern with the countries of the Caribbean. In Cuba, Nicaragua, and the Dominican Republic, they found the United States a major influence in establishing rules and procedures as well as in some of the outcomes of political competition. Anxious to remedy past abuses and lacking the sobriety which experience might have provided, they seemed to believe that solutions lay in the substitution of benevolent activism for what they saw as arbitrary and rapacious interference. While denouncing the use of national interest as a cover for private advantage, they easily persuaded themselves that it was necessary, for security reasons as well as on moral grounds, to act resolutely for the establishment of good government. Despite professions of antiimperialism, there were fewer effective restraints upon American commitment under Wilson than there had been under Roosevelt and Taft.

The use of financial support to sustain the client government of Díaz in Nicaragua, proposed but not consummated under Taft, was urged by Bryan with persistence and ingenuity. In the Dominican Republic and Haiti the Wilson administration moved fitfully toward intervention, caught up in a turbulence that they did not think important to understand. In exasperation Wilson formulated a simplistic plan for imposing an electoral process, but actual control came slowly. It took another year and the overthrow of a president to bring about the occupation of Haiti, and it was more than two years (five years after the assassination of Cáceres) before insistence on reform was followed by actually taking charge in the Dominican Republic.

The expansion of commitments that caused the United States to exercise strong direct control in these countries was thus the result of protracted processes of political interaction that produced the outcomes which they did because of the extreme incapacity of indigenous government to resist imposition and because there was no effective opposition in the United States. Even in its furthest surge, this intervention did not represent planned expansion nor did it signify the evaporation of constraining forces and concerns in the politics and values of the United States. It brought United States policies directly up against the constraints which were intrinsic in a relationship to politics in the dominated societies—the ineffectiveness of collaborators and the indocility of those who represented indigenous values and interests.

1.
CUBA

RENUNCIATION: THE TELLER AMENDMENT

The island of Cuba, so close that its destiny appeared manifest, had been by far the most important object of American interest in the Caribbean area during the nineteenth century. Yet in declaring war against Spain in 1898, the United States committed itself to Cuban independence.

Disavowal of "any disposition or intent to exercise sovereignty, jurisdiction or control" over Cuba "except for the pacification thereof" was the outgrowth of a Senate debate over recognition of the Cuban leadership that was leading the fight for independence from Spain. President McKinley opposed recognition on the ground that it would commit the United States to a particular group without sufficient regard to its competence or domestic support. His influence was probably decisive in blocking the proposed resolution.[1] The Teller Amendment, quoted above, emerged as a compromise. Both McKinley and Elihu Root, who as secretary of war became the dominant figure in policymaking toward Cuba, considered it unduly restrictive, but they did not oppose its basic intent.

The motivation for the Teller Amendment is somewhat obscure. Desire to forestall annexation reflected both fear that Cuba could not be absorbed into the American body politic and a more mundane concern to avoid injury to the rapidly growing beet sugar industry, which was important in Senator Teller's state of Colorado. Yet sentiment opposing the annexation of Cuba also was an expression of deeply ingrained American political values. Teller was in sympathetic communication with Horatio Rubens, an American who had gained the confidence and friendship of the Cuban leaders through service as their counsel, but it does not appear that Rubens's influence was decisive. Teller himself later spoke in favor of putting "a strong hand" on the Cubans to "give them a good government."[2]

By the Treaty of Paris Spain simply relinquished sovereignty over Cuba, leaving the United States free to adopt such measures of government as the Constitution and political system of the United States might permit. Having refused recognition to the Cubans who had taken up arms against Spain, McKinley had no choice but to assume control, but he was slow to recognize the necessity for a clear and firm policy. His annual message in December 1898 made it clear that military occupation would continue "until there is complete tranquility in the island and a stable government inaugurated." "At the earliest moment consistent with safety and assured success," however, "aid and direction" would be given in forming a government which would be "free and independent" as well as "just, benevolent, and humane."[3] A year later, while reaffirming the obligation "to leave the government and control of the island to the people," he dwelt on the "grave responsibility" of the United States "for the future good government of Cuba."

The new Cuba . . . must needs be bound to us by ties of singular intimacy and strength if its enduring welfare is to be assured. Whether those ties shall be organic or conventional, the destinies of Cuba are in some rightful form and manner irrevocably linked with our own, but how and how far is for the future to determine in the ripeness of events. Whatever be the outcome, we must see to it that free Cuba be a reality, not a name, a perfect entity, not a hasty experiment bearing within itself the elements of failure. Our mission . . . is not to be fulfilled by turning adrift any loosely framed commonwealth to face the vicissitudes which too often attend weaker States.[4]

The implicit contradiction between the goal of self-government and the application of American criteria of good government contributed to indecision and drift during the early months of the occupation. The first military governor, General John R. Brooke, may have lacked the energy and the executive ability to carry through a vigorous program of reform and construction, but his tolerance of Cuban performance that fell short of American standards of probity and efficiency reflected also the vagueness of his instructions.[5] There was no representative body of Cubans through which the American authorities could find support or guidance, or from which tangible opposition could arise. A so-called Cuban Assembly, which derived from the revolutionary forces, concerned itself mainly with compensation for veterans and dissolved in discord after the United States made clear its decision to limit payments to a distribution of $3 million from surplus funds already appropriated.

Both in Cuba and in Washington talk of the advantages of annexation and disparagement of Cuban capacities raised widespread doubt that the United States would give effect to the pledge of independence. The two outstanding generals in Cuba, Leonard Wood and James H. Wilson, each of whom was eager to succeed Brooke, wanted the United States to direct its policies toward eventual annexation. Both men thought that the Cubans themselves would seek it. Yet their proposed policies, as described by Theodore Roosevelt, were "utterly different."

Wood believes that we should not promise or give the Cubans independence; that we should govern them justly and equitably, giving them all possible opportunities for civic and military advancement, and that in two or three years they will insist on being part of us. Wilson believes we should now leave the Island establishing a Republican form of government and keeping a coaling station, etc., together with tariff arrangements which would include them with us against outsiders, and he thinks that in a very few years they would drop into our hands of their own accord.[6]

The appointments of Root as secretary of war and of Wood as governor marked the end of the period of drift. Root, looking for "a man who could, in the deepest sense, clean up Cuba," was impressed by Wood's medical training as well as by his character.[7] Yet Wood's political program was rejected; Wood said later that the only instructions he ever received were to "get the people ready for a republican form of government . . . to do all we can for them and . . . to get ready to get out of the island as soon as we can safely do so."[8] The contradiction of goals was not removed, but priority was given to withdrawal; promotion of good government would take place within the context of that commitment.

Unrest precipitated this resolve. A rumor that the appointment of a civil governor would mean indefinite prolongation of the occupation produced such strong reaction that McKinley and Root felt the chill of danger.[9] Looking back, Root recalled that he had "an uneasy life for fear that he would read in a morning paper" the news of American troops firing on Cubans. If the Cubans should "take to the hills and begin another insurrection against us," that would mean the ignoble end of America's adventure in altruism.[10] "A Philippine war in Cuba would be too disastrous to contemplate," Root wrote on the last day of 1899.[11]

The clarification of policy did much to prepare the way for Wood's success. Americans who were willing or eager to assume prolonged Cuban dependency and Cubans, probably a large majority, who thought that United States control would never be given up, were relieved of some of their illusions and fears when Leonard Wood took charge of preparations for withdrawal. This goal having been set, Wood was better able to carry through a drastic program of reform. Even so, such hopes and fears could not fully be set to rest, particularly in view of Wood's autocratic methods and the vigor with which he undertook "the building up by Anglo-Saxons, . . . in a Latin military colony . . . of a republic modelled closely upon lines of our great Republic."[12]

Root was able to sound out the revolutionary leaders through Horatio Rubens, their counsel and confidant, who, it happened, had been a law clerk in Root's office. "The revolutionary element is ready to welcome General Wood," Rubens wrote. Thanks to the public statements of McKinley and Root, Rubens found it "needless to make any further statement to the Cubans, so that General Wood will be entirely free to deal with the situation as he may deem proper."[13]

ASSERTION: THE PLATT AMENDMENT

Wood kept tight control of Cuban affairs. His letters were full of colorful references to the "howling" of "agitators" and the need for firmness in dealing with "Latin races." Yet he was not blindly repressive; press criticism, he thought, could be ignored. His criterion for stable government "to satisfy all classes" was "money at six per cent."[14] But he could not stay clear of the turbulence of Cuban politics: the success of his mission depended upon the establishment of an effective Cuban government.

Root and Wood agreed on the basic importance of restricting suffrage, lest "the elements which have brought ruin to Haiti and Santo Domingo" do the same for Cuba.[15] Municipal officers were elected in June 1900, and a constitutional convention was chosen in September with military service, literacy, or property ownership as criteria for voting. Wood was pleased that restriction of the electorate was accepted with little opposition.[16] Yet the elections brought forward the very men whom Wood distrusted, conservatives having withdrawn or been overwhelmed amidst charges of fraud. Wood saw these men as "adventurers" bent on looting the island and found new reason to question the wisdom of full withdrawal.[17] He thought their performance at the convention would

point out the necessity and justification of any steps we may have to take in the future in the way of continuing temporary garrisons or continual supervision. The Convention represents, at any rate, the class to whom Cuba would have to be turned over in case we withdraw, for the highly intelligent Cubans of the land owning, industrial and commercial classes are not in politics. The politicians are in a certain sense doctors without patients. Lawyers without practice and demagogues living on the subscriptions of the people and their friends.[18]

But Wood did not abandon hope that vigorous and resolute administration would bring forth leaders of virtue and moderation.[19] "Let Congress tell these people frankly," he wrote Root in January

that we are going to establish a government here if they want it, but that we will not turn the Island over until competent men come to the fore, men whose ability and character give reasonable guarantee of the stability of the coming government.... Let Congress establish a definite date of withdrawal provided a suitable government exists and I will make every effort to bring the conservative and representative elements to the fore.[20]

At the end of February, with acceptance of the Platt Amendment provisions at stake, he assured Root that

the real interests and the real people of Cuba will support any reasonable demands and if the rascals in the Convention who are attempting to make trouble succeed even to a small extent they will, before the world, absolve us from all responsibility in reference to resolutions (Tellers) [sic] or other matters hitherto agreed upon. I do not contemplate anything of this sort, but it is better to have it than to destroy the island by surrendering it ... to the class of people whom I have always characterized as unprincipled and irresponsible. . . . The political element are an ungrateful lot and they appreciate only one thing, which is, the strong hand of authority and if necessary *we must show it*.[21]

Despite such fulminations, the alternatives were not seen in such drastic terms in Washington, where the desire to withdraw from direct responsibility was strong enough to overcome any inclination to make strict demands or apply rigid standards. Adoption of universal suffrage by the convention was accepted with little demur, although Wood thought that restrictions should be maintained for at least ten years.[22]

Those in authority in Washington did decide to insist, however, that the constitutional convention acknowledge a right of intervention. Root had thought that this might be achieved through negotiation. In his first annual report he wrote that a "representative convention" would "frame a constitution and provide for a general government of the island," and added "When that government is established the relations which exist between it and the United States will be matter for free and uncontrolled discussion between the two parties."[23] However, the authorization of a convention "to frame and adopt a constitution for the people of Cuba," stated that, "*as part thereof,*" it should "provide for and agree with the Government of the United States upon the relations to exist between that Government and the Government of Cuba."[24]

This demand met with strong resistance. "What is really serious," Rubens reported, "is that this is not the wild talk of leaders, but it is very thoroughly backed up in the country districts. This is perhaps the first instance since the intervention that the people in the country districts have become sullen."[25] His talks with "rabid leaders" had convinced him that "you cannot get any body of men to consent formally and publicly to these propositions" but he thought "their tacit consent" could be obtained by an announcement of "determination on this subject at the proper moment."[26]

Instead of insisting that the right of intervention form part of the constitution itself, Wood asked the convention, after framing and adopting a constitution, "to formulate what, in your opinion, ought to be the relations between Cuba and the United States." Then the United States would "doubtless take such action on its part as shall lead to a final and authoritative agreement."[27] But the convention could not be persuaded to accept the onus of making the desired proposal. Before agreement was finally reached, the United States had to make it quite explicit that control would not be lifted until the required terms had been accepted. To this end, the McKinley administration sought and gained the backing of Congress through the Platt Amendment.

It is perfectly clear that the initiative for the amendment and its essential terms came from the executive branch rather than from the Senate. It is quite similar to earlier proposals set forth by General Wilson, but in its actual formulation Root was the principal author. On January 11, 1901, Root told Secretary of State John

Hay that he was considering an assertion of the right to intervene in Cuba and asked him for information on reports that Great Britain was preparing such a device to enable it "to retire" from Egypt "and still maintain her moral control and prevent the backsliding of the Egyptian government."[28]

The fundamental motivation is less clear. Concern for good government cannot be separated from economic and strategic considerations, although it corresponded well with the self-image of Americans. While it might do something to dilute and disguise an imperialist relationship, it could not change its essential tenor. Moreover, it might do more to precipitate intervention than to promote good government; one senator predicted that instead of having the intended "restraining influence" the proposed relationship was likely to have "an exciting" effect in Cuban politics.[29]

Concern that Cuba might fall under the control of another state, perhaps Germany, was a factor.[30] Root developed his case for the amendment on the doubtful and imprudent assumption that a treaty right would give the United States greater ability to respond to a threat against Cuba. This argument was used, for what it may have been worth, in Cuba. Root asked Wood to let it be known that if Cuba should decline the amendment "she will have to look out for herself in case of trouble with any other nation. . . . And we should probably deal with that other nation not on account of Cuba but on our own account." If it should appear "that Cuba is ungrateful and unreasonable," he added, "the American people will not be quite so altruistic and sentimental . . . as they were in April, 1898."[31]

Root was not oblivious to concern that the U.S. would take unjustified advantage of its supremacy, particularly in regard to the economic relationship which would be determined by congressional action. Congress could not be relied upon to make a voluntary concession in the interest of close relations. It seemed clear to Root that if we demanded that Cuba "treat us as kind of foster-mother, on whose benevolent protection she is to rely and to whom she is to give special privileges in the way of naval stations and rights of supervision and intervention," we should not "treat her commercially at arms length just as we do our most unfriendly competitor and grant her absolutely no privileges and advantages." Root was "willing to stay on in Cuba and stand all sorts of misrepresentation and attack so long as we are right and doing what is best for the Cuban people," but not to occupy "a position where we are retaining our hold on Cuba, to the injury of the Cuban people, doing then an injustice, refusing to properly care for them while we prevent them from caring for themselves."[32]

Yet in the end Root decided that the United States must be adamant in demands upon the Cubans because it was "exceedingly doubtful" that Congress would give preferential treatment to Cuban sugar and tobacco. The convention was not to be permitted to require economic concessions from the United States. He thought that the Cuban people must be "brought face to face with the prospect of being abandoned to their own devices," and that "the sooner we have the round up the better."[33] He saw to it, however, that abandonment did not become the available alternative. Wood deplored the "moral cowardice" of the members of the convention, "simply writhing under the responsibility and attempting to wriggle out in any way, honorable or otherwise."[34]

Root felt that the Teller Amendment left the United States in a weak position:

Congress has . . . so tied the hands of the President by its resolution that, unless the Cubans can be induced to do voluntarily whatever we think they ought to do against the expressed determination of the Cuban leaders, . . . the President must either abandon American interests by a literal compliance with the obvious terms of the resolution or must engage in a controversy with Cubans in which they shelter themselves under the resolution of Congress against the Executive, while he has a probably divided country behind him, one part of which is charging him with usurpation and supporting the diverse claims of the Cuban extremists.[35]

It took the Platt Amendment to escape from this bind. After the convention balked at setting forth an acceptable version, Root drafted a formulation which was transmitted by Wood to the Cuban convention, with a copy handed to Senator Platt of Connecticut, the chairman of the committee on Cuba.[36] When, predictably, this merely served to intensify resistance, Congress was called upon to make it clear that "the whole united power of the nation" stood behind the demands.[37] Although Root feared delay, action was quick. By the Platt Amendment the president was authorized "to leave the government and control of Cuba to its people so soon as a government shall have been established in said Island, under a Constitution" which would "define the future relations of the United States with Cuba" in terms which would give the United States "the right to intervene for . . . the maintenance of a government adequate for the protection of life, property, and individual liberty."[38]

Root was prepared, if necessary, to make full use of his new backing. "Many things are true which it would not be polite or kind to say," he wrote to Wood on the day that the Platt Amendment was passed. The Cubans would have to realize that no government of their own could be established "until they have acted upon the question of relations in conformity with this act of Congress." He pointed out that Cuba was dependent upon the willingness of Congress to approve favorable trade relations; an "immense" force of "kindness and sense of moral obligation" might be aroused, but "ingratitude and entire lack of appreciation of the expenditure of blood and treasure of the United States to secure their freedom from Spain" would risk the loss of any preference.[39]

It took further suasion and a period of attrition to overcome Cuban resistance. Root softened the impact somewhat by assurance, on behalf of the president, "that the intervention referred to in the Platt Amendment is not synonymous with interference or intermeddling with the affairs of the Cuban Government, but the formal action of the United States, based upon just and substantial grounds."[40] Senator Platt gave a similar interpretation.[41] In accordance with a suggestion from Rubens, who told Root that the Cuban leaders would not believe indirect promises, and as a face-saving device, a committee of the convention was received in Washington.[42] Although no formal concessions were made, Root stated that the right of intervention "does not impair the sovereignty of Cuba." Intervention would take place "only in case that Cuba is left in a state of anarchy which will signify the absence of all government, and in case of a foreign menace."[43] Root seems to have been surprised to find that the Cubans "really suspected" that there was a "purpose to make their independence merely nominal."[44] In May 1901, the convention agreed by one vote to accept the amendment on the basis of interpretive statements, but once again it was told that acceptance must be in full, without change or qualification. The pill was finally swallowed on June 12 with one additional vote in the affirmative, but with absences to produce a margin of five. A treaty that formally established the right of intervention on the international plane was signed on May 23, 1903.

POLITICAL BEGINNINGS AND REOCCUPATION

Before the occupation could be ended, a government had to be established. The constitutional convention was elected by the vote of 30 percent of a restricted electorate. Cubans who wanted a gradual transition to independence or hoped for eventual annexation did not take part.[45] Under the new constitution, providing in effect for universal manhood suffrage, a general election was held on December 31, 1901. The presidency was almost uncontested. General Máximo Gómez, a national hero supported by a majority of the constitutional convention, declined nomination. Acclamation then shifted to another patriotic figure, Tomás Estrada Palma, a scholar and educator who had represented Cuban interests in the United States. An opposition candidate, General Bartolomé Masó, withdrew after failing to gain the support of either of the two leading parties.[46] The new president was installed on May 20, 1902. General Wood left the island on the same day. A small number of United States troops remained in Cuba until February 4, 1904.

Beneath a thin facade of order and rectitude provided by Estrada Palma's presidency, Cuban politics lacked stable substance. In the congressional elections of February 1904, the Conservative Republicans controlled the provinces of Matanzas and Santa Clara, where an ambitious general, José Miguel Gómez, was governor, while the National Liberals were predominant in Havana and Oriente. The National Liberals, charging fraud, boycotted the congress. As the presidential election of 1905 approached, the Conservative Republicans split. Those opposed to the candidacy of José Miguel Gómez formed the Moderate party, while Gómez and his adherents joined with the National Liberals in an arrangement worked out by Alfredo Zayas to form the Liberal party. The Moderates turned to Estrada Palma. In hope of preserving constitutionalism and salvaging some of the accomplishments of his administration, the president allowed himself to be brought into the partisan fray.[47]

The politics of Cuba, rather than the policies of the United States, led to a resumption of America control in 1906. Although the likelihood that the United States could be induced to intervene contributed to the political impasse, there is no evidence that United States leadership worked to this end or welcomed it. On the contrary, there were repeated expressions of dismay, and feverish efforts were made to head off intervention.

Cuban politics had not been able to generate stakes other than the lucrative spoils of office. Party competition quickly degenerated into tests of cleverness, boldness, and ruthlessness. In the words of the president, Cuba was a republic without citizens.[48] Estrada Palma's honesty and frugality built up the treasury into a rich prize, but his political aptitude was not equal to the task of safeguarding it. After taking a partisan role in order to push for legislation to provide for fair elections and an independent judiciary, he found that his supporters were content to follow the usual practices of taking control of local electoral boards and padding the lists of voters. The Liberals, not themselves strangers to electoral abuse, gave up the contest and sought means of redress. They urged the United States to insist on free elections and claimed that Estrada Palma was able to hold office only because of the belief that a revolution would be put down by United States forces.[49] Receiving no response, after the uncontested election the Liberal leaders decided to attempt a coup that would be quick and decisive enough to avoid any intervention which would support the government. Before they could perfect their plans, armed revolt broke out in Pinar del Rio and soon spread to other provinces. No one doubted that the United States would be the ultimate arbiter. The chargé d'affaires reported the view of the press that "the revolution must, if not quickly ended, bring about one of two results, both equally deplorable, namely, American intervention or the discrediting of the Platt Amendment."[50] Two days later he reported that one of the rebel leaders, hoping for "a new American intervention that will guarantee future legal elections," threatened to begin a campaign which would endanger foreign property.[51]

Thus the prospect of intervention contributed to the very insecurity and instability which the right to intervene was intended to guard against. Reluctance to intervene increased the likelihood that destructive measures would be taken to bring it about. Yet readiness to intervene would invite competitive maneuvers to manipulate it advantageously. Cuban national sentiment was not so strongly opposed to intervention that the onus of causing it would outweigh any probable gain. With the emphasis that the United States placed on free elections, there was no reason to fear that American occupation would be so ruthless and prolonged that no group could gain from it. For a weak government, intervention became the alternative to defeat, while the popularity of the opposition enabled it to hope for eventual success through elections under American control.

Estrada Palma's appeal for intervention was made through the consul general of the United States, Frank Steinhart. Steinhart had been the principal aide of General Wood during the first occupation, had remained in Cuba as a prominent businessman, and was "quite intimate with President Palma and with members of his administration."[52] In a cable of September 8, 1906, Steinhart transmitted a request for the dispatch of naval vessels to Havana and Cienfuegos and said that "our forcible intervention" would soon be asked for. In reply, Robert Bacon, who acted as secretary of state while Elihu Root was traveling in Latin America, emphasized "the reluctance with which this country would intervene" and the importance of demonstrating that the Cuban government had "exhausted every effort in a serious attempt to put down the insurrection" or "to come to a working agreement which will secure peace with the insurrectors." But in indicating that "shape" and timing were in doubt, Bacon implied that intervention would ensue. The ships were sent.

On the next day Bacon informed Steinhart that the president believed "actual, immediate intervention would be out of the question."[53] But the United States could not control the drift of events. Estrada Palma burned U.S. bridges along with his own. Having accepted mediation by a group of veterans, he rejected their proposals on the same day that he requested assistance from the United States.[54] On September 12, the day of the arrival of the cruiser *Denver,* he asked through Steinhart that two or three thousand men be sent "with the greatest secrecy and rapidity . . . to avoid any catastrophe in the capital."[55] Steinhart sent word that the Cuban president had "irrevocably resolved to resign and deliver the Government of Cuba to the representative of the United States as soon as sufficient American troops had been landed."[56] At the request of Estrada Palma he brought a battalion of one hundred men from the *Denver* to a central position in Havana. Yet no sooner had this been done than explicit instructions arrived that forces were not to be landed. A few hours later the men were back on ships.[57] The emergency abated and a truce was declared on the seventeenth. American forces that had gone on shore in Santa Clara province remained there, in friendly juxtaposition with the rebels.

Poised on the brink of intervention, American officials were unable to persuade Cubans that they must help them to avoid it. Cuban factions tried to make the United States serve their interests, while Americans did their best to avoid any commitment that would have been to the advantage of one side or another. Fearful of becoming involved in a guerrilla war, President Roosevelt made the critical decision not to support Estrada Palma. He then had to overcome the contrary impression created by the dispatch of ammunition and ships to Havana and find means of reconstituting the government of Cuba without handing a victory to the rebels. Moreover, he had to keep his policies credible and acceptable in American public opinion.[58]

On September 14 Roosevelt sent a letter to the Cuban ambassador, which he made available to the Cuban press as "the best way of communicating not merely with the supposed governmental authorities, but with the Cuban people.''[59] It asked ''all Cuban patriots to band together, to sink all differences and personal ambitions, and to remember that the only way that they can preserve the independence of their republic is to prevent the necessity of outside interference, by rescuing it from the anarchy of civil war.''[60] Thus, while Cuban politicians of both sides were trying to bring on American intervention, the American president was telling the Cuban people that in their own interest they should be trying to avoid it.

Roosevelt's message had alternative purposes: either to make intervention unnecessary or to make it acceptable to the American public. In urging Cubans to put patriotism above faction, he was trying to evoke national sentiment against foreign control, even though it might be directed against his own country. But if there were no miraculous change in Cuban attitudes, the message would lay the groundwork for eventual intervention in terms acceptable to the American public. The political culture of the United States placed great value upon self-government. Cuban political incapacity might justify and even require intervention, but the preferable outcome would be the achievement of effective national politics. The appeal to Cuban patriotism was unavailing. Cuban politics shaped itself to the threat (or the promise) of intervention rather than to more tangible domestic issues.

President Roosevelt sent William Howard Taft, the secretary of war, and Robert Bacon, assistant secretary of state, to Cuba to help achieve a ''cessation of hostilities and some arrangement which will secure the permanent pacification of the island.''[61] Taft and Bacon spent eleven days in Cuba, talking at length with representatives of both political parties, before they found it necessary to undertake full-scale intervention.[62] Taft came very quickly to the conclusion that effective support of the government would require ''forcible intervention against the whole weight of public opinion in the island.''[63] The insurgent forces could have been driven back and dispersed by the six thousand or so men who the United States had available within a few days, but suppression of guerrilla warfare ''would have been a work of a year or more and would have cost much blood and money.''[64] He did, nevertheless, warn the Liberal leaders that American troops would be landed if their forces came closer to Havana.[65]

Hope for a compromise depended on the willingness of Estrada Palma to remain in office while other officeholders of his party resigned and the Liberals were persuaded to lay down their arms. The Cuban president refused to do so. Taft concluded after five days that it was ''quite evident that Palma, and I fear the Moderate Party, are determined to force armed intervention by us.''[66] Roosevelt tried another appeal to Cuban patriotism, asking the president ''for the sake of your own fair fame, not to conduct yourself so that the responsibility, if such there be, for the death of the Republic can be put at your door,'' and warning the insurgents that if the United States should be forced to intervene they would ''forever stand as the authors of the destruction of the Republic.''[67]

Compromise failing, the United States had three choices: it could switch support to the revolutionists, provide the necessary backing to the Cuban president, or take control out of Cuban hands. Roosevelt inclined to the former course and Taft to the latter, while Bacon "preferred to uphold the Government, permitting the malcontents to assert themselves at a future election," despite the risk of civil war.[68] If it was the obstinacy of the Moderates which was blocking settlement, Roosevelt suggested, perhaps intervention should be "aimed at them," the insurgents being told that if they would lay down arms the U.S. would agree to a new election. He did not "believe we should, simply because Palma has proved obstinate, put ourselves in the place of his unpopular government and face all the likelihood of a long drawn-out and very destructive guerrilla warfare."[69]

Taft, stressing his desire to avoid any appearance of aiding the insurgents, showed how difficult it was not to take sides. The suggested resignation of Moderate officials other than the president, he reported, was being represented as a great victory for the Liberals. But the Moderates, despite their earlier disposition to negotiate, were now "taking the ground that it was our duty to support the Government at all hazards and put down the insurrection at all cost.... No one can be more impatient of armed resistance to constituted government than I," Taft went on, "and no one more conscious of the dangerous precedent of temporizing and compromising with rebels, but we did not make and were not responsible for the situation which we found." Yet the thought that "an undisciplined horde of men under partisan leaders" might be treated as a de facto government made him "shiver at the consequences." Although the insurrectionist movement had "the sympathy of a majority of the people of Cuba," its supporters were "of the poorer classes and uneducated." He thought the United States must "provide fair elections . . . and then turn the country over to the people duly elected," but first there would have to be a more thorough restoration of order than would result from "mere surrender of the rebels."[70]

Roosevelt agreed that it was "undoubtedly a very evil thing that the insurrectionists should be encouraged and the dreadful example afforded the island of remedying wrongs by violence and treason to the Government." But in the circumstances he saw no better course than to play into their hands. The government's refusal "either to endeavor to remedy the wrongs they have done or to so much as lift a hand in their own defense" meant that it would be "the least of two serious evils" for the United States to carry through the program on which Taft and the insurgents had agreed. He saw only "a slight chance" that despite this precedent "the people who grow discontented with the new government will refrain from insurrection and disturbance some time in the future." But if, after all, the sequence of events should repeat itself, at least "our duty" would be clearer and better understood.[71]

In Taft's view, if intervention were to be "clean," avoiding entanglement in Cuban partisanship, it should be complete. It would be a mistake simply to replace the president, because desperate Moderates might start another revolt or a "mulish Moderate" might come to the presidency and resist compromise. "Clean intervention," he argued, was "better because in that case the insurgents would surrender and we would soon restore order and constitutional government, and by fair elections quickly bring about the same result as compromise."[72] Roosevelt, alluding to public sentiment, was inclined to grasp any opportunity to avoid taking control or to look for "additional proof that intervention is inevitable,"[73] but he told Taft "to do anything that is necessary, no matter how strong the course, but to try to do it in as gentle a way as possible." He was willing "to incur any criticism and run any risk" to bring about a satisfactory result in Cuba.[74]

Taft thought that the Moderates would make intervention "as awkward as possible" by objecting to a provisional government, but he was prepared to go through with it nevertheless. Actually, as he saw it, both sides wanted intervention, "the Liberals because they can earn their victory in the holding of new elections, and the Moderates because if the elections have to be held they want them held under the auspices of the United States, and because Moderates are in favor of annexation generally."[75]

As it happened, Estrada Palma resigned under conditions which made it impossible to choose a successor. The United States could then base its assumption of control on the ground that Cuba had no functioning government. The Cuban president rejected compromise because it would place the government "on an inclined plane of interminable concessions, initiating an era of successive insurrections." He preferred "a political dependence which assures us the fecund boons of liberty . . . to a sovereign and independent republic discredited and made miserable by the baneful action of periodic civil wars."[76]

It remains uncertain as to whether his government could have survived if the United States had given early and firm support. A leading Cuban historian held that the United States had "exacted of the government of Cuba . . . that it abdicate before an armed insurrection."[77] Bacon said, just before leaving Cuba: "I am not satisfied. I shall be ashamed to look Mr. Root in the face. This intervention is contrary to his policy and what he has been preaching in Latin America."[78] The next American minister concluded that the occupation had placed a premium upon revolution.[79] On balance it seems evident that occupation became the alternative to prolonged disorder because of decisions which were made by Cubans.

A few marines were landed to surround the treasury on September 28, and on the next day, before any large contingents had been landed, Taft issued a proclamation establishing a provisional government. Extreme efforts were made to claim that there still existed "a Cuban government, conforming, as far as may be, to the constitution of Cuba." On Roosevelt's insistence, the Cuban flag continued to fly over government buildings. The minister remained at his post.

Cuba entered into international agreements during the period of occupation. The provisional governor, Charles E. Magoon, who succeeded Taft on October 13, went so far as to write in his annual report:

The Government was not changed, but continued in full force and vigor, exercising the same sovereignty and maintaining complete independence. There is in Cuba a provisional administration, but the Government continues to be that of the independent sovereignty of the Republic of Cuba.[80]

Yet Taft and Bacon, having determined that the elections of 1905 were ''so tainted with fraud as to render them illegal,'' suspended the Congress and proclaimed that legislative powers would be exercised by the provisional governor, basing this upon authority possessed by the Spanish governors-general.[81]

Under Magoon detailed codes were prepared and put into effect by decree relating to the organization of municipalities, the conduct of elections, the judiciary, and the civil service. They were drawn up by a commission that included members of the major political groups in Cuba under the diligent and able chairmanship of Colonel Enoch H. Crowder. The commission professed ''the firm intention of respecting the constitution'' of Cuba, with emphasis on democracy and decentralization.[82] However, any attempt to ensure fair elections was probably foredoomed. The bipartisan boards whose job it was to interpret and apply the complicated election rules found it easier simply to accept the decisions of the parties as to who ought to be elected and to distribute the votes accordingly.[83]

The major goal of the occupation was restoration of peaceful political life. Roosevelt asked Taft to assure the insurgents that an election would be held ''immediately'' and Taft's proclamation said that provisional government would ''be maintained only long enough to restore order and peace and public confidence.''[84] In December Roosevelt told Congress and, indirectly, the Cubans:

If the elections become a farce, and if the insurrectionary habit becomes confirmed in the Island, it is absolutely out of the question that the Island should continue independent; and the United States, which has assumed sponsorship before the civilized world for Cuba's career as a nation, would again have to intervene and to see that the government was managed in such orderly fashion as to secure the safety of life and property.[85]

The thought that elections could be held within a few weeks soon had to be abandoned. At Roosevelt's insistence, however, a firm deadline was set and the occupation was terminated on January 28, 1909, after twenty-eight months.

The American political authorities, desiring neither annexation nor continuing intervention, were anxious to find and to nurture patriotism and self-reliance among the Cubans. The army officers who were charged with administration felt, however, in the tradition of Leonard Wood, that there was no hope of lasting gain unless the United States sponsored thorough reform over an extended period of time.[86]

Provisional Governor Magoon was "a hopelessly conventional American civilian," without any of the imperiousness of Leonard Wood.[87] According to so close and astute an observer as Colonel Crowder, he was controlled by Steinhart in dealings with the Cubans.[88] Magoon tried to further the development of political parties through patronage, but found great difficulty. "Party ties set lightly on individuals in Cuba." There were "few, if any, issues involving national policy or political principles." "A large proportion of the business and property-owning classes" were not Cuban citizens and few were politically active. Many of the aliens and "a small number of Cubans who own property and fear a recurrence of disorder" wanted annexation. Indeed, an alliance of convenience existed between annexationists and radicals, which for a time threatened to precipitate revolt.[89]

In public Magoon mustered the optimism which his situation seemed to demand; the nationalism of "the overwhelming majority" gave promise that Cuba could "achieve good and stable government."[90] But he told Roosevelt that stability would depend on bringing "the property owning and commercial classes" into active politics. This would only happen if Cubans were made fully responsible for the conduct of their government, without any prospect of intervention. "The authority granted by the Platt Amendment should not be perverted into a menace to the object it was intended to conserve."[91]

Although the resurgent Liberals were given control of many municipalities, Taft refused to appoint their nominees to the principal departments of the central government and instructed Magoon to oppose Liberal efforts to dominate the elections.[92] A split developed between adherents of Gómez and of Zayas, to the consternation of the provisional governor, who was dependent upon local advice in the distribution of positions.[93] In trying to satisfy the competing demands of amorphous factions, he issued a large number of pardons and sinecures, for which his administration was bitterly attacked by Cuban historians. It was neither a nonpolitical nor a partisan regime. In attempting to distribute the rewards of politics impartially, it nourished partisanship without requiring the discipline of political responsibility. Cubans came to assume that the Magoon administration was reaping its share of booty and went so far as to blame it, implausibly, for being the source of the corruption which plagued Cuban politics.

After the discredited and demoralized Moderate party dissolved, Magoon encouraged a conservative alternative, hoping that competition would help to bring the feuding Liberals together.[94] Local elections gave impetus to a combination of Liberal forces. Since the Zayas faction was considerably weaker, Gómez was nominated for president and Zayas for vice-president. The Conservatives put up General Menocal, who had led the mediation efforts just prior to intervention. The result was a decisive Liberal victory in an election without incident in November 1908.

Reoccupation had a deeply demoralizing effect on Cuban politics. The apparent failure of "the forces that represented the best hopes and dreams for a healthy, honest, and vigorous republic" released "latent elements of irresponsibility and immorality" and there seemed to be no strong nationalistic force that could assert itself.[95] The occupation left behind "a far handier tool for waste and oppression" than had previously been available.[96] A more effective means of coping with insurrection was clearly needed. The Liberals, opposing enlargement of the small rural guard, which had been controlled by the previous government, suggested the creation of a new permanent army which could be staffed to their advantage. Despite the objections of American officers attached to the rural guard, the occupation authorities gave their approval. The army "became the fiscally rapacious and politically potent institution the American officers predicted."[97]

2.
NICARAGUA

Nicaragua became a center of concern for the United States for two main reasons: as a site for a canal and because its central location and the bitterness of its political divisions made it a source of disorder within and among the five Central American countries whose political currents had always intermingled. If the Nicaraguan canal route had been chosen, the United States would have been involved even more deeply. What this might have meant is subject for speculation. It is a revealing comment on American attitudes that in a discussion of alternative routes no attention was paid to probable political disturbances while the likelihood of volcanic eruptions was a major consideration.

With a partial exception in the case of Costa Rica, politics in Central America had never settled into institutional channels. An assumption that the five separate states constituted one political entity was demonstrated periodically in attempts at constitutional integration and almost continually in the conduct of politics. Within individual countries bitter factionalism split the small ruling class. Conservative and Liberal parties were led by dominant personalities through cycles of revolt, repression, intrigue and counterrevolt, with little regard for stable objectives or state boundaries.

In Nicaragua factional disputes traditionally pitted the Liberals of Leon, where lawyers and doctors tended to set the tone, against the Conservatives of Granada, who were mostly merchants and landowners. Liberals provided the leadership for a Central American Republic which managed to exist from 1824 to 1839 though plagued by civil war. A British agent, Frederick Chatfield, provided important support for the unified republic as long as it represented a convenient avenue for influence, but after its collapse his intrigues were aimed at preventing its revival.[1] Between 1839 and 1871 Conservatives prevailed through most of Central America, taking advantage of the dominance that President and dictator Rafael Carrera established over Guatemala. During this period, the American filibusterer, William Walker, came onto the scene on the side of unionist Liberals and was president of Nicaragua for almost a year in 1856 and 1857. The Conservatives regained control there after Walker's defeat and were able to remain in power until 1893, although the overthrow of Conservative regimes in Guatemala and Costa Rica left them without effective outside support after 1871. A period of over thirty years of unprecedented stability came to an end in 1893, when a split in Conservative leadership opened the door for a successful Liberal revolt which brought José Santos Zelaya to the presidency.

By accepting support first from one faction and then from another, Zelaya held precarious political ascendancy for sixteen years, during which he became the principal source of turmoil in the politics of all of Central America. Zelaya used his power freely for personal benefit and was regarded by the State Department as a spoilsman and troublemaker, but the opinion of many Central Americans was more favorable. He gained renown as a nationalist in 1895 when, with some help from the United States, he was able to deprive Britain of its role as protector of the Mosquito reserve. In 1902 he held up negotiations with the United States over canal rights by refusing to concede jurisdiction to American courts. He presented himself as an advocate of Central American unity, although it appeared that his interventions were to his own primary advantage.

THE OVERTHROW OF ZELAYA

After the canal project began to become a reality in Panama, the United States was anxious, as Elihu Root put it, "to get the little Central American countries into a better shape and to do it in such a way as to win their respect and kindly feeling."[2] Root was eager to avoid direct intervention, but when the United States took a hand in Central American disturbances, it could not escape political entanglement.

After fighting broke out in 1906 between Guatemala and El Salvador, Mexico was persuaded to join the United States in helping to arrange an armistice and to set up a Central American peace conference at San José. Nicaragua did not take part because Zelaya, who was engaged in a claims controversy with the United States, rejected outside interference in Central American affairs. Within a few months, in the name of Central American unity, he overturned the government of Honduras and invaded El Salvador. A memorandum prepared by Second Assistant Secretary of State A. A. Adee suggested that "some kind of constraining intervention" by Mexico and the United States would be necessary, but Secretary of State Root resisted direct involvement. United States naval ships were much in evidence, protecting foreigners, sometimes with excessive zeal, but they were not used for political objectives.[3]

The United States chargé d'affaires at Tegucigalpa used his personal good offices in working out a peace treaty between Nicaragua and El Salvador that provided for an acceptable government in Honduras, but this project was never carried through. The State Department inadvertently encouraged Zelaya when it gave a strong letter of introduction to an American named Washington Valentine, president of the largest mining company in Honduras, who then claimed that the United States and Mexico would be happy to see Zelaya set up a military government in Honduras and work toward the consolidation of all of Central

America.[4] Root's real attitude was quite the opposite. But although he thought Zelaya was "bent on conquest," he was unwilling to undertake the "long period of armed intervention" that would be needed to settle Central American problems.[5] Yet he did not believe the United States should stay aloof. Costa Rica was "an exception," so close to Panama "that we must not let her be overturned," and he "would be pretty urgent" in support of El Salvador "for Salvador is pretty decent." He concluded that "we must do what we can and answer any calls upon us to promote arbitration."[6]

Root's pessimism appeared to have been exaggerated when, in 1907, with United States and Mexican mediation, the Central American presidents agreed to a conference in Washington to work out principles and procedures for the conduct of politics. In his opening address Root recalled the history of failure ("The trial has often been made and the agreements which have been elaborated, signed, ratified, seem to have been written in water.") and urged the delegates to "devise ... practical methods ... to secure performance."[7] Honduras and Nicaragua held that nothing less than Central American union would "insure stable and efficient peace and order," but Costa Rica and Guatemala opposed this, and the conference went ahead on the premise of separate governments.[8] The states agreed, in effect, to put an end to the politics of violence across boundaries. They would prevent the organization of revolutionary movements against their neighbors and would withhold recognition from a government which came into power through revolution. "In case of civil war," no government of Central America would "intervene in favor of or against the Government of the country where the struggle takes place." Honduras, the most frequent "theater of Central American conflicts," was to maintain a neutrality which the other states bound themselves to respect. A Permanent Central American Court of Justice was set up, with compulsory jurisdiction, to support and emphasize the "national conscience of Central America."[9]

These commitments had little discernible effect. Nonrecognition of revolutionary regimes could only be made effective by actions of the United States.[10] Yet an active American role would entail deep and intensifying involvement in Central American politics. Whether or not there was a "national conscience" to which the court might give expression, there was something like a national politics of Central America. Political contention regularly spread from state to state. Root nevertheless persisted in attempts to limit the effects of instability. In collaboration with Mexico, he moved to prevent war from arising out of revolutionary invasions of Honduras from El Salvador and Guatemala in 1908, hoping that the Central American governments would invite Mexico and the United States to become joint guarantors of the neutrality of Honduras. "Such a guarantee," he thought, "would be the pivot upon which the whole political life of Central America would turn and ... the Zelayas and Cabreras, unable to get at each other and confined in their own dominions, would be speedily disposed of by their own people."[11]

But before the prudent diplomacy of Root could meet the test of Central American turbulence, it was superseded by the more bumptious "dollar diplomacy" of his successor, Philander C. Knox. Knox and his principal adviser on Latin American affairs, F. M. Huntington Wilson, had similar goals of national interest and of political stability, but, lacking Root's patience and skill, his sensitivity to Latin American attitudes, and his awareness of the entrapments of an interventionist propensity, they were much quicker to equate these goals with the economic interest of American investors. They soon undertook to establish financial control in the more turbulent countries, on the pattern of the customs receivership which had been established in the Dominican Republic in 1905, and sought to sustain American influence by prompting and supporting private investment.

The organized and articulated relationship between private investment and national policy which quickly became known as "dollar diplomacy" was described by Huntington Wilson shortly after he left office. He placed emphasis on the subordination of private advantage to national interest, but premised his views on a biological notion of destiny which afforded little basis for distinguishing necessity from advantage: "Nature, in its rough method of uplift, gives sick nations strong neighbors and takes its inexorable course with private enterprise and diplomacy as its instruments. And this course is the best in the long run, for all concerned and for the world. . . . The startling breadth" of presidential authority in foreign relations, Wilson continued, should be used in directing "a measure of the national prestige and power entrusted by the people to his care" toward "the protection of foreign enterprise." He gave clear priority to "strengthening American influence in spheres where it ought to predominate over any other foreign influence," and supported "those investments or enterprises which most promote vital political interest." The "proper" degree of support to "legitimate and beneficial American enterprises" must be determined by the secretary of state in "careful consideration of subtle measures of national advantage." The objective of Central American policy "was 'to substitute dollars for bullets,' to create a material prosperity which would wean the Central Americans from their usual preoccupation of revolution." He cited Nicaragua as "a case where the political and economic advantages are both of the first rank and where, therefore, the measure of governmental support should be at its highest."[12]

A more assertive United States policy ran directly afoul of the activities of Zelaya. For some time the State Department had seen him as the principal disturber and antagonist in Central America. Zelaya showed no interest in changing this impression. Indeed, his attitudes and actions repeatedly confirmed it. The Taft administration moved quickly to isolate and oppose him, ordering naval forces to stop his filibuster expeditions and practically breaking off diplomatic relations.[13] But Zelaya was able to float a loan in London and Paris, while Washington was trying to arrange loans for the three neighboring countries.

Within a short time United States opposition to Zelaya as a fomenter of revolution became itself an encouragement to revolt, despite the commitments at the Washington conference.[14]

In 1908, for the first time, an American minister had been separately assigned to Nicaragua, but within a few months he resigned, alleging personal insult in the arrest of several Conservatives who carried United States flags in a demonstration.[15] A short while later Knox withdrew the chargé d'affaires, leaving a vice-consul, a Nicaraguan hostile to Zelaya, as the only representative of the United States in Managua.

Revolt began in Bluefields, a Caribbean port dependent upon economic ties with outside investors, in October 1909. At the very least the outbreak was premised on knowledge that relations between the United States and Zelaya were unfriendly, and it was probably prompted by more or less subtle suggestions from United States naval officers and businessmen, but there was no active involvement of the State Department.[16] The governor in Bluefields, General Juan J. Estrada, a Liberal, was persuaded to throw in with the Conservatives. General Emiliano Chamorro and Adolfo Díaz provided the active leadership. Díaz, who had been employed at a modest salary as secretary of a mining company, the largest United States private investment in Nicaragua, managed to gain credit for contributing $600,000 to the revolutionary cause (and to have it repaid to himself after he became president). Knox, before becoming secretary of state, had been counsel to the corporation which owned the mining concession.[17] Knox's nephew, who in 1908 had been United States consul at La Ceiba, Honduras, and was temporarily deprived of his exequatur in the belief that he had given support to a revolutionary movement, visited Nicaragua in the summer of 1909 when plans for a revolt were presumably under discussion.[18] These ties must at least have given encouragement to leaders of the revolt. There is no evidence, however, that Knox was directly involved.

The consul in Bluefields, Thomas C. Moffat, impressed an American admiral as being "less an American consul than an agent of the Estrada faction."[19] He had prior knowledge of the revolt and reported its success with evident relish and anticipation:

the entire population is jubilant...and in anticipation of very great prosperity;... foreign business interests are enthusiastic.... [O]verthrow of Zelaya appears absolutely assured, and...it is intended later to separate Republic of Nicaragua, consolidating Pacific Coast States into a separate Republic, both Republics to be under the control of the conservative party.... [I]mmediate reduction tariff is assured; also the annulment of all concessions not owned by foreigners.[20]

To Senator Borah, who became the leading critic of involvement in Nicaragua, it was "as clear as the noon-day sun that Mr. Moffat was entirely familiar with and a part of the organization of the revolt of 1909."[21] The consul had occasion later to describe his influence over Estrada:

He ever looked for advice and sustaining. Some have been so ungenerous as to say that all he accomplished was initiated or dictated by me. This is far from the truth. While I have been his adviser and friend and have ever found him amenable to advice, still I have ever observed that he is alert to question and prob [*sic*] any suggestions that might be offered ere he accept them.[22]

It should be noted, however, that Moffat was disliked by Americans in Nicaragua who thought that he was "prejudiced in advance against many of the concessions" which they sought.[23]

Huntington Wilson expressed sympathy with the revolt to diplomats from other Central American countries, but the State Department instructed its consuls in Nicaragua to "observe strict neutrality and abstain from any action or expression of opinion which might be imputed or constructed as an indication of this government's opinion."[24] Formal neutrality was soon abandoned. When two American demolition experts who had been hired to aid the revolt were executed by Zelaya's forces (an action, according to Moffat, "unprecedented in Nicaragua in the last 50 years" and taken "not so much because they were revolutionists, but because they were Americans"), the department seized on the opportunity to pose unmeetable demands.[25] Within two weeks, the United States broke off diplomatic relations, denouncing Zelaya in the strongest terms in a note which had "the undisguised purpose" of forcing a change of government.[26] It suggested that the "burden" which the United States might "impose" upon Nicaragua in consequence of the executions would depend upon "whether the Government be one entirely dissociated from the present intolerable conditions and worthy to be trusted to make impossible a recurrence of such acts."[27] Zelaya resigned on December 19, 1909.

Collaboration with Mexico had already broken down when Mexico resisted pressure on Zelaya with what the State Department considered "contemptible motives."[28] A provisional president suggested by Mexico, José Madriz, was elected by the Nicaraguan Congress, but the United States refused recognition, holding that this was not a sufficient repudiation of Zelaya.

The State Department gave serious consideration to a plan to occupy the chief port of Nicaragua and possibly the capital as well in order to establish an acceptable government. The idea was set aside because it was thought to require congressional action. President Taft's annual message made reference to "future steps," perhaps to be made known in a special message.[29] When it appeared that the revolutionists might take Managua, the State Department drafted a note through which Estrada would ask for a loan, to be secured by a customs receivership like that in the Dominican Republic and parallel to one which was planned for Honduras. The note was not actually delivered, because it was thought that it would imply recognition in violation of the 1907 treaties and that customs control might precipitate a new uprising, but the objective was not questioned.[30] A few months later a resolution was drawn up in the department by which Congress would authorize intervention to set up a free and stable government in Nicaragua.[31] No further action had been taken, however, when a turn of events brought to power a friendly government that would seek United States assistance.

It appeared early in 1910 that the revolution would not win an easy victory. Indeed, after a lost battle on February 22, it seemed that it might collapse. The State Department held back from covert assistance because this would have violated international law, but it kept pressure on the government, including seizure of a customs house, to make reparation for the killing of the two Americans.[32]

The United States navy and marines effectively protected the revolutionists in their possession of Bluefields even after government forces had taken the nearby bluff, which was considered the key to the port. They forbade an attack on the town because it would have endangered foreign lives and property and refused to permit a blockade on the ground that the government vessel had forfeited full belligerent rights "by deceiving the authorities at a port of the United States."[33] The officer in charge of the marine detachment wrote later that, knowing "that Washington would like the revolutionists to come out on top," he had told the government forces they were free to take Bluefields "if it could be managed without shooting" and had "suavely" pointed out that the defenders need not be prevented from using their weapons because they would be shooting outwards while the attackers would be firing toward the town.[34] The protection given to Bluefields freed the revolutionists to undertake offensive action elsewhere and did serious damage to the morale of the forces supporting the government.[35]

That failure to take Bluefields would be quickly followed by the demise of the government was not foreseen. New uprisings encouraged the revolutionists to make another attempt in the western part of the country, where they won two engagements in August and entered Managua with Madriz in flight. This outcome may have been as unwelcome as it was surprising to the original instigators of the revolution. Moffat reported "bitter dissensions" among the leaders. Estrada, "with the native Creoles, Mosquito Indians, the best class of Nicaraguans and all the foreigners" was "fighting for the separation and supremacy of the coast," while Chamorro and his Conservative allies cared only for "the interior and Managua."[36] Any plan for an independent coastal state was destroyed by an excess of victory.

DÍAS: CLIENT AND SUPPLICANT

The State Department was not slow to respond to the new situation. It drafted conditions for recognition which Estrada accepted almost as written. As suggested, Estrada asked for a loan which would be secured by customs and requested that a commission be sent to make the necessary arrangements. The new government accepted these terms with some reluctance, but it was so eager for recognition that it claimed that status before the State Department intended that it should.[37]

Thomas C. Dawson, who had set up the customs receivership in the Dominican Republic, was sent to establish the new relationship. Under his guidance, the revolutionary leaders drew up agreements regarding succession to the presidency, a claims commission, and the guarantee of a loan by customs receipts. Although he had been instructed that constitutional government should be established on the basis of free elections, Dawson concluded that it would be ''impracticable and dangerous to peace'' to hold a direct popular vote for president. Instead, a constituent assembly was elected by the victorious revolutionists, which proceeded to designate Estrada for a two-year term as president, with Díaz as vice-president and presumptive successor. The State Department accepted this when Dawson reported that it was the only procedure that offered ''a chance of continued peace.''[38] It was comforting to believe, as Huntington Wilson wrote later, that Estrada, the political leader ''most friendly to the United States,'' was also ''the most successful.''[39] The United States congratulated him on his ''popular mandate, unanimously expressed through the constituent assembly.''[40] But it became evident that he actually had no solid basis of support. The department asked Dawson to express its ''concern that so little progress has been made toward formulating a reassuring policy'' and to give warning that unless ''the present condition of disorder tending to anarchy'' should be ''corrected'' it ''would appear to be inevitable'' that ''outside pressure'' would be brought to bear.[41]

The Estrada government could not resist the greed of its members and supporters any more than it could reject the demands of the United States. The treasury was soon exhausted by large grants to prominent clients who claimed various injuries under Zelaya, and the currency was inflated by paper money, most of which apparently went ''to those in power and to their friends and relatives.''[42] In setting forth its program, the government acknowledged dependence upon ''the esteem of which the United States has given us so many proofs.''[43] Its subordinateness became evident when the United States was able to reject the inclusion of a neutral arbiter on a commission to settle claims against the Nicaraguan government, insisting on ''an umpire appointed by the Department of State.''[44] Although the commission acted with integrity in awarding claimants only about 7 percent of their demands, it is scarcely surprising that such a dependent regime lacked domestic support or that Estrada was soon suggesting that the United States assume a protectorate.[45]

A new minister, Elliott Northcott, was soon aware that Estrada was ''being sustained solely by the moral effect of our support.'' He felt ''the natural sentiment of an overwhelming majority of Nicaraguans'' to be ''antagonistic to the United States'' and found ''a decided suspicion, if not distrust, of our motives'' even on the part of some members of the cabinet. Moreover, ''close alliance with the United States'' would be ''antagonized by practically all the Central American Republics." Yet he thought the attempt to sustain Estrada was "at least worth a thorough trial," since it might be a long time before there would come "another such opportunity to prove our good faith in Central America."[46]

The constituent assembly proved to be under the control, not of Estrada, but of the ambitious Conservative general, Emiliano Chamorro. Estrada's adviser, Moffat, concluded it had been a mistake to have insisted that this body be chosen by election.[47] In an attempt to recoup his losses, with the support of the legation, Estrada dissolved the assembly, rejected the proposed constitution, and called new elections.[48] Northcott, denying any intent to "interfere with matters that were purely internal," tried in vain to persuade Chamorro to support the president. The State Department instructed him to remind the leaders "that by their agreements transmitted to Dawson they have assumed a responsibility toward this Government of working harmoniously and in a cooperative spirit." Under this pressure Chamorro left the country after telling Northcott that he would find out that he should have insisted that Estrada accept the constitution as prepared by the dissolved assembly.[49]

Shortly after the new assembly convened, Estrada precipitated his own downfall by arresting the minister of war, Luis Mena, an act which was reported to have been "done in a fit of drunken insanity" on the advice of a Liberal cabinet member who was to emerge as president seventeen years later, José M. Moncada. Northcott then gave up on Estrada. The State Department acquiesced, on assurance that there was "no anti-American sentiment apparent" (although Northcott cabled also that a "war vessel" was "necessary for the moral effect") and that the assembly would "confirm Díaz in the presidency" according to any one of three plans which the department might choose.[50] Fear was expressed, however, that the overthrow of Estrada had removed "practically the only hope for stability of government." Estrada, as a Managuan Liberal accepted by Conservatives, might have combined the various elements essential to political survival, but Díaz was a moderate Conservative, lacking support from either Chamorro or the Mena Conservatives, with no control over the army, in a country "overwhelmingly Liberal."[51] If Díaz should resign, the State Department feared, the succession of Mena would probably throw the country "into the turmoil of a three-cornered revolution, affording opportunity for the re-entry of Zelaya into politics." Far from deferring to private interest, the department was anxious to frustrate "the machinations of the United Fruit Company, and the schemes of different Americans in collusion with corrupt Central American politicians" which it saw as "the greatest external contributions to the situation the United States seeks to avoid."[52]

Mena's control of the army and his strength in the assembly made it necessary to conciliate him. The United States urged Díaz to maintain "harmony . . . so as to execute effectively the pledges signed by him and Mena and delivered to Dawson."[53] Díaz's political weakness and lack of resolution were apparent. Northcott persuaded him not to resign, but he plaintively confided to a new chargé d'affaires, a young man of only twenty-six, that his position was "that of a figurehead, ignored by Mena's followers," with "no voice in decision on any executive act."[54] Yet he objected to the attention which the Americans paid to Mena.[55]

Díaz sought to relieve the impasse by an advance commitment that Mena would succeed to the presidency, contending that free elections were "hopelessly impracticable" and threatening to resign if the plan were rejected. The chargé d'affaires pointed out that this would mean "immediate approval" of financial arrangements that were desired by the United States. The State Department did not object when the assembly went ahead to elect Mena, fifteen months before the date of succession.[56]

This did not put an end to the factional rivalry which pitted Díaz and the more popular and ambitious Conservative, Chamorro, against the Mena-dominated assembly. At the end of the year Díaz conveyed his discouragement to the department. He had "disconsolately" concluded that Nicaragua could not attain "lasting and stable peace, order, economy, moderation, and liberty" without "more direct and efficient assistance from the United States, like that which resulted so well in Cuba." He therefore suggested a treaty "permitting the United States to intervene in our internal affairs in order to maintain peace and the existence of a lawful government," Secretary of State Knox expressed "intense gratification" but thought that such an important proposal would require "deep and careful consideration."[57]

Promulgation of a constitution became an issue of prestige. The chargé d'affaires wanted it delayed until the arrival of a new head of mission who might seek various amendments. The minister for foreign affairs, who was an uncle of Chamorro, tried to hold it up by refusing to sign it, because it would confirm the election of Mena. Chamorro, having returned from exile, told the chargé d'affaires that he would start a revolution if the Dawson Agreements, which provided for popular election of the next president, were not carried out.[58] However, a few days after a meeting in which President Díaz and the chargé d'affaires confronted Mena and the president of the assembly, a "strong anti-American wave" arose. The assembly ordered promulgation, making explicit reference to the "exceptional interest" which the United States had taken in delaying it and the "insult to the national autonomy and the honor of the Assembly" which had been conveyed by "this interposition."[59]

The State Department immediately adopted a stern attitude, instructing the chargé d'affaires to "summon Mena to the Legation and inform him" that he was expected, "as a patriotic Nicaraguan, strictly to abide by and support" the Dawson Agreements and, with menacing implication, that "his failure to do so would only result in internal disorder."[60] There is no report of this instruction having been carried out. The new minister was George T. Weitzel, who had been assistant chief of the Latin American division. Weitzel concluded that the Constitution was not so objectionable as "to justify at this time any effort to influence the Assembly in rescinding its action."[61] Economic improvements should be given priority.[62] The State Department hoped that by avoiding political commitment it could keep the factions expectant of its favor and keep its involvement limited.[63]

Once Díaz became president, a loan treaty was quickly drawn up, following the recommendations of a financial adviser sent by the State Department. Although the Knox-Castrillo Treaty was held up in the Senate, the adviser, Ernest H. Wands, found New York bankers willing to do their part without assurance of a customs collectorate. The State Department wanted customs control, however, for its contribution to political stability. Eventually, with senatorial action deferred, the bankers worked out arrangements that did include a customs collector nominated by them and approved by the State Department.[64] Colonel Clifford D. Ham held this position throughout the time of direct American involvement in Nicaragua. Further loans were soon needed; to secure these, the bankers assumed management of the national railroad.

Secretary of State Knox visited Nicaragua in March 1912. Avoiding any explicit reference to the aspirations of Mena, he emphasized the importance of "faithful observance of the pledges made by the leaders of all parties."[65] Díaz welcomed him effusively as a representative of a government "which abhors tyranny not only within its own frontiers, but in every place to which it may carry the beneficent influence of its policy." He referred to the denunciation of Zelaya as that "famous note, in which, as the mouthpiece of civilization, you pronounced the doom of tyranny before the world." The "triumph of justice and the establishment of order and lasting peace in Nicaragua" would depend on help from the United States. "As an admirer" of American policy "by reason of its evident results in other fortunate Latin countries," it was his "firm intention of accepting that friendly influence." Knox replied that the United States had been "happy promptly to respond" when called upon "for assistance in the regeneration of Nicaragua."[66] He added, in a later speech, that with its "well-known policy" as to threats "from beyond the sea," the United States was "equally desirous that there shall be no failure to maintain a republican form of government from forces of disintegration originating from within" and would "always be found willing" to help "preserve the stability of our sister American republics."[67]

Currents of hostility were evident, however. The train which carried Knox to Managua was preceded and followed by armed guards and went at full speed through Leon, where large crowds had gathered and "inhospitable epithets were seen painted or chalked on walls."[68] When Knox appeared before the assembly, he confronted a body which was controlled by Mena, "whose party," the chargé d'affaires had reported, "is uniformly anti-American."[69] The president of the assembly made arch and studied reference to "fears and misgivings in timid minds" who saw "peril to our autonomy," quoted antiimperialist pronouncements of earlier American spokesmen "which eliminate all tendency to expan-

sion or to interference in foreign dominions,'' and repeated Washington's injunction that "attachment of a small or weak toward a great and powerful nation
dooms the former to be the satellite of the latter.''[70]

Weitzel was disturbed in May at rumors that the Liberals were "organizing a
concerted uprising, . . . with the declared object of defeating the loan." With the
Liberals "in such a majority," he thought it advisable to station a war vessel at
Corinto "at least until the loan has been put through.''[71] In June he saw no reason
for "serious apprehension," despite "the opposing aims of the President and his
Minister of War." He thought Díaz should not bring matters to a head until he
could gain greater support from the public employees by paying their back
salaries. He trusted that "the moral influence in favor of constituted authority
exerted by the United States" which had "been the strongest if not the sole factor
in the preservation of peace and order" would "continue to be effective to that
end for the present.''[72]

ARBITRATION BY MARINES

A little more than a month later, Mena's moves appeared more menacing.
Weitzel warned that "certain influential European subjects" among his advisers
were encouraging him to take over the presidency.[73] Troop movements led Díaz
to fear an imminent seizure of La Loma, the fortress at Managua. Díaz himself
took initiative against the secretary of war, on July 29, 1912, assuming command of the armed forces and appointing Chamorro, Mena's principal antagonist, general-in-chief. Weitzel explained later that a loan from New York bankers,
arranged through the good offices of the State Department, had so strengthened
Díaz "that he resolved to assume real as well as nominal responsibility for the
Government.''[74]

Díaz's move left Mena besieged in a barracks. After accepting conditions for
ending hostilities, conveyed by Weitzel, Mena took advantage of control of the
police to have the lights cut off and to make his escape. With civil war pending,
control of the railroad and of lake vessels owned by the railroad became the
immediate American concern. Díaz asked the United States to "guarantee with
its forces security for the property of American citizens" and "extend its protection to all the inhabitants of the Republic.''[75] A detachment of sailors was
quickly brought to Managua, and a marine battalion was ordered in from the
Canal Zone. Managua suffered four days of bombardment before the arrival of
the marines. After they had come through from the coast, rail communications
were temporarily broken by the revolutionists' domination of Leon, but reinforcements soon succeeded in opening the line.

The admiral in command at first refused to permit either side to use the
railroad, but this order, which would have forced the contenders to seek a settlement, was soon reversed. From the State Department Huntington Wilson urged
Taft to work "very strongly for the elimination of such elements" as Mena and

the Zelayistas. "If the United States did its duty promptly, thoroughly and impressively in Nicaragua," he argued, "it would strengthen our hand and lighten our task, not only in Nicaragua itself in the future, but throughout Central America and the Caribbean and would even have some moral effect in Mexico."[76] A few days later the minister was authorized to issue a policy statement denouncing the revolution. By its "uncivilized and savage" actions, the Mena group had taken on "the attributes of the abhorrent and intolerable Zelaya regime." The United States "could not countenance any movement to restore the same destructive regime." In addition to responsibility for the protection of American lives and property, under the Washington conventions it had "a moral mandate to exert its influene for the preservation of the general peace of Central America."[77]

Huntington Wilson prepared a memorandum for President Taft which would remove the misapprehension that appeared to underlie Admiral Southerland's "mild attitude" and his references to "strict impartiality." The "sharp distinction" should be clear "between a case of two recognized factions and the present case where the United States . . . desires to see the constituted Government regain at the earliest moment full control of the country." "The leaders of the present disturbances," he wrote, have taken on "the character of bandits rather than of revolutionists fighting for a principle." Deployment of American forces to protect the cities should enable the government "to bring most of its forces directly to bear upon the suppression of the uprising."[78]

Marine Commander Major Smedley D. Butler got the message: "With our government in Washington unofficially but definitely taking sides against the rebels, it was necessary to make a swift and concerted effort to restore law and order—also unofficially."[79] With marines boldly in the fore, the rail line was cleared to its terminus in Granada. Mena, who had been stricken with serious illness, was confronted there and taken to the Canal Zone as "a quasi prisoner of war" until it was decided in December that he was "no longer dangerous to the peace of the country."[80] After a brief fight the remaining revolutionary force was defeated in Masaya, and Leon was occupied after street fighting. United States forces were then used to prevent reprisals; Admiral Southerland ordered that no government troops should come within two miles of the towns formerly under revolutionary control.[81]

The bulk of the marine force was removed in four months, but a legation guard of 100 men was left in Managua after the minister advised that the "withdrawal of all marines would be construed as the tacit consent of the United States to renew hostilities." Moreover, the presidents of Guatemala and El Salvador might attempt to unify Central America by force "if the restraining influence of the United States were removed."[82] The guard was maintained until 1925, becoming a symbol of American commitment which could neither be removed without encouraging revolt nor maintained without a deterrent effect.

The use of United States forces to help suppress a revolution appeared to represent a general commitment "to uphold constituted governments." In Nicaragua "this meant that the conservatives would stay in power, though everyone, including the State Department, knew that they were a minority party."[83] It also meant that American officials had to decide what should be accepted as constitutional. One document concluded that Mena had been "constitutionally and legally elected President of Nicaragua for the ensuing term," but a higher officer in the State Department used his pencil to insert "un-" and "il-" and to put a question mark in the margin. Those who believed that Mena's election was legal were not prepared to give him further support. Since it seemed "clearly evident" that the assembly was opposed to "the lawful, orderly and peaceful regeneration" of the country, the Latin American division was "disposed to concur" with Weitzel and "those Nicaraguans representing the best elements" that "the constitutionality of the election of Mena, and the existence and fruits of the present Assembly should be, and are, disregarded."[84]

In the wake of the turmoil, with Mena out of the picture, the presidential "election" was held on November 2, 1912, "by popular, direct and public vote," as the Dawson Agreements had provided and as the minister urged, but without any real contest. Chamorro, who was often referred to as the most popular political figure, had incurred strong enmities and was persuaded, largely by Weitzel, not to seek either the presidency or the vice-presidency, "thereby removing even the appearance of militarism in the new administration." This left Díaz as the leading candidate despite his "little inclination to continue in office."[85] Weitzel, who had earlier thought that Díaz lacked political strength, was hopeful that the "premium on warfare and militarism could be removed by limiting the candidates to civilians." "Diaz is a civilian," J. Butler Wright noted in the margin.[86] The presence of American marines made practical the candidacy of a man who lacked both popular and military support, but who was widely acceptable for that very reason. As Weitzel noted, Díaz was not identified with "the extremist element in either Granada or Leon," since he had lived as a businessman in Bluefields for about twelve years.[87]

The elections were not supervised and the Liberals did not take part. It is not clear whether they abstained voluntarily. Dana G. Munro wrote in his book of 1964 that they "decided not to participate." In an earlier work he had written: "the three or four thousand voters who were *allowed* to participate unanimously approved the official ticket."[88] In advising against supervision, Weitzel argued:

Neither party would willingly acquiesce in an adverse result however fair and we would have to bear the burden of criticism without the power to justify our course by assuring an honest administration. The fact is the cry of fair elections in Nicaragua is not sincere. The majority of the people are satisfied with Díaz and the malcontents are more desirous of securing the Presidency than of having honest elections.[89]

He saw no need for the United States to undertake to govern Nicaragua. What might "be necessary to insure order and protection to life and property . . . could most probably be controlled as in Panama by moral influence.'' Wright noted, less optimistically, ''Our *present* influence is certainly not the same (nor as strong).''[90]

DÍAZ SUSTAINED

The new tenure of office which Díaz was given did not relieve the desperate financial situation because the Nicaraguan congress rejected the bankers' terms, and the bankers were unsure of the policies of a new administration in Washington. At the end of 1912, however, Díaz and the American minister agreed to an arrangement whereby in exchange for $3 million Nicaragua would grant the United States rights to build a canal and establish naval bases on both coasts. The basic motivation for this appears to have been the desire to give support to the Díaz government, rather than to secure the concessions for their own sake.[91] It was a form of foreign aid with a wrapping and label made necessary because aid was not then considered legitimate. Its sponsors hoped that the treaty would affirm the commitment of the United States to the maintenance of peace in Central America, remove any lingering threat of foreign influence, and enhance trade and prosperity. A rather frantic attempt was made to secure ratification before adjournment of the expiring Senate, but the project carried over into the Wilson administration and was a focus of controversy until a revised version, the Bryan-Chamorro Treaty, was ratified on February 18, 1916.

The election of Woodrow Wilson raised doubt as to whether the United States would continue the policies of financial support through which it had sustained Díaz. By blocking the treaty, Democrats in the Senate had prevented establishment of the financial control in Nicaragua which the bankers demanded as the basis for a substantial loan. The minister reported that they would not ''advance another dollar nor entertain a new proposition until they are certain that the incoming administration in Washington will continue the present policy.''[92]

Although Wilson had said virtually nothing about Latin America during the campaign, he was impelled by events in Mexico just one week after taking office to issue a statement that has sometimes been thought to represent a vital change in policy. It combined a strong expression of desire ''to cultivate the friendship and deserve the confidence of our sister republics'' with stern notice that the United States would attempt to establish the basis for ''mutual respect'' by supporting ''the orderly processes of just government based upon Law, not upon arbitrary or irregular force.'' He further stated:

We can have no sympathy with those who seek to seize the power of government to advance their own personal interests or ambition. We are the friends of peace, but we know there can be no lasting or stable peace in such circumstances. As friends, therefore, we shall prefer those who act in the interest of peace and honor, who protect private rights, and respect the restraints of constitutional provisions.[93]

There was nothing new in this unless it was the implication that the United States had means of influence (and objectivity of judgment) such that it could be insistent. Believing that dictatorship and revolution in Latin America had been made worse by outside economic interests that exploited political weakness, Wilson had reason to believe that the abandonment of ''dollar diplomacy'' would do much to remove these evils.[94] But the policy objectives of Taft had been very similar to those set forth by Wilson. Wilson's eventual acceptance of some of the same techniques and his acquiescence in conditions which had defied improvement under Taft did not so much mean that he had changed his goals as that he encountered some of the same obstacles. It was, as Wilson's biographer Ray Stannard Baker suggested, ''a significant commentary upon the implacable nature of the forces which, under the existing social and economic order, determine the foreign policies of states.''[95]

Both the Díaz government and the Latin American division worked hard to impress upon the new secretary of state the urgent necessity of financial assistance to Nicaragua. The minister of finance came to Washington and employed a friend of Secretary of State William Jennings Bryan, Charles A. Douglas, as counsel and intermediary. Douglas argued quite explicitly that ''financial relief'' could not be obtained unless the United States were empowered ''to take such action as it might find advisable,'' using ''moral suasion, . . . or physical force, or both.''[96] The Latin American division warned that unless ''protection and support'' were promised to the bankers ''much of the good that has already been accomplished will be lost and Nicaragua will probably look to Europe for a new loan.'' It suggested, however, that ratification of the canal treaty might relieve the stringency.[97]

Once the situation came to his attention, Bryan showed no inclination to deny either the importance or the propriety of financial support. Not questioning the conclusion that Zelaya and his supporters were unfit to rule, he accepted the legitimacy of the Díaz regime,[98] although it was dependent upon both military and economic assistance from the United States. In some regards he appeared to be more eager than his predecessor to enhance the American role in Nicaragua.

Bryan's approach differed from that of Knox in the naiveté with which it was assumed that democracy would result if exploitation by private interests were prevented. The ''dollar diplomacy'' that Bryan and Wilson opposed would promote stability by accepting or even facilitating corrupt and despotic rule, but Bryan thought that direct and open pursuance of national interest by the United States could avoid this pernicious effect. This belief weakened resistance to intervention.

In a proposed note expressing opposition to European relations with Huerta in Mexico, Bryan suggested that the United States assert in a new corollary to the Monroe Doctrine, ''its unwillingness to have an American Republic exploited by commercial interests of our own or any other country through a government resting upon force.'' In a memorandum to the president, five days before Wilson delivered the celebrated Mobile speech in which he renounced "material interest" as a determinant of foreign policy, Bryan wrote:

If our country, openly claiming a paramount influence in the Western Hemisphere, will go to the rescue of these countries and enable them to secure the money they need for education, sanitation and internal development, there will be no excuse for their putting themselves under obligations to financiers in other lands. I believe it is perfectly safe and will make absolutely sure our domination of the situation.[99]

Wilson was also given a rationale for intervention by Robert Lansing, then counsellor of the State Department, who later succeeded Bryan. Lansing was primarily concerned with the "danger of European political control" as a consequence of economic activity.[100] He expressed no dismay that the connection between economic influence and political control which he saw in European activity would also result from United States investments.

While Knox had allowed Díaz's offer of a protectorate to rest under "deep and earnest consideration,'' Bryan sent forward a treaty draft prepared by Douglas which would give the United States the right to intervene to maintain "a constitutional government" in Nicaragua, as security and encouragement to the bankers. In remarkable innocence of Central American intrigue, he was seemingly oblivious to the interests of Díaz and Chamorro in securing a guarantee against revolution and hopeful that evidence of Nicaraguan initiative would make such a clause acceptable to other Central American countries.[101] It appeared, as the *New York Times* put it, that "the dawn of a new era in our Latin American relations," which Wilson had proclaimed, would "be due to a cheerful acceptance and amplification . . . of the much-condemned dollar diplomacy of his predecessors."[102] Paradoxically, Bryan's primary concern, contrary to that of his less idealistic predecessor, seems to have been national security interest in gaining the canal option and a naval base in the Gulf of Fonseca, to exclude European influence.[103]

Bryan tried to obtain the approval of the Senate Foreign Relations Committee before signing the proposed treaty. A majority, mainly of his own party, refused either to accept the provision for a protectorate or to give immediate approval to a treaty without this provision. Bryan then devised a plan which would deal with the financial problem of Nicaragua more directly as a matter of natural interest by enabling it (and certain other Latin American countries) to borrow at less than bankers' rates on the credit of the United States.[104] Although the idea was unprecedented, it does not appear to have made extreme demands upon existing attitudes and institutions. This plan, he thought, would have the added advantage of giving "our country such an increased influence . . . that we could prevent revolutions, promote education, and advance stable and just government." But despite Wilson's professed distrust of the bankers, the president was unwilling to support an approach which "would have to be a long time canvassed" and which he feared "would strike the whole country . . . as . . . novel and radical."[105]

Under pressure from Díaz, Bryan resorted to the expedient that he had been trying to avoid: approving another temporary loan from the New York bankers that gave them control of the national railroad and the national bank.[106] Wilson questioned the expediency of pressing for the treaty against the opposition of other Central American countries "just now when we are trying to gain a certain moral prestige."[107] When it came before the Foreign Relations Committee again a year later, Bryan was subjected to criticism for having become the dupe both of Wall Street bankers and of Nicaraguan politicians in a project "based upon deception, misrepresentation, fraud, tyranny and corruption."[108]

Elihu Root, the respected elder statesman who had done the most to shape Latin American policy after the war with Spain, was a member of the Senate at this time. He accepted the assertion of a limited right of intervention, but was anxious not to give unnecessary alarm to other Latin American countries. He was unwilling to accept "a grant of power which I felt certain the people of Nicaragua could not and ought not to approve" and "troubled" as to "whether the Nicaraguan government which has made the treaty is really representative of the people of Nicaragua and whether it will be regarded . . . as having been a free agent in making the treaty." The marine commander had not minced words in reporting that "The present government is not in power by the will of the people; the elections of the House of Congress were mostly fraudulent." Root did not doubt that the presence of United States Marines really maintained the government in office:

Can we afford to make a treaty so serious for Nicaragua, granting us perpetual rights in that country, with a president who we have reason to believe does not represent more than a quarter of the people of the country, and who is maintained in office by our military force, and to whom we would, as a result of the treaty, pay a large sum of money to be disposed of by him as president: I should be sorry to see the United States get into that position.[109]

Root was also concerned about the reaction in other Central American countries. If they should become "convinced that we wish to rule them by force . . . it would mean the end of all our attempts to benefit them and help them along as we have been trying to do."[110]

Costa Rica and El Salvador complained that the treaty would be in flagrant violation of their treaty rights—contentions which the Central American Court of Justice upheld in 1916 and 1917 at the cost of its own demise. The government of Costa Rica objected to what it construed as a "demand" from Bryan that certain Nicaraguan revolutionists, including Zelaya and Mena, be requested to leave the country.[111] The Salvadorean minister of foreign affairs gave assurance, however, that his government "would not permit" the hostile sentiment "among the masses throughout the Republic . . . to assume proportions which it would be unable to repress."[112]

Had the United States broadened its concern beyond the commitment to an unpopular Conservative government in Nicaragua to consideration of the rest of Central America, its basic interest in stability might have found better expression and response. Movement in this direction occurred in 1915, when discussions were held with the five governments on proposals for several treaties providing for naval bases, financial stabilization, and economic and educational assistance. Its sponsors hoped that these proposals "would stand as a proof of the Department's wisdom and disinterested regard, and as a silent rebuke to those who have attacked the Administration" on the treaty with Nicaragua, but they were not pursued.[113]

As time passed, with the bankers holding back from further commitments, while the effects of war in Europe drastically reduced customs receipts, the financial condition of Nicaragua required further attention. On August 5, 1914, Bryan and Chamorro had signed a new treaty which omitted the "Platt Amendment" provision, but it was another eighteen months before ratification, and it was not until Díaz's term of office had expired that payments were made. Despite a recommendation that the people should be given "ocular demonstration" and employment to distract "their minds from revolutionary pursuits,"[114] two-thirds of the $3 million was applied to past debts, mostly to United States banks, with nearly all of the rest used for back salaries and claims.[115] In "long and painful negotiations," the State Department worked out an agreement between the bankers and a Nicaraguan government that showed considerably more strength and self-confidence than Díaz had been able to muster.[116]

3.
THE DOMINICAN REPUBLIC

The large island which lies between Cuba and Puerto Rico has attracted the attention of the United States more because of the turbulence of its political life than through any enticement or apprehension created by proximity. Its instability was heightened by the relationship between the two countries that share the island. Santo Domingo, roughly the eastern two-thirds of the island, was ceded by Spain to France in 1795, was repeatedly invaded after 1891 from Haiti, the more populous country to the west, and came under Haitian rule from 1822 to 1844. Dominican political figures connived at various times with Haitian factions and repeatedly sought support from Spain, France, and the United States, offering concessions and even annexation. Spain took over the government from 1861 to 1865. A thread of patriotism could occasionally be seen, but it was always intertwined with personal and factional intrigue. The party in power usually sought foreign protection, hoping thus "both to save the country and perpetuate its own rule, while independence was invariably supported by the opposition, which bristled with patriotic indignation and the fear that it might be permanently excluded from the banquet table."[1]

The first of several approaches to the United States was made in 1850, after President Buenaventura Báez had failed to attract French support. During the Grant administration Báez, again in power, concluded an annexation treaty, only to have it defeated in the Senate. On several occasions Dominicans of various factions tried to gain revenue and support by making Samaná Bay available to the United States.

THE ATTEMPT AT PACIFICATION THROUGH CUSTOMS CONTROL

Political turbulence was held in abeyance during the relatively long dictatorship of Ulises Heureaux, who came to power with help from the uncle of the American vice-consul and managed to put down or buy off opposition from 1882 until he was assassinated in 1899. Heureaux did nothing, however, to improve the country's ability to conduct an autonomous political life. Like his predecessors, he engaged in repeated efforts to secure funds from outside sources. Although he did not succeed in leasing Samaná Bay, he was able to secure loans that increased national indebtedness tenfold, with little if any benefit to the people.

Heureaux's increasing reliance on the United States was challenged in 1892 by an attempt to put together a European syndicate, but the cabinet member who sponsored it was imprisoned and eventually murdered. In 1893, an American enterprise, the San Domingo Improvement Company, acquired from Westendorp and Company of Amsterdam a right to collect customs revenues that had been granted in 1888.[2] During Heureaux's last years, "an unmitigated reign of terror," public sentiment was aroused against the United States because of the prominent influence of the Improvement Company.[3] In 1898 Heureaux suggested that the United States seize Samaná Bay or negotiate a secret cession with accompanying payment. In 1899, two weeks before he was murdered, he secretly proposed a United States protectorate. The State Department reprimanded the minister for having forwarded the project to Washington.[4]

The two principal opponents of Heureaux became the leaders of rival factions following his death.[5] General Horacio Vásquez, one of the group which planned the assassination, was proclaimed provisional president, but he supported Juan Isídro Jiménez in the election a few weeks later. As president, Jiménez incurred bitter criticism by his vacillating policies toward the Improvement Company.[6] A vote of censure was soon followed by an outbreak of revolution. Vásquez gave up a prolonged effort to avoid an open split, quickly defeated the president's forces in April 1902 and once again became provisional president. But he was soon confronted with widespread revolution, due largely to an attempt to discontinue payments to local *caciques*. General Woss y Gil, who had been vice-president and minister to the United States and had been released from confinement through the intervention of the American vice-president of the Improvement Company, was proclaimed provisional president. After sharp fighting, Vásquez, incapacitated by illness, went into exile.

The new government, lacking popular support, was defenseless against rival creditors. The president revived the tactic of offering Samaná Bay to the United States, while the foreign minister was reported to prefer an arrangement with Germany.[7] Before any such ideas could be carried forward, however, revolution broke out again, with *jiménistas* and *horacistas* jostling for advantage. In November 1903 the capital fell to forces commanded by General Carlos Morales, who proceeded to renounce loyalty to Jiménez and announce his own candidacy for president, in alliance with the *horacistas*. After some six months of fighting, opposition faded and Morales, a man "erratic and impulsive far beyond the border line of sanity," according to Sumner Welles, was elected president.[8] The price of *horacista* support was control of the cabinet and most of the provincial governorships.

United States forces had been landed in April and again in November 1903 to protect the consulate and a large sugar estate. The presence of American forces may have contributed to the defeat of Jiménez. Commander Dillingham of the *Detroit* claimed two years afterwards that he had been "entirely responsible for the placing of Morales in power."[9] This seems to have been exaggerated, however, since Morales's initial success occurred before Dillingham reached Dominican waters.[10]

There is no evidence that the United States took sides in order to gain special advantage, although this could readily have been done, since both sides were willing to bid for support. Jiménez, spurred by defeat, thought the United States should assume "more or less" the same relationship that it had toward Cuba under the Platt Amendment.[11] The new government eagerly sought support. The minister, William F. Powell, who had for several years been trying to persuade the State Department to undertake an active supervisory role, extended recognition to Morales before the department had made up its mind to do so and encouraged presidential overtures.[12]

State Department officials were increasingly concerned that prolonged disturbances would attract "foreign attention in a way somewhat similar to the Venezuelan affair."[13] As they saw it, Dominican politics was shaped by access to revenues. Each province "tended to become a virtually independent semi-feudal principality" the expenses of which were "paid directly out of the proceeds" of the local customhouse. "A Dominican revolution might be briefly defined as the attempt of a bandit guerrilla to seize a custom house."[14] If customs revenues and foreign loans could be put out of reach, they reasoned, the domestic conflict which led to intervention could be greatly reduced, for there would be little for which or with which Dominican factions could fight. A sophisticated observer noted, however, that revolution also had an essential political function. "The real campaigns and expressions of the people's will have . . . been the revolutions, and politics and revolutions have thus come to be regarded as going hand in hand."[15]

President Roosevelt moved reluctantly to undertake a supervisory role. He sent Assistant Secretary of State Francis B. Loomis on a special mission to Santo Domingo, but it is not clear whether he intended him to conclude an agreement for customs control.[16] After Loomis was on his way, Roosevelt wrote to a friend that he wanted "to do nothing," or, if it were "absolutely necessary to do something, then . . . as little as possible."[17]

As a result of the Loomis mission, the Morales government proposed that customhouses be placed under custody of the United States. The president held back, however, with reference to "precedents which would be equally inconvenient and undesirable for both countries."[18] Roosevelt had concluded that the United States should take "partial possession" of the Dominican Republic, but he wanted to defer action until the necessity should become more clear to the American public.[19]

The rationale for intervention was publicly set forth in a letter from Roosevelt to Root on May 20, 1904, which was read at a banquet in New York. It took up and broadened the theme of the Platt Amendment: "Brutal wrong-doing, or an impotence which results in a general loosening of the ties of civilized society, may finally require intervention by some civilized nation, and in the Western Hemisphere the United States cannot ignore this duty."[20] This came to be known as the Roosevelt Corollary to the Monroe Doctrine after it was set forth in the annual message to Congress the following December.

As evidence of the new seriousness of concern for the Dominican Republic, Thomas C. Dawson, an able diplomat and scholar, was appointed on April 28 as full-time resident minister. His predecessor had also been minister to Haiti and had resided in Port-au-Prince. The issue of finance soon came to a head. With support from the State Department, the Improvement Company had negotiated an agreement for compensation on terms to be fixed by arbitration. The arbitral award, fixed on July 14, 1904, provided for monthly payments to an agent appointed by the United States, to be secured by customs revenues from the northern ports. The agent was empowered to take over these ports in case of default.[21] This was not unprecedented. The company had controlled customs collections before January 1901, and the same man who had previously represented it was appointed financial agent. In September default occurred and the agent took charge of the customhouse at Puerto Plata.

This arrangement gave the Improvement Company a privileged position that was likely to be resisted by European creditors. Just how strongly they were prepared to act is not clear. Sumner Welles wrote that Germany, instigated by the *jimenistas,* "had under consideration the project to purchase the Spanish, Belgian and Italian claims . . . and secure control of the Republic by occupying the customs houses."[22] Roosevelt told Congress a year later that there had been "imminent danger of foreign intervention."[23] Dana G. Munro concluded, however, that the real purpose of the Europeans was to secure American intervention and found no contemporary "indication that the German government was taking a hostile attitude."[24]

On December 30, 1904, following Roosevelt's pronouncement that the United States might be forced, "however reluctantly, in flagrant cases of . . . wrongdoing of impotence, to the exercise of an international police power,"[25] Secretary of State John Hay instructed Dawson to see "whether the Government of Santo Domingo would be disposed to request the United States to take charge of the collection of duties and effect an equitable distribution."[26]

It was not as easily done as Roosevelt might have hoped. Although Dawson had reported that most Dominicans appeared to favor "some form of American protection,"[27] he found that "deeply grounded prejudice against any sort of American intervention" caused "great difficulties."[28] Although within four days the principal cabinet members gave their consent, prolonged negotiation was necessary. Dawson's efforts were supplemented by Commander Dillingham. After the acceptance of a definitive agreement on February 7, Dawson noted that the presence of naval ships had "had a powerful moral effect on the rash and ignorant elements, who unhappily are in the majority and who do not yet understand the real benefits the country will receive from the arrangement.''[29]

The revised agreement was in treaty form. Roosevelt submitted it to the Senate with a lengthy explanation. It was essential to place ''the custom-houses beyond the temptation of insurgent chieftains.'' Thanks to ''the prudent and far-seeking statesmanship of the Dominican Government,'' the solution was at hand. Advantages would be ''indirect, but nevertheless great, for it is supremely to our interest that all the communities immediately south of us should be or become prosperous and stable, and therefore not merely in name, but in fact independent and self-governing.''[30]

When the Senate held up ratification, the Morales government again faced imminent revolution, but Roosevelt went ahead to establish a collectorship on executive authority. Three months later Dawson noted with satisfaction that the 45 percent of revenues reaching the central government gave it more cash than at any time in the five years when receipts from the ports had been disposed of by local authorities. Moreover, for the first time since the death of Heureaux there had been ''a cessation of active plotting against the established government.''[31]

Putting an end to revolution was clearly to the advantage of the government. It was not clear, however, what the United States would do if revolution should break out. The hope that this question would not have to be faced proved vain. ''Repeated efforts at revolution occurred throughout the spring and summer of 1905,'' and in November there was a major outbreak.[32] Before the end of the year, authority had so thoroughly dissolved that President Morales, increasingly isolated and impotent in his own administration, himself left the capital and joined the revolutionists!

Roosevelt was determined in September ''to stop any revolution,'' regardless of ''technical or red tape difficulty.''[33] In December, however, when Dawson asked for authority to land forces, Secretary of State Elihu Root refused to use either protection of Americans or maintenance of the customs collectorship as a pretext for further intervention.

We cannot take any part in differences between factions or officers of Dominican Government. No troops are to be landed except when absolutely necessary to protect life and property of American citizens, and if landed they must confine themselves strictly to such protection, which will extend to the peaceful performance of duty by the Americans who are collecting revenue in the custom-houses so long as the Dominican desires them to continue that service. If Dominican Government determines to end the modus vivendi and the collection of duties by Americans nominated by President of the United States, protection will extend to their safe withdrawal with their property.[34]

Landing of United States forces, it appeared, might have jeopardized rather than protected resident Americans. The French chargé d'affaires offered to bring up a warship from Martinique to do what the United States could not safely do for itself—an ironic reversal of the assumption that American intervention was impelled by the need to prevent European involvement. In this situation protection could only have been a pretended cause for the landing of American forces, and Root would have none of it. He cabled Dawson that his previous instructions were to be followed strictly. There was to be "no landing of troops under any such circumstances as to justify apprehension of danger to lives of foreigners."[35]

Root's desire to limit direct involvement appeared also in his acceptance of a proposed amendment to the pending treaty, providing that a request for help in maintaining order would have to be approved by the Dominican congress. He pointed out that "the unconditional power of interference would practically destroy Dominican sovereignty, which, of course, none of us wishes to do."[36]

Morales held out only briefly before giving himself up, with a broken leg, to the Spanish chargé d'affaires and going into exile aboard an American naval ship. The vice-president, General Ramón Cáceres, a cousin and close associate of Horacio Vásquez, succeeded to the presidency. Although the *jiménistas,* who had been conceded control of the northwestern province, kept the revolt alive for several months, Dawson optimistically concluded that "the revolutionary classes" were "discouraged" and the political leaders frustrated by the absence of opportunities to seize power and revenues.[37] A few months later, however, he noted that "back of the danger" caused by the "professional revolutionary class" there was "the possibility of a revolution caused by sheer poverty."[38]

A debt settlement was worked out by an American economist, Jacob H. Hollander, and the Dominican finance minister, Federico Velásquez. Hollander readily acknowledged that obligations had been contracted "under circumstances that smack always of extortion and often of fraud" and were "swollen . . . by extravagant, and sometimes incredible, items for commissions, publicity, and kindred charges."[39] A new treaty, providing that the United States would appoint a general receiver to collect and disperse customs duties, was quickly approved by the Senate in February 1907.[40] The American purpose appears to have been improvement of administration rather than "extension of further control over the Republic's internal affairs."[41]

Ratification by the Dominican Republic was held up until Root agreed to certain "clarifications," but the revolution predicted by the American Consul at Puerto Plata did not occur.[42] Instead there followed nearly five years "of peaceful, stable and orderly government" and dramatic economic growth under the presidency of Cáceres and the energetic administrative direction of Velásquez. The government's armed forces were well enough paid, fed, and led, and internal transportation was sufficiently improved so that sporadic efforts at rebellion were quickly put down.[43]

RELUCTANCE ERODED

By 1910 it began to be evident that no panacea had been found. Horacio Vásquez charged his cousin, Cáceres, with resorting to repression rather than responding to popular demands. Although Vásquez was unwilling to lead an open revolt, others vied to do so. When former President Morales told the State Department that he intended to move against the president, the department alerted Cáceres and had Morales arrested in Puerto Rico. In telling Cáceres of this threat, Huntington Wilson appended a blunt warning against any interference with the present system of customs administration.[44]

Containment of revolutionary ferment ended suddenly on November 19, 1911, when Cáceres was shot to death, like Heureaux, whom he himself had killed twelve years before, and Trujillo, fifty years later. The vice-presidency having been abolished in 1908, there was no automatic succession. The assassin was pursued and killed by the guard. Its commander, Colonel Alfredo Victoria, too young to become president himself, secured the election by congress of his uncle, Eladio Victoria. But the Victorias were supreme only in the capital; the countryside "relapsed with incredible rapidity into a state of complete anarchy."[45]

Such turmoil did not restrain the rhetoric of Secretary of State Philander C. Knox. On tour of the Caribbean, Knox told the Dominican congress that he rejoiced to see that the "dark cloud" of Cáceres's assassination had not disturbed "the normal march of your people in the orderly path of self-control." When he reached Nicaragua he claimed that American protection of customs had successfully "cured almost century-old evils" in the Dominican Republic.[46]

Vásquez and Velásquez came together in St. Thomas to promote revolutionary activities along the Haitian frontier. Huntington Wilson warned Haiti that the United States expected it to prevent operations "subversive of Dominican peace," but Vásquez slipped ashore at Port-au-Prince and was quietly aided by the Haitian president.[47] The government of Victoria, confronted by "the open opposition of all factions," quickly exhausted its resources.[48] Everything that had been accomplished through the customs agreement was rapidly being destroyed. In this situation the United States began to urge the government "to make friendly overtures to the leaders of the revolution."[49]

More drastic measures were soon under consideration in a State Department which was no longer dominated by the competence and sensitivity of Elihu Root. Sumner Welles described the contrast:

In place of the courteous, helpful, considerate spirit manifested both by President Roosevelt and by Secretary Root . . ., there was now assumed by the Department of State an omniscience in all that concerned the solution of the domestic problems of the Republic. A policy . . . was formulated . . . which ignored the advice which would readily have been tendered by a great number of competent Dominicans of prominence in public life, had the Department of State shown any sign of desiring such cooperation.[50]

The minister, William W. Russell, saw no hope that disorder and destruction could be ended by victory for either side; the fighting was "purposely prolonged by the Government military chiefs, who are enriching themselves at the expense of the troops.'' The State Department was determined to find a means of "definitively curing the present deplorable situation.'' Russell thought this should "dictate a policy beneficial to the country.'' The Victoria administration was "extremely unpopular and very detrimental,'' while the success of the revolution "would be disastrous.'' "Intelligent Dominicans'' were looking to the United States to make good the promise of the convention. "Only complete control by our Government would permanently insure order and justice, but any degree of control would be beneficial; indeed, without our effective control, one administration here would be just as good as another.''[51]

Huntington Wilson prepared a recommendation for President Taft. To avoid failure of "its whole Dominican policy'' and "the wreck of the broad policy pursued in Central America,'' the United States would have to "enforce its demands by such measures as the breaking of diplomatic relations, the forcible protection of the customhouses, and perhaps the withholding of the customs revenues.''[52] Immediate action should be taken to set up a border patrol under the customs service and secure the removal of the president's nephews from control of the armed forces, together with a decree of amnesty, backed by a threat of marine landings. Taft appointed the chief of the bureau of insular affairs, General Frank McIntyre, and the chief of the Latin American division, William T. S. Doyle, as special commissioners, to proceed to Santo Domingo on the U.S.S. *Prairie* together with some 750 marines.

They found "a very hard situation.'' The president and his ministers were "wholly unable to meet the requirements of ordinary normal government.'' They could not put down the revolution, but seemed able to prevent its success. It was generally believed that Victoria's election had been "obtained by bribery and intimidation,'' despite "the appearance of legality.'' "The apparent majority'' wanted Vásquez to become president, but "a smaller number of perhaps a more intelligent class'' preferred Velásquez. "A still smaller'' group wanted "a direct American intervention.'' Many felt, as did the commissioners, that "a fair election'' might achieve no better result than "the irregular methods heretofore in use,'' because of the "low average of intelligence and integrity'' among the electorate. Vásquez seemed "unable to accomplish anything except the fomenting of an insurrection.'' "Adequate remedy . . . would require prolonged intervention and controls,'' but this was "practically impossible.''[53]

The commissioners centered their efforts on securing resignations first of the president's nephews and ultimately, when it seemed that there was no other way to end the fighting, from the president himself. Lacking support from any significant faction and dependent for revenue on the customs, Victoria resigned on November 26, 1912. The commissioners meanwhile met with Vásquez and smoothed the way for designation by the congress of the Archbishop of Santo Domingo, Monseñor Adolfo A. Nouel, as provisional president. The marines remained on board the *Prairie*. A new loan of $1.5 million was arranged, with American officials to control its expenditure.[54]

Archbishop Nouel lacked the political skill and force to master the contending factions. He was voted into office only because his election had been indicated by the American commissioners as the one means of ending the civil war without "the direct intervention of the United States."[55] Within two weeks he was ready to resign, but Knox importuned him to remain.[56] In January 1913 the minister reported that Nouel was urging the United States to take "an active part in controlling elections." In reply Taft specified several reforms which would make it "easier . . . for the United States to lend its aid." Considering the extreme weakness of Nouel's government, this could hardly have been regarded as helpful. Nouel's next communication had a less inviting tone: he trusted "earnestly" that the United States would not have "occasion" to fulfill its obligations "in a manner painful to the Dominican people."[57] Then, at the end of March, the archbishop resigned the presidency.

The new administration in Washington thus faced a situation that no longer sustained the hopefulness which had accompanied the customs arrangements. The stakes and methods of Dominican politics had not changed significantly, although efforts were concentrated more upon the national government. The contenders still had regional bases of strength, and factional rivalry continued to dominate political life. The State Department had concluded that more extensive controls were needed and had suggested that free elections would break the cycle of violence, but no serious thought had been given to how the change might come about.

THE ATTEMPT TO ENFORCE POLITICAL VIRTUE

Wilson and Bryan "had a genuine compassion for the victims of the unending instability of the Caribbean republics" and believed that constitutional democracy was an attainable alternative. Once the necessity and apparent promise of intervention were accepted, however, nothing stood in the way of deepening involvement—neither power, nor law, nor scruple. "There was a certain self-perpetuation about the working out of policies of helpfulness."[58]

Inclined as they were to assume the efficacy of good will, Wilson and Bryan did not take Caribbean problems seriously enough to value diplomatic competence and experience. There was a complete change of policymakers in the State Department, except for the perennial A. A. Adee, who served as second assistant secretary of state from 1886 until 1924, and legations in the Caribbean area went to Democratic politicians of relatively advanced years and no diplomatic experience. In the case of the Dominican Republic, the new minister, James M. Sullivan, may have owed his appointment to the lobbying of an American promoter who had lost out on banking deals.[59]

Following the resignation of Archbishop Nouel, the congress, unable to settle upon any of the factional leaders, chose a well-regarded former partisan of Vásquez, General José Bordas Valdés, to serve as president for no more than one year. Lacking at the outset any following of his own, Bordas maneuvered to gain the backing of Desiderio Arias, "the most powerful and dangerous of the local *caudillos*," and of Jiménez, by taking the Central Dominican Railway out of the hands of the *horacistas*.[60] The provincial governor who had been the beneficiary of railway revenues promptly went into revolt, and in September 1913 Horacio Vásquez proclaimed himself provisional president. The Wilson administration, with slight information, denounced this "pernicious revolutionary activity."[61] The new assistant secretary for Latin America, Boaz W. Long, naively relied on the Dominican chargé d'affaires's opinion regarding Vásquez. It was misleading to characterize him as "one of the most unruly of political agitators," a "Professional Revolutionist" who "caused the last administration no end of trouble," but it was convenient in the reforming spirit of the new administration to identify a particular source of evil.[62]

It was not until later that a thoughtful summation was received from the consul at Puerto Plata which cast quite a different light on the revolution. The consul, a Ph.D. from Yale, saw the movement as a continuation of that of 1912, which had been stopped by American action. Apart from personal interests, "its underlying object and justification" was "genuine civil government, . . . as against the tyrannical military rule of the Victorias." Vásquez and his followers had been willing since 1912 "to submit their fortunes to an election" and were "reluctant to take up . . . arms" again. But the consul warned of difficulty:

Until . . . good government is guaranteed from outside (and they who undertake to guarantee it must have infinite patience and firmness coupled with intimate knowledge of the people and affection for them. . . .), I see no end of the scourge of revolution, no end of bloodshed and suffering for the defenseless poor. . . . If there be intervention, which, like that of 1912, does not go to the root of the matter, it can be but of temporary effect. . . . Halfway measures will not suffice, and, if such are taken, the Dominican people will be left worse off—as most seem to think they have been since the abortive American intervention of 1912—than if left alone to deal with the situation by their own anarchical methods.[63]

Bryan composed, in an instruction to James M. Sullivan, the new minister, a prescription of virtue which paid no regard to actual conditions:

You will carry with you a copy of the President's statement of last March which sets forth fully, and in such a way as to leave no doubt, his position on two important points, namely: First, that we can have no sympathy with those who seek to seize the power of government to advance their own personal interests or ambition: and, second, that the test of a republican form of government is to be found in its responsiveness to the will of the people, its just powers being derived from the consent of the governed.

It is not to be expected that those in power will be able to avoid mistakes but mistakes should be corrected by constitutional means. Neither is it to be supposed that reforms will in all cases be brought about as soon as they ought to be, but the remedy of this is agitation—not insurrection. Say to any who may feel aggrieved or who may be disposed to violence that the good offices of this Government can be counted upon at all times to assist in the establishment of justice, in the remedying of abuses, and in the promotion of the welfare of the people. We must depend, therefore, upon all the people of Santo Domingo, of whatever party or faction, to join together in securing justice through law and in the election by free and fair ballot of officials whom the people desire. . . .

I am sure that when the disinterestedness of our Government is fully understood, its friendship will be appreciated and its advice sought.[64]

More tangibly, Bryan warned the revolutionists that the United States would deny them recognition, should they come to power. Customs receipts would be withheld, the convention of 1907 would be invoked to prevent any increase in the debt, and any move to increase taxes would be regarded "with disfavor."

Minister Sullivan, who tried to give effect to these instructions, was hardly a paragon of democratic virtue. The circumstances of his appointment, the contract-seeking activities of a cousin to whom he was indebted, his disregard for the dignity of the Dominicans, and his impulsiveness made him the central figure in unflattering anecdotes and rumors. Bryan's apparent willingness to use the customs service to provide jobs for "deserving Democrats," contrasting with proclamations of disinterested concern, did nothing to curtail cynicism.

Sullivan had hardly reached Santo Domingo when he cabled jubilantly that "the revolutionists had yielded to the American declaration that force of arms can never settle any question, and it is understood by all parties that the last civil war of the country is over." Just four days later, however, after the revolutionists rejected a settlement, he was equally unrestrained in the opposite conclusion, asking the State Department to "fortify" him "with instructions to take the most drastic measures."[65] He informed the consul at Puerto Plata of his advice to Washington that the revolutionists should "be stamped out," warning that Americans should "prepare to leave town." When two warships arrived, the rumor spread that they were about to bombard the city. As it turned out, there was no direct commitment of American arms. Government forces recaptured the key ports, and the revolutionists signed a peace treaty. But the price of peace was a deepened commitment for the United States. The consul reported that the revolutionists had accepted the agreement "with the clear understanding that the carrying out of it is guaranteed by the United States down to the last syllable and that they may appeal to the United States whenever they think they are being wronged."[66]

Sullivan soon besought the State Department for "explicit instructions in regard to carrying out the promise I made on behalf of the American Government that in the event of revolution being abandoned, a fair election would be ensured. . . . They ask me to put into practice now my preaching about free speech and free press in the public square."[67]

The State Department was slow to respond. Sullivan then recommended, in conjunction with the naval commander, "a non-interfering scrutiny . . . by open agents appointed by the Department" in the scheduled election of a constitutional assembly. The Dominican Gcvernment should be warned that unless the balloting "expresses the will of the people as a whole the American Government will take full control of the presidential election that follows." Bryan acknowledged that an American commitment to "fair and free elections" had been "the condition upon which peace was restored." Sullivan was instructed to urge the adoption of regulations to ensure free access to the polls, a fair count, and freedom of speech.[68] With some hesitation Bryan also approved "non-interfering scrutiny." Members of the department anticipated resentment and were doubtful that "scrutinizers" could "tell whether men voted freely or not," but it might at least be possible, they thought, to eliminate the prevailing practice of forcibly enlisting soldiers in order to have them vote "early and often."[69]

When Dominicans questioned the right of the United States "even to suggest what shall be done," Sullivan insisted that President Wilson's declaration of principles concerning Latin America reserved the right to enter any Latin American country to see that the people's rights were not lost by force or fraud. He thought "the non-interfering features of our plan could not hurt the tenderest sensibilities," but warned that "objection to the commission would naturally raise grave doubts as to the intentions of the Dominican Government."[70] The Dominican minister in Washington questioned the basis for supervision, since the revolutionists had continued to fight after the statement regarding free elections. Moreover, it "could be exploited by provokers of revolutions, who would endeavor to make the Dominican people believe that the Dominican Government had consented to the despoiling of our sovereignty."[71] President Wilson typed out a reply which denied that the United States contemplated a supervisory role.[72]

Three young officers of the Department of State and thirty agents from Puerto Rico were received as observers. Although arrests held down the vote in the capital, no tangible evidence of intimidation or coercion was found elsewhere. An opposition majority indicated that the election had not been controlled by the government (however much it may have been dominated by local *caudillos*). The observers happily reported praise from both the government and the opposition. They saw hope, if similar action should be taken in other elections, for acceptance of the ballot to become an alternative to "more radical interference."[73]

A period of deadlock and attrition ensued. The minority that supported President Bordas prevented a quorum in the constitutional convention, and his opponents in congress held up financial relief, "hoping," as Sullivan put it, "to starve the Government from office."[74] Sullivan thought that factional struggle was intensified by belief that the United States would "stand behind the next elected Government." The politicians did not seem to "realize that the Department intends to prevent the wholesale stealing of the past."[75]

Arias, the *caudillo* of the northwest, emerged as the most serious threat to American objectives. He suggested to the consul at Puerto Plata that the United States would do well to let him run the country: "he could guarantee many years of tranquility.''[76] But the Americans would not consider such a deal. Sullivan was unrestrained in his denunciation, urging ''action that will eliminate Arias and his gang.'' He identified Jiménez and Velásquez as ''oratorical candidates of the respectable type,'' but considered Bordas ''the best possible agency for implanting American ideas of good government.'' If Bordas could take advantage of a pending loan, Sullivan suggested, it would make his reelection almost certain and enable him to deal with Arias.[77]

The State Department was concerned ''whether a serious revolution might not result'' from actions which Bordas might take ''to eliminate Arias.'' Bordas told Sullivan that ''his attitude toward Arias'' could only be decided by the United States. If Arias were to be treated as an outlaw, the government would have to be supported in a campaign against him.[78] Sullivan pressed for resolution, but the State Department maintained a bland approach, seemingly fatuous, which might provide the basis for a later commitment.[79] With Bordas on the way to meet Arias on an American vessel, it asked him to ''assume that Arias is sincerely interested in his country's welfare and . . . talk to him as one patriotic citizen would talk to another.'' He should ''point out'' that the United States would ''not permit'' revolution and would ''use its influence to reward those who show themselves deserving.''[80]

The meeting with Arias did nothing to win him to patriotic docility. Bordas sought a showdown by calling for an early election and dismissing governors who could prevent him from controlling the result. Again Sullivan asked the State Department to support the president, but it objected to ''putting funds into Bordas hands so same may be used prior to or during election.'' Sullivan responded forthrightly that ''forcing Arias out of Dominican affairs for ever was of 'supreme importance.' '' He thought it to be ''proper, necessary and expedient that the interests of decency should be permitted to enjoy incidental benefit that can be hoped for through the proper distribution of funds prior to and during election time.''[81] The State Department, clinging to what it considered its proper role, told Sullivan to ''use caution'' in political expressions. But it would have no truck with Arias, ''a smuggler and a revolutionist.'' The daily stipend to Bordas was increased for a fifteen-day period to finance the military campaign against the obstreperous *caudillos*.[82]

Perplexity in Washington can hardly have diminished when Sullivan punctuated alarmist dispatches with the optimistic conclusion that ''the application of Wilson's Latin American policy'' had brought about ''a wonderful improvement. . . . The lesson that the Department has taught by the President's and your pronouncements against revolutions is being learned to the dismay and chagrin of the band of generals who have lived in the past upon revolution.''[83]

Just four days later he cabled that the key northern port had gone over to the rebels. With Puerto Plata in hostile hands, the United States found that its desire to avoid damage conflicted with its support of the government. United States naval vessels prevented the government from blockading the port and on one occasion the U.S.S. *Machias* fired on government artillery to silence its bombardment of the city. The government protested that the United States "must take responsibility openly" if it should continue such action.[84]

Thanks to divisions among his opponents, Bordas was able to extend his original term when it became impossible to hold elections. There was no way, however, for him legally to hold office beyond the expiration date of the term to which Cáceras had been elected. The State Department still felt "in honor bound . . . to use its best efforts to see that [elections] are as free as possible," but the only device which it could suggest, short of using marines, was to avoid a contest. If the prominent candidates should all give support to "some honorable and upright citizen," the United States would do its best "to see that the election is carried out in the fairest and freest manner possible." It suggested that Arias be arrested on a smuggling charge.[85] By then it was too late, however, to prevent Bordas from staging elections in those places which he controlled. His supporters hopefully conducted an inaugural ceremony, but the whole procedure was too fraudulent to resolve the crisis.

By this time Bryan had endorsed the idea of finding a nonpolitical president and had concluded that the United States could not "remain passive any longer."[86] Further action was delayed because of events in Mexico and Haiti,[87] but in late July the United States undertook a peremptory move to establish a new government. Sullivan, perhaps because of personal financial concerns, had kept trying to muster support for Bordas, but the State Department had learned to discount his advice.[88]

President Wilson himself prepared a plan for "immediate reconstitution of political authority" based upon a memorandum from the State Department. A three-member commission took the plan to Santo Domingo under instruction to give "no opportunity for argument." It called for designation of "some responsible and representative man to act as Provisional President" pending an election in which he would not be a candidate. If necessary the United States would "name, . . . sustain, . . . and support him." An observed election would be held at the earliest feasible date. If it had been "free and fair," the United States would recognize the new president and congress and "support them in the exercise of their functions and authority in every way it can." Otherwise, better elections would be held. The United States would "feel at liberty thereafter to insist that revolutionary movements cease and that all subsequent changes in the Government of the Republic be effected by the peaceful processes provided in the Dominican Constitution."[89]

A fifteen-day armistice was already in effect, and talks had begun when the commission arrived. Bordas made one last effort to take advantage of the American presence to save his position, but the commission stood firm, with support from President Wilson, who typed out a brief instruction:

Yield nothing; insist upon full and liberal compliance with plan. . . . Bordas should be given distinctly to understand that the United States means business. This government will not brook refusal, changes of purposes, or unreasonable delay.[90]

A physician and professor, Dr. Ramon Báez, was accepted as provisional president by all of the significant leaders except Arias, who took no part. Báez was inaugurated within a few days and was immediately recognized by the United States.

The assertions and actions through which Wilson tried to establish orderly constitutional government had no explicit basis in treaty rights. The president made reference to "tacitly conceded obligations as the nearest friend of Santo Domingo in her relations with the rest of the world." Rather than seeing contradiction between his peremptory insistence and the emphasis upon equality, in his Mobile speech Wilson relied upon benevolent intent ("the feeling of sincere friendship") and the claim that political strife left no alternative.[91]

The immediate obstacles to implementation of the Wilson plan were overcome without coercion. Bryan wanted to lay down an ultimatum to Arias which would lead to the marines arresting him, but Báez, anxious to avoid any landing of American forces,[92] persuaded the commission that he could handle the problem.[93] This had a paradoxical sequel in the presidential election. Jiménez, the aging leader of one of the major factions, reached an agreement with Arias which resulted in the *caudillo* whose elimination Bryan thought necessary not only having his regional power confirmed, but becoming minister of war. Jiménez gained also the backing of Velásquez and profited from the sympathy of Báez, although the provisional president accepted American observers and did not seriously abuse his authority.[94] The *horacistas* were not able to match this combination.

The department advised Báez to proclaim the election of Jiménez, even though the *horacistas* might prevent a quorum in Congress. Báez, swayed by suggestions that he cling to office, objected to overriding the requirement of a quorum, preferring, as the chargé d'affaires reported, "that solution of crisis shall come from Washington," but gave way to the State Department's insistence that "the will of the majority expressed at a free and fair election" be respected.[95]

The chairman of the commission believed that Jiménez was "fairly in sympathy with the United States, . . . a man who, if necessary, will ask us to protect the Dominican Government."[96] It remained to be seen whether, with American backing and guidance, Jiménez could conduct the administration which the election had placed in his hands. The United States would provide protection, impose controls as needed, and bring military force to bear if it should appear that the president lacked the strength and pliancy to put through reforms and to put down revolt.

TAKING CHARGE, 1916

It soon appeared that in trying to govern in accordance with American expectations, Jiménez could not hold the support that had brought him to office. Much as with both Morales and Bordas, the United States was tied to an increasingly isolated individual who became reliant on its support against forces from traditional Dominican politics, which were strengthened by patriotic sentiment.

Jiménez was under such pressure that he asked for "reassurance" in a plan for "assumption of dictatorship in case of attempted impeachment."[97] The State Department assured him of support "in the suppression of any insurrectionary attempt." "A Government chosen by the people having been established," " no more revolutions" would be permitted. Moreover, "any assistance . . . necessary to compel respect" would be provided against attacks "direct or indirect, open or in secret." Both Arias and Vásquez would be held "personally responsible" if they should "attempt to embarrass the Government." "A naval force" would be "sent whenever necessary." But the government was under tight injunction: "changes advised" by the United States were to be put promptly into effect.[98]

The principal demands were for American officials to take control of internal revenues, customs, and public works, and to organize a constabulary which would replace the Dominican army.[99] These measures were blocked in congress by supporters of Vásquez and Arias. A flavor of patriotic resistance could be sensed amongst claims for patronage and subsidy.

To stern admonition, Vásquez returned succinct rebuff, in sharp illustration of the difficulty of squaring Wilson's commitments with his ideals:

I believe that not by means of threats but through tried and respected institutions will the country obtain a lasting peace. The threats and conduct of Minister Sullivan in support of the indefensible administration of Bordas contributed not a little to one of our most disastrous wars. Moreover, I do not believe that President Wilson has the right, under any pretext, to violate the sovereignty of an independent people.[100]

The United States used its control of revenues to keep the Dominicans on short ration. Reduction of trade due to war in Europe enhanced the stringency. The Dominican government had little incentive to avert revolt because there were "extraordinary opportunities for graft" in expenditures for rations and supplies.[101] The chargé d'affaires suggested that it would be better for the United States to take an active part.[102] The government contended that its own forces were sufficient; if the United States were directly involved, "national sentiment, urged on by interested sources," might "convert the assistance into a situation of hostility." The chargé d'affaires thought this was a posture taken "for internal political purposes alone," since it contradicted the attitude of the president in private talks.[103]

Sullivan's assurance, as he left the legation under charges of malfeasance, that "the Department's policy is finally accepted here," "the leaders of all factions and parties" being in agreement "that revolution is no longer a means of power," bore no resemblance to reality.[104] As local rebellions and prolonged deadlock between president and congress blocked the fulfillment of Wilson's plan, direct American control became imminent.

By the autumn of 1915 the Dominican problem could be attacked with greater professional competence, Bryan having been replaced by Lansing and Sullivan by the reappointment of his predecessor, the early "apostle of 'Control'," William W. Russell.[105] A treaty with Haiti, the product of an involvement which had largely replicated the earlier experience in Santo Domingo, provided a pattern.[106] "Just as the Americans had believed that they could impose customs supervision in Haiti because they had done so in Santo Domingo, it seemed to them after September, 1915, that they should be able to establish a more general control over Santo Domingo, as they had done in Haiti."[107]

American objectives were premised on a charge that the Dominican Republic had repeatedly failed to live up to its obligations in the 1907 agreement. The debt was mounting rapidly, while "extreme peculations . . . in the collection of internal revenues" were taking place and "the civilian employees of the Government go unsalaried and unfed." The United States wanted a new treaty with a right to intervene on the lines of the Platt Amendment, but if this were unattainable, it would insist on an interpretation of the existing treaty to provide for a financial adviser, a larger customs guard, and a new constabulary.[108]

Russell concluded that the Dominican Congress would never approve new treaty obligations. "Executive imposition" would require a man "more dominating and forceful" as president. The Convention of 1907 had been imposed by a president, Cáceres, "who inspired the opposition with abject terror."[109] Russell therefore tried the alternative of insisting on expanded interpretation of the existing agreement, although he feared that this would stimulate *horacista* "propaganda to start revolution" and might even lead to the resignation of Jiménez and the "terrible calamity" of Arias being chosen by Congress.[110] (A short time before this he had written that while Arias had had "more experience as a professional troublemaker, and just at present has a little more power," he was "no worse than any of the rest of them.")[111] Jiménez rejected the proposal in a note which argued that it would not achieve the results intended; foreign support "must be of that character which does not wound the susceptibilities of the Dominican people."[112]

The State Department showed more eagerness than despair as it concluded that force would have to be used to compel acceptance.[113] Lansing summarized for Wilson on November 24 his

firm belief . . . that no substantial permanent improvement in conditions in the Dominican Republic can be assured unless the treaty of 1907 is amended in line with the treaty with Haiti. . . . If President Jiménez should resign or a revolution break out for any cause, we should be justified in landing forces to prevent bloodshed and to give the Dominican Congress an opportunity [!] to ratify an amended convention.[114]

Action was delayed. Wilson did not want to jeopardize the treaty with Haiti which was already before the Senate.[115] It seemed best, moreover, to continue a waiting game as long as Jiménez's survival in office left open the possibility that he might be pressured into compliance. If open revolt should develop, it would be a pretext for military intervention.[116] Harassed by sporadic revolt and the threat of a major outbreak, unable to control his own administration because Arias, the minister of war, held a large enclave of power, Jiménez was denied financial support for a military offensive unless, in the words of Welles, he "consented to an interpretation of the Convention of 1907 which public opinion . . . unanimously considered violative of the Dominican Constitution and an infringement of the sovereignty of the nation."[117]

Finally, in April 1916, Jiménez tried to gain control of the army by arresting two generals who were partisans of Arias. Arias himself took charge of the fortress in the capital city. Jiménez was kept from resigning by efforts of the minister, but the long-threatened impeachment was voted on May 1.[118] Jiménez, claiming that the vote was illegal, managed to muster a small force outside the city. United States marines waited on board two vessels offshore.

On Russell's urging, Lansing directed that the president be afforded "all support."[119] But Jiménez would not accept a puppet's role. Although pressed to accept American help, he tried to advance on the capital with his own forces. After running out of ammunition, he approved an American offer to take the city but then quickly changed his mind, asking in vain for guns and ammunition to resume the attack. On May 7 Jiménez resigned, announcing that he preferred "his own immolation" to returning "among ruins to enjoy a power re-gained . . . by foreign bullets" under "the humiliation of a North American intervention."[120]

The United States thus found that its strength and resolve could not be harnessed to Dominican politics. Unilateral force was quickly applied after Lansing told Russell to proceed with "such action as you may deem advisable."[121] Arias, given an ultimatum, decided to withdraw, enabling American forces to enter the city without opposition. If it had come to a fight, Russell thought, the government forces might have joined in resistance.[122] Within a few weeks, with only minor skirmishes, the principal northern cities were also occupied and Arias was arrested.

Russell thought that the presence of American military forces would lead to acceptance of "the permanent reforms under negotiation," but it was far from clear how this might be brought about. A "constituted government" had only the most tenuous existence, lacking both strength and inclination to give effect to the American program. "Anti-American sentiment" was "considerable."[123]

Four members of the Jiménez cabinet remained in office, persuaded by Russell that the alternative would be an American military government.[124] The constitution provided for choice of an interim president by Congress, but Russell feared that Arias would control the selection. He thought that the "final elimination" of Arias "as a political or military factor" was essential. The department suggested that Jiménez's resignation might be declared invalid, but Russell advised against any attempt "to rehabilitate" him.[125]

Russell asked the Congress to delay for two or three days, while advising that an election should not be permitted until the entire country should have been pacified. The lower house would not be put off, however. It voted to elect as president a favorite of Arias, the chief justice of the Supreme Court. Russell and Admiral William B. Caperton, who commanded the naval forces, demanded that the Senate postpone action, hoping to avoid an arrest of senators and the "international criticism which might follow."[126] Lansing told Russell that if the Congress refused "to agree on a desirable candidate," the Council of Ministers might be assured support in dissolving it and proceeding "to the election of a new Congress which will properly represent the country and elect a President who would be acceptable to the country and carry out the reforms desired by the United States."[127]

The Council of Ministers apparently took the initiative in deciding to put several senators under arrest. Russell, given short notice, suggested to the State Department that to "uphold the Ministers" would be the only way to prevent the election of an undesired president "unless we ourselves arrest senators."[128] On the next day, however, he concluded that the arrests had created an "untenable position for us" and the senators were released.[129]

The department nevertheless persisted in its refusal to countenance the election of anyone who would not accept its demands. The chief justice withdrew his candidacy in a statement which protested American interference. Velásquez refused to let himself be considered.[130] The two houses were deadlocked until July, when they agreed to designate for five months as provisional president the brother of the chief justice, Dr. Francisco Henríquez y Carbajal, a nonpolitical figure who had lived in Cuba for several years. Russell had no chance to seek a commitment from Henríquez and no plausible basis on which to oppose his inauguration. It was evident that the choice was an act of defiance. Russell reported that members of Congress congratulated Arias and that with but one exception the new cabinet members were "probably all anti-American."[131] Nevertheless, the minister argued that it would be wrong to violate the constitution. Even if the result should be the election of Arias, we should be as insistent "upon its being observed in the matter of changes in the Government" as in our opposition to "revolution of any sort, whether peaceful or armed."[132] The logic of this was more consistent than its application in the Dominican Republic and elsewhere. The State Department found an excuse for denying recognition to Henríquez because he did not take a formal oath of office until after the session of congress which elected him had terminated.

Against the "most categorical" protest of the council of ministers, the United States had used its military supremacy to place internal revenues as well as customs duties in charge of the receiver of customs.[133] Russell insisted that the new president accept by decree "the existing financial control" and dissolve the army in favor of "a rural constabulary to be organized along lines suggested by the United States." Payments would be withheld until acceptance of the desired treaty interpretations "or until the present Dominican Government has been recognized by the United States." Publication of the American note of the previous November aroused strong but futile protests.[134]

In private talks Henríquez acknowledged the necessity for reform but pleaded that the demanded decree "was absolutely outside of his faculties." He thought his personal acceptance ought to suffice, but Russell feared the influence of his "anti-American advisers." The State Department insisted that recognition and revenues be withheld "until proposals are definite and it is assured that revolutionary influences in Cabinet are terminated."[135] Ironically, the cabinet included capable and respected figures and had unprecedented support from the major political factions in its attitude toward the occupying power.[136]

Henríquez had one counter of limited value—the threat of resignation. But a government which could not govern was hardly better than none. While he remained in office, banditry increased and the economy suffered, with the United States taking most of the blame.[137] Efforts of the marines to seize arms and to stifle the press, together with "the insolence and overbearing manner of a few officers" intensified a hostility toward Americans which the foreign minister described as universal.[138] Russell reported that suspension of payments was creating "a condition of internal disturbances that we must suppress." We could not "tell where to look for support of our policy." An ultimatum should be issued. If it were not complied with, we should "take charge ourselves until the country is pacified."[139]

Full and direct control by the United States, which had been so long pending, was like a wave about to break in the fall of 1916. When the Dominicans tried to deflect it by arranging to elect new members of Congress, it only loomed higher. The legation feared that Henríquez would be chosen for a complete term, thus enabling Arias to gain full power.[140] It became increasingly significant that Arias was notoriously pro-German.[141] The State Department and Russell concluded that nothing would be gained by further deference to the constitution. They would no longer accept rebuff and evasion.

Russell was recalled for consultation at his own request, and on October 31 a meeting of state and navy officials tried "to find a practical solution."[142] Russell prepared a summarizing memorandum, premised on the need for "complete control." This could be attained either through "a *de facto* government of the best elements" or by a military governor. He thought the latter would be "too extreme," but suggested a convenient tactic:

We could state at the proper time that... the United States had determined that revolutions shall cease in Santo Domingo; that... the American forces will pursue all men known to be revolutionary leaders or chiefs and that all arms hidden in the country will be searched for. In doing this our forces are sure to meet with opposition. . . . This opposition will necessitate the placing of the whole country under martial law and we will have force enough to accomplish this; due regard to be had to pretext for criticism of our action by the other Latin American Republics.[143]

The conference recommended instead a direct approach. All agreed that there was no alternative to military law and occupation, "basing this on the interpretation which the United States has given to the Dominican Convention of 1907 and also upon the present unsettled conditions in the Republic." There was no mention of a German threat. President Wilson gave his approval "with the deepest reluctance," after striking out a sentence which authorized removal of judges (although he conceded that it might become "necessary to resort to such extreme measures").[144]

A proclamation of military occupation was issued by Captain Harry S. Knapp on November 29. It was done, Knapp explained, "with no immediate or ulterior object of destroying the sovereignty of the Republic of Santo Domingo," but to help it "in returning to a condition of internal order." An official protest was brushed aside. Russell reported that "the only people dissatisfied" were "disappointed petty politicans." He thought that an American-controlled government "should go right ahead for a year at least working out complete reforms necessary with the voluntary aid of patriotic Dominicans." The country might then be placed under "*de facto* government presided over by a junta of the best native element" until after a "period of trial" it should be "ready for elections."[145]

4.
HAITI

Haiti, the densely-populated country which occupies the western third of the large island of Hispaniola, between Cuba and
Puerto Rico, was not a significant concern of American diplomacy during the first century of its independence. Although it was the first
independent state in the New World following the United States, diplomatic
relations were not established until 1862, when defenders of slavery had lost
influence in Washington. The instability of Haitian politics engaged only
sporadic attention because of the poverty and isolation of the country. Lasting
financial engagements did not develop. As a site for naval bases Haiti afforded
little advantage over other locations which were less encumbered by political
complications and uncertainties.

The United States had several chances to acquire Môle St. Nicolas, on the
narrow passage separating the island from Cuba, but did not persist at the price of
entanglement and opposition. In 1868 Secretary of State Seward rejected a proposal that would have entailed involvement in civil war. President Arthur turned
down a similar offer in 1884. Secretary of State Blaine attempted to exploit the
political weakness of Haiti by negotiating for lease of the Môle in 1891, while a
naval force held target practice off of Port-au-Prince, but Admiral Gherardi's
"combined threat and bribe" to President Hyppolite was unavailing.[1] When the
United States later took an interest in Haiti, strategic concern was slight because
control of the Windward Passage had been gained through Guantánamo.

By 1908, after intervention in Cuba and the Dominican Republic, the United
States undertook to rectify wrong-doing and disorder in Haiti whether or not
there was a threat to be countered or a base to be gained. Theodore Roosevelt
looked for a pretext for intervention "in the name of humanity, morality, and
civilization."[2] Secretary of State Elihu Root, concerned that "any interference"
might arouse "an outcry of protest," confided that he had "been watching every
move in Haiti for several years very closely" in hope that "the psychological
moment" would arise "in which we could . . . give . . . help in such a way as to
establish the right sort of relations."[3]

A revolution in 1908 did not bring intervention, however. Root earned the
gratitude of the beleaguered government by firmly denying the right of asylum.[4]
Neither did Taft's "dollar diplomacy" bring the United States into Haiti, al-

though steps were taken toward financial supervision. A loan arrangement that placed American bankers in partial control of the national bank was made without State Department sponsorship.[5] The bank, which had been dominated by French investors since its establishment in 1881, had been deprived in 1905 of most government deposits. In 1909 the State Department opposed a proposal actively backed by the French minister that the bank restore treasury service. It also denounced a plan for a new bank that would be dominated by French and German interests, with only token American participation, as "derogatory to the sovereignty" and "inequitable to the people of Haiti" as well as "detrimental to American interests."[6] But when participation was broadened to include the National City Bank and the contract was amended so that the new bank would not collect customs duties, Knox decided to drop the objection.[7]

The National City Bank representative in Haiti, Roger L. Farnham, was "adept at playing on the State Department's desire to avoid French or German interference."[8] Paradoxically, Farnham's influence became strongest during the Wilson administration, despite its repudiation of economic self-interest. But even with the leverage of a skilled operator who could arouse larger concerns, economic advantage did not become the basic cause of American intervention in Haiti. Rather, it was the turbulence of politics and the belief that the prestige and the available forces of the United States could and should be drawn upon to establish political stability that brought the United States into Haiti.

The politics of Haiti was a series of struggles among constantly shifting factions. A succession of self-anointed monarchs and dictators gave way after 1869 to "election" for a limited term, but no president left office voluntarily. Only one civilian attained the presidency, in 1913, and he was overthrown after nine months. Constitutionalists held office from time to time before 1879, but the relatively honest election of that year, which was won by the opposition, marked the end of any semblance of responsive government.[9] Before 1879, a small elite, largely mulatto, numbering less than five thousand in a population of about two million, controlled the government. Those who seized power in later years usually were men of little or no education who were dependent on support from the peasantry, particularly from those called *cacos,* who made revolution a way of life. Cruelty and cupidity prevailed. In the words of a reflective participant, "Authority . . . lost among us all moral prestige, all solid basis, and [was] transformed into ephemeral, malevolent, sanguinary, or grotesque preponderance."[10]

In the years preceding American occupation, there was a quickening spiral of political disorder, engendered by incompetence and corruption. This left its mark in the chronicle of American naval actions. Warships were sent to Haiti in 1868, 1869, 1876, 1888, 1889, 1892, 1902, and in every subsequent year through 1914, with the single exception of 1910. In 1889, in a typical Haitian power struggle, the outcome of which was ratified by an election, Florvil Hyppolite emerged victor over François Légitime, who had been recognized by France and Britain. Many Haitians believed that Hyppolite had sold out to the United States, but he stood firm against pressure and almost lived out his seven-year term. His successor, Simon Sam, served nearly as long before being deposed. The next president, Nord Alexis, succumbed more to senescence than to his opponents; he was over ninety when he resigned in 1908. This administration mustered enough vigor to conduct a trial for fraud in which the previous president and no less than three men who were later to become president were convicted. The next incumbent, Antoine Simon, was overthrown after three years in 1911. By April 1915, five other presidents had either been killed or otherwise removed. Bankruptcy was averted only by loans at increasingly exhorbitant terms. The poverty of Haiti is indicated by a comparison of export values; exports per capita for Cuba in 1913 were worth \$63.54; for Puerto Rico, \$40.50; for the Dominican Republic, \$15.00; and for Haiti, \$5.66.[11]

MOVING IN

Political disorder might have led to intervention on either economic or strategic grounds, but neither was an effective precipitant. American economic interests were not substantial nor were they closely tied to any faction. Strategic threat was not acute, although German merchants had learned that they could turn a neat profit by financing revolutions, and there was reason to believe that the German government was working to obtain a naval base or coaling station in Haiti.[12] The Wilson administration dispatched an assistant secretary of state on a secret mission to see whether Môle St. Nicolas could be acquired, but when President Michel Oreste rejected any idea of cession, Secretary of State Bryan was content with a promise that it would not go to any other power.[13]

The eventual landing of American forces was preceded by an extended period during which the Wilson administration was pressed by the Bank of Haiti to establish control of customs revenues as had been done in the Dominican Republic. When Oreste was overthrown in January 1914, having foolishly cut off payments to the *cacos,* Farnham of the National City Bank appealed to Bryan's humanitarianism, with the support of Boaz W. Long of the Latin American Division. The evils inflicted upon the masses might be eliminated, Long argued, if the United States should take control of customs.[14] Long's deputy, J. Herbert Stabler, suggested that the time had come for the United States "to gain that influence which for many years we have desired and needed in the Republic of Haiti." He thought that by supporting "a suitable candidate for president" the United States could get access to the Môle and could effect a change in the Haitian constitution so that aliens could "undertake the cultivation of some of the extremely rich portions of the republic." He conceded that "popular sentiment" was strongly opposed to permitting foreigners to acquire land.[15]

Oreste Zamor was elected president without prolonged disorder and in correct form, thanks to his military strength. The minister reported that he did not need "to use bribery or threats to obtain votes. That he held the situation in his hand was realized by everybody.''[16] Protracted discussions involving President Wilson led to a decision not to demand financial control.[17] In tentative fashion, Bryan did say, in response to Farnham's suggestion that Zamor might let French bankers take over, that the United States would be willing to help administer the customs and that support for the government would depend on its worthiness. This brought angry charges led by Zamor himself that the bank was working to impose an American protectorate.[18]

When Zamor was confronted with a revolutionary challenge after only six weeks, Long resumed his argument that the customhouses should be placed beyond reach of the ''outs.''[19] Stabler held that financial stability would quickly attract investments in cotton and bananas, while without customs control any honest government would be overthrown by revolution. He thought the United States should provide assurance that in case of popular demonstration it ''would immediately preserve order.'' Once the people learned ''that foreigners are not all slave traders'' and the ''political agitators were shown the strong hand of the United States,'' opposition would be slight.[20]

The bank threatened to shut off revenues, hoping, the minister reported, to force the government to ask for help ''in adjusting its financial tangle'' and eventually to accept control of the customs.[21] On June 25, 1914, President Wilson, endorsing what was called the ''Farnham Plan,'' asked the department to prepare a draft treaty similar to that with the Dominican Republic. It appeared for a time that Zamor would accept an implicit offer of American support and protection in return for a customhouse agreement, provided it should appear that he had no choice, but Bryan and Wilson were unwilling to appear insistent, and Zamor lost interest when German sources persuaded him that other means of financial support could be found.[22]

In late summer of 1914 the administration took a bolder approach based on the ''Wilson Plan'' for the Dominican Republic. The cycle of revolution was no less vicious in Haiti. Indeed, Zamor's principal opponent, Davilmar Theodore, was linked to Desiderio Arias, the Dominican *caudillo*. Extolling the plan, Bryan asked the minister in Haiti to let Zamor know that the United States was prepared, on request, to provide such help as might be needed to insure constitutional government.[23]

President Zamor did not rise to this bait until his situation became utterly desperate. In October, when he was already defeated, he and his brother offered ''to have adopted the views of the United States Government'' in return for effective help ''to triumph over the revolution.''[24] Four days later decisive moves began. Bryan gained Wilson's support in increasing naval strength in Haitian waters, both to protect foreign interests and ''as evidence of the earnest intention of this Government to settle the unsatisfactory state of affairs which exists.''[25] Eight hundred marines and the battleship *Kansas* were ordered to Port-au-Prince. The department knew that this was at best a last-ditch rescue operation; if the president had already left the country, the minister was to afford ''every protection" to his brother, presumably a refugee in the consulate. The minister was authorized at his own discretion to ask the marine commander "to take charge of Port-au-Prince" and to "restore Charles Zamor to his cabinet functions." It was too late. The minister cabled that the capital was "in complete possession of the revolution," with the president already on board a Dutch ship and his brother in the Dominican legation, preparing to embark also.[26]

President Wilson and the State Department persisted in the attempt to put the "Wilson Plan" into effect in Haiti until they had to realize that it was utterly inapplicable. There was no basis for meaningful elections in party organization or in political awareness.[27] The planned procedure for "immediate reconstitution of political authority" assumed that the president would be elected together with the legislature, but the constitution provided for choice of the president by the legislature. The next election was not due until 1916.[28]

Despite disorder, Theodore emerged quickly, if only briefly, as a duly chosen president and the State Department faced the issue of recognition. It tried to impose strict requirements: the government must accept a customs convention and settle with the bank and the American railroad, must protect all foreign interests, and must not give base rights to any European power.[29] Compliance was blocked by intense opposition in the legislature. When the foreign minister advanced an alternative "avoiding the irritating and offensive idea of customs control," the Senate "rose in a body" to drive him from the platform.[30] He resigned the same day. Bryan then changed his tone, stating that the United States had "no desire to assume responsibilities in regard to Haiti's fiscal system except in accordance with the wishes of the Government" and offering recognition if the government could prove itself able to maintain order and meet foreign obligations.[31]

The next proposal from Haiti was an offer of economic advantages. This gave Bryan the opportunity to avow disinterest.

While we desire to encourage in every proper way American investments in Haiti, we believe that this can be better done by contributing to stability and order than by favoring special concessions to Americans. . . . Our obligation to the American people requires that we shall give all legitimate assistance to American investors in Haiti, but we are under obligations just as binding to protect Haiti, as far as our influence goes, from injustice or exploitation at the hands of Americans.[32]

The marines, who had arrived off Port-au-Prince just after the fall of Zamor, were used only for one operation, the removal, on the Bank's request, of $500,000 in gold, about half of an amount that had been brought to Haiti a few months before for backing of a new currency issue. The action was denounced by the government.[33]

The political wheel kept turning. Means of gaining power in Haiti were far more reliable than those of keeping it. Disappointed revolutionists whose rewards did not match expectations were quick to turn to a new aspirant. Theodore's grasp was particularly weak because the treasury was empty, while the meager revenues were almost all pledged to foreign creditors. An order of paper currency was slow to arrive from New York; meanwhile the army was paid in locally-produced paper which did not look like money and was not accepted except when men with guns demanded that it be.[34]

Revolution began, as always, in the north, where, in his haste to take the capital, Theodore had left several "important strongholds" in the hands of "the old Zamor party." As soon as the new movement took Cap Haïtien, Guillaume Sam, its leader, was "considered as the future President," although it was about a month before he reached the capital. Theodore was forced out when water and food supplies for Port-au-Prince were cut off. Congress then followed the practice by which, as the minister explained, upon entrance of a successful military leader into the capital, "the Chambers are convoked and he is invariably elected."[35]

The advance of Guillaume Sam was shadowed by an American naval force under Admiral William B. Caperton, whose mission was to prevent looting and burning in the port cities. Caperton was on guard against attempts by projected losers to induce intervention. He was given a proposal of ten senators that the United States insist on an election. He "ignored all such advance and . . . refrained from showing by any word or action any disposition to favor any man or party in Haiti."[36]

President Wilson was more and more "convinced" that the United States had a "duty to take immediate action." He thought the contending leaders should be told "as firmly and definitely as is consistent with courtesy and kindness that the United States cannot stand by and permit revolutionary conditions constantly to exist there." He wanted, "as in Santo Domingo, to insist upon an agreement for a popular election under our supervision."[37] The same two men, J. Franklin Fort and Charles Cogswell Smith, who had undertaken a mission to the Dominican Republic, agreed to make a similar attempt in Haiti.[38]

Before the commissioners could go to work, however, Bryan and Wilson seem to have acknowledged that a scheme to establish democratic politics could not be put into effect in Haiti. Wilson must have been taken aback by the minister's reply to an inquiry regarding the electorate. "Elections as understood in America do not exist in Haiti . . . the population generally takes no part . . . the voting being done by soldiers acting under instructions. Few voters who vote many times."[39] Because Guillaume Sam refused to negotiate without recognition and perhaps also because life in the Haitian capital was unpleasant, the commissioners' stay was brief and accomplished nothing.[40]

Guillaume Sam was challenged almost at once by another revolution, under a former minister, Dr. Rosalvo Bobo, supported, it was thought, by Desiderio Arias across the border. He did not fall immediately, largely because he could disburse the currency issue which Theodore had ordered and had access to current revenues that had been taken out of the hands of the bank.[41] He was able to take advantage of Bryan's belief that Bobo showed "manifest hostility towards the United States."[42]

Rumored threat of European influence stirred the American authorities again into action. With almost incredible credulity, Bryan and Wilson reacted to a story from Farnham that French interests were cooperating with their wartime enemies, the Germans, to drive Americans out of Haiti and gain control of Môle St. Nicholas. Wilson thought the "sinister" implication of this made it essential to "sustain and assist" American interests "in every legitimate way." He called on Bryan to devise "a plan of controlling action which we can take . . . before the tangle gets any greater—while the threads can be pulled together rather than cut."[43] Bryan was reluctant to use force, although it might be "necessary to compel a supervision which will be effective,"[44] but Wilson was impatient to "get our plans going in Haiti for a stable arrangement that will preclude anxieties such as we have recently felt."[45]

A proposal taken by special emissary to Guillaume Sam offered recognition and a treaty promising the use of "such force as may be necessary to prevent insurrection and ensure stability," demanding in return nothing more precise than acceptance of advice and renewal of the understanding that the Môle would not be alienated. It did not mention a customs collectorship. The Haitian president wanted advance assurance that American forces would be withdrawn on request. The emissary reported that while Haitian leaders were afraid to take responsibility for an agreement, most Haitians were in favor of American protection. He thought that the president would come around.[46] Wilson and Lansing, the new secretary of state, were weighing their next move when another revolution broke, this time convulsively, with little warning.

TAKING CHARGE

Although Guillaume Sam was able to prevent his opponents from sweeping down from the north in the usual fashion, he lived under constant threat. Repressive measures became more rigorous and vengeful when he suspected that conspirators in the capital were giving aid to rebel forces. About two hundred men were imprisoned, and many more took refuge in various legations or went into hiding. On July 27 a group of fugitives surprised the presidential guards, seized their guns, and besieged the palace. Guillaume Sam managed to escape to the French legation next door. When this uprising occurred, orders were given to kill the prisoners and about 167 persons were slaughtered, "the best people of the city," according to Admiral Caperton. On the next morning, having learned that an American admiral was nearing the port, perhaps to rob them of vengeance, the populace surrounded the president in his place of refuge and literally tore him to pieces after he was thrown over the fence. "The wildest disorder" then "prevailed in all the city."[47]

When the palace was besieged and the prisoners massacred, the chargé d'affaires put in a call for warships. The cruiser *Washington* under Admiral Caperton was entering the harbor when the mob seized the president. Caperton decided on his own to land forces, but before he actually did so an instruction arrived from Washington.[48] Marines and sailors went ashore that afternoon, although no Americans had been killed or injured.

A revolutionary committee had formed, according to usual practice, and members of Congress wanted to proceed with the election of Bobo as president. Caperton, however, persuaded the committee to accept his authority and held that military control was necessary because there was "no government or authority in town." Refuting press dispatches which suggested that the State Department was under a misapprehension, he cabled, "All government functions at present undertaken carried on by committee citizens acting practically under my direction." He reported that the "professional soldiers called Cacos" who "practically control politics" were demanding the election of Bobo, and "Congress, terrorized by mere demand," was "restrained by my request. Stable government" would not be possible "until Cacos are disbanded and power broken. Such action" was "imperative" if the United States desired "to negotiate treaty for financial control." He thought he could "control Congress" and disband the *cacos* with the help of an additional regiment of marines. He was unsure, however, just what his superiors wanted to accomplish: "As future relations between United States and Haiti depend largely on courses of action taken at this time earnestly request to be fully informed of policy of United States."[49]

Pending explicit instructions and strengthened by a regiment of marines, Admiral Caperton moved briskly to control the choice of a new president. Bobo had boarded an American naval vessel at Cap Haitiën after negotiations with the revolutionary committee under the guidance of an American officer. He was a person of impressive education, both a lawyer and a practicing doctor. Caperton's chief of staff, Captain E. L. Beach, considered him intelligent and honest, but so greatly lacking in judgment and so dependent on *caco* support that he should not be permitted to become president. Expecting to be greeted as president, Bobo was brought to the Admiral's ship to be told by Beach that as a revolutionist he was "a menace and a curse" to Haiti. Distraught, he agreed to renounce his candidacy and disband his army.[50]

Caperton had already reported on August 5 that the alternative to Bobo was Sudre Dartiguenave, the president of the Senate—"a man of personal honor and of patriotism" who "has never been connected with any revolution, is of good ability ... realizes Haiti must agree to any terms laid down by United States, professes to believe any terms demanded will be to Haiti's benefit," and "says he will use all his influence with Haitian Congress to have such terms agreed upon by Haiti." Congressmen were anxious to avoid "humiliation." Any president, Caperton reported, would have to be "sustained by American protection."[51]

Lansing and Wilson were already prepared to take such control as might be needed to establish orderly government. Timing and justification had not been settled, but neither man was disposed to resist the momentum that had put American force in control of the capital. Fear of German intrigue had been a factor in building up their concern for Haiti and was alluded to retrospectively by Lansing in 1922 as a real influence on the actual decisions, but it is not clear that this was of decisive importance at the time.[52] Lansing was making calculated response to a critical Senate inquiry; Sumner Welles had advised that "stress" be placed "upon the position assumed by the German Government just prior to our intervention."[53]

In 1914 Lansing asked himself whether American concern for the quality of government in Caribbean countries should have a broader object than defensive necessity.

Should a new doctrine be formulated declaring that the United States is opposed to the extension of European control over American territory and institutions through financial as well as other means, and having for its object, not only the national safety and interests of this country, but also the establishment and maintenance of republican constitutional government in all American states, the free exercise by the people of their public and private rights, the administration of impartial justice, and the prevention of political authority from becoming the tool of personal ambition and greed, the chief enemies of liberal institutions, of economic development, and of domestic peace?[54]

While European control was still linked to American action in this formulation, the logical basis for the link was removed. The note which Lansing sent to Wilson after receipt of Admiral Caperton's request for policy guidance expressed uncertainty "what we ought to do or what we legally can do," but suggested that humanitarian duty might justify the United States in rectifying the political and economic situation.

Wilson was in no mood to be prevented by legalities from doing what he had already concluded would be right and necessary. He thought the United States must "take the bull by the horns and restore order." It should "absolutely control" Port-au-Prince and the surrounding country from which it drew its food supply, should demand that "the present Congress . . . put men in charge of affairs whom we can trust to handle and put an end to revolution," and should "insist on constitutional government," if necessary by taking charge of elections.[55] Lansing asked the solicitor of the department to "show that the United States has ample justification for whatever acts it may be necessary to do in order to solve the perplexing difficulties in Haiti."[56] Such a rationale was never prepared, because the solicitor decided that events rendered it superfluous.

Lansing's advisers pressed for decisive action, although they were unsure what it might accomplish. One memorandum predicted stability and "quick growth" if "the prize in money for which all wage war" were removed from reach.[57] Another was less sanguine, citing "lack of public opinion," absence of a "sense of public responsibility," "complete political incompetence," and "growing demoralization generally." It called for "complete forcible intervention" for thirty-three years. At that time and after "each succeeding 33 years, it shall be decided by the President and Congress as to whether the United States shall withdraw."[58]

On August 6 Lansing asked the navy to take control of Port-au-Prince and the principal customhouses. Caperton was instructed to proclaim that the United States had "no object in view except to insure, establish, and help to maintain Haitian independence and the establishment of a stable and firm government by the Haitian people."[59]

Admiral Caperton soon reported that he had "curtailed the power of the revolutionary committee" because it did not "keep faith." Although his orders were "gladly accepted and executed," he thought it was "extremely desirous" to "permit Congress to elect a President."[60] The secretary of the navy quickly cabled approval of an election "whenever Haitians wish" and bluntly asserted, "The United States prefers election of Dartiguenave."[61] The State Department asked the chargé d'affaires, together with the admiral, to "let Congress understand" that recognition would be accorded only to a man "whose abilities and dispositions give assurances of putting an end to factional disorders." Candidates should understand that the United States expects "such financial control" as it "may deem necessary for an efficient administration."[62]

On the day before the election, the revolutionary committee tried to prevent a vote by dissolving Congress and sealing the doors of the chamber, but Caperton quickly announced that "they would be considered public enemies of United States if they . . . further menaced United States policy." A last-minute attempt to put forward as a candidate J. N. Léger, a former diplomat who was "easily in popular esteem Haiti's first citizen," was rebuffed when Léger sent word that he must "be in a position to defend Haiti's interests" in case United States demands should be "unreasonable."[63]

On August 11 Captain Beach addressed the Congress, presenting an "exact, direct, authoritative message" from the United States, and ordered acceptance of its "demands."[64] This was achieved, and on the following day, with Beach on the floor, Dartiguenave was elected president on the first ballot. Beach sat beside the new president in the inaugural procession, with marine escort.[65] The exigent presence of the United States aroused little open opposition. The rebel leader had also been willing to bargain for favor; Admiral Caperton reported that "the Bobo crowd" offered the cession of Môle St. Nicholas "and anything else I wanted."[66]

Admiral Caperton maintained later under senatorial questioning that U.S. preference for Dartiguenave was not made known to the Haitian Congress.[67]

There seems, however, no reason to doubt that the choice was made in acute awareness that it was expected. Surely this was true if the Americans in Haiti carried out their instructions. Only in the narrowest possible sense can credence be given to Caperton's claim that the "Haitians themselves, without any outside influence or pressure or bargaining made [Dartiguenave] . . . their president."[68] On the other hand, there is no evidence to refute Munro's judgment that the choice was approved by a majority of the congressmen.[69] It was "realized by everyone in touch with the situation," as the chargé d'affaires put it, that the government could exist only through "the support of the United States."[70] The new president, chosen by a legislature composed mainly of the elite, which was free for the first time in decades from the menace of armed revolutionists, was the first southern mulatto to occupy that position since 1879.[71]

As soon as the president had been chosen, the State Department pressed for acceptance "forthwith . . . without modification" of the treaty to give the United States rights of control. Lansing was determined not to permit delaying negotiations. The chargé d'affaires was authorized simultaneously to extend recognition and to sign the treaty. The terms were considerably more stringent than those of the earlier draft of July 1914 "in view of the friendly attitude of the Haitian Government."[72] They combined the most far-reaching features of the treaties with Cuba and the Dominican Republic, and included financial controls which were not in effect in Santo Domingo. The United States would appoint both a general receiver and a financial adviser. A constabulary "organized and officered by Americans designated by the president of the United States" would control arms and ammunition throughout the country. Haiti would take such measures as the United States might consider necessary for sanitation and public improvement. Provisions were included for claims settlement and to prevent any surrender of territory to a foreign power. Finally, by Article XIII the United States would have "the right to intervene for the preservation of Haitian independence and the maintenance of a government adequate for the protection of life, property and individual liberty." A decision not to develop a base at Môle St. Nicholas was the only concession made by the U.S. The State Department alluded to this "as an evidence of its good faith and unselfish motives."[73]

Presented with this draft, the Haitian government balked, threatening resignation. The chargé d'affaires thought the main concern was to avoid customs control and urged the State Department to make no concession. Lansing responded by arming him with a two-fold threat to be used "discretely"; rejection would result either in "a military government until honest elections can be held" or in "permitting the control of the government to pass to some other political faction representative of the best elements of Haiti."[74] After extended discussions, the chargé d'affaires concluded that the president was not "a man of sufficient force to control Cabinet and Chambers." Caperton saw "both the Congress and the members of the Government" as "cowed and intimidated by fear of sentiment throughout the country."[75]

While the treaty was under consideration, financial pressures were intensified. Contrary to his own judgment, Admiral Caperton had been instructed to take over the customshouses. Preferably this was to be done on request, but "whether President so requests or not," the Admiral was to proceed. After a short delay, they were taken over one by one in ten ports until the process was completed on September 2.[76] Caperton saw this as a more blatant violation of Haitian sovereignty than any previous action.[77] President Dartiguenave may privately have given his consent; publicly, he disclaimed responsibility.[78] The president did secretly request that martial law be proclaimed—an action which Caperton took on September 3 "in order better to support the present Government."[79]

Caperton warned the Navy Department that it might be necessary to conduct "offensive operations" against the *cacos* in the north, unless resumption of railroad construction should induce some of them to "desert their chiefs and go to work." Secretary Josephus Daniels in return cautioned him not to act without consulting the navy "unless absolutely necessary to prevent loss of life or property."[80] It appeared that American objectives would require an increasing resort to force.

However, the various pressures took effect. The declaration of martial law "greatly strengthened" the position of the government. Forced resignations of the two cabinet members who led the opposition improved the "treaty situation."[81] "Military pressure" was effective "at propitious moments in negotiations." The prospect of "offensive operations" was a source of "additional pressure." In retrospect, however, Caperton insisted that "there was no actual military movement made against the congress ... if there was any pressure brought to bear at all, it was only on the enemies of the government, which I was there to support."[82]

When further obstacles developed, Caperton avoided any appearance of "using force to secure ratification, believing it to best interest of both countries that treaty be ratified after full discussion following Haitian rules of procedure."[83] Economic suasion was not eschewed; upon ratification the United States would help in securing necessary loans.[84] The chargé d'affaires was concerned, however, that the position of the president would be weakened if revenues were withheld. Noting that Dartiguenave appeared "utterly discouraged," he urged the State Department to make essential funds available.[85]

The State Department agreed to relax its insistence that the treaty be approved "without modification" on assurance that a redraft would "concede all demands ... in a manner less humiliating to Haiti."[86] The word "demands" was for internal use; the department objected when the Haitian foreign minister so designated the treaty draft, even while reiterating its determination:

The phrase "United States demands" is not in consonance with the voluntary offers made by those who, after the carnage at Port au Prince in August last, upon seeing the national existence threatened and descending into anarchy, undertook to head a government only after receiving the assurance that the marines would remain on the ground and preserve life and order. The things which the United States considers to be necessary for the rehabilitation of Haiti fall far short of the offers freely made by these Haitians to Admiral Caperton on August 7, 1915. [Presumably in reference to the cession of Môle St. Nicholas]. The Department therefore expects that this cable will put an end to questions of further amendment and result in the immediate conclusion of the treaty as herein described.[87]

In the treaty redraft explicit reference to intervention was replaced by a promise of "efficient aid for the preservation of Haitian independence and the maintenance of a government adequate for the protection of life, property and individual liberty." The chargé d'affaires conveyed the interpretation that this implied "the lending of . . . armed force should internal strife or uprising endanger the existence of Government."[88]

When the treaty was signed on September 16, the United States extended formal recognition to Dartiguenave. The chargé d'affaires expected prompt ratification. Reports of opposition aroused by "certain members with presidential aspirations" led the State Department to "let it be known" that it would not "countenance" any attempt to overthrow Dartiguenave.[89] To Caperton's displeasure, funds were withheld, partial resumption of salary payments being made only the day before the lower house approved the treaty.[90] Senate action was held up in committee until early November. Lansing was worried by a report that some members were hoping that delay until the next session of the United States Senate might produce "a political situation . . . which will result in the withdrawal of the American marines." Admiral Caperton, on instruction from the secretary of the navy, let it be known that the United States intended "to retain control in Haiti until the desired end is accomplished."[91]

The Haitian Senate approved the treaty on November 11, 1915. Despite the need for pressures and threats, it may have had majority support among the urban, privileged Haitians. Admiral Caperton reported "great relief and general rejoicing."[92] American protection promised to restore the security and the dominance of the educated elite by eliminating the politics of revolution through which the black peasantry made its strength felt in the capital.

The treaty did not formally go into effect until after the Senate of the United States consented to ratification, but a *modus vivendi* was instituted. Under martial law legal niceties could be circumvented. The eventual approval of the Senate on February 28, 1916, was unanimous.

Hopes that ratification would lead to withdrawal of the marines, once a gendarmerie had been set up and the treaty services placed in operation, were not born out. "Instead for nearly twenty years the ultimate authority in Haiti was vested in the senior American naval officer rather than in the president of the republic and was derived from Caperton's proclamation of 'martial law' rather than from the treaty or the Haitian constitution."[93]

Part II
EXERCISE AND LIMITATIONS OF CONTROL

INTRODUCTION

In each of the countries covered in this study, the United States assumed a degree of control that exceeded the norms of interstate relations but stopped short of annexation and which was not expected to be permanent. It is difficult to draw clear lines that set off the period during which strongest influence was exercised from the stages which preceded and followed it. (In the case of Cuba the periods of occupation when the United States took over completely have been dealt with as parts of the prolonged adjustment to the outcome of the war with Spain, establishing the terms of a more lasting relationship.) The period of strongest influence may be conceived of as that time when policy goals were fixed neither on gaining a dominant role nor on relinquishing it, but on maximizing the values which it was expected to serve. These values related to the maintenance or achievement of conditions favorable to "life, property, and individual liberty" (not quite synonymous with stability and American investment), with components both in material progress and in the conduct of politics. The basic rationale for American control was deficiency of political capacity. The uses to which it was put should therefore have been not only to make up for the effects of this deficiency but to contribute to the achievement of a stabilizing politics. The U.S. gave repeated attention to promoting free elections in Cuba and Nicaragua, without notable success, but in the Dominican Republic politics was eclipsed for five years and in Haiti it was stifled for a decade and a half.

Stable self-reliance in the conduct of politics was an elusive goal. Patterns of political dependency deepened and extended themselves as long as the United States accepted a responsibility and role conducive to intervention. To avoid inter-meddling, as Root had promised for Cuba, invited an intensification of dis-order and chaos, which would demonstrate that intervention was necessary. The alternative role of guardian and mentor, while inhibiting revolution, consolidated a dependency that became in some respects mutual; a client government could resist pressures and demands that might appear to threaten the stability which it represented. Economic advantage, although of minor proportion except in Cuba, became more of an end and less of a means in a patron-client relationship that served the immediate needs of those on both sides who were directly involved.

Periodic tests of the relationship arose at election time. In the American view, elections were essential; without electoral choice, political stability would totter between repression and revolution, tainted by illegitimacy and jeopardized by reactions both in the country concerned and in the United States. The American role was a delicate one, because whatever the United States did or failed to do, whatever statements were made or were obviously withheld, could be used by one side or another. A government trying to control an election would profit from silence on the part of Ameri-can representatives and would suffer if openly pressed for improvement of its electoral practices. By and large, in Cuba and Nicaragua the pattern was one in which governments were reelected under conditions that suggested that a fair election might have gone the other way. This en-hanced incentive for revolt and increased the pressures on the United States to be more insistent.

In Cuba during a period which extended from 1909 to 1933, shadowed by the experience of occupation and by the Platt Amendment, the United States exercised a "preventive policy" of surveillance and advice that was intended to promote stability and avoid another interventionist takeover. Deterrence of revolution, by an evident readiness to support the govern-ment should it occur, was complemented by efforts to limit electoral abuses. This left the government in a strong position to resist reform—particularly because, although lacking popular support, it was regarded by influential Americans as a more reliable guardian of American interests than the opposition. In 1917 electoral fraud did lead to revolt and to limited intervention by United States forces, with the government prevailing. The pattern shifted around 1920 without change in its basic character. Cuban politics was fluid enough to permit high-level adjustment and shallow enough to prevent manipulation and corruption from arousing mass dis-content. After reform attempts by General Enoch Crowder ended with the dismissal of an "honest cabinet" that lacked political strength, it was de-cided in Washington that moralizing activism was self-defeating. After 1924 it seemed that a fortunate confluence had taken place under President Machado, whose political base seemed strong, who drew on the support of a moderate nationalism, and whose policies the United States found sound. By the end of the decade, however, discontent and disorder led an American ambassador again to look for means of pressuring a Cuban president toward reform, while his superiors in Washington had concluded that nothing short of a collapse of government would justify resumption of "intermeddling."

In Nicaragua, where the presence of marines took the place of a treaty from 1912 until 1925, the United States protected a government that lacked majority support, while advocating free and fair elections. In 1916, with help from the navy, the State Department managed to avoid a contest at the polls by pressuring the Liberal candidate to withdraw. In 1920, as in Cuba, it affirmed principle but acquiesced to fraud. Dimensions of paradox in benevolent intervention were revealed when a movement in the State Department to exert effective pressures toward reform as a means toward withdrawal met with the rejoinder that this would constitute an improper extension of intervention. Withdrawal of the marines, projected to follow the election of 1924, took place after some delay despite the weakness of a Liberal president, who was left without the protection of an effective military force. The Conservative general and former president, Chamorro, who had previously enjoyed American support, seized power and defied nonrecognition. The incongruity of opposing on procedural grounds a president whom the United States was otherwise inclined to favor contributed to a stalemate, which ended only with the return through American mediation of the original client president, Díaz, and a revolution which brought the marines into the country again.

In the case of Cuba and even in that of Nicaragua, where the United States role in the revolution had left Díaz in power under the protection of marines, the existence of competitive politics in which parties and elections had recognized functions enabled the United States to pursue its objective through indirect means. In the Dominican Republic and Haiti this was hardly possible. When the Wilson administration tried to insist on fair electoral procedures, it found that there was no indigenous authority that could either put them into effect or successfully maintain itself without them against American pressure. While in Cuba and Nicaragua American policymakers could concern themselves with the effects of pressures on the strength and balance of local forces, in the Dominican Republic and Haiti political contention lacked a structure which could adapt itself to the introduction even of superficial practices of orderly change. The Dominican Republic was deprived of both the experience and the example of self-government by being placed under military control, while in Haiti open manipulation of the election of the president, amendment of the constitution, and the staging of a plebiscite showed that the occupation force could be as cynical as Haitian leadership with regard to democratic procedures. Yet the U.S. provided no more than a temporary suspension of the need for local governments that could with some degree of effectiveness and legitimacy represent the societies of these countries.

5.
CUBA

PREVENTIVE SURVEILLANCE, 1909–1919

Roosevelt hoped that after the second withdrawal of United States control the Cuban government would seek help in public finance, in maintaining order, and in guaranteeing fair elections. He hoped for understanding of "the exact truth, . . . that our sole and genuine purpose is to help them so to manage their affairs that there won't be the slightest need of further interference on our part."[1] The incoming secretary of state, Philander C. Knox, authorized the minister to state, when he could be "sure speech would be opportune and silence equivocal," that the United States was "unwilling to intervene again in Cuba unless it becomes absolutely necessary after an existing Government has actually shown incapacity."[2]

No formal supervision was arranged, but the State Department undertook to do "everything in its power to induce Cuba to prevent any reason for possible intervention."[3] In pursuit of a "preventive policy," the United States became involved in issues primarily of domestic concern and opened itself to the charge of "intermeddling" in the face of Root's assurance in 1901. The minister found himself regarded "as kind of a moral adviser to President Gómez" but without authority to prevent "improvident and ill-advised" legislation.[4] He argued that more decisive steps would eventually be necessary. A "popularly elected, theoretically independent Congress" could not be controlled "merely by moral suasion," and a president could not "submit to foreign dictation and remain in office."[5] In 1912 the minister urged Knox to salvage as much as possible from the "rapidly disintegrating financial and legislative wreck" by demanding "broad supervisory powers." Knox responded by warning the Cuban government that its fiscal policy would "ultimately lead to a situation requiring intervention" and cancellation of fraudulent concessions to supporters of the government.[6] The Zapata Swamp concession, in an area later known to history as the Bay of Pigs, which occasioned Knox's warning, was not found on investigation to be improper, but it was evident that the rectitude of the Gómez government left much to be desired.

The United States let it be understood that in case of a revolt, its intervention would be in support of the government. By making it difficult for opposition to gain credit or support, it permitted the government to abuse its powers with little concern for protest. Policy was tested early in 1912. Agitation by a group of veterans led the minister to suggest that if "our intention to support the President were made known, those helping to provoke intervention by revolt would be discouraged." But Knox was less clear, urging that efforts be made "to prevent a threatened situation" which would compel consideration of intervention.[7] Some months later, when a group of blacks protested a law which outlawed parties based on race or color, the minister reported a "prevalent belief . . . that the movement was initiated for the express purpose of provoking an American intervention."[8]

On this occasion troops were sent "to protect the lives and property of American citizens." Knox insisted that this was in accordance with "uniform custom," adding bluntly: "This is not intervention." When Gómez replied that such actions "do not seem anything else," the State Department maintained that there was an "absolutely evident distinction . . . between 'intervention' and . . . the landing of marines if necessary in sporadic cases to prevent or suppress jeopardy to American life or property."[9] The Cuban foreign minister stubbornly objected that "the intervention" had been ordered "quickly and unjustly," and would "discredit [the government] without purpose and without even advantage to anybody."[10] The government succeeded in putting down the revolt without further involvement by the United States although American forces remained on Cuban soil for several weeks.

The presidential election of 1912 took place without serious incident. The Conservative candidate, Mario G. Menocal, the manager of an American-owned sugar estate, defeated the Liberal, Alfredo Zayas, with the help of dissident Liberals. The change of party control did not mean the democratic process was in operation, since Gómez was quite content that Menocal should win, once his own hope for reelection had been frustrated.

In the face of a continuing threat of revolution, Wilson's minister to Cuba, William E. Gonzales, urged the State Department to counter memories of "the quick intervention . . . and the favorable consideration of the rebels" at the time of "the made-to-order revolution against Estrada Palma" by indicating "that horse-thieves and anarchists, in assaults upon orderly chosen governments, would not be smiled upon by the United States."[11] Enoch L. Crowder, who had been legal adviser under Charles E. Magoon, had articulated the other horn of the dilemma: it was important for the United States to avoid being "made the blind instrument for fastening an undesirable or fraudulent government upon a people for whom we profess to be preserving a free government."[12]

President Wilson condemned revolution in terms that may have encouraged Menocal, contrary to precedent and advice, to seek a second term in 1916. The Liberals were not deterred, however, from thinking hopefully of 1906 and of the interventions recently undertaken in the Dominican Republic and Haiti.[13] Anticipating that Menocal, who was well-disposed toward the United States, would "lack the personal strength and the political support necessary to assure his reelection," J. Butler Wright of the Latin American division suggested that it would have "a wholesome effect" if Cubans were told that "constituted authority" must "be upheld and law and order be maintained at all costs."[14] Wilson had such a statement published in a Havana newspaper.[15]

When it appeared that Menocal was about to lose to Zayas, with fraud common on both sides, returns were interrupted. The Supreme Court ordered new elections, however, in a few districts where the vote was missing, enraging Menocal. The chargé d'affaires suggested that action was needed to head off trouble, but Gonzales, who was in Washington, objected that to intervene because of fraud would invite attempts to reverse the result of every election.[16] The minister concluded later that controlling the vote by ruthless means "even without a revolution, would be a disaster for Cuba," but he was authorized to say only "that any action which would cause disturbance . . . would be decidedly regrettable."[17]

The Gómez faction of Liberals plotted revolt rather than wait for the special elections, while the Zayas group favored a request for American supervision.[18] The minister later suggested that the uprising amounted to a coup against Zayas as well as against Menocal.[19] Once revolt had broken out the United States made clear "its confidence and support" for a government "established through legal and constitutional methods."[20] Preparation for war with Germany sealed the United States commitment to Menocal.

The Liberal plot relied upon support from army commanders, but it misfired in Havana and the western provinces. The Cuban government in 1917 did not suffer the incompetence and demoralization that had been evident in 1906. Menocal did not ask for support from United States forces, although military supplies were sent and marines were landed, as they had been in 1912, where property was threatened. The "moral support" that Menocal did request was forthcoming through strong notes which were given wide distribution. The minister reported that they had a "most clarifying effect" and that government officials were "deeply grateful."[21] Meanwhile, against advice from the United States, a special election was held in Santa Clara, with a predictably one-sided result.

In eastern Cuba American naval and consular officials dealt with the Liberals who had seized control. Spurred by threats to property, they arranged a truce and attempted mediation.[22] A proposed settlement was objected to in Havana, however, by both the minister and the president. "Anything like compromise," Gonzales thought, "would be acclaimed victory by the revolutionists."[23] He also questioned any attempt to challenge the Santa Clara election on the ground that hundreds of "similar or more gross frauds" may have helped the opposition.[24] Any further challenge to the ascendancy of Menocal was brought to an end by the defeat of Liberal forces.

The activity of radicalized remnants of the revolutionary movement caused concern, as the United States moved to war, for the supply of sugar and as avenues for possible German influence.[25] In August 1917 a regiment of marines was sent to eastern Cuba, despite Menocal's reluctance to receive them. In order to minimize the political effect of an implication that government forces were unable to maintain order, the pretext of a training mission was maintained.[26] Some forces remained in Cuba until 1922. When a Senator inquired about them in 1919, State Department officials found the questions "rather awkward," and responded evasively. Within the department, it was clear that they had been "protecting the sugar crop, the railroads, and quelling any strikes or disorders which might arise," but the Senator was told that the purpose was "to train for European service," pursuant to an "invitation from the Government of Cuba." It was acknowledged that American interests had been aided "when the sugar crops were menaced by revolutionary activities."[27]

ATTEMPTED DIRECTION, 1919–1923

The Liberals' resort to force strengthened Menocal's resistance to electoral reform. It was evident, however, that if the "preventive" influence of the United States were to promote good government and forestall intervention, fair elections were of critical importance. The elections of 1920 were preceded by nearly two years of intermittent pressure on the Menocal regime. In January 1919, the Department of State asked for "immediate assurances" of electoral fairness and tried to persuade Menocal to ask for American assistance. Gonzales was reluctant, as he had been in 1916, to involve the United States in the electoral process. He agreed that General Crowder should be asked to help in drafting a new iron-clad law, but thought that if "fairly honest elections" did not result, "it would be much preferable frankly to take over the Government for a long period and institute the many reforms possible under such conditions, than to undertake the doubtful, endless and thankless task of guaranteeing honest elections."[28]

The minister had cultivated a close relationship with Menocal and his associates, relying on "suggestions and hints in personal conversation" instead of "ominous notes."[29] On this occasion, however, in the minister's absence, the more formal method was employed. Menocal quickly rejected the suggestion that he request a supervisory commission, contending that it would be "a disturbing and unsettling element" and would be seen as "an expression of lack of confidence." After several talks with the president, Gonzales was able to repair some of the damage. General Crowder would be invited to help improve the existing electoral code. Despite the rejection of a stronger statement, the minister thought that Crowder would be able to "retain direction if considered desirable."[30] Within the State Department there was strong disposition toward major rectification:

[F]ifteen million dollars a year are wasted in Cuba; . . . there is immense graft received by an army of office holders who never go to their offices, and . . . it is the duty of the United States under the Platt Amendment to put an end to this whole thing[31]

The electoral situation provided a focus for reform, but the difficulty was far less with the law than with the practices of both parties. Crowder found an instance at hand. The Supreme Court had just annulled the elections of 1918 in a majority of the precincts of Santa Clara. It was acknowledged that most of the names on the voting lists "represented imaginary or fictitious persons, knowingly and intentionally inscribed" by officials "who carried out in form substantially every requirement of the law."[32] In the special elections soon to be held, "President Menocal seemed to contemplate . . . with equanimity" repetition of the fraud, with but one change:

Few, if any, electors will present themselves at the polls, and the college boards will make up and cast the ballots of the individuals named on the registration lists to elect the candidates heretofore agreed upon between the political parties, except that this time they will mark and fold the ballots so that the Central Electoral Board and the Supreme Court can entertain the presumption that the individual elector did cast his ballot.

Crowder found this "somewhat embarrassing" but felt that he had to ignore it.[33]

Crowder saw "parity of elections" as "the controlling factor in the maintenance of stable government." Changes in the laws would be of limited value, however, unless Cuban politics should gain more genuine vitality. "Reorganization of the political parties from the bottom up" was of "vital importance." "A wholesome public conscience in favor of honest elections" would have to develop in the barrios. Crowder advocated only a limited "measure of supervision." Could not the minister, "without intermeddling or giving offense to the Cuban Government, call the attention of that Government to any evasion or violation of the new Electoral Code and advise the authorities to correct the evils in their incipiency?"[34] To prevent control by "the same political crowds," the new law provided that nominations be made in special assemblies or conventions during the year of the election.[35] Crowder tried also to make it more difficult for courts to reject electoral complaints on narrow technical grounds.[36]

In response to Liberal party urging, the State Department told Gonzales that supervision might be necessary to avoid "serious political disturbances." The most "natural" course would be "for Cuba to invite General Crowder . . . to interpret and apply the new law."[37] As Gonzales predicted, Menocal refused, rejecting also a milder alternative of inviting Crowder simply as an observer, lest his opponents herald this as a rebuke. In reporting Menocal's attitude, Gonzales called attention to Liberal frauds and recommended a strong declaration against revolution. The State Department again turned the coin over when Gonzales denied reports that Crowder was to supervise the elections: it thought that this would be construed as injuring the Liberals.[38]

The candidacy of José Miguel Gómez, the former president and leader of the revolt in 1917, provided the focal point in the electoral politics of 1920. He had been disliked and distrusted in the legation and in the State Department.[39] Before going to Cuba, General Crowder urged "that we should cause it to be felt in Cuba that we could not approve the accession of this man to the presidency." The department avoided such a commitment[40] and also rejected a suggestion that Menocal be given confidential guidance in the choice of a candidate to oppose Gómez.[41] Menocal and the Conservatives lost some of their support when Norman H. Davis, who had been an active investor in Cuba since 1908 and was a friend of Gómez, became undersecretary of state,[42] and Gonzales was replaced by Boaz W. Long.

The Conservatives found hope of continued power in the ambition of Zayas, the perennial Liberal candidate, whose split with Gómez was beyond repair. However, the electoral law had to be amended to permit nomination of the same candidate by more than one party. Contrary to the State Department's advice, Menocal signed the revision, arguing that it would have passed over his veto and that passage of this limited measure would reduce the danger of "pernicious amendment."[43] The department rebuked the president for "undue haste ... especially as he was aware of the Department's attitude," but was unwilling to chastize him publicly. Further amendment proposals caused the Gómez Liberals to threaten withdrawal. Secretary of State Colby warned that such action would be regarded "as tending to undermine the foundations of popular government" and would "in no way influence the policy of the United States to regard the result of a free election as expressive of the national will."[44]

The final move in the department's attempt to preserve the validity of the election was to draft a statement for the Cuban president that linked rejection of supervision to "assurances ... that a free and fair election would be held" and called attention to remedies "clearly set forth in the Election Law."[45] This put pressure both on the government, to avoid abuse and keep open channels of complaint and investigation, and on the opposition, to expect no redress except through accepted procedures. It also implied that gross violations would not be accepted. This attitude was made explicit in a supplementary statement from the legation:

The Government of the United States does not propose actually to supervise the elections. However, *it is by treaty pledged* to "the maintenance of a government in Cuba adequate for the protection of life, property and individual liberty." It is, therefore, unalterably opposed to any attempt to substitute violence and revolution for the processes of government. I am desired to emphasize the fact, however, that it is no less opposed to intimidation and fraud in the conduct of elections as such procedure might be effective in depriving the people of Cuba of the right of choosing their own government.[46]

The essential terms of the draft statement were publicly accepted by Menocal only after almost three months of persuasion and pressure. Meanwhile the State

Department decided to appoint agents to observe the elections in each province, but it appeared that stronger methods would be needed if Gómez were not to be deprived of an electoral victory, with revolt a likely consequence. Crowder advised "radical measures" and Sumner Welles, chief of the Latin American division, was willing to send him to Cuba even if this should cause Menocal to resign.[47] Welles wanted to "make every effort to avoid" another intervention in response to revolt precipitated by electoral abuse.[48] Once again the Liberals threatened to boycott the election, making revolt all but certain, and were dissuaded by the State Department. But the unwillingness of the United States to insist on direct supervision left the Conservatives free to disregard much of the law and the advice which the Americans pressed upon them.[49] Crowder was not sent to Cuba. The government took advantage of the army's fears of a Gómez administration.[50] With the same man in charge of the War and Interior Departments, "military supervisors" were sent to municipalities that were considered unreliable, ostensibly to be prepared for revolt.

As election day approached, the minister was instructed to have President Menocal publicly proclaim responsibility for the operation of the Electoral Code. The content of the proclamation was prescribed, although the minister was not to "attempt to dictate its phraseology."[51] It came out, as suggested, four days before the election. President Wilson asked the secretary of war to have an army division ready for possible use in Cuba.[52]

The election result was no surprise. A slow count put the Conservatives ahead in every province except Havana, but the observers reported that intimidation and trickery had disenfranchised many Liberals.[53] Liberal leaders pressed the United States to have the elections annulled, but the State Department insisted that they seek redress in the courts.[54] A sharp drop in the price of sugar just before the election brought an end to the "dance of the millions" which wartime prosperity had made possible. At the end of the year, without prior notification to President Menocal, General Crowder was sent back to Cuba on the battleship *Minnesota*, where he kept his headquarters for several months, charged, as special representative of President Wilson, with helping to resolve both political and economic problems.

While the State Department hoped that the electoral process would provide an alternative to revolt, conservative opinion in the United States openly preferred minority control. *World's Work* claimed that the Liberal majority consisted largely of "Negroes and 'poor whites.'" As in the South following Reconstruction, "the educated and propertied classes" had resorted to illegal methods rather than permitting "the party of ignorance . . . to rule indefinitely." It advocated a new intervention which would last "long enough, twenty-five years if necessary, to bring up a new generation of Cubans."[55]

Menocal objected to Crowder's "being sent on a warship without our first observing the formalities customary among friendly nations," but the State Department insisted that "the special relations" with Cuba made prior consent unnecessary. "A receptive attitude" would make it possible to avoid "measures which could be construed as intervention or as supervision of Cuba's domestic affairs."[56] The secretary of the navy, Josephus Daniels, commented tartly in his diary, "Truth is we put Menocal in 4 years ago when he had not been elected and he thought he could bluff it through again."[57]

Menocal was soon persuaded to receive Crowder. Expressing "great satisfaction" with the mission, he asked for help in resolving the electoral dispute. State Department policy was "to surround with adequate safeguards" partial new elections.[58] Although results were confirmed in several disputed districts, the courts invalidated enough returns to make a Liberal victory possible. Crowder insisted that to avoid "active intervention," disputes should be resolved quickly and duly elected officials should be sworn in at the proper time.[59]

Crowder did not believe that either candidate would be good for Cuba. When a deadlock seemed possible, he suggested that an alternative might be agreed upon. Sumner Welles came to Havana and placed Carlos Manuel de Céspedes, the minister in Washington, at the head of a list of men who would be amenable to "suggestions or advice,"[60] but the State Department held back, loftily instructing Crowder that the plan was

not one in which this Government should participate or as to which it desires to express an opinion. . . . The people of Cuba should not be permitted to feel that we claim any voice in their selection of a president or other public official, or that this Government expects them in any way to be influenced by any preferences on our part as to candidates. We shall endeavor not even to feel a preference and scrupulously to refrain from expressing one.[61]

The Liberals boycotted the special elections, following incidents that Crowder found to have been staged. They would have been satisfied, he reported, by nothing less than "exclusive American supervision and control of both electoral machinery and armed forces."[62] Gómez and his supporters did their best to persuade both Crowder and Secretary of State Charles Evans Hughes that the entire election should be reheld, with an interim president to be chosen by Congress, but the United States maintained that "safeguards and recourses" had been available "without partiality or discrimination."[63] Gómez gave up the struggle, rather, as he put it, than to endanger the safety of the Republic by another American intervention and died a few weeks later.[64]

Cuba's dependence upon the United States for financial survival enabled Crowder to exert immense influence during the early part of the Zayas administration. He remained in Cuba as "Special Representative near the Cuban Government," while the accredited minister languished, left the country, and finally resigned. The State Department instructed Crowder to advise Zayas "that there is implicit in the Treaty of 1903 the obligation on the part of the Republic of Cuba to maintain an honest and efficient government" and to impress upon him the importance of appointing "men of the highest ability and unquestioned honesty." Zayas accepted this interpretation and several policy commitments by "signed O.K." and stated publicly his intention "to utilize the valuable and disinterested services" of his American adviser.[65]

The project of a $50 million loan became the fulcrum for Crowder's efforts. The Department of State was unwilling to seek the "complete control by officials of this Government of the national finances of Cuba," which it thought the Morgan banking house wanted. Sumner Welles told the bankers that an attempt to constitute "a receivership general of Cuban customs similar to that now obtaining [*sic*] in Santo Domingo or Nicaragua" would cause the resignation of the Cuban government. Intervention, "which the President desired, at almost any cost, to avoid," would then become necessary and "the impression created in Latin-America as a whole would be exceedingly unfortunate." The bankers accepted a more limited degree of "effective control."[66]

Trying to maximize the leverage of the loan, the State Department construed Article II of the Platt Amendment as requiring assurance that revenues would cover current expenses and the service of the public debt. Article III was also invoked. Crowder held that "stable government . . . is as much imperiled by insolvency as by armed revolution. . . . Our policy of noninterference" had "permitted extravagance and corruption to expand to the point of constituting a danger for the existence of the Republic." We had "the authority and duty to intervene" either with "preventive" or "remedial measures."[67] When it appeared that Zayas and the Congress would try to avoid compliance by resorting to an internal loan, they were told that this also would violate Article II.[68]

Crowder stressed the importance of abolishing the lucrative plums of Cuban politics, *botellas,* or jobs without work, and *colecturias* of the lottery, which enabled the holders to sell tickets at inflated prices.[69] Thus both greed and patriotism were aroused among Cubans who had benefited from these perquisites. The United States was unable to establish links with a Cuban reform constituency. An emergent reform movement refused to identify its goals with the demanded "normalization," and when it appeared later that American insistence on reform had given way to complicitous acceptance of corruption as the price of stability, the impetus to reform contributed to the further radicalization of Cuban nationalism.[70]

After several weeks during which it became apparent that the budget law as proposed would leave loopholes for evasion, Crowder suggested that "a Government of American Intervention" would have little difficulty in imposing "its solution."

I fully appreciate that the Department is most anxious to avoid intervention. . . . In his present mood (created for him largely by a hungry political following) it is certain that [President Zayas] will continue to obstruct many of the reforms . . . unless coerced into a compliant attitude by pressure from Washington.[71]

In October, with funds too low to meet the payroll, the State Department offered to approve a temporary loan of $5 million, provided Zayas would limit the budget to $65 million and "demonstrate conclusively to its satisfaction" the necessity for any sum larger than $50 million.[72] For several weeks there was a test of will. Pressure for the loan was brought to bear from the secretary of commerce, Herbert Hoover, who wanted to relieve "apprehension of Cuban government bankruptcy and social chaos."[73] In January 1922 Crowder and the State Department approved the temporary loan, having secured budgetary reductions.

During the same month Crowder helped to prepare a long statement of the rights and duties of the United States toward Cuba, giving notice that he would "at times offer suggestions and recommendations regarding needed fiscal measures and appropriate legislation" and would insist upon "free and full access to any and all sources of information." He followed this up in March by asking the department to approve "certain demands for specific reforms, to be accomplished within specified time limits." The "recommendation for an ultimatum" was soon cast in two memoranda, which were to be the first of a series.[74]

Following emphatic instructions from Secretary of State Hughes, Dana G. Munro, acting chief of the Division of Latin American Affairs, advised against "giving the communications referred to the character of an ultimatum or... threatening intervention." He could envisage "a situation which would force this government to consider very seriously... some form of intervention," but "a continuation of the present financial situation" would not be "sufficiently disastrous."[75] Accordingly, Crowder's draft was toned down; instead of stating that noncompliance would "place my Government in a position in which it could no longer avert the natural consequences," it read that such failure "could not but be regarded... with the gravest concern."[76] It bristled nevertheless with peremptory phrases: "my Government is firmer than ever in its insistence that the total amount of the budget... must not exceed fifty-five millions of dollars; ... it is now time that Congress be awakened to its duty and held to compliance therewith;... my Government now considers the present situation to permit of no further delay."[77]

Crowder pressed for further action with a memorandum on "Graft, Corruption and Immorality in the Public Administration," which he acknowledged to be deficient in evidence (and which, he later said, he recalled with "a sense of shame" when he "witnessed the corruption of municipal politicians" in Chicago).[78] He thought "insidious corruption" had "so extended itself as to render futile any hope that the evils will be remedied by the Cuban people through the ordinary agencies at their disposal." The State Department's response was again cautious: Crowder should avoid "any appearance of threat or any demand so insistent that the Department would be embarrassed by the failure of the Cuban Government to comply immediately" and should stress the financial needs of Cuba more than the Platt Amendment.[79]

Crowder finally gained agreement to appoint new men as secretaries of three graft-ridden departments and to reform the lottery.[80] The "honest cabinet" took office in June 1922. A few days later the Cuban Senate asked the United States to maintain "the spirit and the letter" of Root's interpretation of the Platt Amendment as "not synonymous with intermeddling or interference in the affairs of Cuba."[81] Crowder's attempts to press for enactment of the reform program were stridently contested in the Cuban press. One of his memoranda to Zayas somehow leaked, coincident with a report of a ten-day ultimatum. The State Department felt constrained to deny that there had been an ultimatum and to warn Crowder to avoid statements which could be so construed. Crowder subsequently reported that the denial had been taken to mean that his program might be obstructed "without serious consequences."[82] Enough was enacted, nevertheless, for approval of the long-pending loan. The secretary of state decided not to condition it on commitments regarding an amnesty bill or retention of the "honest" ministers.[83]

Under prodding from Crowder, Zayas agreed to keep the cabinet members "indefinitely in their offices, as convenient for the total realization of the moralizing program."[84] But financial stringency having eased, with the loan in hand and the price of sugar improving, he was able on April 3 to dismiss with impunity four of the "honest" men "who were closer to the American ambassador than to himself."[85]

Hope that national pride might be enlisted against corruption in Cuba had been frustrated. Instead, scoundrels found refuge in patriotism. Yet a concept of public interest was emerging. Those who used patriotism cynically ran the risk that eventually it would be turned against them.

The lottery reform was repealed in the name of nationalism. The Lower House overrode a gentle veto. Supporters of repeal argued, as Crowder reported, that "a policy of interference contrary to the principles of self-government" would "take on dangerous proportions unless all unite to carry to the Government and Congress of the United States the firm impression that Cubans would feel deeply wounded in their sentiments if said interference should be attempted."[86]

Shortly afterwards, when the Cuban chargé d'affaires complained about statements "that even seemed to contemplate intervention," the Secretary of State, in denying any such intention, expressed "great disappointment" at the lottery resolution and objected to its offensive language. If Cuba persisted in "a downward path" contrary to "caution and advice, . . . she could not in any way hold the United States responsible for the inevitable disaster which would follow."[87]

It was clear that the United States would no longer be prepared to step in to prevent such an outcome. The time for "strong action" had passed. Possibly, it was thought in the department, if Crowder had been withdrawn when the "honest cabinet" was dismissed, the Cubans might have "set their house in order." But a belated gesture would appear to support the opposition. The United States would "stultify itself" if it kept giving advice which the Cuban

Congress rejected. The department thought that Crowder, after a vacation, should limit his role to that of an observer. We could "draw up a comprehensive indictment . . . should the Cuban politicians unfortunately bring their country into a condition where the United States would be obliged under the Treaty . . . to intervene."[88]

Crowder's efforts to promote reform were henceforth sporadic and unavailing, although, with the title of ambassador, he remained in Cuba until 1927. The State Department concluded that if promotion of rectitude would jeopardize stability and risk deeper involvement, stability was the value which the United States should promote. As a general rule for the Caribbean area, the chief of the Latin American division suggested, the United States should

let the natives work out their solution with help and assistance from our diplomatic representatives, but without tying our hands to any given course of action should the people of the country be able to come to some solution which gives promise of affording a period of stability even though it should not fall in with our idea of a democratic constitutional government and even should it not be in accordance with their own written constitution.[89]

RESIGNATION AND AGGRAVATION

Having acquiesced to Zayas's throwing off the reforms that Crowder's pressure had introduced, the United States left no doubt that it still rejected revolution. Crowder reminded the secretary of state that the United States bore some responsibility for corruption that it did not permit to be remedied through revolt.

The people argue, with some force, that as no relief against corrupt government can come through corrupt elections, and as the right of armed revolt against such a government has been denied them by the policy of the United States here and elsewhere in Latin America, the responsibility for the continuance of corrupt government here lies with the United States and that relief can only come through a much more aggressive attitude of our Government.[90]

But when a reform and protest movement touched off a small revolt in April 1924, President Coolidge immediately denied arms to the revolutionists while the war department approved sales to the government. This put an end to "moralization." Cuban politicians "henceforth felt there was no further need for them to restrain themselves in the pursuit of private fortune at the expense of the state."[91]

In the election of 1924 the popular choice was not opposed by the government. Electoral abuses were therefore limited, and the danger of revolt did not become acute. The United States took no part. Zayas, who did not control the army and "had never been either a fool or a fighter," was unable to hold the Conservative nomination. The Liberals nominated General Gerardo Machado after a contest with Colonel Carlos Mendieta, who stood against corruption and in favor of "going hand in hand" with the United States but made little effort to cultivate support. Zayas withdrew in favor of Machado on the promise that he could name three members of the cabinet. Menocal, the Conservative candidate, could not this time rely on governmental resources to overcome the Liberal majority. The government, not needing to abuse its authority in support of Machado, did so with comparative moderation. Machado polled nearly 60 percent of the vote. The State Department was able to avoid any statement that could be construed as favoring him.[92] Hopeful speculation was heard as usual from the losers that revolt might bring intervention, but they decided to concede. The State Department congratulated Crowder for "having induced Menocal to take the peaceful method."[93]

Machado, who was closely connected with United States business interests as a leading figure in public utilities, claimed allegiance to the growing force of nationalism in a manner which the State Department could approve. Rather than lead a political movement, he was content to control the reins of power while expressing a national sentiment in mild tones. "A wise patriotism," he held, would make the Platt Amendment "an organ without functions, a dead-letter law, that can be laid away in the tomb."[94] Ostensibly in order to avoid intervention, he made use of the army to suppress strikes.[95] Policymakers in Washington, having failed themselves to overcome malfeasance and disorder either by close supervision or by open intervention, had reason to be hopeful. Crowder was anxious to cultivate Machado's disposition to cooperate. He wanted to offset "the reputation of a somewhat hard bargainer" and to make Cuba an "entering wedge into the good will of this hemisphere" by offering "proof of American altruism."[96]

Machado brought up the Platt Amendment with President Coolidge. While "all the Cuban people understood" that it "was a benefit," he contended, "it did a certain amount of moral damage" with nations that really enjoyed less independence than Cuba. He "simply wanted" Coolidge "to have this matter under consideration and some time before he left office turn it over in his mind and see whether he thought something should and could be done."[97]

It soon appeared that little had changed in Cuban politics. Crowder's attempts to reform electoral procedures had little lasting effect, and the Congress was brought under presidential control by astute use of patronage. As the election of 1928 approached, Machado looked for a way to remain in office without violating his repeated denunciation of "re-electionism." He ostensibly proposed an extension of term until 1930 coupled with a rule against reelection, but a constituent assembly decided that he should be allowed to run for a new six-year term.[98]

American reactions were ambivalent. Earlier, noting Machado's desire for the "closest possible cooperative relation," Crowder had recommended that he be given "informal assurance" that reelection would be accepted. But measures "savoring of dictatorship," as Crowder put it, were a threat to stability.[99] The Latin American division feared "popular resentment and consequent disorder" but concluded that Crowder had apparently committed the United States "to a policy of quiescence for the moment."[100]

There was talk from some Latin American countries of boycotting the Inter-American conference in Havana, and it was rumored that Machado feared opposition, but when he visited Washington he encountered nothing more than mild reproach. Crowder concluded that "nearly all that may properly be said" had been said.[101] Shortly afterward Crowder was replaced by a political appointee, Noble Brandon Judah.

Machado, having been nominated by the three existing parties, while the constitutional revision prevented the establishment of any new party, was reelected easily. Opposition meetings were broken up by the police. The chargé d'affaires recommended that official congratulations be withheld to show that Machado did not have "the wholehearted support which he is apparently trying to have the people of Cuba believe he is receiving,"[102] but Secretary of State Kellogg was unconvinced. Indeed, rejecting also the advice of undersecretary J. Reuben Clark, he appointed a special representative to the inauguration.

When the documents were reviewed in the Department of State several years later, it seemed clear that

both the Department and the Embassy put a premium on "order" in Cuba. Any qualms that may have arisen over those factors of the Constitutional Amendment Bill which made the Government less responsive, instead of more responsive, to the people were quashed, for President Machado had brought internal peace to Cuba for the first time since 1917. Both Ambassador Crowder and the Department indicated that their passivity to the constitutional amendments was due to their hope that under Machado peace, order, and "political cooperation" would continue.[103]

Reluctance to appear to interfere in Cuban affairs was also shown in connection with a loan repayment proposal in 1928. Rather than take direct issue, the Department of State suggested that the ambassador indicate orally that "an unfortunate impression would be produced" if a Special Public Works Fund were drawn upon, but Judah refrained even from this: an amendment of the budget "would give rise to considerable talk and our interference [would be] at least guessed at."[104]

The State Department was not yet prepared, however, to retract its extensive claim to the right and duty of involving itself in Cuban politics. In 1929, very soon after Henry L. Stimson became secretary of state, it acted to prevent passage of a bill to penalize Cubans who might seek foreign intervention either by direct appeal or by propaganda. The ambassador was instructed to point out that the measure would be seen as an "affront by Cuba directed at the United States." The department held, quite bluntly, that its responsibility required "free access to the sources of information" and made particular reference to the importance of "citizens of Cuba" providing information as to "whether the Government of Cuba, at a given time, is adequate for the protection of life, property and individual liberty." It rested its case, moreover, upon ground broader than the Platt Amendment: Judah was told that he might tell Machado

that the rights of intervention inhering in the United States . . . date back to the general obligations which the United States assumed before the world by expelling the Spanish Power from Cuba and turning the government over to the Cubans, and to the specific obligations which the United States assumed in the Treaty of Paris, and are not necessarily comprehensively stated in the Treaty of Relations with Cuba.[105]

Machado had no chance to respond to this suggestion; when he gave assurance that the bill would not be passed, Judah refrained from raising the general issue. The bold assertion of interventionist obligation was not repeated.

Machado, who had represented a hope for stable order, became in his second term a hated figure, surviving in office only through increasingly ruthless resort to force. His control of political parties meant that tension and despair generated by the depression found no political outlet. The president, along with the majority in Congress whose fortunes were linked to his, stood in increasing isolation, sustained by the police, the army, and unofficial gunmen.

J. Reuben Clark, the undersecretary of state, assessed the situation early in the Hoover administration. With the Platt Amendment in effect, a corrupt president could "impose such a rule upon Cuba as would not be possible except for the armed force of the United States which stands behind him." He thought "we may not properly blink our responsibility of knowing what is actually happening there and of taking the steps necessary to correct any inequitous conditions." Should investigation sustain charges of "corruption and despotism" we would be "face to face with a problem as serious as has ever faced this Government in connection with Cuba."[106] Stimson preferred, however, to avoid any avowal of American responsibility.

The new administration was anxious to cultivate good will in Latin America by making a break with the interventionist pattern. Hoover wanted to include a lengthy "definition of our relation to questions of intervention" in his inaugural address, but was dissuaded by Charles Evans Hughes, who thought any discussion of that subject was bound to be misinterpreted.[107]

The ambassador during most of the Hoover administration was Harry F. Guggenheim. Through "unofficial advice" based on research by an expert staff, he hoped to be quietly effective in providing "friendly support" to the Cuban government.[108] Guggenheim was aware that an oppressive regime could take advantage of any apparent sign of American support. He moved to prevent a visit by two warships to Havana at the time of a mass rally against Machado, when it might have been viewed as an attempt to intimidate the protesters. According to the ambassador's account, the visit had been arranged through an American businessman close to Machado.[109] During 1930, before intransigence and bitterness had reached their peak, Guggenheim was active in trying to mediate between Machado and his opponents, particularly Colonel Mendieta and former President Menocal, but he "consistently refused to have anything to do with" a demand for a presidential election within three years. He thought the president "made every reasonable concession" and that his opponents were "most stubborn and uncompromising." Professing idealism, they only wanted "to satisfy their personal ambition and get into office."[110] While they disavowed any desire for military intervention, they were eager to provoke American demands that would ruin Machado politically.[111]

In September 1930 Guggenheim asked for a clarification of policy, quoting the Root interpretation of Article III of the Platt Amendment and suggesting that the embassy should not go beyond "unofficial expert advice and assistance" unless there should be a "complete breakdown" of government or "in the case of foreign aggression."[112] Shortly afterwards Stimson set forth the basis of United States policy in a background conference with correspondents. Surprisingly, he had been unaware of Root's formulation until it was brought to his attention, but he found that it provided a convenient rationale. He insisted that we had "never intervened in Cuba except once in 1909 [sic] when there was no government there." With regard to the possibility that American forces might be used to support the government, Stimson suggested at first that the correspondents "could say that has never been done in the past. American forces have never landed in Cuba when there was any regime to maintain. The only times we have gone into Cuba was when there was no government." He concluded, however, that such a statement might be taken as "an encouragement to revolt." He asked the press to say instead that "it was pointed out at the State Department that while it is true there was never an intervention in Cuba to support a government, every case in the future will be judged on its merits and a situation might exist which would distinguish it from the preceding one." He was "perfectly willing" that they should use the rediscovered words of Root to describe "the national policy of this government."[113]

Machado's opponents blamed Ambassador Guggenheim for the inaction of the United States, but the United States was determined "after years of trying to cut down interference in Caribbean states" to avoid any suggestion "that the United States intervene either by diplomatic pressure or by force to oust an established government."[114] Guggenheim was provoked by Menocal to express surprise "that he should advocate American interference in Cuban affairs since the Embassy's records were full of protest from him during his Presidency against such interference."[115] When he circumspectly offered "unofficial good offices," Stimson warned him not to say anything which might encourage the opposition.[116] Increasingly, Guggenheim was embarrassed by rumors which played upon "what seems to be a fixed impression among the Cuban people—that the United States intends to support the Machado Government." To the contrary, he reported, the embassy had "taken particular care" to avoid "any semblance of political partisanship for Machado"; he had refrained "from even the innocent public praise that is so often bestowed upon a President by the head of a mission accredited to him."[117]

Guggenheim was more ready than was Stimson to urge Machado to adopt "a policy of reconciliation."[118] State Department officials left no doubt that their prime objective was to avoid deeper involvement. When the solicitor of the department, referring to reports of imprisonment without trial, suggested that the government might not be "adequate for the protection of life, property and individual liberty" and the embassy supplied evidence of its inadequacy, the State Department considered the evidence inconclusive and prevented further inquiry. Assistant Secretary Francis White informed Stimson that he did not see how such information could be obtained without the inquiry being "heralded as indicating that the United States is withdrawing support from Machado."[119]

Stimson did tell the Cuban ambassador that the American people were deeply opposed to arbitrary arrest and detention. Evident failure of the Cuban government to maintain the adequacy referred to in the Platt Amendment would bring "immediate pressure . . . on the Secretary and he would be charged with dereliction." The ambassador replied that Cubans were "not imbued with the sense of legality that prevails in this country." Leniency "was damaging to Machado's prestige," but "it was impossible to get a conviction" because "the upper classes were strongly against Machado." Machado had "worked hard for the good of Cuba" and "for the sugar interests and the tobacco interests." Stimson acknowledged Machado's problems and accomplishments. "The thing that he wanted most to avoid was a revolution with its concomitant a possible intervention on our part."[120]

In May 1931 the restraint on mediation was slightly relaxed and Stimson approved a memorandum which modified the policy of support for an established government; if fighting should break out, the United States would limit its interference to protection of American lives and property, but if government should cease to function, military occupation would be considered.[121]

Resisting demands for constitutional reforms, Machado threatened to resign "and let the army run the country," but Guggenheim considered this a bluff. To Machado's suggestion that the United States would be bound to oppose "proposals for a modified parliamentary form of government," Guggenheim replied that "this was a question for the Cubans to work out in their own way." Machado told Guggenheim that he would "let the press enjoy the same freedom as it does in the United States, regardless of what it might say," but censorship was imposed a month later.[122]

Open revolt broke out in August, led by Menocal and Mendieta.

Guggenheim's view that they were motivated by political opportunism was accurately reported in the press.[123] There was no public statement of support for the government, however.[124] The revolt collapsed quickly, and its leaders were taken captive. A spokesman in New York bitterly complained that Guggenheim had worked to keep Machado in power rather than in the interest of justice.[125] Guggenheim objected that "reports given out by the Department" were being interpreted in the press "as indicative of American support of the Machado Government," arousing distrust among the Cuban people.[126]

There is no doubt that American policymakers were eager for Machado's political survival. Guggenheim congratulated him "on his successful campaign against the revolutionists and on the efficiency and loyalty of the army."[127] He wrote later, to be sure, that the "widely accepted opinion" that the United States was unalterably opposed to any resort to violence or revolution was a misunderstanding, noting that it "did not even place an embargo on munitions of war entering Cuba" in 1931.[128] But the Cuban government had been dissuaded from requesting an embargo on the understanding that shipments were "being prohibited as effectively as they would be under a formal proclamation."[129]

Guggenheim did try to persuade Machado to take steps toward "moral peace," and suggested that he offer to resign two months before the 1932 elections. He went so far as to draft "a suggestion for the appropriate presentation" of a reform program.[130] When Machado claimed that such steps would cost him the support of the army, Guggenheim secured from the chief of staff of the army, "a friend of long standing," a statement that if "the politicians refused to pass the reforms," they "must be forced" to do so.[131]

Machado would not agree to resign, but he did present to his Congress a reform program which had been worked out by the American ambassador and the secretary of justice. Guggenheim believed that his role as "spectator" would "act somewhat as an incentive"[132] in keeping the program intact, but Machado showed unexpected tenacity in resisting pressure for reform. He had a collaborative relationship with United States banking interests, which the State Department, professing nonintervention, was unwilling to disturb. Until it became impossible to do so, he took care to meet loan payments, at the cost of defaults on salaries and greater repression. Stimson did nothing to counteract the appearance that by not insisting on reform the United States was preferring bankers' profits to the welfare and liberties of the Cuban people. Guggenheim's plea for a statement to show that Machado could not rely on continued support was rejected, in part because "the bankers, who had [sic] a big stake in Cuba, are working hard on a scheme which they hope will work out satisfactorily."[133] Ruby Hart Phillips, the wife of the New York Times correspondent, claimed matter-of-factly that "the Chase National Bank . . . was determined that President Machado should remain in office as long as he continued to make payments on the public works loans."[134]

Having rejected early resignation, Machado tried to maintain his power through "specious gestures of conciliation" and by preventing the organization of an effective opposition. Guggenheim embarked on a major effort to induce a change of United States policy. Once revolution had failed, instead of facing "an intransigent opposition unwilling to accept reforms" the United States confronted "the consequences of a Government intent on perpetuating an unpopular grip on the country." The economic situation had worsened "following the disregard of our advice" and "the faith of the Cuban people in the ability and disposition of the President to restore moral peace" had been "wholly lost." Machado's renewed intransigence responded to "his growing feeling that the United States Government is not interested in . . . the question of political liberties in Cuba." It was not too late to "save Cuba from the fate of so many of the Latin American Republics." But Machado would not yield unless "circumstances" (among them "the attitude of our Government") forced him to do so. Although the embassy had been "strictly impartial," it was widely believed, partly because of "the shadow" of past policy, that we were "maintaining him in power." Guggenheim asked the department to give stronger support to the embassy's attitude of avoiding "any appearance of supporting Machado or of sympathizing with his policies." The Cuban Ambassador to the United States, Orestes Ferrara, had been reassuring Machado. To make clear to Ferrara "our lack of sympathy" with his present policies "would at least tend to relieve our Government from responsibility" for their "inevitable consequences."[135]

This forceful plea brought no response for two months. Meanwhile, Guggenheim met Menocal and Mendieta and reported "a growing realization of the impartiality of the United States." He considered it "of the utmost importance that everything should be done to maintain and foster this opinion in Cuba."[136]

Stimson rejected any initiative which would put pressure on Machado and lend encouragement to the opposition. He thought that to tell Ferrara that we lacked sympathy for Machado's policies would be "a radical departure from an attitude of strict impartiality." Cuba should try to achieve a "Cuban solution" to its problems as Guggenheim had "so frequently and consistently advocated in the past." To the thought that an expression of disapproval of Machado would tend to relieve the United States of responsibility, Stimson icily responded, "The Department cannot acquiesce in the view that the continuance of its policy of non-interference in Cuba's internal affairs involves our Government in any responsibility for any consequences of the policies of the Cuban Executive."[137]

During the year which followed, there was a precarious balance between repression and sporadic outbreaks of violence while the Cuban people festered in hatred of the government and despair at their impotence. The Root interpretation had become a "doctrine of self-denial"[138] serving to shield a Cuban government that could avoid chaos and prevent damage to United States citizens or property. A State Department spokesman told a delegation headed by the historian, Mary Wilhelmina Williams, that to send a commission of investigation to Cuba "would be intermeddling imperialism of the most flagrant sort."[139] Stimson told

Representative Hamilton Fish that Article III of the Platt Amendment imposed no obligation "but only set forth the willingness of the Government of Cuba that the United States may intervene for the attainment of certain objects."[140]

The State Department refused to invoke the Platt Amendment against refinancing loans despite Guggenheim's warning of "serious reaction" against apparent "moral support to financial arrangements made by American bankers for the perpetuation of the Machado dictatorship."[141] When asked by Guggenheim to take a position on a plan worked out by the Chase Bank with three oil companies, which in effect would divert tax receipts into loan repayment, Stimson replied that disapproval "would constitute an unwarranted interference in Cuban affairs."[142] Belief among Cubans that the main concern of the United States was to support banking interests and that noninterference was a convenient rationale for indifference to reform intensified as the economic crisis continued. As long as the United States renounced political objectives, it was vulnerable to the charge that it was subordinating them to financial concerns.

When Sumner Welles took over the embassy in Havana, with somewhat more responsive superiors in Washington, he found Machado so convinced of his dependence on "the American banking groups" that he refused to take any initiative toward a moratorium. The new administration did nothing to change this impression. The State Department responded, on the authority of President Roosevelt, that it could not take initiative toward a suspension of payments and that it was convinced that "the bankers, having legal or moral responsibilities towards the bondholders, would not be disposed to suggest" any such move.[143] It appeared in Cuba, to Machado perhaps as clearly as to anyone, that if at a time of extreme economic and political crisis the government of the United States did nothing, then the purposes of American policy were being carried out.

As Guggenheim's ambassadorship drew to an end, he argued that the basic cause of difficulty was the treaty right of intervention. The Cuban government would not respond to "friendly suggestions" unless it believed that failure to do so would lead to intervention, to the loss of a needed loan, or to political defeat. The opposition was tempted to acts of despair that might provoke intervention but was deterred from taking effective steps of their own. Guggenheim wanted, however, to make one final attempt to apply the Platt Amendment constructively. Abrogation "should be made contingent upon certain constitutional reforms and the re-establishment of truly representative government in Cuba." This "interposition in Cuban affairs," would, he thought, be "fully justified as an exceptional measure, and 'the United States would have the satisfaction of again starting Cuba on the road to democratic government, but this time only after disposing of an obligation that is both irksome to Cuba and useless, if not actually harmful, to the United States.'"[144] The dream died slowly.

Both Stimson and Guggenheim were visited by Charles W. Taussig, an adviser of Franklin D. Roosevelt. Stimson thought that Machado could "hold the country safe and suppress revolution''; a proposal to supervise a special election would be unnecessary and impractical. Guggenheim conveyed his view that the next ambassador should be allowed to play a more active role than had been permitted to him under Stimson. Taussig concluded that Machado had lost the support of the Cuban people and should be induced to resign.[145]

6.
NICARAGUA

CHAMORRO IN POWER

As Díaz's term of office drew to an end, it was evident that the State Department would be in large measure responsible for the outcome of the impending 1916 election. According to Dana G. Munro,

It was generally recognized that Díaz had been able to stay in office only because the continued presence of the legation guard meant that the United States would not permit another revolution, and it was clear that Díaz' group would remain in power by controlling the election if the United States took no action. This would be unsatisfactory for several reasons.... [T]he political situation was clearly unstable and continuing rivalry between Díaz' friends and the *chamorristas* made the conservatives' hold on the government precarious. More especially, the State Department was sensitive to charges that it was supporting a minority government by force, and it would be further criticized if the same group continued in power by stealing the election.[1]

The Díaz government, beholden to the United States, had earned such unpopularity that the chargé d'affaires, without fear of rebuke, referred to "that powerful oligarchical ring that, working through the President, have been strangling Nicaragua for these four years past and who, without outside help, can only be overthrown by revolution."[2]

The State Department was intensely distrustful of the Liberals, considering them still tainted by association with Zelaya. An extraordinary discussion was carried on, nevertheless, with the leading Liberal contender, Julián Irías, through the intermediacy of J. Reuben Clark. Clark had become counsel for the Nicaraguan Liberals after service as counsellor of the Department of State,[3] on condition that the Liberals agree to "carry out the policy of the United States." Irías tried to show that he and his party could be "as loyal to American interests in Nicaragua as has been the present government." He was willing to accept treaties that would provide for a canal option, a right of intervention, and supervision both of finances and of a rural guard.[4]

The department, however, preferred General Emiliano Chamorro, a Conservative candidate who it was thought could win without open fraud and suppression.

Chamorro's withdrawal in 1912 had probably entailed the understanding that he would have the nomination in 1916.[5] The argument for supporting him was set forth by the new acting chief of the Latin American division, J. Butler Wright.[6] Wright castigated Irías, "than whom no one could have been more anti-American in past years," and the Liberal party, which was "undoubtedly tainted" with the strain of Zelaya ("whom this Government ousted from office in 1909"). The Díaz administration was dominated by the minister of finance, Eulogio Cuadra, whose attitude had changed from "grovelling gratitude" to "superciliousness" toward the United States. His brother, Pedro, the candidate of this faction, was unreliable. On the other hand, Chamorro was "a disinterested patriot, a man of undoubted honesty and a sincere friend and admirer of the United States." Wright did not concede that the Liberals were clearly a majority in Nicaragua; he thought that numerically the two parties were about equal, but in quality the Conservatives, "comprising men of commerce and finance, merchants and that portion of the middle class who perceived at first hand the beneficial results of our intervention in 1912" more than offset the Liberals, "composed in great part of the ignorant masses of the people who either do not appreciate the intentions and policies of this Government or who are readily susceptible to political oratory."

In considering policy alternatives, having rejected withdrawal, Wright ruled out supervision of the elections on the ground that it would have to be imposed against the will of the government, although a few weeks earlier he had held that "we can not do otherwise, in accordance with democratic principles and in fairness to all concerned." A third possibility was to maintain the legation guard "for the assurance of law and order but in no way to support the Government in an arbitrary military control of the situation." If this should result in the triumph of the Díaz-Cuadra faction, it would give rise to violent criticism. But the course that he favored differed from this in little more than the choice of candidate. He thought the United States should let it be known "by such means and channels as may subsequently prove opportune," that in its opinion "General Chamorro best reflects the policies of his party and . . . is now entitled to recognition." With Chamorro as candidate, Wright was quite willing to let the presence of marines redound to the advantage of the government party. Logic, he conceded, appeared to "demand that a Government whose disinclination to accept the proposal of the United States to supervise its elections strongly implies fear of the result, should not receive even the tacit support of the presence of the American Marines at the time of the election." But "exigencies" appeared "strongly to indicate that we can well afford to dispense with logic in an illogical situation."[7] A short time before this, Chamorro had "admitted smilingly that he recognized as well as we did that ideal free elections were impossible in his country."[8]

President Wilson noted that the matter was of "grave importance" with regard to relations with Latin America, but he did not attempt to specify its significance.[9] Chamorro was brought back from his post as Nicaraguan minister in Washington on a United States warship. The American minister warned the Liberals that the United States would not recognize anyone who had been associated with the Zelaya regime and made no protest, despite the intercession of Clark, when Díaz refused to allow Irías, the exiled Liberal leader, into the country.[10] Díaz, having agreed to let the secretary of state choose the Conservative candidate, was not permitted to veto the designation of Chamorro. It put an astringent icing on the cake when, after this interference, the department went on to demand guarantees that the election would be free and warned that if it were not, recognition of the victor would be withheld as contrary to "the spirit of this Government's attitude toward Nicaragua."[11]

Everything threatened to come unfixed when the minister's choice of a Liberal candidate was rejected as too pro-American, and it appeared that Díaz had turned, after all, to Irías as a means of blocking Chamorro. Following the appearance of two additional American warships, however, the political leaders were "less inclined to fractiousness," as Admiral Caperton put it. The minister, who "made a special point" to have the admiral at his side, set forth to Irías the demand that a Liberal candidate must prove that he had taken no active part in Zelaya's administration or in any subsequent revolutionary movement.[12] Irías withdrew and Chamorro was elected without significant opposition. The Liberals protested that the minister, "completely annulling our sovereignty," had "placed the Republic under a depressive [sic] guardianship" through demands "backed by a powerful regular force from the United States ready to land in Corinto to make the imposition effective."[13] The American army officer who observed the elections of 1920 considered it a matter of fact that in 1916 "the American Government, to all practical purposes, nominated and elected General Emiliano Chamorro as president of Nicaragua."[14]

Chamorro was neither as effective nor as compliant as his sponsors had hoped. The naval commander complained that his "attitude is apparently far from what should be expected as [sic] one who owes his choice to the United States Government. . . . Frequent and unexpected visits of ships," he thought, would "have a tremendous influence toward reminding the Nicaraguans that we have not relinquished our interest in the maintenance of good government in their country."[15]

As the election of 1920 approached, the State Department felt that it was important to avoid any gross illegality. It had been embarrassed by the survival of the Tinoco regime in Costa Rica in the face of nonrecognition, while it opposed revolution as a means of deposing him. In Honduras and Guatemala revolution seemed to be the usual means of political change. If it should appear that the electoral process was simply a method of giving tenure to incumbents, the United States could not hope to oppose revolution by appealing to principle.

The Nicaraguan minister, inquiring about the attitude of the United States toward Chamorro's reelection, was told that the constitutional provision that prohibited reelection "must be complied with.'"[16] The nomination went instead to the president's aging uncle, Diego Chamorro. The opposition, mostly Liberal but calling itself the Coalition, nominated a wealthy coffee planter and business man to whom the State Department had no objection.

Feeling that the United States should relieve itself of its role as the dominant force in the politics of Nicaragua, "a new group of officers" in the Latin American division recommended that some form of supervision of the election be insisted upon, but their proposal was rejected by Assistant Secretary Adee, who held, despite the effects of the presence of a marine garrison, that this would constitute improper intervention.[17] The matter was not seriously considered at a higher level because of the president's illness and Lansing's resignation as secretary of state. The department officers then asked General Enoch Crowder, who had gained prestige and experience in Cuba, to review the Nicaraguan electoral code.[18] On the basis of Crowder's conclusions, the minister was asked "tactfully" to "suggest . . . the desirability" of inviting him to come to Nicaragua and propose reforms. After Chamorro termed this "inconvenient" and unnecessary, the department tried to make it clear that it would not repeat the biased role of 1916.[19]

The State Department's concern was strengthened by a warning from two moderate Liberal leaders that fraudulent election would probably lead to revolution.[20] Three days later, the new chief of the Latin American division, Sumner Welles, prepared a memorandum which urged preventive action so that "the United States should not, once more, because of a revolution, be forced to intervene in Nicaragua in order to preserve order." It appeared to Welles that the Liberals had the support of a large majority. He thought that the Chamorro faction could be deterred only by "fear that the United States will not look favorably upon any administration which is brought into power by fraud and which does not represent popular sentiment." To enable the State Department to "form an opinion as to the conduct of elections," he arranged to send as an observer a former subordinate of Crowder's, Major Jesse I. Miller.[21]

Miller reported that registration was "enormously padded" and recommended that each voter be marked with indelible ink. The State Department thought it "unwise" to inflict this "personal indignity," but Miller saw no alternative. To compensate for underregistration of the opposition, Miller suggested that all lists dating back to 1906 should be considered valid, but the department thought that verified names should be added individually to the last authentic list. Miller's attempts to persuade Chamorro to relax registration procedures led him to express "surprise" that he had been asked to violate the law and constitution of Nicaragua in a way that "would make null and void our form of Government." Just before the election, however, the president made concessions which Miller considered "fairly satisfactory." Although the votes of those unlisted would not be counted, they could be cast and the State Department would take them into consideration in deciding what action to take.[22]

Miller concluded, after the election that there had been such "gross fraud" that it was "absolutely clear" that the victory of Diego Chamorro was not "expressive of the popular will." Without "some measure of relief," a Liberal uprising would occur. The United States would then "be forced to throw the weight of its influence to the maintenance in power of a minority element" or Nicaragua would "again be thrown into the throes" of civil war. There was no immediate resort to violence, Miller reported, because neither side considered the result final until the Department of State passed on it.[23]

The department recommended acceptance of the returns. To withhold recognition merely on the ground of electoral fraud would be "an unwarranted interference" and "would create a most unfortunate impression throughout Latin America."[24] But it attached great importance to assuring the opposition that it would have a fair chance in 1924. It warned Chamorro that there would be serious danger of revolution unless there were immediate electoral reform.[25] Having received assurance that a new law would have no retroactive effect, the outgoing president requested the help of General Crowder. Diego Chamorro was inaugurated with the American minister in attendance. Crowder himself did not go to Nicaragua because of his return to Cuba, but Harold W. Dodds was sent instead. A law based on his proposals was enacted in 1923.

Diego Chamorro's term of office was punctuated with disorder that threatened to engage the marine guard. In 1922 seizure of La Loma by a group of Conservatives brought stern instructions to the minister, a political appointee whose discretion had not been tested, to avoid any involvement by the guard in local political affairs. The State Department was anxious to prevent any test which might demonstrate that its presence "was little more than a bluff, which might be called at any time with embarrassing consequences."[26] Within the department there developed a firm resolve to withdraw the marines as soon as this could be done without it being taken as an invitation to revolt. If the election of 1924 could be "so free and fair that the people would be contented," they could be withdrawn and order could be maintained by an "efficient constabulary" which the United States "would assist in any proper way" to establish.[27]

The perennial issue of Central American unity kept arising in the interplay of revolution and counterrevolution and became a vehicle for anti-American sentiment. In 1917 a unity movement initiated by Costa Rica, which expressed resentment against the Bryan-Chamorro Treaty, was countered by Nicaragua's insistence that any meeting should include Panama and should be held either in Washington or in Panama.[28] Three years later the overthrow of Estrada Cabrera in Guatemala led to a pact of union, but Nicaragua withdrew when the other countries refused to include an express validation of the Bryan-Chamorro Treaty. The United States denounced any interference in Guatemala in the name of the Union, lest silence be taken as acquiescence. Secretary of State Hughes gave notice that the United States "would view with the greatest concern any attempt by one Central American country to interfere in the internal affairs of another, either by invasion or by assisting one political party.''[29] Munro feared that under a federal government "quarrels and disorders" would be no less frequent than in individual states and would be likely to involve the United States "in constant interference and probably occasional armed intervention" in the affairs of all of Central America.[30]

The United States tried to strengthen sanctions against revolution by sponsoring another conference of Central American states at Washington in 1922-23. This produced a treaty of peace and amity in which the commitments of 1907, not to intervene in civil wars and not to recognize governments that came to power through unconstitutional means, were renewed in more detail. Although, as in 1907, this was largely initiated by the Central American countries, its outcome came to be regarded as an imposition that gave the United States at least a veto power in the choice of presidents.[31]

In a convention on limitation of armaments, each of the countries agreed "to establish a National Guard to cooperate with the existing Armies," to be organized with help from the United States. While this would not eliminate existing armies, it could do something to curtail the use of armed forces for partisan and personal advantage.[32]

Since the treaty attempted to eliminate the traditional means of political change in Central America, it would fortify the power position of existing governments unless means of political change other than revolution could be introduced. With marines standing behind the government in Nicaragua, the State Department considered it essential to press for free elections and withdrawal. The department acknowledged that their presence cast doubt on the government's legitimacy, referring delicately to "the assertion, however unjustified it may be, that the United States Government is maintaining in office a government which would otherwise perhaps not be strong enough to maintain itself against the attacks of its political opponents." Setting January 1925 as a target date for withdrawal, following the election and installation of a new president, the department offered assistance in electoral preparations and in training a constabulary. Emiliano Chamorro, the former president, then again minister in Washington, objected that the plan would be regarded as supervision "and would cost the Conservative Party many thousands of votes," but the department went ahead.[33]

CHAMORRO AS OPPOSITIONIST AND USURPER

The sudden death of the president, Diego Chamorro, brought a radical change in the conditions under which the election would be held. The new president, Bartolomé Martínez, was not prepared to give support to Emiliano Chamorro. His own candidacy appeared to be barred by the constitution, but Chamorro supported it in order to curry favor, expecting a veto from the United States. The Department of State tried to avoid taking a position, while supporters of Martínez construed evasion as consent and the inept minister floundered in uncertainty.[34]

Eventually the State Department told Martínez in confidence that it wanted to avoid any question regarding eligibility. When he replied that his candidacy might unify the country and suggested ways of getting around the constitution, the department threatened to make its position public. Martínez acceded, saying resignedly that he was "well aware of the helplessness of an 'intervened' state and would make no complaint," although he did not make the renunciation public until after American objection had been made public.[35]

Martínez's support went to a Conservative of the faction opposed to Chamorro, Carlos Solórzano. Juan B. Sacasa, a Liberal, was the candidate for vice-president on this ticket. Most of its backing came from the larger faction of the Liberals. Chamorro had to undertake the unfamiliar role of running against the government. Presumably he knew well what this would mean. His attitude toward supervision of the election was quickly reversed.[36] The State Department tried to be neutral, but it could not avoid a rebuff to Martínez, when asked whether it would favor the government candidates. It replied that it desired "only that free and fair elections may be held. . . . [T]ransference of the center of political activity of Nicaragua to Washington," it concluded, "would be detrimental to the Government's interests."[37]

Preparations for the election went forward with the help of Dodds and three assistants, but only one of the assistants was permitted to stay until the election. The department tried to persuade Martínez to give Dodds a stronger role, but when he demurred, it did not insist, considering supervision no longer essential because the Liberals were not excluded from influence.[38] The government-supported candidates won decisively. Dodds wrote later that the election was "considerably better than former," but was "tainted with some of the old-fashioned practices."[39] The chargé d'affaires reported that votes were cast and counted under conditions which "render the published statements of the result unworthy of acceptance." Probably, however, a majority of voters supported the winning candidates.[40] It may be that Martínez made a mistake in not permitting supervision.

Any implied threat that the outcome might not be recognized turned out to be completely hollow, as astute Nicaraguans doubtless foresaw. The department, having "very carefully considered the whole Nicaraguan situation," concluded

that it is not feasible to demand new elections because it is not in a position to take the strong measures necessary to ensure compliance with the demand and even should the Government readily consent to new elections they would be valueless unless very closely supervised by this Government which would also mean armed intervention which is not to be contemplated.[41]

It found "merit of fairness" in the Liberals becoming beneficiaries of "the same tolerance shown the conservatives after the elections of 1912, 1916, and

1920.''[42] Once again the United States tried to gain ground prospectively by securing a pledge of fair conduct for the elections of 1928.

When January arrived, when the marine guard was scheduled to be withdrawn, nothing had been done to organize the nonpartisan constabulary that was to stand alongside free elections as the basis for constitutional order. The chargé d'affaires reported that it was being "announced by foreigners and Nicaraguans alike, that once the marines have gone a revolution will be inevitable.''[43] In reply to a request from Solórzano that withdrawal be postponed until the establishment of an efficient National Guard, the State Department held that ample notice had been given. The Nicaraguan government would be responsible "for any unfortunate developments which might result from the failure to make adequate preparations to meet the situation.''[44] Yet the United States did finally agree that the marines would remain for a few months while the new force was being organized.

When a constabulary plan had been prepared, efforts were made "to vitiate" it, the chargé d'affaires reported, because the government had "been given to understand" that it was "not especially important or urgent and that the withdrawal of the Legation Guard has not actually been decided upon.''[45] The constabulary was to be "trained free from political influence as a national institution," with "the object of entirely replacing the existing national police, navy and army." The marines were to lend service in training, with "full and complete authority." After withdrawal, Americans designated by the United States would manage the training branch. The senior officer would be an American subordinate only to the president of Nicaragua.[46]

A counterplan approved by the Congress in May provided for continued existence of the army "independent of the National Guard" and made no reference to American direction.[47] The chargé d'affaires objected that it would place the constabulary under "absolute control . . . of the Minister of Gobernacion," a post to which expresident Martínez had been appointed, and thus would become "a strictly political agency." He thought the government was trying to avoid withdrawal of the marines and recommended that it take place at once. Unless there were clear safeguards against political control, no American instructors should be appointed. The department accepted the Nicaraguan plan, however, believing that no more could be done than to give "the American instructors full authority over the constabulary school and authority to inspect and make recommendations regarding the constabulary proper." "Ultimate control" would have to "rest with the Nicaraguan Government.''[48]

By this time less than three months remained before the marines would leave. A former officer of the Philippine constabulary, Major Calvin B. Carter, signed a contract as chief of the constabulary and of the School of Instruction. The State Department pointed out that "all arrangements" were made "without intervention by the Department." The new constabulary would be more likely to succeed if it should be "regarded as a purely Nicaraguan institution." A last-ditch effort by the Nicaraguan government to involve the marines more directly and perhaps induce a delay in their departure was rebuffed by the chargé d'affaires with the approval of the department.[49] Withdrawal took place on August 3, 1925. Major Carter had gathered together a sufficient force to occupy the barracks. Even though the constabulary was new and green, the absence of any army worthy of the name gave it a chance to develop quite quickly into an effective instrument.[50]

The vacillation and confusion that attended the establishment of a constabulary were caused by pressures upon President Solórzano, whose personal strength was negligible, since he commanded no military force. Solórzano's two Conservative brothers-in-law controlled the key military positions. They made an attempt to control the new guard and were only prevented from doing so by the intervention of their sister in support of Major Carter.[51] Within a month of the marines' withdrawal, one of the brothers-in-law, General Alfredo Rivas, sent a rowdy band of troops into a reception in order "to liberate President Solórzano from the domination of the Liberal element in his government."[52] In the presence of the American minister, they arrested several prominent Liberals. Major Carter offered to support the president in a showdown, but rather than risk bloodshed, Solórzano agreed to remove several Liberals from his cabinet in exchange for release of the prisoners. For $4,500 and the promise of the consulate in Los Angeles, General Rivas surrendered the fortress that dominated the capital.[53] On request of the president, American war vessels were sent to the two principal ports, Bluefields and Corinto. The minister reported that their presence "extricated President Solórzano from a difficult position and stopped temporarily at least the tendency toward anarchy and revolution."[54]

It is not clear whether General Chamorro instigated the arrest of Solórzano's Liberal associates, but he soon appeared in Managua, ready to take advantage of the situation. By one account, the American minister, through an intermediary, asked Chamorro to try to quiet the people, in terms that could be construed as "an invitation to seize power."[55] Yet the minister urged Solórzano to place the guard in control of the key fortress of La Loma, and it was his refusal to do so that gave Chamorro his chance. On October 25 a friendly colonel opened the rear door of the fortress to him, and Chamorro took control. Solórzano, who was quite literally a captive of his rival, soon appointed Chamorro commander of the armed forces and handed him a resignation statement, which Chamorro could use once he had maneuvered himself into the position of legitimate successor.[56] The constabulary, having no orders from the president and no machine guns, did nothing and came under direction of the usurper who had denigrated it. Major Carter was exposed to the judgment that he "succumbed to Nicaraguan tradition" and "actively comforted and aided Chamorro."[57]

Sacasa, the Liberal vice-president, became the principal target of the Chamorro forces. He fled to Honduras, sending the State Department a note of protest which invoked the Washington treaty of 1923. The minister thought revolution would occur as soon as the Liberals could gather an army.[58] In response to his request for specific instructions in the event of Solórzano's resignation, the State Department said flatly that the United States "would not employ its armed forces to place Sacasa in power." Moreover, to bring him back "might create an embarrassing precedent, and "be misunderstood." Nevertheless, the United States considered Sacasa "the Constitutional Vice President" who had "merely sought refuge outside the Republic when armed troops without warrant were dispatched to arrest him."[59] Delineating its dilemma, the Department told the minister that "while the United States would not recognize the usurping government, yet it is under no obligation to oppose such a regime with force and to put a constitutional government in office. . . . Nicaragua's political problems must be solved by the Nicaraguan people themselves."[60] Sacasa was given a similar message:

[A]lthough the Department desired to render any proper aid to the republics of Central America in the solution of their political problems nevertheless it believed that the regeneration should come from within through a desire of people for constitutional government; that although the Department would lend its support to any element seeking this end yet it would not assume the responsibility of seeing that this is accomplished. To be more specific, as long as the people of Central America feel that the "last word" comes from the Department the attainment of political stability will be postponed.[61]

Chamorro apparently thought first of turning the presidency over to Díaz, but when he asked the minister "to recommend a solution of the local problems which might prove satisfactory to the Department," he was given no encouragement.[62] Having been assured by his adviser in Washington, a highly connected former State Department official, Chandler P. Anderson, that it would be difficult for the department to refuse recognition to a government which had been reorganized by Constitutional procedure, "especially after it is an accomplished fact,"[63] Chamorro determined to take office himself. The effectiveness of a threat of nonrecognition was limited by a decision, of which Chamorro knew, that the Americans who controlled the customs would not withhold funds from the new occupant of the presidential office.[64] Denial of recognition would not mean denial of revenue.

Secretary of State Kellogg reviewed Chamorro's actions and intentions in a note to ministers in the other Central American governments. His accession to the presidency should be regarded as based on force, despite any veneer of legality. The other governments were asked publicly to make clear their intention to deny recognition.[65] Chamorro went ahead nevertheless. He had himself elected to fill a vacancy in the Senate, had the packed Congress delcare the vice-presidency vacant (pressure and intimidation not having procured Sacasa's resignation), was chosen as first designate, and took over the presidency after Congress gave Solórzano a leave of absence in January 1926. Threats and bribery finally brought

Solórzano to submit a formal resignation, which was accepted by Congress in March.[66]

For several months Chamorro tested the resolve of the State Department. Sustained by access to revenues, he was impervious to efforts of the minister and of Lawrence Dennis, the brash and able chargé d'affaires (who later gained notoriety for his advocacy of American Fascism) to persuade him that he could not hope to be recognized. The minister reported in April that after three months of what appeared to be "benevolent non-recognition," Chamorro was "arrogant."[67] In June Dennis complained that as long as the Americans controlling revenues continued to turn them over, apparently "under the Department's high approval," Chamorro and his followers would be "confirmed in the belief that our non-recognition means nothing. . . . He has virtually told me this." Dennis complained also of the attitude of Major Carter.[68] The State Department took the position that it could not interfere with these officials, since their obligations were to the bondholders and to the Nicaraguan government.[69]

In a game which seems to have been relished by both, Dennis and Chamorro fenced for advantage. Chamorro counted on the reluctance of the State Department to take overt action, while Dennis tried to deprive him of political support by telling Conservative leaders that the United States counted on "the force of moral persuasion" to restore "the principle of constitutional succession."[70] Chamorro told Dennis that "he would have to be forced out," while complaining that Dennis's stand amounted to incitement to revolt.[71] Dennis pointed out that Chamorro and his partisans were expanding American disapproval of revolution "into the assertion that the United States will protect his regime against revolutions. What more could any unconstitutional dictator in Central America ask?"[72] Chamorro could boast almost openly that he knew the State Department too well to let himself be pressured out of office:

He has intimated that the best policy for a Central American President is to disregard anything the Department may say based on altruistic principles which may run counter to his interests, but at the same time to treat American representatives, American citizens and American interests with every consideration. Such a policy will . . . render entirely ineffective any attempts on the part of the Department at moral suasion, because American public opinion and financial interests only allow intervention in defense or support of an injured or threatened American interest.[73]

Chamorro's case found support in antiimperialist sentiment in the Senate and the press. The acting editor of *The Nation* questioned the propriety of promoting "counter-revolution" and was assured by Joseph C. Grew, the acting secretary of state, that the United States had no intention of going beyond "informal and friendly good offices in assisting to find peaceful and satisfactory solutions when requested to do so."[74] But the department was unwilling to lapse into passivity.

"What is needed in this situation," Dennis reported, "is not American assistance toward a settlement but American insistence on a settlement." This drew a marginal "Yes" from the assistant chief of the Latin American division.[75]

Sacasa, denied support in Washington, might perhaps have gained recognition if he had accepted the risk of returning to Nicaragua without American protection. A Liberal revolt broke out in eastern Nicaragua early in May, only to be deprived of control of the customs in Bluefields by the landing of United States forces. The Liberals did succeed in making away with $161,000 in government funds from the East Coast branch of the national bank, and Secretary Kellogg instructed the consul at Bluefields that American forces should not "be used in the interest of either faction to protect revenues or moneys belonging to the Nicaraguan Government."[76] Revolt broke out again in August in several parts of the country, with support from Mexico, where Sacasa had taken up residence in June.

By this time Chamorro was running short of money. The State Department tried to precipitate a settlement by warning that jeopardy to lives and property might necessitate protective action and suggesting a conference of political leaders of all parties. Chamorro showed no inclination to oppose the United States; indeed, he said that he "would cheerfully turn over government" to American forces. But he was determined "to maintain his position against all Nicaraguans." He agreed "to discuss and elaborate a plant of conciliation" based on his resignation in favor of a Conservative to be designated by the Congress.[77]

Secretary of State Kellogg intervened at the last moment with a "rush double-priority" message instructing Dennis to avoid any involvement which might be construed to make the United States responsible for a settlement, but Dennis was unshaken, and meetings took place on the United States cruiser *Denver,* with Dennis as neutral chairman.[78] The Liberals insisted that Sacasa was president by constitutional right, but their case was weakened by dependence on aid from Mexico. Dennis asked the State Department for "a clear, forceful statement" which would "smash the doctrine of constitutional restoration by means of foreign aid to revolution, once and for all." The department warned Sacasa, then in Guatemala, that "any faction or party which solicited or accepted" aid from another country "could count upon the firm opposition of the United States government."[79]

THE RETURN OF DÍAZ AND OF THE MARINES

The conference on the *Denver* ended without agreement. The United States acquiesced to Conservative rejection of a Liberal proposal that Sacasa resign in favor of a respected neutral figure, being unwilling to attempt to compel acceptance. As evidence emerged of Liberal ties with a Mexican government that was considered to be dangerously radical, Kellogg and the State Department became receptive to a Conservative proposal whereby Liberal congressmen, judges and other officials would be reinstated, with a promise of two members in the cabinet and eventual free elections, while former president Adolfo Díaz would be designated to complete the term for which Solórzano had been elected.[80] The department indicated that, while it did not desire "to suggest or favor any candidate," it felt that Díaz "would be a wise choice" and told Dennis to make "judicious use" of this information, taking "the utmost care to avoid any criticism that the United States is endeavoring to direct Nicaraguan internal politics." Arrangements were worked out for Díaz to be recognized quickly and to request "a mission of United States Army officers to organize and instruct the constabulary."[81] As Dennis wrote later, the State Department, "much to its dislike," was "obliged to commit itself in advance to the recognition of a given man under certain specified conditions."[82]

Chamorro first resigned in favor of an ailing senator, Sebastián Uriza, who had been second designate. Uriza was refused recognition on the ground that, like Chamorro, he had been improperly chosen. The choice of Díaz was then made by essentially the same Conservative majority, after eighteen members previously expelled had been invited to return (only three of these actually took their seats, six others being represented by alternates). The State Department thus concurred in a procedure which was almost identical to that which Chamorro had followed and which again rewarded the man whose dependence on the United States as president in 1912 had given rise to the prolonged occupation. Opposition to Chamorro had been "against the grain"[83] of American support for friendly Conservatives in Nicaragua. The reemergence of Díaz restored the familiar pattern. Inevitably, it was suspected that Díaz had played an important role all along in Chamorro's maneuvers, but this was probably not the case.[84]

Although Sacasa refused to resign, the United States held that his continued absence had deprived him of the right of office. Should he attempt to challenge the Congress's choice, the State Department indicated, it could not consider him "other than revolutionist."[85] Recognition of Díaz was delayed briefly to enable the other Central American countries to act at the same time (having scrupled to inform them of its intention before the new president had been designated).[86] Chamorro remained in charge of the army for a short time, but the United States refused to resume arms aid until he was removed. For an advance of salary and expenses, he undertook the task of representing his country in Great Britain, France, Italy, Spain and the Vatican.[87]

Díaz's recognition was accompanied by an expression of hope that the Liberals would accept "overtures of peace and general amnesty."[88] Instead, however, Sacasa returned to Nicaragua claiming to be head of the legitimate government. On December 2 the department received a note from the "minister of foreign affairs," from Puerto Cabezas. "Constitutional order having been restored," it blandly stated, there is "reason to believe that by the same fact the cordial friendship and official relations that have united our peoples and Governments are to be considered as restored.'' Recognition of Díaz was dismissed since it took place on the assumption that the vice-president was absent from the country.

The only obstacle to peace is Don Adolfo Diaz who in agreement with General Chamorro has rebelled against the constituted authority but the Government proposes to subdue them in a short time relying on the support of legal and moral forces, and on public opinion, and on the moral force which it is to receive from the express recognition of Your Excellency's Government.[89]

The Sacasa government gained recognition only from Mexico, although Guatemala and Costa Rica withheld it from Díaz.

Dennis meanwhile submitted an alarming report that government forces were resorting in desperation to ''forced contributions, looting and plundering,'' while Mexico was ''furnishing military leaders, arms and supplies to the revolutionists on a scale unprecedented in the history of Central America.'' In retrospect, he somehow saw the downfall of Chamorro as ''brought about neither by our non-recognition nor our diplomacy but by the pressure of Mexican arms.''[90] Dennis was to become a bitter critic of ''the Communist advance in Mexico'' and of ''the Diplomacy of Righteousness'' or ''moral imperialism'' which attempted ''to reform Latin Americans by the use of non-recognition and pontifical utterances by legalistic Liberals in our Government.'' Better, he thought, to ''obey the commands of our destiny'' by exerting influence in Latin America through ''a native ruling class.''[91]

On the day after his inauguration, Díaz addressed a note to Dennis which stated that with ''open hostility'' Mexico was mounting irresistible ''elements of attack'' which made it impossible for his government to protect the interests of Americans and other foreigners. Noting that the United States had always assisted legitimate governments (''in order to enable them to afford a tranquil field of labor for foreigners which is needed for . . . growth and prosperity''), he asked for ''support'' by ''whatever . . . means'' might be ''chosen.''[92]

The State Department rejected the sweeping assertions of Dennis and responded with caution to the effusive overtures of Díaz. It expressed ''regret that there appears to be a tendency'' to rely upon the United States for protection and asked Dennis, if Díaz should expect armed assistance, to ''state plainly'' that recognition did not ''imply any such obligation.''[93] At the same time, however, a spokesman alerted the press to the department's concern over Mexican efforts to foster Bolshevism in Central America and made public the essence of Díaz's request.[94]

The department clung as long as it could to an optimistic view, registering surprise and dismay when alarming reports kept reaching it from Managua. The secretary wondered how a crisis could have developed so quickly after ''the Legation's report that President Diaz could count on the support of a substantial majority of the people of Nicaragua and that his designation by Congress seemed to confirm this understanding.'' The minister replied that while Díaz apparently did still have majority support, help from Mexico would enable the Liberals to prevail if the government were not strengthened. The desperate financial situation might cause a sudden collapse of authority.[95]

Consternation and uncertainty were evident in the State Department. Chamorro's adviser, Anderson, collaborated in a memorandum urging that marines be used more widely to protect American property.[96] Beginning with the landing at Bluefields in the spring of 1926, marines had established neutral zones on the east coast. On December 23 forces were landed and a neutral zone declared at the town of Puerto Cabezas, or Bragman's Bluff, owned by an American lumber company, on the edge of which was located the seat of Sacasa's "government." The Liberals in the zone were ordered to give up their weapons or to depart within twenty-four hours. Sacasa disarmed his forces rather than leave, protesting his relegation "to indefinite inaction." Because there was no danger to foreign capital, he thought it evident that the "real motive" for declaring a neutral zone was "protecting the de facto government of Adolfo Díaz."[97]

But the department was unwilling to take sides openly. A new chief of the Latin American division suggested informally that the navy establish its neutral zones in places where they would cut off the Liberals. Yet when a telegram from Admiral Latimer made it bluntly evident that he construed American policy to be one of supporting the government, Secretary of State Kellogg asked that he undertake nothing beyond protecting lives and property (adding "I assume this is all he has done") and urged "great care . . . to preserve the strictest neutrality." The admiral could note with satisfaction, however, that his "action up to date was fully approved."[98]

Within a few days, Kellogg's opposition to intervention collapsed, due to fear that Mexico was gaining ascendency through its support of the Nicaraguan Liberals. Díaz was supported by Anderson and the American economic interests in Nicaragua in stressing this influence.[99] After the Conservatives suffered a bad defeat in the east, members of the Díaz government showed their desperation in a meeting at the American legation on the last day of 1926. They could hope to hold out, they claimed, only by resorting to drastic and destructive measures: "inflation of the currency, capital levies on Liberals first and then indiscriminately and ultimately suspension of payments on foreign debts." With calculated bravado, they proclaimed that they would "fight to the finish" rather than accept "surrender to Mexico," even though it "might mean the complete ruin of the country and of foreign interests here." Foreign intervention "would be preferable to Mexican domination." The minister reported that Díaz "would prefer resignation or peace at any price" to such extreme measures, but that other Conservatives would "either impel Diaz to go to extremes or put another in his place who will stop at nothing."[100]

Kellogg's policy shift was evident in a January 3 telegram suggesting the return of a marine guard to Managua. Orders were issued, on the basis of Díaz's requests, even before a reply had been received. The guard arrived in the capital on January 6.

In a lengthy message to Congress, President Coolidge set forth the history of commitments in Nicaragua and the evidence of Mexican support for Sacasa. Without any "desire... to intervene," he held, we were "in a position of peculiar responsibility" and must "view with deep concern any serious threat... tending toward anarchy and jeopardizing American interests, especially if such state of affairs is contributed to or brought about by outside influences or by any foreign power."[101] To career officers in the State Department, his emphasis on the protection of economic interests and on canal rights was exaggerated and in conflict with recent policy goals.[102] Under-Secretary of State Robert Olds saw the situation as a test, however, as to "whether we shall tolerate the interference of any other power (i.e., Mexico) in Central American affairs or insist upon our own dominant position."[103]

Kellogg, defending the intervention before the Senate Foreign Relations Committee, picked up the theme of a Communist menace. His statement on "Bolshevik aims and Policies in Mexico and Latin America" came under devastating attack in Congress and the press. It contained no evidence of actual involvement of the Mexican government in Communist activity. Indeed, most of the allegations referred to attempts of Communists in the United States to organize in Latin America. The *Baltimore Sun* thought it doubtful "that ever before in the history of the Nation has the head of the State Department appeared in public in a state of such utterly indecent intellectual exposure." Senator Borah, chairman of the committee, who had been a critic of intervention in Nicaragua since 1912, made a strong case for the legitimacy of the Sacasa government. It seemed to some that in intervening in Nicaragua President Coolidge was really maneuvering for war with Mexico.[104]

While political controversy erupted in Washington, the State Department was urging Díaz "to deal with the opposition in a broad and generous spirit."[105] When he talked of resigning, however, pressures were evidently brought to bear by more militant Conservatives to persuade him against the compromise which his resignation would entail.[106] The State Department again told Sacasa that he could not hope for recognition, even should his forces emerge victorious, but held out the prospect of effective supervision of the 1928 election.[107]

Early in February the fighting spread to the western part of the country. Two American aviators, employed by the constabulary unbeknownst to the State Department, played a prominent part. Kellogg informed Admiral Latimer that American forces were not to "become involved in any direct action against the revolutionists."[108] On February 16 the minister reported that a Liberal force under General Moncada was advancing from the east coast. It was "increasingly evident that without complete intervention there is no likely prospect of an early restoration of order."[109] Four days later American forces were landed to control the railroad and permitting its continued use by the government.[110] Marine forces, soon numbering more than two thousand, were deployed to all of the principal centers to thwart revolutionary military objectives.[111] It was not until April, however, that gunfire was exchanged between Americans and Nicaraguans.

In mid-February, when the decision was made to bring in more marines, Díaz again submitted the proposal, first advanced in 1911, that the United States should accept a formal protectorate. Intervention, which had been "found inevitable," should be given "a well-defined de jure status with clearly stated responsibilities and apparent benefits for the intervener and the intervened."[112] The United States should guarantee the independence of Nicaragua and be empowered by treaty "to intervene in order that there be maintained a constitutional government adequate for the protection of life, property and individual liberty which would have its origin in a vote of the people in a free election." There should be a financial plan to develop "economic interests" and to open up "a field for the activities" of American and other foreign interests. Provision should also be made for a national guard "organized and disciplined by a corps of officers of the United States Army."[113]

This project was objected to by Liberal members of the Congress, but the minister reported that many prominent Liberals actually favored it, as did "all people ... irrespective of party" who are "heartily tired of war." The State Department warned him not to encourage a belief that such a treaty would be acceptable, in order "to avoid any possible charges in the future that President Diaz was misled or deceived."[114] An American journalist found no evidence "that one party in Nicaragua is more friendly to the United States than is the other." There were few among the "politicians of both parties" who were "ardently pro-Nicaraguan."[115]

7.
THE DOMINICAN REPUBLIC

IN CHARGE, 1916–1921

All branches of the Dominican government were soon brought under the administration of United States naval and marine officers.[1] Captain Knapp, the military governor, claimed later that he had not intended to supplant the entire Dominican cabinet, but found that the members "had cleaned out their desks" in "an evident case of desertion."[2] Their departure took place, however, only after they had been told that they would have to serve without recognition or salaries. When back salaries of permanent officials were paid (in checks which could not be endorsed to others, a provision which resulted in losses to legitimate creditors as well as to speculators), those of cabinet members were withheld on the ground that the government had not been recognized by the United States—an interesting exercise of retroactive authority.[3] Members of Congress were suspended from office. The military governor legislated by decree. U.S. control of the courts was authorized by President Wilson in October 1917.

In form the assumption of authority by American military officers did not alter the status of the Dominican Republic. It continued to conduct diplomatic relations. It concluded a postal convention with the United States and proclaimed neutrality when the United States went to war against Germany.[4] Moreover, although the government was conducted by armed forces of the United States, it was not closely directed from Washington. With war in Europe the dominant concern, "the Department of State modified very materially its original insistence that questions of policy be submitted to it for its approval before action was taken by the military authorities. With but nominal supervision from Washington, the Military Governor reigned supreme."[5]

Some amusing episodes ensued. The military governor, who was backed by the Navy Department, objected, much as had the previous government, to being entirely dependent upon the will of the general receiver of Dominican customs (a subordinate of the War Department's Bureau of Insular Affairs) "for the necessary funds to carry on the government." The resulting army-navy dispute was mediated by the legation. The War Department reluctantly gave in, although it noted that a subsequent Dominican government might feel offended if control were reimposed.[6] The secretary of war undertook to define the situation as follows:

(a) The Dominican Republic may be described as not altogether extinguished but temporarily suppressed and, for the time being, in a state of suspended animation.

(b) There is no existing Government of the Dominican Republic in the ordinary acceptation of the words.

(c) The governmental attributes of the Dominican Republic are, for the present, merged or submerged in the Military Government of Santo Domingo, an agency of the Government of the United States.

(d) Under existing circumstances, therefore, in all that relates to the administration of the national government affairs of the Dominican Republic, the Government of the United States and the Government of the Dominican Republic are in fact synonymous.[7]

Captain Knapp regarded the "unexpected evolution"[8] that threw the government of the Dominican Republic almost entirely into the hands of American naval officers as "most fortunate," because of their "intelligence and zeal" as well as their "integrity and freedom from affiliations here." Their authority, he wrote, was "resented only by the class which has brought the Dominican Republic to the low plane which has made it a reproach."[9]

Government by Americans made valuable contributions in reducing banditry and gunplay, in building roads, in education, and in adjusting the debt, disposing of claims, and settling land titles (although this was sometimes to the advantage of large estate owners, at the expense of small cultivators). Peace was generally achieved except in two provinces where the removal of experienced officers for service in Europe contributed to a climate of mutual hostility that produced a number of atrocities.[10]

The military governor urged the State Department to give no encouragement to cooperation. Knapp's successor, Rear Admiral Thomas Snowden, declared without authority that the occupation should continue "until the generation of Dominicans then in the cradle had reached adult age."[11] Lacking his predecessor's regard for Dominican sensitivities,[12] he heavily censored critics whom he regarded as "visionaries or socialists" or "at any rate . . . irresponsible."[13] He opposed even local elections which might activate "the old political parties, a mercenary, grafting, vicious, office-seeking clan." Reacting to a proposed law to regulate parties, he commented that "not the founding of political parties . . . but the effacement of them, is necessary for the good of the country."[14] His disdain for politicians left him dependent for information and advice upon officers who were mostly ignorant of Spanish and "studiously refrained from associating with Dominicans."[15]

TURNAROUND

The Department of State renewed attention to the Dominican Republic when conditions there came under criticism from other countries, particularly in Latin

America. As early as January 1919 the department argued that a strictly military government was no longer needed, only to meet with a flat rebuff from the Navy Department, which held that the United States was "no where near ready" to bring civilians not "amenable to military discipline" into the cabinet. The chief of the Latin American division tried, apparently without effect, to point out "that in Santo Domingo the Navy Department was carrying out an international policy . . . as emanating from the State Department."[16]

Former President Henríquez lobbied at the Paris peace conference and was received informally by the division chief. The former president, who was perceived as "not rabidly anti-American," denounced "the degenerate militarism" of his country's politics and set forth a program of "total reform aimed to free the soul of the people from all the oppressive, constrictive and restrictive bonds in which it has lived." Foremost in this program was the formation of political parties. He pointed to the Cuban intervention of 1906 to 1909 as an example of "tact, prudence, generosity, fairness and self-respect" resulting in the restoration of free government through popular elections. He suggested as a first step the appointment of a consulting commission of Dominicans.[17]

When the State Department suggested that Henríquez take up his ideas with the military governor (whose first reaction had been that they "would result in anarchy and early ruin"),[18] he objected with calculated blandness that a military governor could only pass suggestions "through the proper superior organs." He complained that censorship kept "the thought and will of the people . . . secret" or led to the use of "underground channels of divulgation," despite an "unmerciful system of espionage."[19]

The military governor urged the State Department to give no encouragement to Dominican agitation. Snowden wanted a declaration that the occupation would continue "until such time that the people of the Dominican Republic have developed the character and ability to govern themselves. . . . A minimum period of twenty years would be necessary."[20] He was authorized to state only that in the view of the State Department "up to the present time nothing has occurred to alter in the slightest the present situation."[21]

Meanwhile a critical report was prepared for the State Department by Judge Otto Schoenrich, a man of long experience in Dominican affairs. He did not think that the occupation had "reflected the highest credit on the United States." No one had shown the same administrative qualities that Wood had demonstrated in Cuba. Most of the officers had "done their work with sympathy or interest," but a few had been "overbearing tyrants." The provost courts had "gained the reputation of being unjust, oppressive and cruel." Some of their judgments were "outrageous." Censorship was "arbitrary and ridiculous." Certain words such as " 'General' (as a title for a Dominican), 'national,' 'rebellion,' and phrases such as 'freedom of thought,' 'freedom of speech,' " were prohibited. "Not the slightest comment on the work of the military government or its officials" was allowed.[22]

On the department's initiative an advisory board of four prominent Dominicans was appointed in November 1919 in order, as Snowden saw it, to appease the Dominicans.[23] Its members included the perennial presidential aspirant, Velásquez, and a former president, Archbishop Nouel. Henríquez remained out of the country, although a place was reserved for him. This attempt at cooperation broke down almost at once. The advisers recommended suspension of censorship and restriction of the jurisdiction of provost courts, but Snowden put into effect new and more severe regulations.[24] They resigned in protest on January 9, 1920. Shortly afterward prominent Dominicans formed a journal, *National Union*, which dominated opinion at home and worked hard to generate sympathy and support throughout Latin America. Its stand against cooperation became a major obstacle in further attempts to bring Dominicans into responsible governmental activity. Although the military government brought about this impasse, Sumner Welles thought the State Department was also at fault because of its failure to play an active supervisory role or to develop clear policy. When the situation began to affect relations elsewhere in Latin America, the department finally asserted itself.[25] One of its first steps, which initiated prolonged controversy, was to instruct Russell, the minister, to gather "all available information" on censorship and the suppression of the right of assembly.[26]

The military government, claiming to abolish censorship, nevertheless forbade publications or speeches that might lead to disorder or revolt, including "those which teach the doctrines now commonly known as Bolshevism or anarchy," are "hostile in tone towards the Military Government," "hold up to scorn, obloquy or ridicule the conduct of the United States Government," and "describe present conditions . . . in a manifestly unfair or untruthful manner." The arrest of a well-known poet, Fabio Fiallo, produced outrage in Latin America and distress in Washington.[27] Revised regulations against "sedition," "defamation," or "insult" amounted to defiance of the State Department on the part of the military governor. The acting secretary complained to the secretary of the navy that they were "peculiarly objectionable as breathing a spirit foreign to American ideals and actions." Snowden was instructed to annul them and to issue a conciliatory proclamation.[28]

Within the State Department, where Leo S. Rowe and Sumner Welles had taken charge of Latin American Affairs, the conclusion had been reached by the summer of 1920 that the people of the Dominican Republic should be given "at least partial control of their Government."[29] With the president's approval, the department set forth and the military governor proclaimed the intention to "inaugurate the simple process of . . . rapid withdrawal." A commission was to be appointed to prepare amendments to the Constitution and to draft an election law. The State Department prepared a list of nine prospective members who would be "representative," but after a press campaign denounced anyone who would serve in this capacity, the military governor went ahead with the appointment of only five members from the list, four of whom had constituted the previous advisory board.[30] These men posed conditions regarding the composition and powers of the commission and when these were rejected, refused to serve. The State Department "regretted exceedingly" the action of the military governor in making the appointments, and "even more" in rejecting the conditions, which actually conformed quite well to the new policy. Its "very grave apprehension" was alleviated, however, when the five did finally agree to participate and two others, not on the original list, were chosen to complete the membership of a body that ended up smaller and less representative than the State Department had hoped it would be.[31]

8.
HAITI

STAGNATION AND DICTATION

The U.S. relationship with Haiti, which was established through occupation and defined by treaty, had as professed goals strengthening of amity, remedying the condition of revenues and finances, maintenance of tranquility, and the carrying out of plans for economic development and prosperity.[1] In an expansive view Admiral Caperton stated, "The benevolent unselfish, and helpful purposes" of the United States would mean, "if there is genuine cooperation on the part of Haitians," that

Haiti will be a land free from violence, with President Dartiguenave guiding the destinies of his country. With the support of his people, justice and prosperity will mark the life in Haiti, the country's fertility and possibilities will be developed, there will be plenty of work and good wages for the country's peasantry, and employment for the abilities and intelligence of the upper classes. It is easy to see that instead of misery and desolation, with misfortune knocking at every door, Haiti will be a land of honor, peace, and contentment. Haitians will do this for themselves; the United States will stand by as an elder brother to help and support.[2]

Rhetoric deflated, it was the belief of most Americans that a government which followed the direction and advice of the United States could not fail to transform the lives of a people plagued by poverty and violence. Colonel Eli K. Cole, one of the commanders of the marine brigade, expressed the idealism and pragmatism of the American approach in testimony before a Senate committee.

I believe [the United States] had a moral duty to clean that place up and establish decency down there, because it did not exist. You have no idea of the conditions, if you have not been there, that did exist when we landed in Haiti. The Aegean [sic] stables were Paradise compared to it.[3]

Yet the treaty did not specify control of education or of the system of justice, areas where much of the effort to transform Haiti would have to be directed.

The occupation worked no miracles. Indeed, during the first five years and more, only the most rudimentary tasks were accomplished—policing, road building, some sanitation projects, and the collection and disbursement of revenues.

Not all of this was done well. The financial advisers were regarded as incompetent. Within a few months the minister in Washington was complaining that no progress had been made toward the promised goal of "a true economic transformation of the Haitian nation."[4] In 1919 the minister set forth a summary of grievances:

Work on reconstruction and restoration is barely outlined, and . . . we are still waiting for the most important reforms, such as the consolidation of the public debt, the building of public schools, professional and agricultural schools, the revision of the custom tariff, all of which are needed for the upbuilding of the Haitian finance and the making of new generations that must be prepared to have a part in the evolution of the country.[5]

In 1920 President Dartiguenave told American reporters, "No effective aid had been brought to Haiti for the development of its agricultural and industrial resources, and no constructive measure has been proposed, for the purpose of placing its finances on a really sound basis."[6] In 1921, Roger L. Farnham, the agent of the National City Bank who had been active in arousing official concern for Haiti, attributed "renewal of revolutionary conditions" to "the failure of the United States Government . . . to present some well-defined plan" of development. American officials "always seemed . . . to be drifting and waiting for some plan to be presented to them."[7]

Under the best conditions the occupation could not have implanted democracy and prosperity in Haiti. But little effort was made, despite the high promises. The war in Europe helps to explain the neglect and contributed to limiting the economic growth which might otherwise have been achieved. Order was improved and graft reduced. But essential elements of concern and attention on the part of the United States were missing.

Fragmentation of responsibility and direction among U.S. officials prevented any concentration on major reform. While Admiral Caperton was in Haiti, his rank and energy helped to compensate for the absence of a determined directing authority in Washington, but he and his successors in command of the Caribbean squadron had their headquarters at Santo Domingo after May 10, 1916, leaving control in Haiti to the colonel of the marine brigade.[8] Military authority was also represented by the marine colonel in command of the gendarmerie, who was technically on detached duty with the government of Haiti. The minister, spokesman of the Department of State, could claim to outrank the other officials, but Wilson's appointee was ineffective.[9] In the absence of Admiral Caperton relations with the Haitian government were often conducted by the commander of marines without directions from either the Department of State or the Navy.[10]

The "treaty official" positions of general receiver, financial adviser, engineer for public works, and engineer for sanitation were filled by nominees of the president of the United States. After these positions had been held for several months by naval officers, civilians who were outside any clear line of authority were appointed. It was not until July 1918 that the Department of State moved "to effect greater coordination" by calling for weekly meetings at the legation, "to be presided over by the American Minister." The minister was to decide whether "any difficulties or differences" should be "presented to the Haitian Government" and was responsible for the presentation.[11]

The most significant accomplishment was to remove opportunity and incentive for revolution by abolishing the army and making revenues inaccessible.[12] The gendarmerie, which took orders both from the president of Haiti and from the occupation officials, was officered by marines, many of whom were noncommissioned in American service. The plan of training Haitians as officers was quickly set aside when the first group, chosen from the elite, refused to comply with such requirements as grooming horses and stripping for a physical examination.[13]

The role of the Haitian government was a source of continual friction and confusion. Although its powers were severely limited, it could not be ignored, and it was a source of obstruction, delay, and harassment. Colonel Cole, who would have preferred out-and-out military government, complained, "We could not get cooperation from them; the minute we took our eyes off of them they were off doing something that was a waste of money, or a waste of time, or a grain of sand or two in the bearings."[14]

The government had no chance, under occupation, to develop a responsive relationship to the people. It was continually subject to the demands of the treaty officials, the marine commander, and the minister. The Americans found it convenient and even essential to work through the president. Unable to secure cooperation or even compliance from other political figures, the United States backed Dartiguenave in a series of moves that made a mockery of democratic procedures. While "not unaware of his embarrassments" the Americans looked "to him to carry out the necessary measures of cooperation under the Treaty as being himself the Government."[15]

The legislature quickly became bitterly antagonistic toward Dartiguenave. It was rumored that he would be censured and impeached. He seized the initiative by proposing constitutional changes to cut the number of senators and deputies in half, to formally designate the gendarmerie to take the place of the army, and, as a spur to investment, to permit foreign acquisition of property. He counted upon the United States for essential support:

Should Congress be hostile and refuse there will be but one thing to do. I do not ask the American Government to advise me to do this, nor to express any opinion on this matter, but I request the forward assurance of Admiral Caperton that my Government will receive complete military protection. I shall declare both chambers dissolved. I will call for a constituent assembly which will be formed of about 50 representatives, patriotic Haitians, who will revise the constitution according to present needs.[16]

Caperton asked for and received authority to back the president against the Congress. When the Senate assembled in defiance of Dartiguenave, without a quorum, on April 5, 1916, he dissolved the body, convened the Chamber of Deputies as a constituent assembly, and created an appointed council of state to help draw up constitutional revisions. The president of the Senate denounced the "flagrant violation of the constitution" and asked whether the United States was "upholding this revolutionary act."[17]

The answer was prompt, unequivocal, and unabashed. Caperton informed the legislature that he must "comply with my orders to support the Government of Haiti."[18] Already, the gendarmes had closed the legislative building and the marine commander had defied judicial decrees which called for it to be opened.[19] After Caperton's statement the presidents of the two houses were told by the marine commander that an attempted meeting would lead to violent expulsion. Colonel Waller proclaimed:

No political agitation will be tolerated which tends to provoke manifestations against the express declaration of Admiral Caperton regarding the decree of April 5, 1916, and to compromise, contrary to the terms and spirit of the convention, the stability of the Government of President Dartiguenave, which is the free expression of the vote of the National Assembly.[20]

Similarly, Admiral Knapp was instructed in January 1917, after "conference between Navy and State Departments," that no attempt to overthrow the president of Haiti or to annul his decrees would be countenanced.[21]

Dartiguenave hoped that a new legislature would approve the constitutional revision, but the marine commanders prevented him from controlling the vote. He did not pass up the chance to chide his mentors. As Colonel Cole recalled, "On a number of occasions afterwards the President said that we had forced them to have a fair election . . . that the President formerly would have been in a position to have expended money, but we would not allow that, and consequently his hold over the national assembly was gone."[22] This is not to suggest that the election was free—it was controlled by local politicians who opposed the president.

Colonel Cole tried to have a cabinet put together that would be competent and "more or less nonpolitical" but yet "somewhat along the same political lines as the National Assembly." There was probably no chance of success. The particular cause of failure was Cole's determination to include the incumbent minister of finance, Dr. Edmund Heraux, "probably the only minister who really was in favor of . . . American management of Haitian affairs." When Heraux became the target of "vicious attacks," Cole was even more insistent, concluding that if he were thrown aside no one would be willing to work openly with the United States.[23] The occupation authorities did succeed, after cabinet resignations, in extending the duration of the treaty from ten to twenty years, in order to attract a needed loan. In 1919 in connection with the establishment of a claims commission, the contemplated loan was given a term of thirty years, with provision for control of revenues by American-nominated officers during the life of the loan after expiration of the treaty. The bonds were not actually issued until 1922 and 1923.

As a token of defiance ("in order to swat the United States," as Cole put it) the new assembly refused to declare war on Germany.[24] It was not until June 12, 1918, that Haiti formally joined the war effort.

The new Congress was strongly opposed to constitutional proposals that the United States considered essential. Haitian law had long prohibited foreign ownership of land, a concept deeply rooted in the emotions of the people. The government resorted to every device possible to shift responsibility for the removal of this prohibition to the United States. The Americans were equally determined that the Haitian government should openly support that which its members privately considered necessary. Dartiguenave, transmitting the views of the United States to the national assembly, said, in effect, as Colonel Cole saw it, "This is not our recommendation, but here is what practically amounts to dictation from the United States. Now, see what you can do with it."[25]

When Dartiguenave decided there was no chance that the constitutional revision would pass, he asked Cole what should be done next. Cole opposed "drastic action" and urged the president to "come out in the open."[26] But it soon became apparent that the legislature would insist on prohibition of foreign land ownership. Only dissolving the body could prevent inclusion of such a provision. Cole had "little doubt" that the president had "consistently worked" toward dissolution of the congress. His own preference was to dissolve "the entire Haitian Government" and establish military rule. Dartiguenave told Cole that an elected national assembly could not be satisfactory in Haiti. A cabinet and council of state should put into effect a constitution "in accordance with the ideas of the United States" and govern under it "until such time as the country had gotten out some of the influence of the politicians."[27]

Two days later Colonel Cole notified Washington that he intended, if necessary, to have the assembly dissolved, "through President, if possible," unless otherwise directed. The Navy Department asked him to try to avoid the use of military force. Dartiguenave delayed in signing a dissolution decree until he had been told by Smedley D. Butler, the marine colonel who was serving with the rank of general-in-command of the gendarmerie, that if he did not sign, Cole would suppress the assembly himself and recommend a military government. The assembly meanwhile was rushing passage of the objectionable draft amidst renewed talk of impeachment. Cole "directed that the doors be closed with the members and spectators being inside" and "directed Gen. Butler to proceed immediately to the national assembly and deliver the decree to the President of the assembly." The account continues:

The president of the assembly refused to accept the message or to announce it to the assembly as it was not delivered to him by the cabinet or by a member thereof. . . . Gen.

Butler then took the decree, promulgated it to the national assembly, and directed, in accordance with my orders, that the chambers be cleared and members and spectators be released.[28]

The State Department was only partially in touch with these proceedings. When informed of the imminence of dissolution, it cabled: "Take no action until arrival of State Department's message." But Colonel Cole concluded that his decision should stand. "If we had stopped," he said later, "our usefulness there would have ended."[29]

Butler later gave a colorful account. President Dartiguenave would not sign the dissolution decree until four of the five cabinet members (the other being out of the city) had been brought together to share responsibility. Two of them were forcibly apprehended by the gendarme corporal who served as Butler's chauffeur. Butler agreed to present the decree himself because a cabinet member might be met by violence. Gendarmes in the chamber had to be restrained from using their weapons in his behalf when he came under verbal attack. In legal form, however, the deed was done by the Haitian government.[30]

Attempts to maintain a legal government led to further absurdity when the minister of education resigned, and it was necessary to find a replacement. Haitians who were politically alert were not willing to expose themselves to attack as members of a cabinet under American domination. A Haitian gendarme recruited his illiterate barber as minister so that he could get back fifty dollars that the man owed him. Butler told the tale with gusto.[31]

Drafts of a new constitution were worked over for several months. The State Department had a hand in this, and even the Haitian government made some contribution. Colonel Cole indicated that the major work was done by Admiral Knapp, the chargé d'affaires, and himself, after they had concluded that "we probably were better informed as to the needs of Haiti than anyone else."[32] (Franklin D. Roosevelt's claim during the campaign of 1920 that he wrote the Haitian constitution as assistant secretary of the navy was without foundation.)

The Haitian government suggested a procedure of ratification which would bypass the assembly. The new constitution was submitted to the people in a plebiscite. There was a historical precedent for this, but nothing of the sort was provided for in the existing constitution of 1889.[33] Despite the blending of tyranny and force which it represented, the Department of State "recognized finally the wisdom of the suggestion."[34] Lansing went so far as to set forth suggestions based on a plebiscite in Uruguay. Gendarmerie officers "could explain and discuss the proposed constitution, especially with the illiterates." Ballots could be cast in the form of colored cards. "The national colors of Haiti being red and blue, it is suggested that the cards bearing the affirmative vote in Haiti be a vari-colored red and blue, while the cards which signify the negative vote be made of sombre hue."[35] Alexander S. Williams, the gendarmerie commander who succeeded Butler, "had never heard" of a plebiscite, but he faithfully carried out his assignment. The officers were instructed to conduct a "campaign, which was frankly proconstitutional." The orders combined inducement ("funds for refreshments and barbicues [*sic*]")[36] with threat: "Opposition to the constitution exists. Where this takes the form of public expression and the public expression tends to incite distrust or more in the minds of the people, the persons guilty will be treated as disturbers of the peace and arrested for scene or scandale publics [*sic*]."[37]

The votes were cast openly, in the presence of gendarmes. Less than 1 percent were negative. Colonel Russell, the marine commander, reported that practically all of those who opposed did not vote, that the vote from "the intelligent class" was small, that "no enthusiasm whatever" was displayed on the streets of Port-au-Prince, and that the voting was done "largely by countrymen and the half-clothed ignorant class," many of whom had no idea what they were voting for.[38]

The new constitution placed the president in a dominant position. He could determine in what year legislative elections would be held. Until such time legislative power rested with an appointed council of state, as did the choice of a president. It was not until 1930 that an elected assembly began to function.

RESISTANCE

The increased power of the president of Haiti did not eliminate friction with the United States. The president and his cabinet were anxious to avoid being held responsible for unpopular actions and to devise gestures of independence. The State Department, on the other hand, wanted to minimize Haitian recalcitrance. In their desire to keep Heraux as finance minister, some officials held that the treaty implied the right to dictate cabinet appointments, but the legal adviser did not accept this interpretation.[39] Heraux was replaced by Louis Borno, who resisted demands of the financial adviser.

The end of the war in Europe and President Wilson's support of self-determination gave Haitians the chance for a hearing. Soon after the armistice the minister in Washington complained of "the vexatious and unfair tyranny of American officials" just "when, thanks to the might of the United States the holy principles of right, justice, respect of small peoples triumph in the world."[40] The Americans in Port-au-Prince dismissed this as the work of Borno, but his removal from the cabinet brought only an abatement of antagonism. The foreign minister initiated an appeal to the American peace mission in Paris, with the suggestion of a threat. Wilson and Lansing "should surely deem it best, at this hour, that the voice of a feeble nation like Haiti should not be raised in the presence of all the nations assembled to complain, with just reason, of the injustice of the powerful Republic of the United States."[41] Lansing's reaction showed that the point was not lost. He concluded that the end of the war had removed any necessity for military control of Haiti. To continue the occupation without change would subject "the United States to much criticism particularly as the rights of smaller nations are being kept to the fore and in the light of the President's utterances.'' The gendarmerie, he suggested, was effective enough so that the marines could be limited to a legation guard.[42]

In Haiti, however, this was not a time for quiet change. The officials in Port-au-Prince reported that the gendarmerie could not control brigandage. To withdraw "would undoubtedly result in a serious revolution.''[43] For several months political differences were put aside while marines and gendarmes fought Haitian peasants.

Military operations against "the Caco bandits" had been going on since 1915. Four months after the occupation began they had reached such a scale that the Navy Department, "impressed with number Haitians killed,'' instructed Admiral Caperton to avoid "further offensive operations" except in case of urgent necessity. Caperton characterized the *cacos* as "bandits pure and simple, owing no allegiance to the Government or any political faction" while admitting that their movement appeared to have been "of a revolutionary nature against the present Government and the American occupation, as well as brigandage.'' He urged that "any diminution in the protection and support offered the Government and the people of Haiti by the United States will greatly harm our prestige.''[44]

The gendarmerie had been hastily established from a nucleus of former police and army officials and had become responsible for law enforcement as early as February 1916, when Dartiguenave, hoping to embarrass its sponsors, had dissolved the police. It had had considerable success; the number of Haitians reported killed declined from 212 in 1915 to 50 in 1916, only 2 in 1917, and 35 in 1918. Before the end of 1918, however, sizable armed bands were in active revolt. During the following year, 1,881 Haitians were reported killed, more, probably, "than had occurred in a typical revolution before 1915.''[45]

Banditry and terrorism were nourished by peasant grievances, particularly against abuse of the corvée, forced labor on the roads, and by resentment of American control. The corvée had been officially abolished, but the order was not carried out in the district where disorder was greatest. A leader named Charlemagne Peralte gave the outlaw movement some semblance of the style and trappings of government until he was shot by a marine who had infiltrated his headquarters. The Haitian minister in Washington noted that "the outlaw movement" was assuming "a character of a struggle for freedom, of an active claim for ignored and trampled rights. '' He thought its "daring and success" were due to a change in the sentiment of the rural masses. At first they had been "glad of being rid of the tyranny of Haitian military chiefs,'' but they were repelled by "the brutality and injustice of the Haitian gendarmes.'' Moreover, they were encouraged by "selfish politicians" who "themselves find support in the discontent of the people of the towns.''[46]

The State Department ignored the contention that the revolt was in part a response to real grievances. It stressed the "constantly obstructive" attitude of the Haitian government and disparaged both the people and the gendarmes:

The Gendarmes have been recruited from the best element of the Haitian population and while their experience is below what would be desired, it is hoped that with years of training it may be found possible to obtain an intelligent and well disciplined force.[47]

A former commander testified in contrast, that the gendarmes were drawn "from the lower class almost entirely," and went on to say:

The old Haitian police had enjoyed such a reputation that anyone who joined it practically announced his criminal tendencies. This made it very difficult for us in the beginning to even recruit the necessary educated material which we had to have in order to develop noncommissioned officers, who must know how to read and write.[48]

As the fighting subsided, verbal encounters continued with new force. The controversy focused on attempts to tighten controls. The State Department insisted on an agreement that "proposed legislation bearing upon any of the subjects of the Treaty" (later interpreted to mean *all* proposals) be submitted to the minister prior to enactment for information "and if necessary for discussion between the two Governments."[49] The demanded procedure amounted to a veto right. When laws were passed without submission, the Haitian government was informed that they "would not be recognized as law" by the United States.[50] In the summer of 1920, when the council of state passed a law on ownership of real property by foreigners over the "violent protest" of the minister and refused to accept a regulation demanded by the financial adviser to prohibit the importation of foreign currencies, the minister took the drastic step of suspending salary payments "until change of attitude and proper action by Haitian Government," and suggested, when the government refused to give in, that "the necessary steps be taken to have the military commander in Haiti, Colonel Russell, take over the Government of Haiti until such time as it shall have been reorganized."[51]

The State Department was taken aback by this deadlock and rebuked the minister for having acted without instructions, but it accepted his explanation that the action was within the terms of the treaty and added its own complaint regarding "the recent and marked change in the attitude of the Haitian Government."[52] Dana G. Munro concluded that the department should establish "that measure of control" over both the treaty officials and the government "which is necessary to accomplish the legitimate objects of the United States in Haiti."[53]

The Haitians protested with new force and eloquence as the Wilson administration dragged to a close:

The Government cannot admit the universal competency assumed by the American Minister and the Financial Adviser, who believes they have the right of *sovereign* decision on all questions—legislation, finance, commerce, public works, and public instruction—for a people with whose manners, needs, and aspirations they are unacquainted.[54]

The State Department was sufficiently concerned to arrange for "the introduction of a new personality"—Admiral Knapp, the former military governor of the Dominican Republic.[55] Knapp's instructions stressed the importance of avoiding any action "which might ultimately lead to military intervention,"[56] but he pressed hard for compliance with the demands of the American officials. To "save the susceptibilities of the Haitians," he accepted their oral assurances, but stood ready to insist, if necessary, that the president "surround himself with a Cabinet and a Council of State that will keep faith with the United States."[57] The State Department rebuked the minister and, by implication, Knapp, for resorting again to suspension of salaries, wanting to avoid any appearance that "the subsequent carrying out of the program would have been in response to coercive pressure."[58] The measures at issue were finally enacted, but Knapp reported an unhealthy and worsening relationship between the American officials and the Haitians who constituted the formal government.[59] In one of his recommendations he was clearly ahead of his time; he thought Congress should pass an enabling act for a loan to Haiti from the treasury of the United States. This would provide "a means of pressure upon the Government of Haiti" superior to any private loan and would minimize dispute. A State Department official made the marginal note: "Excellent. Have tried to effect this for 3 years.!!"[60]

REDIRECTION

With the advent of a new administration, Haiti gradually came to the attention of Congress and the American public. In one of his campaign pronouncements from Marion, Ohio, Warren G. Harding said that he would not

empower an Assistant Secretary of the Navy to draft a constitution for helpless neighbors in the West Indies and jam it down their throats at the points of bayonets born by United States marines, nor . . . misuse the power of the Executive to cover with a veil of secrecy repeated acts of unwarranted interference in the domestic affairs of the little republics in the western hemisphere.[61]

President Dartiguenave reminded the new president of the United States that he had "nobly demanded justice and kindness for the people of Haiti," asking that the occupation be reduced to "a mere military mission" and be withdrawn as soon as the gendarmerie should be able to preserve public order.[62] The Haitian president had been empowered to decide when a national assembly should be elected. Dartiguenave suggested that elections should be held if the outcome could be controlled:

The Government must not and may not stand aloof from the election. It is a sacred duty entailed upon it to assist by honest means the candidates whom it believes apt to promote the welfare of the nation. There must be no impediment to its action as there was in the election of January 10, 1917.[63]

Although Harding was apparently impressed by this appeal, the State Department had plans for "strengthening rather than weakening American control." Secretary of State Hughes was able to gain approval for a program which entailed continuing occupation.[64] The suggestion regarding elections was met with a cool rebuff: the United States could not agree to an election in which "the results . . . would be determined in any manner other than by the will of the Haitian people freely expressed."[65] Hughes acknowledged the likelihood that a legislature "anti-American in sentiment," would be chosen, but he thought that "any connivance" would work against the "consistent effort to help the Haitian people establish a democratic, stable and constitutional government."[66] Dartiguenave was told, however, that the choice of president might be left to the Council of State that he had appointed.[67]

Pressure against the occupation was building within the United States. A group of Haitians formed a "Patriotic Union" which published charges against the occupation. Allegations of atrocities were given wide publicity. A select committee of the Senate expressed "its chagrin at the improper or criminal conduct of some few members of the Marine Corps" while also condemning the exploitation of "individual instances" by "biased or interested individuals and committees and propagandists" who were trying "to bring into disrepute the whole American naval force in Haiti."[68]

The Senate committee did not limit its concern to specific instances of misconduct. It found that accomplishments in Haiti had been woefully meager. The United States had failed "to develop a definite or constructive policy." Not enough care had been taken to find "men who were sympathetic to the Haitians and able to maintain cordial personal and official relations with them." The committee called for a "policy of constructive service" in justice, education, and agricultural assistance and appealed for the cooperation of "patriotic Haitians." The alternative was "the abandonment of the Haitian people to chronic revolution, anarchy, barbarism, and ruin."[69]

The situation in Haiti came before the Senate in June 1922 through a proposed amendment that would have prevented expenditure to maintain marines in either Haiti or the Dominican Republic.[70] Senators William H. King of Utah, William Borah of Idaho, and George W. Norris of Nebraska, supporting this proposal, quoted a report endorsed by twenty-four prominent lawyers, including Zachariah Chafee, Jr., Raymond B. Fosdick, and Felix Frankfurter. It concluded:

The methods employed by the United States in Haiti to force acceptance and ratification of the treaty framed by the United States, namely, the direct use of military, financial, and political pressure, violate every canon of fair and equal dealing between independent sovereign nations and of American professions of good faith.

The maintenance in Haiti of any United States military force or of the control exercised by treaty officials under cover of the treaty of September, 1915, amounts to a conscious and intentional participation in the wrong of the original aggression and coercion.[71]

Only nine senators, however, voted to force an end to the occupation.[72] Secretary of State Hughes ignored the lawyers' charges and was sustained by a memorandum from Munro which held that the American forces had been "dealing . . . with irresponsible political leaders who had come into prominence as the leaders of armed uprisings."[73]

The Harding administration postponed its plans to reform the occupation until after the Senate investigation, but in February 1922 it appointed General John H. Russell as a "guiding authority" to supervise the work of the treaty officials, with the title of high commissioner.[74] Russell had served as commander of the marine brigade for more than three years in two separate assignments. The appointment had the appearance of an extension of military government, but Russell was given the personal rank of ambassador and received instructions from the State Department.[75] He held office until 1930.

Russell had set forth his ideas in a memorandum of October 1, 1921. He thought the United States should be clearly in charge:

The absurdity of a dual control, or of two nations administering the affairs of a country, is too obvious to need comment. Two men can ride a horse but one must ride behind. If the United States is to ride behind in its conduct of Haitian Affairs it had better withdraw entirely and let the country revert to a condition of chaos when, after a time, the United States would be forced to occupy Haiti or permit some foreign nation to do so.[76]

He thought a high commissioner would be able, with "discretion and tact," to "*guide* (his emphasis) and support the Constitutional Government." He should take part in cabinet meetings, without a vote, but with a veto on all legislation, subject to appeal by the president of Haiti to the Department of State. Although Russell's formal authority did not extend as far as he advocated, he was able to establish the rapport that he desired with Dartiguenave's successor, Louis Borno.

Hughes was manifestly hopeful that a corner could be turned. Russell was to bear in mind (the language is that which Root had drafted for the first Philippine Commission in 1900) that the intervention and occupation had been "designed neither for the satisfaction of the United States, nor for the promotion of any selfish purposes or ambitions on the part of the United States," but for the advancement of "the happiness, tranquility and welfare of the Haitian people." Any measures he might urge upon the government "should conform to the customs, habits, and even to the prejudices of the Haitian people, so far as may be consistent with the accomplishment of the indispensable requisites of stable and efficient government." To make an early withdrawal possible, Russell was instructed to pay particular attention to the gendarmerie.[77]

"Outstanding needs" were identified as judicial and educational reform. Neither of these had been brought under the control of American officials. The lower courts, notoriously lax and corrupt, were often bypassed by provost courts or simply ignored. The educational system had shown no "tangible improvement," and illiteracy remained estimated as high as 98 percent.[78]

The Russell-Borno collaboration did not overcome the obstacles to judicial and educational improvement. After several years, the courts were adjudged to be, "if such could be possible, less effective than ever and their inefficiency and incompetency more notorious."[79] By constitutional amendment in 1928 the president of Haiti gained a power of removal which brought hope for "purification of the judiciary," but improvement was hardly discernible.[80] In education, cultural differences between Americans and the elite were a major obstacle to progress. Under Dartiguenave, the occupation officials had opposed greater expenditure because, lacking supervisory authority under the treaty, they were convinced the funds would be wasted.[81] Russell was instructed to negotiate a new article conveying the right to "control education," but the obstacles to treaty-making could not be surmounted. The Haitian president was willing to cooperate on a less formal basis.

Instead of trying to improve the existing educational program, the occupation directed its efforts to agricultural and industrial training through the Department of Agriculture, under an American agricultural engineer. In a conscious attempt "to eliminate or 'absorb' the Haitian schools," appropriations for traditional education were held almost constant while general revenues increased by about 75 percent.[83] The expenditure per student was about $50.00 in the American-directed schools, as compared to $4.50 in the Haitian-controlled system, with three-fourths of school age children attending neither.[84] The stress on vocational training was an attempt to break away from a cultural pattern that valued education as a mark of status. The importance of making education relevant to the needs of the people was evident. But rejection of the cultural aspirations of the small class of educated Haitians could only alienate those who would dominate an elected legislature and inherit power when the occupation came to an end. An American educator commented:

It has taken the American Negro twenty years to understand that both academic and vocational training are necessary and to admit that in some sections of the country peculiar emphasis can be laid on vocational training without implying the inherent inferiority of the Negro. If the Occupation cannot so direct the thinking of the Haitians as to avoid this chasm, it will have learned nothing from the thinking of its own subjected people. Before 1915 the Haitians considered vocational training as beneath them. The apparent attempt is now being made to convince them that vocational training, in the eyes of the American, is the *only* kind that should be served up to them. [Unless Haitians could think of the two systems as coordinate rather than in conflict, he continued,] . . . our educational policy in Haiti will have been as disastrous as was that of the Haitians themselves prior to 1915.[85]

Collaboration between the high commissioner and the president of Haiti was made possible by recognition that the United States had settled in for an extended period. Dartiguenave was passed up for reelection by the council of state, which he had appointed and which he tried to control through calculated replacements. To Russell's apparent surprise, it turned, instead, to Louis Borno, a candidate whose possible presidency had been regarded as "very disastrous" in 1918.[86] Bribery may have been a factor.[87] There is no evidence that American officials tried to influence the choice. Russell was importuned to let it be known which candidate he preferred, but he confined himself to a booster role: " 'Push for Haiti' should be the slogan, the watchword of all.' "[88] However unexpected, the choice proved to be fortunate from the perspective of the State Department. With the appointed council of state as the only body, apart from the occupation, to which he was responsible, President Borno was able and proved willing to collaborate with the high commissioner in what has been called "joint dictatorship."[89]

Opposition, which came to include practically every politicized Haitian who was not an officeholder, found in Borno and the United States a single target. Lacking parliamentary or electoral channels through which to operate, the opposition displayed an extremism which could be used to justify postponing elections. The State Department saw little merit in "an election in the usual Haitian style" to produce "a hostile Congress which might cause incalculable difficulties."[90] Having accepted deferral in 1924, intending to insist that elections be held in 1926, the Department agreed to put them off until 1928, pressing meanwhile for revision of the rules.[91]

Borno held out little hope that the electorate could make a meaningful choice. The rural population, "almost totally illiterate, ignorant and poor, . . . would be the easy prey of those bold speculators whose conscience hesitates at no lie," while in the towns most of those who could vote intelligently were too "disgusted by the immoral maneuvers and the insolent frauds" to participate. This left "the small group of professional politicians, with their followers of every sort, who are mainly illiterate." He announced, nevertheless, that a new electoral law would create "the rational and necessary foundation of democratic suffrage, . . . parties with platforms.' "[92]

After he had jailed the principal spokesman for the opposition and replaced eighteen of the twenty-one members of the council of state, Borno was elected by that body to a second four-year term in 1926.[93] During the following year he submitted a series of constitutional amendments, one of which would give the President a six-year term. The State Department opposed this, fearing "internal disorders" that would involve the United States.[94] This aroused Borno's indignation since he had relied on what he thought were contrary assurances by Russell.[95] Changes were made as the State Department directed, including a prohibition of reelection that would prevent Borno from taking advantage of a six-year term. The amendments were made subject to a plebiscite, as the constitution provided. In spite of widespread and bitter opposition to the president, the voting was peaceful and the outcome clear: 177,436 in favor, 3,799 opposed.

No election having been held in 1928, the end of Borno's term approached without there being a legislative body, other than the appointed council of state, which could elect a successor. Borno had hinted that "on the eve" of the expiration of his term, he might authorize election of "the Chamber and Senate," but he concluded that the attitude of the opposition had made this "a vain hope.... [B]linded politicians condemned to remain the slaves of their passions" had "created by their machinations ... a dangerous state of mind favorable to the worst impulses of disorder."[96] The decision again to defer elections agreed with the views of the high commissioner, although, believing that opinion in the United States might "outweigh the logical conclusion," Russell had told the department previously that he favored elections. He noted that a legislative body, once established, could not legally be dissolved, changed, or even guided, and feared that it might damage or destroy "the development and progress" which "many years of hard work" had achieved.[97]

The State Department agreed not to insist that the president "go against his better judgment," but gave notice that he would not be permitted another term.[98] Munro, who was among those responsible, concluded that an election would not be meaningful and thought that an elected Congress would "obstruct or destroy the constructive programs which we were trying to carry out." But hindsight suggested that this policy may have been unwise.[99] The choice of a president in 1930 was of crucial importance, for he would still be in power when the treaty, which was the basis for the occupation, would come to an end in 1936. "To Haitians of the Opposition, it became in the fall of 1929 a matter of 'now or never.'"[100]

Part III
DISENGAGING

INTRODUCTION

The change of purpose that brought the United States to seek means of reducing and removing rather than increasing or taking advantage of its presence and control in Caribbean countries was more readily accomplished than was the actual withdrawal. This change was precipitated by three interrelated factors: disillusionment with results and increasing awareness of political and moral costs, protest and criticism from all sides, and a postwar mood which rejected idealist activism and found no other compelling reason to persist in efforts that were more onerous than gratifying. From the beginning interventionist policies had been presented as temporary expedients, justified only as long as they could plausibly be considered either necessary for reasons of security or effective in promoting indigenous political competence. When criticism and protest developed and it became evident that no major or lasting accomplishment could be claimed, there was no acceptable rationale through which these policies could be continued except in order to do as much good or as little harm as possible in the process of withdrawal.

The goal of promoting free government was not quickly and easily abandoned. Prolonged efforts were made to deter or dissuade incumbents from avoiding or rigging elections and to transform the military into a nonpolitical, stabilizing force by establishing constabularies under professional control. Failure was due both to the intrinsic difficulty of altering practices rooted in culture by organizational improvization and to the impatience and inattentiveness of American policy as it tried to find its way out without stumbling over the scattered debris of its own principles. Somoza, Trujillo, Batista, and the Haitian elite were not imposed upon their respective societies by conscious intent of the United States, although American influence enhanced their ability to grasp and hold power. The only alternative to continuing intervention was to defer to political power. This meant accepting the perverted results of policies that had tried by superficial measures to make effective government possible.

In the Dominican Republic and Haiti American military rule was strongly challenged after the end of the European war. The navy fended off State Department efforts toward restoration of indigenous government in the Dominican Republic, but its position became untenable when unreasonable censorship was revealed and as it became apparent that there was no program of accomplishment that might justify arbitrary rule. The commitment to restore indigenous government was made, and the first steps were taken before the end of the Wilson administration, but it was 1922 before military government came to an end and 1924 before the marines withdrew. Negotiations for the transfer of authority broke down over the issue of American control of revenues and of a guard, but were resumed after the United States had demonstrated its determination by proclaiming a two-year extension of the occupation. In March 1924 the provisional government held a presidential election in which, thanks to the persistence of Sumner Welles, the advantage in strengthening authority of endorsing a "national candidate" (the veteran contender, Horacio Vásquez) was combined with the benefit in demonstrating democratic procedures of a contested vote. But Rafael Trujillo was in position to prevent any consolidation of political freedom.

In Haiti, after the crudities and cruelties of rule by marines had been revealed in a Senate investigation, the dominant role of the United States was carried forward through close collaboration between a former marine general as high commissioner and a Haitian president who was permitted to postpone elections. The Hoover administration was moved by an outbreak of violence to insist on an active search for means of exit. To the consternation of the State Department, the administration refused to be dissuaded by evidence of Haitian incompetence or by the knowledge that withdrawal would leave control in the hands of a small and unrepresentative group of politicians. The occupation was prolonged until 1934 due to complex interplay between U.S. determination to withdraw, shaded by concern for a competent guard and financial safeguards, and the reluctance of a Haitian government that hesitated between the onus of keeping marines on hand and the risk of losing protection.

In Nicaragua, where the first attempt to leave a competent government standing without the prop of marines had been frustrated, withdrawal was put off until after a new outbreak of fighting. Henry L. Stimson tried to break out of the cycle of repression and revolution by insisting on a free election, much as Wilson had done in the Dominican Republic, but with calculated simplicity rather than real naiveté. Fortunately, the ingredients were present for a majority choice. Confronting the imminent defeat of the U.S.-favored Conservatives unless sustained by American arms, Stimson was able to work out an accommodation with the Liberal revolutionists. Due in part to the necessity and possible advantage of appeasing the United States, their leadership gravitated to General Moncada, who had collaborated with the Americans many years earlier. After a show of determination by Stimson, insisted upon by Moncada to reduce the appearance of complicity, an agreement was reached for a supervised election, won handily by Moncada, and the organization of a reliable nonpartisan guard. Stimson wanted electoral supervision to continue indefinitely, but the American admiral who supervised the presidential election of 1932 reported that he had lacked the means to ensure fairness and recommended emphatically that the United States not again commit itself to the validation of an election.

Meanwhile, despite the best efforts of Stimson, military engagement was prolonged. One of the revolutionary commanders, Sandino, went back into the hills. It was expedient to call him a bandit, but he had a political and ideological vision and gained recognition as an authentic representative of national sentiment.

It became increasingly evident that domestic pressures and Latin American policy required withdrawal. To respond to this intensifying demand while the fight against Sandino was still not won, the United States accelerated the training of the guard and hurriedly procured Nicaraguan officers. When command was turned over on January 1, 1933, it was not to a nonpolitical, professional force that might stand as guardian for democratic procedures, but to an instrument for the seizure of power, controlled by men whose adherence to traditional goals and values was stronger than any indoctrination to disciplined restraint.

Cuba provided the most difficult test of the ability of the United States both to escape involvement in the politics of Caribbean countries and to absolve itself from the consequences of abstention. While Machado clung to power, the United States could not credibly dissociate itself from his rule. So strong was the conviction in Cuba that Machado enjoyed U.S. support that any emphatic statement of disclaimer would give his opponents the chance to claim that American officials were collaborating with them for his overthrow.

Activity under Franklin D. Roosevelt that hastened the demise of Machado and denied recognition to Grau San Martín appeared to go against the trend of abdication, but intent and eventual results were in accordance with it. Sumner Welles tried to mediate a settlement that might both relieve the immediate impasse and make it possible to remove the United States from its role as mentor and guardian in Cuban politics. The key to this was the resignation of Machado. When Machado and those around him proved stubborn, Welles suggested that military intervention might be necessary and recommended the drastic step of withdrawal of recognition. Without the necessity of such action, however, a decisive shift took place in the attitude of the army. Machado was forced into exile. To Welles's great disappointment, the moderate successor government never gained footing. It was kept off balance by two strong new forces— the army and a radical movement under student leadership. In a coup which removed both the government and the officer corps, a "sergeant named Batista" became the potential key to the existence and survival of a radical Cuban government headed by Dr. Grau San Martín.

Welles wanted to unite, reassure, and invigorate Cuban resistance to the radicals who claimed control of the government, by using the armed forces of the United States. Roosevelt and Hull rejected direct intervention except in dire emergency. But Welles fell back on the tactic of withholding recognition. This was kept within the framework of nonintervention by the claim that in the peculiar situation of Cuba, still subject to the Platt Amendment, recognition of a government which did not represent the will of the people would in itself constitute intervention. This made sense if the United States did not by nonrecognition deny a government the chance to gain and to demonstrate support and if an alternative regime were to be held to the same test. These conditions were not met; while the radicals could never prove that they had popular support, the government that restored conservative leadership was assumed to have it. Both Welles and Hull placed their hope in Batista. Although he hesitated to move against Grau, persistent American pressure brought him to endorse a more traditional government under Mendieta in January 1934. The United States immediately extended recognition. Abrogation of the Platt Amendment took place soon afterwards.

9.
THE DOMINICAN REPUBLIC

Secretary of State Charles Evans Hughes was sensitive to the impact of the Dominican occupation upon his effort to improve relations with Latin America. After a new military governor, Rear Admiral Samuel S. Robison, had replaced Snowden, a proclamation was issued on June 14, 1921, setting forth a detailed plan for restoration of constitutional government. It did not contain provisions advocated by Sumner Welles that would have specified a right to intervene and kept control of finance in American hands.[1] Assuming "helpful cooperation," it contemplated withdrawal of American forces within eight months. Electors chosen as provided for by the Constitution in supervised voting would choose a Congress. Through a convention of evacuation, negotiated with "certain Dominican citizens" appointed by the military governor, acts of the military government would be ratified, a final public works loan concluded, the duties and powers of the receiver of customs extended, and assistance provided in maintaining "an efficient Guardia Nacional" with American officers. The electoral colleges would choose a president only after the Congress should have confirmed the convention. The president would give his approval "at the same time" as taking office. The military government would then come to an end and American forces would be withdrawn, "assuming . . . a condition of peace and good order."[2]

The proclamation aroused "a hot blast of protest from the press" and was rejected, in Welles's opinion, "almost unanimously" by the Dominican people.[3] An attempt to show that the proposed safeguards were necessary and not intended to perpetuate American control did nothing to nullify the opposition.[4] The Dominicans broke off discussions. Elections were postponed indefinitely when it became clear that they would be boycotted.[5] Welles thought that Admiral Robison had confined himself too rigidly to his instructions; "frank discussion" might have resulted in acceptable adjustments.[6]

During several months of deadlock, the financial situation again deteriorated. At the end of January 1922 "the Military Government had practically ceased to function, except spasmodically, owing to its financial straits and the refusal of the Department of State to authorize a new loan."[7] The secretaries of state and the navy tried to put pressure upon the Dominican political leaders by warning that the withdrawal plan would be given up unless they asked for the elections to be held. Military government would then continue until urgent public works had been completed and an adequate constabulary was functioning—a time "estimated to be not longer than two years from July 1, 1922." To allay resentment, they suggested that the elections might be supervised by "Dominican citizens recommended . . . by the Dominican political leaders." As a "final concession," the United States would not insist on a military mission; it would suffice to maintain an assisting legation guard until the Dominican constabulary should be able to safeguard public order.[8] A new loan of $10 million would be floated, entailing extension of the receivership general.

After meeting with the Dominican leaders, the veteran minister, William W. Russell, reported that they were determined "to accept nothing." All who had attended reiterated their "unswerving protest" against the occupation. Russell thought that they feared "attack in the press." They readily accepted the arrangement for permanent financing, but evaded "responsibility therefore," and it was "quite evident" that they would "never accept anything in the nature of the military mission." They claimed that "continuance of the occupation for a hundred years" would be preferable to "a condition similar to that in Nicaragua."[9]

A proclamation "Providing for the Continuance of Military Occupation until Approximately July 1, 1924," was issued on March 6. With the United States committed to the organization of a constabulary and a new loan, the two veterans of Dominican politics, Vásquez and Velásquez, whose parties, according to Russell, controlled the country, were willing to discuss elections.[10] Meetings were held in Washington, away from the military governor.[11] Sumner Welles, who had resigned from the Department of State shortly before, took an active part on behalf of the secretary.

Vásquez and Velásquez approved a plan to set up a provisional government, which would be chosen by a committee from the four leading parties or groups. In addition to the two parties for which they spoke, the remaining *jimenistas* were included, together with a group of *nacionalistas,* consisting of "all those opposed to these three political parties," whose leader was "presumably" former president Henríquez. Establishment of a provisional government would make it possible to entrust electoral supervision to Dominicans.[12]

Welles doubted "the political strength of these gentlemen." It would be "a serious error to permit the Provisional President, who can control the subsequent elections, to be placed in power by a group which may represent only a minority of the Dominican people." He wanted to determine "whether an agreement can, in fact, be reached between political leaders representing a majority of the electorate upon a Provisional Government."[13] A "Plan for the Withdrawal of the Military Government" was signed, nevertheless, by representatives of the three parties (not including the Nationalists), without any such investigation.[14]

Shortly afterwards Welles visited the Dominican Republic's nine principal cities and towns and found "overwhelming" approval for the program. The people of country districts followed "instructions . . . from the local bosses who are without exception affiliated with one of the major parties." Only in Santo Domingo and Santiago was there "real opposition," but this was by "extremist agitators" without any following.[15] In *Naboth's Vineyard,* Welles later portrayed himself more as an advocate of the plan than as an impartial fact finder and did not dismiss the opposition as readily, stating that *nacionalista* orators "fanned the antagonism of the more excitable elements of the population to fever heat"; agitation was "very great." But he thought that opponents of the plan, however vocal, were a small minority; "the saner elements" were convinced "of the desirability of acquiescing in the project."[16]

Welles used his diplomatic skill to see the agreement through. He was willing to omit an explicit assertion that orders of the military government had been "laws of the Republic from the date of their publication" and interceded with the secretary of state to block proposals by the military governor which he thought would be so strongly resented that they would "inevitably destroy all the work of the United States."[17] After Admiral Robison adamantly rejected a Dominican request that off-duty marines be kept out of the cities during elections, Welles persuaded Hughes to the contrary.[18]

The Dominican commission of representatives agreed upon Juan Bautista Vicini Burgos as provisional president. He had not been politically active and was "favorably disposed towards the American Government," Welles happily reported. Following the choice of a provisional cabinet, the new government was installed on October 21, 1922.[19] Further movement toward a constitutional government was delayed by disputes over an electoral law and registration of voters. Welles blamed the delay on the political activities of members of the commission.[20] The alliance between Vásquez and Velásquez was challenged by a coalition led by Francisco J. Peynado, who resigned from the commission to plunge into the presidential campaign. Peynado was tagged as the favored candidate of American sugar interests. Welles feared that the campaign would "develop along pro-American and anti-American lines," causing a loss of "influence . . . with the coming Constitutional Government."[21]

Welles's hope to remain benignly neutral and aloof was further threatened by a breakdown of the carefully arranged procedure for electoral supervision. The central electoral board, with a zeal for propriety that seems to have been both whimsical and calculated, rejected the Vásquez ticket in an important province on the ground that the nominations were not submitted in duplicate.[22] The board apparently stood ready to take the same action elsewhere, thus in effect deciding the election results on this technicality. Welles tactfully commended the board's "independence and moral courage" and suggested the "simple" solution of preparing a duplicate copy.[23] He was at pains, however, to avoid "any open intervention." Unfortunately, the provisional president declined to assume responsibility for remedying this electoral technicality and thus subject himself to partisan attack; he would only "propose the solution as coming from the American Government." As a further complication, impeachment charges prevented the electoral board from functioning, and an attempt to reconstitute it foundered on the inability to find "an impartial professor." Welles pointed out to the commission that "technical advantages" had accrued to both sides. The elections were postponed while balanced adjustments were worked out.[24]

It was evident that Vásquez would win, but it remained to be seen how broad his support would be and how much bitterness and obstruction would remain. Welles was discouraged by the low quality of congressional candidates. He was attracted by a suggestion that Vásquez be accepted as national leader in exchange for minority representation; this would bring "the ablest men" into government, "making it possible for the majority of the old school politicians who are responsible for the disastrous history of this country to be permanently eliminated from participation in public affairs.[25] But when Peynado suggested that Welles force Vásquez to give way to a candidate acceptable to both parties, Welles rejected any such maneuver.[26]

The assessment that Welles made at the time strikes a rather different note from his retrospective judgment. He assured the secretary of state that if Peynado should withdraw, "the saner element" would "cooperate with a government headed by General Vasquez," and "only a few" would be obstructive "for purely political ends," but he wrote later that "discontent and unrest would have arisen throughout the country, and the administration of General Vásquez would at once have confronted sullen hostility on the part of all the factions composing the Coalition party."[27]

The elections were held on March 15, 1924, without disturbance and with about a 50 percent higher turnout than ever before. As expected, Vásquez won decisively, with firm control of Congress. Peynado accepted the result.[28] Welles's pleasure was enhanced by the quality of the cabinet—"men of the greatest ability in the country whose capacity and integrity are recognized by all.'"[29] Later, however, he deplored the disappearance of "a healthy opposition. . . . Until political parties have been formed, with principles and policies," he wrote, "personal government is inevitable, and the succession to the Presidency will be dictated by a few politicians.'"[30]

Vásquez visited Washington prior to his inauguration. The convention validating the acts of the military government was signed essentially as agreed upon two years before. A new financial agreement gave the United States control of appointments in the customs service and a veto on borrowing, in terms similar to those of 1907. Embarkation of American forces was completed on September 18.

The marines left behind a Dominican National Guard, which the Americans had created in hope that it would remove the military from Dominican politics. By decree of April 7, 1917, existing forces, mainly under the control of provincial governors, had been replaced by a Constabulary Guard, temporarily officered by Americans. Dominicans qualified to serve as officers would not do so under American command.[31] The problem of leadership was exacerbated when experienced marine officers were withdrawn to serve in the war in Europe and their places were taken by men from the ranks who in many cases inspired fear and loathing rather than respect. Under Snowden little was done to train Dominicans for responsible positions and the guard came to be "generally regarded as a branch, and a subsidiary branch, of the American forces of occupation."[32] During this time, on January 11, 1919, Rafael Trujillo received a commission as second lieutenant.

In June 1921 the force was redesignated the Dominican National Police. Serious attention to the training of Dominicans began with the founding of the Haina Military Academy on August 15. Trujillo was a member of the first class. Welles expected the training program to move rapidly so that when the occupation came to an end the police force could be officered entirely with Dominicans who had received training under American instructors.[33] Trujillo was jumped in rank from second lieutenant to captain in October 1922. Welles managed to obtain statements from the two presidential candidates of 1924 that the police would be kept free from politics. He thought that the regulations for appointment and promotion on the basis of merit provided "a definite guarantee that public order will be maintained after the Occupation is terminated by a well-drilled nonpolitical force."[34] Although a plan to keep American officers in charge of training broke down, it appeared that the goal had been essentially achieved.[35]

As the occupation came to an end, Welles fended off pressures to impose restrictions on the Dominican government. When a financial adviser as in Haiti was suggested, Welles replied that such a proposal would "destroy public confidence in the good faith of the Government of the United States" and would cause the president to refuse to assume office.[36] When the State Department backed the Santo Domingo Water, Light and Power Company in a contract dispute, Welles vigorously objected to an "apparent intention" to force acceptance of an unfair proposition. "Policy of this nature" had fed "suspicion and ill will" in Latin America. It could not be reconciled "with our announced intention of assisting the Dominican people in every way possible to establish a stable government and to increase the prosperity of the Republic."[37]

10.
NICARAGUA

STIMSON AND MONCADA 1927–1928

To resolve the impasse which threatened to draw the United States into a new commitment in Nicaragua, President Coolidge turned to Henry L. Stimson, a former secretary of war and a close associate of Elihu Root. Stimson was given "the utmost latitude."[1] His competence and prestige enabled him to assume "the policy-making initiative."[2] Should the mission fail, the Stimson diary reveals, the United States was prepared to undertake full intervention.[3]

While Stimson was en route, it appeared that the Conservatives had won a major victory. Although experience had made the State Department skeptical of such claims (justly so, it turned out), the possibility that the tide had turned led it to caution Stimson not to characterize his mission "as an act of mediation" nor to take initiative in getting in touch with the revolutionists. The State Department was "not inclined" to press the government to give up any advantage, although it would urge "reasonable generosity toward the revolutionists." While accepting the probable necessity of maintaining marines in Nicaragua "for a time to constitute an effective guarantee of stability," the department hoped that Stimson might be able "to avoid our assuming the responsibility of supervising an election."[4]

Stimson's first appraisal convinced him that the situation had not resolved itself through a government victory and that supervision of the 1928 election was an "absolute necessity." To forbid revolution while the government could control election results would perpetuate existing party control and make the United States the "target of hatred." This approach "treated the symptom and not the disease." The cure, Stimson suggested, would be "gradual political education of Nicaraguans in self-government," through supervising elections in 1928 and "in subsequent years." Military intervention in support of Díaz would be unpopular both in the United States and in Latin America and would produce no lasting improvements:

Such a naked military intervention in 1912, with no vigorous attempt to improve political methods of Nicaragua, proved to be wholly barren of permanent political benefit and peace lasted only 25 days after withdrawal of marines. Therefore I believe we should endeavor to carry out a more constructive effort now.[5]

In his talks with party spokesmen, Stimson introduced "the supposition of American supervision" even before the State Department, convinced that the Liberals had not been defeated after all, indicated that it had not been "excluded."[6] He insisted also upon the retention of Díaz as president. "The only way out was to follow the straight and simple course of driving at the main object of securing a fresh and fair start in 1928."[7] His "very naiveté" in "starting from scratch" and remaining "unshakable" was a source of strength.[8]

General José Moncada, the commander of Liberal forces, had long been "a friend to United States influence in Central America.'"[9] An opponent of Zelaya, he had been a cabinet member under Estrada in 1910 and under Díaz in 1911 and was making regular reports to the State Department in 1916.[10] Moncada told a visiting delegation that if Díaz would resign he would "accept any government in Nicaragua administered by the United States for the next 18 months in preparation for guaranteed free elections in 1928."[11]

Stimson anticipated that a military threat might be needed to persuade General Moncada to accept the retention of Díaz. The hope and expectation were that the threat would suffice, but the United States would, if necessary, undertake "forceful disarming of the insurgents."[12] Stimson thought that "the manifestation of a firm policy" would probably induce responsible Liberals to "terminate organized resistance to our action not later than first contact of forces."[13] But there were a few leaders, including Augusto Sandino, who would be "far better off as insurgents than . . . in time of peace," and might resort to guerrilla warfare.[14] Sandino, it later appeared, was a figure of different stripe. He had joined forces with the Liberal *politicos* and Moncada only through necessity, but his goal was to create a popular movement "with a purpose and a promise" of social reform.[15]

The Liberal emissaries proved to be adamant on only one point—the resignation of Díaz. Stimson had been authorized to accept this "as a last resort," but considered Díaz's role to be "practically necessary" for constitutional settlement. There appeared to be "no other Nicaraguan" who could be "trusted to cooperate," and with every other possible candidate there was "an ulterior expectation of partisanship." The only safe alternative, "a provisional American executive," would cause "legal and constitutional difficulties." Stimson rejected a State Department suggestion that pressure might be put on the revolutionists by threatening to draw back from the commitment to supervise the next election.[16]

A resolute Stimson met with Moncada at Tipitapa, near Managua. He found him "less technical in approving a substantially just compromise than the civilian leaders of his party."[17] Díaz's role was dealt with through a face-saving procedure, the essence of which was well conveyed in Stimson's account to the State Department:

[Moncada] admitted that neither he nor Government could pacify country without help of the United States, but insisted that in honor of the dead of his army who had fought so long against the retention of Díaz he could not consent to a settlement involving such retention. He stated frankly however that he approved all the other terms of proposed settlement. He also frankly told me that he would not oppose the United States troops if we had determined to insist on Díaz issue. I then told him I was authorized by the President to insist on retention of Díaz as essential to the plan of a supervised election and was authorized to state that forcible disarmament would be made of those unwilling to lay down their arms. He agreed to recommend to his troops that they should yield and for this purpose I gave him at his request [a] letter addressed to him [which set forth this intention].[18]

It was an adroit and successful maneuver, undertaken with little risk, given Stimson's understanding of Moncada's position. Stimson later wrote in his diary that he "knew mighty well that the chances were a thousand to one that I wouldn't have to carry . . . through" a threat to use force.[19] He had been authorized to inform Moncada that "forcible disarming may prove to be an alternative to a settlement by negotiating."[20] It was rather grandiloquent, therefore, for him to state in his memoirs that he "would have been extremely embarrassed if Moncada had proved untrustworthy, for he had no authority to pledge his Government to virtual war in Nicaragua."[21]

Despite Moncada's regard for the United States, his proclamation in response to Stimson's demand resounded with nationalism:

The forces of the United States . . . are sufficient to do what they please with our little country. . . .

I am not inhuman. . . . I cannot advise the nation to shed all its patriotic blood for our liberty, because in spite of this new sacrifice, this liberty would succumb before infinitely greater forces and the country would sink more deeply within the claws of the North American eagle.[22]

When Stimson met with Moncada again, some of the Liberal political leaders suggested a plebiscite within the party, but Stimson said bluntly that he found it "very different talking to soldiers" than to politicians "and proposed to settle this with them."[23] A truce and amnesty, collection of arms (with a payment of ten dollars for every serviceable weapon), and the restoration of Liberals to positions that they held before Chamorro's *coup* appeared to have been largely achieved without a serious hitch by the time Stimson left Nicaragua, one month after his arrival. Sandino was the only prominent military leader who held out. Sacasa and a few "personal associates" who had "done no fighting for their cause"[24] left the country.

Stimson was determined that the United States see to it that the election of 1928 be completely free. He persuaded Díaz to propose an electoral commission controlled by Americans, which would have available "the entire police power of the state . . . through the organization of a nonpartisan constabulary under the instruction and command of American officers."[25] This time a new force would replace the army and Americans would command as well as instruct. As "members of our active armed forces" who "had their future record to consider" they would be "above local temptation."[26] A colonel of the Marine Corps was appointed director-in-chief of the Nicaraguan National Guard in May 1927, and the first newly trained detachment entered on active duty in August.

As the means of supervision were taking shape, President Díaz informed the minister of his hope that the United States would maintain its influence. Until the new national guard reached full efficiency, peace should be assured by the presence of marines. He did not doubt the benefits of American occupation, past or future. "Happy results were to be expected because of what had been obtained in the 13 years of peace which Nicaragua enjoyed and which arose from the respect derived by the Constitutional governments from the indirect assistance of the body of marines."[27] Carlos Cuadra Pasos, another leading *americanista,* argued that "considerations of high policy should make the United States favor the Conservatives." Should the Liberals come to power, having relied for support upon Mexico and Guatemala, they would "have to be most anti-American." He argued further, in an elliptical logic which did not impress the State Department, that since "the United States . . . could not with dignity contribute to the support of an opposition party the Conservatives would have to seek aid from Mexico and Guatemala also and become anti-American."[28]

Stimson had concluded, however, that the long-range, principled goal of United States policy—to find the basis for legitimacy and strength in free elections rather than in protection against revolution—was conveniently in harmony with its electoral preference. He thought that Moncada, "our strongest real friend," had earned an advantage by "being brave enough to stand for friendship with the United States and open acceptance of our help." The United States could not "turn around and throw him down even if he is not unnaturally doing his best to cash in his reward politically."[29]

The first objective in preparing for a stabilizing election in 1928 was to prevent the candidacy of Chamorro. Dana G. Munro, who had recently returned to Nicaragua as chargé d'affaires, warned that his participation would arouse such hostility "that the establishment of a satisfactory government would be impossible."[30] The State Department was more than willing to do its part. Chamorro, on the way home from Europe, told the assistant secretary that he would never have taken the presidency if he had known he would not be recognized and offered to see to it that the Conservative nominee would be acceptable to the United States. He was told that the United States did not "pick out candidates for President in a foreign country," but that Chamorro could not hope to be recognized even should he be elected, because his (unrecognized) present occupancy of the position made him ineligible.[31]

Moncada, meanwhile, had announced his candidacy, claiming the backing of all Liberal factions, including Sacasa. He too conferred with the State Department, which, according to the press, found his revolutionary participation no obstacle, since he had not gained office.[32] The Nicaraguan minister complained that public expressions and reports of the State Department's attitude were so favorable to Moncado, that he seemed to have become the "official candidate." The department made a Delphic reply: "It would be unfortunate indeed if a misunderstanding of the true motives of the United States should result in disadvantage to any particular candidate in the forthcoming election."[33]

Confronting the popularity of Moncada, the benevolence of the United States toward him, and the apparent preponderance of Liberal voters (although Munro concluded that the majority was "slight" in municipal elections in November),[34] and lacking a strong candidate of their own, the Conservatives knew that they faced defeat in a supervised election. Chamorro tried to persuade Díaz to resign, so that the executive power would "not be hampered by existing understandings with the Legation." The State Department, prompted by Munro, expressed its "utmost disapprobation" of a tactic that "would strike at the very foundation of the transaction by which peace and order have been restored."[35] A special congressional election, in which it appeared that the count was arbitrarily raised, indicated what might happen. In spite of Munro's warning that it would create "a very bad impression," the Conservative candidates were fraudulently certified and given seats.[36]

President Coolidge designated General Frank R. McCoy, a friend of Stimson with experience in Cuba and the Philippines, as chairman of the commission to organize the elections. Working with Dodds, McCoy drew up a temporary law through which Americans would be given the decisive voice in election boards previously under party control.

Enactment was delayed in the lower house, where Chamorro controlled a large bloc of deputies, on what McCoy and Munro regarded as a pretext of unconstitutionality.[37] Kellogg and Stimson personally informed the Nicaraguan minister that they were "highly dissatisfied" and insisted that "the good faith of everybody involved . . . is plainly pledged to carry out the supervised election under the terms of the agreement."[38] Chamorro, however, held that he was in no way bound by the Tipitapa agreement. After several weeks of unavailing effort to secure its passage, the new law was put into effect by decree, with the Supreme Court electing McCoy chairman of the national board of elections. Ironically, actions instigated by the United States in order to establish a new basis for constitutionalism in Nicaragua were in violation of the existing constitution.[39]

As guarantor of free choice, the United States found that its involvements were manifold. It controlled the constabulary and utilized this force jointly with its own marines. The issue of financial control was not so conclusively resolved. Moncada wanted the United States to take over internal revenue collection, but the State Department preferred to rely on Díaz's integrity and his ability to resist pressure.[40] The legation thought that a loan would provide leverage that was needed precisely because the financial situation was not desperate: without the controls that would go with a loan, available public funds and revenues would constitute a "temptation as far as the election is concerned."[41] If a loan were denied, Díaz might be so "bitterly disappointed" that he could not then be relied upon. Díaz proved willing to set up essential controls, however, "preliminary to the flotation of a loan."[42] Specific arrangements were frustrated later by failure of negotiations with the bankers. After the election the Coolidge administration repudiated any suggestion of financial supervision through control of internal revenue.[43]

Bitter differences between the Chamorro faction and the pro-American Conservatives threatened to prevent a clear-cut electoral choice, but the State Department refused to interfere. When asked whether Díaz should be dissuaded from announcing support for Cuadra Pasos, as the pro-American candidate, the department replied that it preferred "not to have anything to do with the candidates, platforms, or issues in this campaign."[44] The Díaz-Cuadra faction contrived a deadlock so that the United States-controlled election board would have to decide who was the legitimate Conservative candidate, but the board rejected both factional slates.[45] The deadlock was eventually broken when Díaz ceased to press for Cuadra and a *chamorrista* named Benard, "the sugar king of Nicaragua," was nominated.[46] The electoral board rejected two further slates, one of which was headed by a reputed Sandino sympathizer and supported by former President Martínez.[47] The presence of more than two parties on the ballot might have thrown the choice to the Conservative-dominated Congress.

The election ran remarkably smoothly. A total of 906 American supervisors, nearly all servicemen, were under strict instruction to maintain impartiality.[48] Voters had to dip their fingers into Mercurochrome. As expected, Moncada won the presidency. Rather unexpectedly, the leading Conservative newspaper conceded that it had been an "honest, tranquil, correct and honorable" election.[49] But free elections clearly required the vigilant presence of the United States. Both parties had agreed before the voting to ask for the same form and manner of supervision in 1932. The State Department was "most sympathetic," but pointed out that it could not commit the new administration.[50]

The choice of Moncada was welcome to the State Department. To emphasize reconciliation, Sacasa was appointed minister and took up his post in Washington with an effusive statement of the strengthened "disposition . . . toward a fraternal association of our two countries."[51]

SANDINO

There remained, however, the mocking and elusive, occasionally stinging, opposition of Sandino, who had openly revolted against "Yankee imperialism" and the leaders who had accepted occupation. Sandino's bitterness and scorn toward Moncada were extreme. Operating in the mountains adjacent to Honduras, and utilizing, among others, criminals and outlaws, Sandino could plausibly and conveniently be regarded as nothing more than a bandit. Although, as the well-informed *New York Times* correspondent wrote at the time, he "had no record of banditry," in as late as 1947 Henry L. Stimson referred to his "long record as a bandit leader in Mexico."[52] In explaining its intention to call on the marines to restore order, the State Department noted that both political parties regarded "these men . . . as ordinary bandits."[53] Sandino was not lacking, however, in political talents and objectives. He aroused sentiment against the United States in Latin America and his audacity and tenacity gained sympathy within the United States.

Sandino began with verbal taunting but soon showed a more ominous capability by taking possession of the largest American-owned gold mine, both for its gold and for dynamite, and attacking the marine garrison in the provincial capital of Ocotal. In reply to the State Department's worried inquiry, the minister identified Sandino as "an erratic Nicaraguan" who had "preached Communism, Mexican brotherly love and cooperation, and death to the Americans, until the rabble of the whole north country joined him in his plan to massacre Americans there and to set up his own government." Although he had "met with complete disaster," it was "quite possible that in his fanaticism" he would "continue his outlawry."[54] So, indeed, he did. On July 31, 1927, the minister conveyed the belief that Sandino "must soon be annihilated or leave the country." On November 24, Munro reported that his "stronghold" had been located and bombed and that it should soon "be possible to make a decisive attack."[55] But the attacking patrol was ambushed and a relief force was also cut off. Although the "stronghold" was finally taken, Sandino eluded capture. During the months of electoral preparation, enlarged marine forces struggled in vain "to capture Sandino, to kill him, to drive him out of the country, to induce him by negotiations to lay down his arms, to eliminate him in any way possible."[56] The minister was able to report shortly before the election that the "outlaws" had been so weakened that they would be unable to interfere and the election was conducted without obstruction.[57]

Sandino's activities meant that the Nicaraguan guard had to be larger and more of a fighting force than had been intended. The basic agreement establishing the National Guard as the "sole military and police force."[58] was signed in December 1927 and endorsed by the Nicaraguan Congress in February 1929. The legislation set a maximum level of expenditure, which was not accepted by the United States and was exceeded as long as a surplus of revenues was available.[59] Most of the officers were United States Marines, many of them noncommissioned in American ranks.

The growth and improvement of this force made it possible to reduce marine strength. Of about five thousand marines, more than one thousand were withdrawn in January 1929 and another one thousand two hundred in July, with further reductions following. Although Sandino was in Mexico from June 1929 until early the next year, guerrilla activity and banditry continued. As demand increased in Congress for removal of the marines, the minister worked to enable the guard to take over field operations. President Moncada, however, placed more hope in a force of "volunteers" who knew the terrain and could match their opponents in mobility and ruthlessness.[60] Some of its members seemed little more than bandits themselves; the most notorious and effective was a Mexican mercenary named Escamillo. In the view of the minister Moncada was "conspiring" with the marine commander, General Logan Feland, in trying to weaken the guard and its commander, General Elias R. Beadle.[61] The minister, Charles C. Eberhardt, had both officers replaced, but the attendant frictions led also to his own removal and that of Admiral Sellers from command of the naval squadron. The irregular forces were gradually disbanded, but the guard itself was not always under proper discipline and could not be insulated from Moncada's partisan maneuvers.[62]

A new chargé d'affaires (later minister), Matthew E. Hanna (the same man who, at the beginning of his career, had organized the Cuban school system under General Wood), advised against withdrawal of the marines and advocated a vigorous program of road construction. This would open up the disturbed areas and provide employment for "misguided souls who would abandon their present precarious mode of existence if they could escape the influences that are holding them and find some other method of supporting themselves."[63] The State Department was not at first willing to press for such a program,[64] but in 1930, when the depression had brought into question the ability of Nicaragua to pay for an adequate guard, Stimson, then secretary of state, urged Moncada to provide an even larger sum for road-building than Hanna had suggested, in hope "of solving definitely the problem which has been acute in Nicaragua for three years."[65]

By this time Stimson was determined to relieve the United States of the task of maintaining order in Nicaragua. He proferred advice in two long notes to Moncada in November 1930 but "frankly stated" that "the responsibility and obligation . . . rests upon your Government."[66] Stimson's summation at that time was rather different in emphasis from the claim in his autobiography that his mission had established "general peace . . . punctuated only by sporadic outbreaks from the bandit Sandino."[67] Referring to the continuing disorder as a "cancer," he warned Moncada that "no Government can stand," which does not fulfill its "primary duty . . . to maintain law and order."[68] He recalled that at Tipitapa it had seemed easy to suppress

this insignificant force of lawless individuals. But how different has been the event: Nearly four years of constant warfare in the three northern provinces of your country, where these bandits took refuge, has ensued. . . . [T]he fountains of banditry in these difficult locations seem to be indefinitely supplied, and we are as far from peace and settled conditions as ever. . . . There is thus constituted a continuing focus for possibly infecting with disorder the remainder of your country.[69]

In his first note Stimson intimated that continued American cooperation with the guard would depend upon its being maintained at adequate strength with a guarantee of "prompt and regular payment" and upon efforts to solve the "basic problem'' through "funds for road building in the disturbed sections.''[70] In the second, while urging strenuous efforts both in road-building and in education, he agreed to a reduction of costs and served notice that the marines could not "remain later than to assist you in carrying out the elections of November, 1932.'' Public opinion in the United States would "hardly support a further continuance.'' In making his position clear Stimson held that he had "fully discharged the responsibility of the Government of the United States in this matter.'' Now, he wrote to Moncada, "the questions . . . rest clearly with you.''[71]

This premise became the basis for a formulation that was worked out in Washington in January 1931 by Stimson, Hanna, McCoy, and the marine guard commander. The guard, enlarged by men mostly from the mountainous regions, under quickly-trained Nicaraguan officers, would take over field operations by the first of June, leaving marines only in Managua. The marines would be fully withdrawn following the 1932 elections, at the latest.[72] Substantial amounts were to be spent for roads in the disturbed areas from a million dollar National Bank loan, but the destruction of Managua by earthquake on March 31 caused drastic curtailment of these plans.

When armed bands appeared on the east coast in April 1931, the chargé d'affaires ordered a force landed from the cruiser *Asheville,* "contrary to . . . announced policy.'' This precipitated a statement by Stimson that Americans could not count on protection throughout the country. Those feeling insecure should "withdraw . . . at least to the coast towns where they can be protected or evacuated in case of necessity.''[73] Stimson was "concerned lest the Commander of the Guardia feel that the presence of three Naval vessels of the United States on the East Coast relieves him of the responsibility of maintaining order there.''[74] In his diary he described "the American interests on the east coast'' as "a pampered lot'' who "feel that they have a right to call for troops whenever any danger apprehends.''[75] To former President Coolidge, who had expressed concern for the protection of American interests, Stimson recalled that the marines had been sent reluctantly, for the "entirely different purpose'' of ensuring a fair election in order "to end a disastrous civil war and release the American naval forces which were protecting foreign life and property against the consequences of that strife.''[76] Stimson did not intend to permit the administration to be diverted from the intention of withdrawal. A modicum of political stability would be the only requisite.

Little had been done to enable the guard to take responsibility. In November 1931 the marine officer in command described it as "a compact, loyal, and enthusiastic body with a growing *Esprit de Corps,* a consciousness of their usefulness to the nation, and a spirit of patriotism which makes them loyal to the state.'' But to avoid "rapid disintegration,'' a basic law was needed to take it out of politics, to "make it possible for officers to choose it as their profession,'' and to "make it responsible only to the federal authority.''[77] Legislation had to be postponed, however, until after the election.

Meanwhile, steps were hastily taken to make it possible to turn over command to Nicaraguan officers. Less than six months before the transfer no Nicaraguan ranked above lieutenant and only two were first lieutenants. Moreover, no further appointments could be made until after the election in November. The commander of the guard thought it "inconceivable" that a president would permit Nicaraguans "in key positions in the Guardia, of whose personal loyalty to himself and to his party there is the slightest doubt." He recommended that each candidate draw up a list of acceptable men from both parties, so that appointments could be made immediately after the election.[78] This might achieve a balance between "the historical political forces," but it could not establish effective nonpartisanship, nor would it neutralize the influence of the president and/or the commander of the guard. Approval of this device by the United States amounted to abandonment of any hope of "converting guardsmen to political neutrality."[79]

Higher officers were brought in from civilian life, to the detriment of morale. Fear that the guard would be seriously weakened by the sudden change of command in the face of continuing guerrilla warfare led the presidential candidates to ask privately that the withdrawal of marine control be postponed, but it took place as scheduled. Command was turned over to the new officers on January 1, 1933.[80] The new chief was a young associate of Moncada and a nephew of Sacasa's wife, Anastasio Somoza. Somoza had been educated as an accountant in the United States, had become a general in the revolutionary forces, and had ingratiated himself with American officials. He was not Sacasa's preferred choice. Presumably the minister and the guard commander were influential in the appointment; certainly this was the prevailing belief in Nicaragua.[81]

ELECTORAL SUPERVISION

With the termination of military occupation, the United States brought to an end also its mostly unsuccessful experiment in electoral supervision. Early in Moncada's term repressive measures had drawn protest from the State Department, which pointed out that "resentment . . . would be deflected also toward the Guardia and its American officers."[82] The unsupervised municipal elections of 1929 gave rise to bitter complaint. When the Conservatives demanded an American chairman of the election board for the congressional voting in 1930, the Nicaraguan government acquiesced and suggested a permanent cooperation.[83] Without any commitment for the future, the United States assigned a naval captain to this mission. Soon after his arrival he objected to the removal of several Conservative officials, but failed to gain the backing of the minister.[84] The minister urged that the guard be used to preserve order, to avoid an impression that Nicaragua needed foreign soldiers to assure a free and fair election.[85] However, renewed guerrilla activity and the financial obstacle to enlarging the guard made it necessary to utilize marines. The elections were held without major incident, although the Conservatives complained of abuses.[86]

A few weeks after the elections, the arrest of two defeated Conservative candidates, charged with plotting to assassinate the president, led Hanna to suggest that the time had come to "warn this Government that we cannot give our material and moral support to dictatorial and arbitrary methods."[87] Stimson admonished Moncada against resort to measures that appear to be "retaliatory or unjustifiably oppressive."[88] The Conservatives officially boycotted the municipal elections of 1931.

As the presidential election approached, Moncada looked for ways to prolong his influence, if not his tenure of office. He lacked support from his own party; his emergence as the Liberal candidate in 1928 had been due to the belief that the United States would support Díaz against any other Liberal.[89] Moncada's first tactic was a plan to institute minority representation in the government and extend the presidential term to six years, under a provisional president chosen by the Congress. As bait for American support, he offered to support approval of the electoral laws, the guard, and the Bryan-Chamorro Treaty. After the chargé d'affaires, Willard L. Beaulac, reported open boasting by Moncada that the State Department would consent to cancelling the elections, Stimson strongly advised that they be held.[90] Beaulac called attention to "obvious pressures and compulsions" employed by Moncada and suggested "that the Department would not wish to condone the imposition of any candidate," but Stimson urged him "to make every effort to refrain from intervening in these questions of party politics."[91]

In a personal note to Stimson, Moncada eloquently denied any thought of extending his term and complained that a "change of public opinion in the United States" had left Nicaragua "forgotten by the hand of God and exposed once more . . . to civil war." He suggested that an agreement for minority representation would provide a basis for "the mediation of the American Legation in each Presidential election."[92] Stimson gave no encouragement. The United States would supervise the scheduled election "on the pathway of regular and orderly procedure under the Constitution," but would "be unable to continue with its plans" if a constituent assembly were to be chosen.[93]

If he could not gain support, Moncada was not averse to arousing national feeling against the United States. In a final fruitless appeal to his party, he said that the U.S. attitude provided an opportunity "to restore . . . the complete liberty and sovereignty of Nicaragua" by bringing about "the immediate withdrawal of American armed forces."[94]

Rear Admiral Clark H. Woodward was designated to head the American electoral mission in 1932, to the apparent satisfaction of both parties. Unlike in 1930, it was believed at the outset that additional marines would be needed. However, the State Department objected, and Congress prohibited the use of funds for this purpose.[95] A revised plan was drawn up which would not use American personnel in places "where they would not be afforded adequate protection by the Nicaraguan police forces." This led Admiral Woodward to record his opinion that controls would be insufficient to ensure an election which he could certify as free and fair. He found Moncada "stubbornly resentful and hostile" because of the State Department's "refusal . . . to be hoodwinked."[96] A dispute between Liberal factions further jeopardized the supervisory procedures.

To the great relief of the Americans, however, when confronted by the Conservative nominations of Díaz and Chamorro, the Liberals quickly nominated the former vice-president and revolutionist, Dr. Sacasa.[97] Moncada considered a coalition with the Conservatives, but negotiations toward this end were unsuccessful. The Conservatives had no hope of victory. Chamorro, citing apathy and lack of funds, threatened to withdraw but finally acceded to the plea that this would "wreck the admirable progress which has been achieved" and "prejudice the hopes of peace and stability for the future of Nicaragua."[98]

The election went off without serious disturbance or abuse, thanks in part to its onesidedness. The Liberal tally, 76,269, was only 59 votes different from what it had been four years previously. The Conservative vote fell off by about three thousand. Given the lack of change in leadership, the stability of adherence to the two parties, the absence of significant issues, and the predictability of the outcome, Nicaraguans may well have wondered whether this exercise of democratic choice justified the burden of occupation and tutelage. While Sandino continued to be active, moreover, not even peace could plausibly be claimed as a benefit secured by the American presence.

Despite his earlier reservations, Woodward was able to conclude that the elections had been valid and legal. He pointed out, however, that a supervisory mission would have to gain almost complete control over nomination and election procedures in order to insure fairness. He thought the United States should "seek, by every means possible, to avoid again becoming involved" in electoral supervision in Nicaragua.[99]

The traditional leaders were so fearful that renewed contention would bring on general violence that even during the campaign they found a basis for collaboration. They asked again, in vain, that the marines be kept on (the minister reported that "all classes" were "practically unanimous" in this desire) and sought help from the legation in drawing up a plan for interparty cooperation. Although this too was formally refused, the minister encouraged discussions among Nicaraguan political figures, including not only those in both parties who were pro-American, but also a group "generally opposed to the intervention of the United States."[100] The party leaders agreed to divide public offices in a system of "harmonious conviviality" and sent emissaries to Sandino "to negotiate national peace." On February 2, 1933, Sandino signed an agreement to cease fighting. His men were given amnesty and a tract of state land, he was permitted to retain an armed guard, and "the representatives of the two parties 'rendered homage' to his noble and patriotic attitude."[101]

Dana G. Munro, writing with intimate knowledge, hailed the agreements as "impressive justification of the policy inaugurated in 1927":

It was this policy which made possible the growth of the spirit of conciliation which inspired these pacts. . . . With the holding of a series of free elections, the tension between the parties noticeably decreased. The defeated party did not feel the resentment which inevitably followed the installation of a government by force or fraud, and the administration was not compelled to adopt repressive measures to prevent revolution.[102]

But this was a minority opinion. After Sacasa was deposed in 1936 Under Secretary of State Sumner Welles concluded that "over twenty years of attempted assistance in the political realm had brought benefits neither to Nicaragua nor to the United States."[103]

The agreement between the parties showed that the United States had failed in its basic purpose of enabling Nicaragua to develop a competitive political system that would not depend upon outside protection. The moderate figures who had come to the fore under American protection did not have either popular support or military strength. They needed peace with each other and with Sandino to avoid domination by armed force and even this was no guarantee that the guard commander would not seize power.

The United States assumed no responsibility to prevent misuse of the military instrument which it had created. "Withdrawal of the American forces," the State Department insisted, "marks the termination of the special relationship which has existed between the United States and Nicaragua."[104] In December 1933 the foreign minister approached the department regarding a proposal to reorganize the guard and was told that this was "not a subject on which it may appropriately express an opinion." Although the minister had "witnessed the signature" the department explained that "the United States was not a party to the agreement" that provided for a bipartisan force. The new minister, Arthur Bliss Lane, was told, however, that if approached on the matter, he might indicate "orally and informally" that the continuance of the existing organization was "important to the future peace and welfare of Nicaragua." Lane did not take advantage of this instruction because he did not "entirely share the Department's view."[105]

11.
HAITI

STANDING DOWN

A decision by President Herbert Hoover to undertake an inquiry which might lead to the end of the occupation almost coincided with an outbreak of opposition in Haiti, beginning with a student strike. It was a conflict over educational funds that precipitated open protest. Scholarships that had gone to town students at the School of Agriculture were cut back in favor of work opportunities, which were attractive only to students from the countryside.[1] With the backing of opposition leaders, the strike spread. President Borno's announcement that he would not seek re-election did not quell the disorder.

General Russell, the American minister, reported that the strike was "fostered by politicians, the mulatto class who do not desire to see the condition of the peasant improved, and the French Brothers who are opposed to our system of education."[2] He was concerned about loyalty of the guard (formerly the gendarmerie) but believed it could be counted on "as long as it is under the control of white officers." He instructed the marines to show themselves in the streets with their machine guns, and called for reinforcements.[3] When there was a threatening outbreak at the southern port of Aux Cayes, Russell "sent planes to drop bombs in the harbor to overawe the people," but with only "a momentary effect."[4] He ordered prohibition of "articles or speeches of an incendiary nature or those that reflect adversely upon the United States Forces in Haiti or tend to stir up agitation against the United States officials." Offenders would be tried before a Military Tribunal.[5] The State Department, with reference to "the unfortunate effect produced in the United States," asked too late that his orders be withheld.[6] At Aux Cayes, about fifteen hundred country people, hurt by lower prices and a restriction on seasonal labor migration, moved toward the town and were met by twenty marines. Ten Haitians were killed and twenty-four wounded in the firing that turned them back.[7]

President Hoover had already initiated a review of the American role in Haiti. The situation, he told his secretary of state, had "flowed into the White House doors." Anticipating "congressional attack," he suggested the appointment of a commission of "highly important citizens to reexamine the whole of our policies."[8] This plan was made public in the president's annual message early in December. The five-member commission was under the chairmanship of W. Cameron Forbes, the former governor general of the Philippines. It included Henry P. Fletcher, whose extensive Latin American experience included service as ambassador to Mexico and to Chile, as under secretary of state, and as delegate to the Havana conference, and the well-known liberal Republican editor from Emporia, Kansas, William Allen White. Hoover discussed the Haitian situation "very fully" with Forbes and Fletcher before their appointments were announced, but gave them "an absolutely free hand."[9] The principal task of the commission was to decide "when and how we are to withdraw from Haiti" but the president's instructions placed emphasis also on the "need to build up a certainty of efficient and stable government."[10]

The commission held public hearings in which President Borno's adherents "were entirely on the defensive."[11] After only two weeks, with the cooperation of Russell, it had gained acceptance of a plan to transfer power from Borno and his entourage to the politicians who had been the scourge and despair of the occupation officials. An interim president acceptable to the political contenders would conduct elections for a legislature which would choose his successor. "Delegates of patriotic groups" chose Eugene Roy, a man who had been more active in business than in politics, for this role in a meeting at the Parisian theater.[12]

William Allen White was the principal advocate of accepting the leaders of the opposition as spokesmen for Haiti. Having come with a "virgin mind," he was "amazed and puzzled at what he saw" and was soon "convinced that the commission should recommend definite steps" for withdrawal. With support from Fletcher he drew up a statement which pledged to end military occupation as soon as possible, but the State Department vetoed its release. The opposition threatened to boycott the commission, but accepted White's personal assurances.[13] He was well aware that they represented a small elite and thought it was futile to expect them to respond to American good will:

They honestly feel that we are tyrannical and the fact that the occupation is honestly trying to serve the Haitians does not get to them, because we are not serving them in the Haitian way. However, we are trying to serve them after the manner of American civilization and American ideals which they loathe. We are in the 20th century looking toward the 21st. They are in the 18th century with the ideals of the Grand Louis always behind them as models.[14]

The commission was at pains to dispel "delusions as to what may happen in Haiti." It chided the treaty officials for their apparent failure to realize that their work must be completed by 1936. Education and literacy were so limited that the government was "liable to become an oligarchy" and "must necessarily be more or less unstable and in constant danger of political upheavals."[15] The "brusque attempt to implant democracy . . . by drill and harrow" and the "determination to set up a middle class'' reflected "the failure of the occupation to understand the social problems of Haiti.''[16]

The commission placed great emphasis on rapid "Haitianization" of all services. It was particularly critical of past failures to bring more Haitians into high positions in the guard. There were none above the rank of captain and only two of the twenty-three captains on duty with troops were Haitians. An officers' training school had functioned only sporadically.[17]

The commission presented its plan to President Hoover with a warning that the situation was critical. "The responsible leaders of the articulate elements of the Haitian public" had convinced it that if the popular demand "for the restoration of representative government" were not met, bloodshed would be likely.[18] President Hoover accepted the plan almost at once, without the endorsement of Secretary of State Stimson, who was in London.[19]

Objections quickly arose both in Haiti and in Washington. The State Department, reluctant throughout, was particularly disturbed at proposals for Haitianization of the treaty services "which seemed certain to put an end to any constructive work.''[20] It felt that, largely through White, the Haitians had been led "to expect a more complete and immediate change in the whole relationship than the administration at Washington had really contemplated.''[21] It found opportunity for delay in a constitutional issue. By a "permissible construction" an early election could be called, but the opposite interpretation was "likewise permissible." In any case, the decision belonged with the president of Haiti; the United States should neither "object to it" nor "insist upon it.''[22]

With some further prompting from White, however, the plan was carried through. Russell was empowered to warn Borno that he could not expect "any support or protection" if he were to take a contrary course of action.[23] When the council of state refused to vote itself out of power, the president, at Russell's suggestion, adjourned it for several days and replaced twelve of its members. Even after that it was only due to Russell's "astuteness and knowledge of Haitian psychology" that success was achieved in "pushing through the election of Roy.''[24]

Legislative elections were held in October. The State Department announced that the United States, regarding this as "entirely a Haitian affair, . . . would exercise no supervision.''[25] A majority of black nationalists was returned, threatening the dominance of the mulatto elite. The latter managed, however, to elect one of their own, Stenio Vincent, as president.[26] As president of the assembly, Vincent had been a vigorous opponent of the American program for Haiti in 1917.

Dana G. Munro of the State Department was appointed minister, to "represent the President in Haiti in the same manner as did the High Commissioner.''[27] He was instructed to "bend every effort" to make it possible to "withdraw from any participation in the internal affairs of Haiti," provided only that there be "a reasonable hope that there will be no return to the conditions which compelled . . . intervention in 1915.''[28]

The principal issues to be resolved were Haitianization, particularly of the guard, and future financial relationships. Haitians pressed for quick change, but often without firm conviction. Munro, aware of political realities, wanted to preserve a degree of constructive influence by timely and temperate response; the State Department was less realistic. The Vincent government called for Haitianization of the treaty services within one or two years in a plan that Munro refused to take seriously. He thought it would destroy practically everything that had been built up and that the Haitians "would be surprised and perhaps dismayed" if it were accepted.[29] He was impressed with the "very strong desire . . . both in the elite and in the lower classes of the city population, that all Americans should leave Haiti at once" and feared that concessions "would merely encourage new and increasingly bitter attacks."[30]

The difficulty of "maintaining political stability" was illustrated for Munro by the pressure for early withdrawal of the marines. The elite feared the attempt to establish an independent guard free from political interference because it posed a threat of military control. Trujillo's "vicious example across the border in Santo Domingo" did not go unheeded.[31] The State Department insisted that financial services and the guard be excluded from any commitment to rapid Haitianization, because loans had been made in the belief "that law and order should be established and maintained."[32] Moreover, it wanted to use Haitianization as inducement for a new financial treaty, which would be closely similar to the hated treaty of 1915. Munro, reluctant to give the extremists a new issue, thought it wise to accept a less stringent arrangement and preferred to go forward with Haitianization unilaterally or through an executive agreement.[33]

A prolonged dispute over the budget, seen by Munro as "the most serious effort which has yet been made to evade the financial control established by the Treaty," brought a reversion to the threat to hold up payments.[34] The finance minister countered, "Well go ahead and do it. Take the whole country and the responsibility for doing it."[35] The issue was resolved after the United States showed that it could and would handle emergency requirements without caving in on the basic issues. After tedious negotiations, a degree of cordiality was restored.

Munro stressed the importance of concluding a general financial agreement before the American position should be further weakened. It was already evident that an agreement would require "substantial concessions to the point of view and to the political necessities of the Haitian Government. . . . Effective financial control" might require "such compulsion as the United States Government would find it exceedingly embarrassing to exercise." We might eventually have to accept "an arrangement much less satisfactory than we can probably obtain now by friendly negotiations."[36]

The State Department did not attempt to refute this argument, although it was less forthcoming than Munro desired. Draft agreements were prepared regarding financial control and Haitianization of the guard, the department insisting that the latter be dependent on the former. These became protocols attached to a treaty that would end the occupation, "in view of the substantial accomplishment of the purposes of the Treaty of September 16, 1915."[37]

The new treaty was rejected, however, on September 15, 1932, by unanimous vote of the Haitian legislature. The national assembly, although most of its members had been elected as supporters of the president earlier in the year, had already fallen out with Vincent on matters relating to pay, tenure of office, and constitutional powers.[38] Misconstruing the intentions of the United States, perhaps understandably, members claimed that the fiscal representative would be able to control the economic life of Haiti and that a provision to suspend withdrawal in case of unforeseen difficulties might become a pretext for keeping marines in Haiti indefinitely.[39] The chargé d'affaires reported that it would take "great executive pressure" to persuade the legislature to change its attitude.[40]

The State Department tried a hard line, tying withdrawal and Haitianization of the guard to a "definite settlement of all the questions at issue," but it soon specified that Haitianization would "in any case be carried forward" and reiterated its desire to keep financial responsibilities limited.[41] The next hope of the department was to exact an agreement on financial control as the condition for a new loan. The new minister, Norman Armour, thought that such an attempt might cause the president to "return to his previous stand of nationalistic opposition" in an attempt to "regain lost popularity."[42] The essential task was "to build up the President's morale." Legislators were too insecure "to oppose a really determined insistence." An irrigation project in the Artibonite valley might help to generate support, making ratification possible without "exposing the United States to the criticism of having used its special position to exert pressure to obtain it, as was the case in connection with the ratification of the Treaty of 1915."[43]

The new administration of Franklin D. Roosevelt made further efforts to assuage Haitian demands. Haitianization of the guard and withdrawal of the marine brigade would take place within six months of enactment of a new treaty. The proposal for a military mission could be omitted; if retained, "it should be made clear that it is at the request of the Haitian Government."[44] The State Department was willing to consider separate agreements on military and financial matters[45] and to treat the protocol on financial control "as an executive agreement not requiring ratification."[46]

President Vincent's inability to control the legislature increased the difficulty of concluding an agreement and strained existing controls. When Vincent raised the possibility of dissolving the legislature the department expressed reluctance to support unconstitutional methods.[47] The "very delicate internal political situation" was "satisfactorily adjusted," to permit the signature of an executive agreement that was not materially different from the rejected protocols of the previous year.[48] The date of withdrawal was advanced to October 30, 1934. When President Roosevelt paid a brief visit in July, he arranged for the marines to leave the country in August.

Continuation of financial control, due to assurances that had been given to buyers of Haitian bonds, was a cause of continuing agitation. Just before the Inter-American Conference at Montevideo, President Vincent asked President Roosevelt whether it was "really necessary" to maintain this "disparagement" of a member of the great Pan-American family.[49] In discussions with the Haitian delegation, Secretary of State Cordell Hull agreed to support attempts to negotiate an acceptable arrangement with the bondholders. An erroneous report that he had gone farther than this caused embarrassment to the State Department when Vincent, wanting to be sure that credit did not go to his political opponents, pressed for an official statement.[50]

Nevertheless, the commitment to nonintervention, which the United States accepted at Montevideo, meant that there was little point in maintaining a formal government role in debt-collection. As the State Department quite bluntly explained a year later:

Should the present Government of Haiti, or any future Government, during the life of the loan, determine to abrogate these agreements by unilateral action, it would be contrary to the established policy of this Administration to undertake to use force in order to preserve to the present treaty officials the rights and powers now vested in them. [The safety of investments would be greater if they were privately managed and thus] . . . less likely to create opposition on the part of Haitian public opinion.[51]

A solution was soon found. A proposal, already advanced by the Haitians, to set up a private bank as the collection agency, led to an agreement for purchase of the national bank by the Haitian government, with a majority of the board to be nominated by the creditors. Approval was held up by opposition in the Haitian Senate, but Vincent staged a referendum on February 10, 1935, (454,357 votes in favor, 1,172 in opposition) and then removed eleven senators who continued to oppose the agreement on the ground that they were "in open revolt against the sovereign will of the people."[52] Armour believed that the issue was merely a pretext for getting rid of members of the opposition. He wanted to avoid any impression that the United States had actively supported the president in gaining approval of the contract by unconstitutional means.[53] The State Department's refusal to comment on the question of constitutionality caused the National City Bank to doubt the security of its investment,[54] but the formal transfer did go through on July 9, 1935. Thus the end of the occupation, much like its beginning, demonstrated the failure of Haiti to attain constitutional government.

A treaty to permit the bank to assume the duties of the fiscal representative was not approved by Haiti, however. Protracted negotiations, held in abeyance from time to time because of hope for a new loan, did not produce a solution until 1941, when the office of fiscal representative was finally abolished. After 1934, nevertheless, it was clear that in all but form the United States had relinquished its role in negotiating the relations between Haiti and its creditors.[55]

12.

CUBA

WELLES VERSUS MACHADO

Franklin D. Roosevelt's Latin America policy was influenced by the same contradictory impulses which had led Woodrow Wilson to take control of two countries in pursuance of an ideal of self-government, but it was tempered through experience by a strong desire to avoid "single-handed intervention."[1] He believed, as did Sumner Welles, that coercive measures could be avoided by determined and intelligent preventive action. Welles wrote to Roosevelt in 1928:

The value of a policy of preventing the rise of conditions which lead to political disturbances, revolution, and civil war in the Caribbean republics is, to my mind, far greater than the value of a policy which lets matters drift until civil war breaks out and then adopts measures of coercion.[2]

Such an approach was elaborated in an article that was drafted by Welles but which was published with Roosevelt's approval under the name of Norman H. Davis.[3] It took Stimson to task for having abandoned Wilson's "policy of fostering the growth of democratic institutions and orderly government," by "extending immediate recognition to a new government on purely technical grounds."[4]

President Wilson held that it constituted a greater measure of intervention in the domestic concerns of the Latin American republics for the Government of the United States to recognize a revolutionary government before the people had passed on it (because of the fact that recognition inevitably implies financial as well as moral support of that government), than for the United States to withhold recognition until it felt assured that the people, in an orderly and legal manner, had in fact approved the change.[5]

The article expressed no doubt as to the potential efficacy of preventive action or the possibility of orderly and valid expression of the will of the people. It was "the failure of preventive and corrective measures" that had caused repeated intervention and military occupation.[6]

Roosevelt's appointment of Sumner Welles as ambassador indicated in unmistakable terms that Cuba was an urgent problem, a test of his intention to change the tone and spirit of inter-American relations. Welles, although still young, had long experience at policymaking levels and had already been appointed by Roosevelt as assistant secretary of state. His assignment in Cuba was clearly intended to resolve quickly the central issue of restoring legitimacy to government.

Welles's instructions, which he himself must have had a hand in composing, reviewed the steps through which Machado had gained reelection and took note of reports that the United States had given "tacit approval." With rapid economic deterioration Cuba had become embattled:

Political opposition has degenerated into a ruthless campaign of violence against the President and against the members of the Administration. Repressive measures . . . have failed to curb the campaign of terrorism resorted to by Machado's opponents.

Not only all the political leaders of importance, but a great majority of the intellectual leaders of Cuba as well, have been forced to leave the Republic. The University of Havana and the secondary schools throughout the Island have been closed by Government Decree for nearly three years . . . [A] very large percentage of the students are actively engaged in subversive activities notably through such organizations as the ABC. Many of them have been assassinated by the police authorities and many of them have been imprisoned. It is apparent that under conditions such as these, those groups among the younger generation from whom the Cuban leaders of tomorrow must spring are being brought by experience to the conviction that changes in government in Cuba must be effected not by the orderly processes of constitutional government, but by the resort to measures of violence and revolution.[7]

"Such a state of affairs," the instructions continued, "must rightly give the Government of the United States . . . grave disquiet" at the possibility of "open rebellion" which might leave Cuba without a government "adequate to preserve life, property, and individual liberty" and thus trigger intervention. Offers of "friendly advice" in order to correct the "course of events" should "not be construed as measures of intervention" but would be "intended to prevent" it. Mediation was to be aimed at "a definite, detailed, and binding understanding" which would make possible the free election of "a new constitutional government." Coincidentally, Welles was to set forth the prospect of a reciprocal trade agreement.[8] Clearly, no settlement could be reached without the prospect of "a change of administration.'"[9] Despite references to the Root interpretation, "intermeddling or interference" were not excluded, but Welles was to do nothing to make "formal intervention" more likely.[10]

Welles found the situation "both more precarious and more difficult" than anticipated, but he was not dismayed by the equivocal task which he had undertaken: to effectuate a major change in Cuban government amidst unprecedented political turbulence while furthering a noninterventionist Latin American policy. With "any luck at all," he told Roosevelt, it should be possible to avoid an intervention, "either by force of arms or by open diplomatic action," which would jeopardize "that sane and beneficial Latin American policy, which you have often discussed with me."[11] In their first talk, Machado, "very obviously impressed" conveyed to Welles a "definite intimation" that he would resign, at least temporarily, "before the electoral period began."[12]

Welles was cautious in pressing for the replacement of Machado because he feared that any attempt "to anticipate such a change" might cast doubt on the loyalty of the army. With the opposition "divided into factions, . . . general chaos might well result," with "malcontents" trying "to bring about intervention by the United States through the destruction of American property."[13] The preservation of order was too valuable to be placed at risk. Welles was deeply concerned with the tendency toward violence and radicalism among the opposition. He realized that his role was a vulnerable one; political leaders who were "secretly only too anxious to obtain our mediation" were quite capable of appealing "to the more radical element . . . by public announcements that they will not countenance diplomatic intervention in any guise by the United States."[14]

During his second talk with Machado, Welles made evident his intention to play a strong role. He vigorously criticized the opposition's plan. If elections were held too soon, another candidate of the president's party would win and "unrest and agitation" might be even more difficult to control.[15] Welles cast himself as a dispenser of political wisdom, melding practicality with principle to establish the conditions for political stability. Machado can hardly have failed to understand that his "mediation" would be preemptory.

Machado agreed to issue a statement calling for reform of the constitution by representatives of "all shades of public opinion" and restoration of the office of vice-president. Welles went over the text "in order to avoid any possible confusion as to the President's intent."[16] After six weeks in Cuba he was able to report that the various opposition factions had agreed to his mediation. A statement in the name of the president pledged "the moral support of the American people behind these attempts at the peaceful adjustment of Cuban problems."[17]

After several days of negotiations, Welles was optimistic. Although the student groups gave him concern, he saw a "good chance" for "a fair and just solution of the political problem strictly within the lines of constitutional procedure." He asked for Roosevelt's personal support in persuading Machado to agree to resign several months before the 1934 elections.[18] Ten days later, he professed even greater hopefulness; barring a change in Machado's "frame of mind," there would be "no possibility of an unsuccessful outcome." But he warned "that the President changes his mind with the utmost frequency."[19]

In this instance Machado's compliance lasted barely long enough for Welles to draft the report that described it. In "rambling and at times incoherent speeches," before each of the two houses of the congress, he asked for support until 1935 stating that the mediation had been acceptable only because it was personal and spontaneous, not "under the instruction of the United States Government." Welles was so concerned at the effect of this among the opposition that he urged the State Department to "state that while of course my tender of good offices has been made spontaneously as stated by President Machado, it could not have been made other than with the full authorization of my Government."[20] The statement was issued the following day, in just this language, expressive of the contradiction between the goals and the avowed methods of United States policy.

Within a few days the Cuban ambassador complained that Welles was "using the economic distress in Cuba, which could only be cured by a new commercial treaty," in "dictating a policy to President Machado." He foresaw "certain disaster; . . . either President Machado would be shot or American Marines would be landed."[21]

Optimism vanished during the first week of August. A president who at times seemed "utterly uncontrolled" and "unbalanced mentally," faced a general strike, which it was thought had been fomented largely by members of his own government in order to disrupt mediation and cause a return to martial law.[22] Desperately, Machado tried to find shelter in Cuban nationalism, meeting with the strike leadership and at a critical time refusing to see Welles.[23]

Welles reported imminent danger of "utter chaos,"[24] using a word which the State Department had consistently reserved as justification for open intervention. He decided that chaos could only be prevented if the Cuban president would go on leave, enabling a newly appointed impartial secretary of state to form a cabinet including all important political elements. Welles told Machado that unless this were done, "a condition of absolute anarchy" would result. He mentioned the Platt Amendment "obligations," while reiterating that his "whole purpose" was to avoid the United States having to carry them out.[25] At his request, the president backed him up in a message to the Cuban Ambassador. Roosevelt added, however, "that he had no desire to intervene but that it was our duty to do what we could so that there should be no starvation and chaos among the Cuban people."[26] This has been interpreted as a significant weakening of the "intimation" of intervention which Welles had conveyed,[27] but while it did not convey the determination which Welles had wanted,[28] it clearly did suggest that intervention might become unavoidable. Welles's explicit warning that Machado and those around him were "confident that because of the prejudice to our own interests the United States Government will not intervene now under any conditions whatever" did not reach Washington until after Roosevelt had seen the ambassador.[29]

Ambivalence was unavoidable, unless the United States either stood prepared to intervene openly, or, accepting the costs of chaos, renounced not only any obligation under the treaty but also any serious attempt at influence. It was in any event too late to step back. Any attempt to pull out would have major political effect. Collapse of the government was a real possibility. No constructive purpose could be served, nor could deepening involvement be avoided, by reverting to support for Machado. Welles explicitly rejected Stimson's view that the Platt Amendment imposed no obligation. Intervention was to be "avoided at any cost *except* that of failing to comply with our treaty responsibilities."[30]

While Welles was unwilling to divest his diplomacy of the prospect of open intervention, it was of limited use. As a warning of the consequence of chaos, it showed that intervention was regarded as an undesirable last resort. Without explicit support from Washington, a threat to intervene could not be fully credible. Yet even an intimation incurred the risk of creating a mood of defiance. The Cuban ambassador warned that Machado would not be "pushed out." Machado once told Welles to "inform the President of the United States that he would prefer armed intervention to the acceptance" of what he had proposed.[31]

The realization that there could be no solution without Machado's departure became evident during Welles's efforts at mediation. He was able to claim that the proposed solution "represented neither imposition nor interference by the United States, but was . . . a result of conferences" representing "every part of Cuban opinion." He concluded that Machado's determination to cling to office necessitated "forceful and positive action." Specifically, he proposed that "the United States should no longer accord its moral support to the Government of Cuba and should withdraw recognition."[32]

In supporting this recommendation Welles invoked criteria that were broader than the avoidance of chaos and the protection of lives and property. He argued that responsibilities under the treaty were incompatible with "formal support of a Cuban Government which has consistently deprived the Cuban people of their constitutional rights, which has been guilty of atrocities which have shocked the entire continent, and which refuses to consider the acceptance of a fair and Cuban solution of this disastrous situation." He thought withdrawal of recognition would compel Machado to resign, so that, within hours, "a stable government could be installed in strict accordance with the provisions of the existing constitution, . . . provided arrangements to that end are made by me before recognition is withdrawn." This would avoid "even a brief armed intervention." He thought, however, that "two American warships should be in Havana harbor with instructions not to land a man except in the gravest emergency the terms of which should be precisely defined beforehand. . . . The ultimate objective" would be to hold free elections in November 1934.[33]

Neither the president nor the State Department made any recorded reply to the suggestion that recognition be withdrawn. Diplomatic activity intensified as Roosevelt, trying "to be terribly careful not to be in a position of intimating that the Cubans get rid of their President,"[34] suggested a face-saving rationale for Machado's stepping down. The Cuban ambassador thought that Machado "would be freer to make concessions" if Welles were recalled and suggested a liberal loan and commercial treaty to help restore Machado's popularity, preliminary to his retirement, but Roosevelt stood firm.[35] Hull took note of criticism "that the United States is attempting to coerce rather than to persuade," but assured Welles that "both the president and myself appreciate the trying difficulties with which you are faced."[36]

The long-sought abdication took place on August 12, precipitated by the army, when "all of the ranking officers" withdrew support.[37] Cubans have suspected that Welles was behind it, through "a word to the Army commanders," but Welles called it "a spontaneous mutiny."[38] It was immediately preceded by a proposal by Welles to the Cuban secretary of war, Alberto Herrera, a former chief of staff to whom the army was "unanimously devoted," that he should become acting president. The officers were anxious both to forestall intervention and to avoid a mediated settlement, in fear that the armed forces would be drastically reduced.[39] Welles praised Herrera as one who bore no personal responsibility for atrocities, had "refused to permit the Army to be used for political purposes," and was "exceedingly amenable to suggestions."[40] The army leaders decided, however, that his connection with Machado had been too close. With Herrera as a bridge for legality, the presidency passed to Dr. Carlos Céspedes, a "thoroughly impartial" figure who had been born and educated in the United States and had served with the military government. He was Welles's preferred candidate (as he had been in 1921), but Welles denied emphatically that he had anything to do with his selection.[41]

Welles was well aware of both the importance and the difficulty of minimizing his own role. Machado's resignation, he claimed, could not be attributed to "pressure from the United States." Procedure had been strictly "constitutional" (although the necessary documents were approved by three congressmen who met by candlelight, surrounded by three hundred soldiers).[42] He expressed "confidence that the situation has been saved."[43] But avoiding disaster through political improvisation did not represent the stability that was the ultimate goal of United States policy.

While it was not true that the solution had "been worked out solely by the Cubans themselves,"[44] release from a regime that had forfeited public support did provide new opportunity for Cuban control of political life. It remained to be seen whether the political system could gain a legitimacy and effectiveness that would free it from obsessive dependency on the United States and also keep at bay the preemptive potentiality of the armed forces. Welles had found it necessary to take an active part in restoring to power older forces and figures who had no broad or solid constituency. Although he had tried also to reach out to some of the new political movements and to avoid isolation of the army, his presence and role tainted some participants and further radicalized others.[45] Seeking to promote an integrating stability, Welles was caught up in a polarization that represented both the broadening and intensification of Cuban politics and its continued preoccupation with the interests and policies of the United States.

It quickly appeared that the stability of the Céspedes government was threatened on one side by indiscipline in the army, and on the other by what Welles called "the most pernicious element in Cuban public life," the "utterly lawless student groups.'' Moreover, it lacked cohesion among its members.[46] Céspedes included in the cabinet representatives of secret organizations whose program, although ''radical'' included ''salutary'' features—''social reconstruction and honesty in administration with punishment by law of those guilty of malfeasance in office.'' Welles hoped that the ABC group, a clandestine organization opposed to Machado, could keep the students under control, through its ''extraordinary organization.''[47] He did not accept the businessmen's foreboding that the government would give way to a regime installed by ''Communist agitators 'under the pay of Russia.'''[48]

Machado's overthrow brought the military to prominence as a political force. It could no longer be assumed that the United States would hold it in check. The people had seen ''how easy it is for the army to force a change of government.''[49] Yet the army itself lacked discipline. Jubilant fraternization ''juxtaposed military grievances with political discontent.''[50] A rumor was circulating only five days after Machado's overthrow that the students and Communists were ''plotting with the soldiers'' against the officers.[51]

Welles remained hopeful for a few days. One week after the new regime took office, he asked that his mission be terminated. He thought the new government had the confidence of the people and that ''grave political disturbances'' were unlikely. The role into which he had entered was ''bad for Cuba and bad for the United States.'' His ''intimate personal friendship'' with Céspedes and his ''very close relationship'' with the cabinet meant that he was asked to make ''decisions on all matters affecting the Government of Cuba.'' Both the political opposition and ''the sincere opponents of American influence'' were bound to find in this ''a means of political attack.'' His designated successor, Jefferson Caffery, would ''obtain all of the needed influence'' without it being ''apparent to the public.''[52]

WELLES VERSUS THE RADICALS

It proved to be more difficult than Welles had hoped to withstand ''the popular agitation for revolutionary government.'' By August 24 ''a general process of disintegration'' led him in a mood of despair to suggest that elections should be held within about three months on the premise that the constitution of 1928 was illegal, even though ''disturbances'' would ''take place in many parts of the Republic.'' Conditions were ''almost anarchic,'' with ''groups of so-called students and radicals of every shade . . . breaking into houses, promoting lynchings, forcing resignations from Senators and Congressmen and other public officials.'' The political leaders agreed that the existing Congress could not resume its functions. Labor discontent was rife on the large sugar plantations.[53] Roosevelt had already decided that Welles should stay in Cuba until September 15. A new period of crisis kept him there until the middle of December.

Demoralization and indiscipline in the army precipitated a broad movement against the Céspedes government. Noncommissioned officers were upset by proposed pay cuts and by abrogation of a law under which sergeants could become officers. What began as "an insubordination" was soon joined by students and other civilian opponents of the government. The moderate regime in which Welles had placed his hopes was quickly swept aside by an unstable mixture of barracks revolt, social radicalism, nationalism, and opportunist improvisation, in which Fulgencio Batista emerged as the only person who could effectively command support.[54] Batista's first concern seems to have been to protect himself and his fellow mutineers, but he wrote later that he had "kept up his courage" by telling himself:

My steps mark the path of victory for the humble; ... this is the straight road to the restoration of the sovereignty of a people whose independence has been threatened by the imposition of a regime of "mediation" by a foreigner who exercised a right which must be destroyed."[55]

During the early morning of September 5 Welles reported that "a revolutionary government" had been established "composed of the most extreme radicals in Cuba." The army had come "under ultra-radical control," with all officers removed and "a sergeant named Batista" installed as chief.[56]

No concerted attempt to regain command was made by the ousted officers, due in part to hope that if there were no blurring of the radical character of the new regime, the United States would intervene against it. Welles may have contributed to this attitude. One of the officers claimed that, through a military attaché, Welles "prevented" them "from returning to their commands."[57] Welles's judgment on the prospects of the new regime, maintained for four months while it clung to power in the face of nonrecognition and the withholding of economic relief, was expressed only a few hours after its emergence, in the language of the intervention provision of the Platt Amendment:

It appears hardly likely that a so-called revolutionary government composed of enlisted men of the Army and radical students who have occupied themselves almost exclusively during the last 10 days with the assassination of members of the Machado Government can form a government "adequate for the protection of life, property and individual liberty."[58]

Welles's first effort was to rally the traditional leadership that had opposed Machado. In what amounted to "an invitation to organize a new opposition," he suggested that "they determine whether they can devise any plan to prevent the utter break-down of government which in my judgment is inevitable under the present regime."[59] In the case of Machado, he had helped to give effect to an emerging consensus; in this instance, with new forces in play, he took vigorous action at the outset to deny their legitimacy and to concert and energize an opposing alternative. Nor did he limit his efforts to the mobilization of internal forces. He made a strong and urgent plea for the use of military force. The morning after the revolt, he told Hull that there should be a show of naval strength; nearby destroyers "should go on in" to Havana harbor despite the chance that they would be fired on, and a battle cruiser should be sent without delay.[60] Toward evening of the same day, he suggested that troops be landed.

When asked how he would "define our policy that would contemplate what you suggest," Welles replied that it "would simply be on the ground of protection of the American Embassy and the protection of American nationals." But the real purpose would be to support a counterrevolt. Welles reported that political leaders advocated an American landing and did not equate it with intervention. They were said to agree "that the only possibility of avoiding American intervention" was to install "a government composed of all the chiefs of all of the political groups," and that the only way in which such a government could be "maintained in power, until a new Army could be organized" was for marines to maintain order at key points. There was a general belief that in a few days "the present revolutionary group" would be "forced to give way to an out and out Communist organization."[61]

Roosevelt and Hull would not approve a landing, "for the moral effect," of the fifty or so men immediately available, unless the embassy staff were "in physical danger." Welles was to hold off until the battleship *Mississippi* should arrive.[62] On the following day, after conferring with representatives of the four largest Latin American countries, Roosevelt announced that "the United States has absolutely no desire to intervene and is seeking every means to avoid intervention."[63]

Hull told Welles that "the landing of men" should be avoided unless absolutely necessary. It "would in all probability mean intervention," with the prospect that "we will never be able to come out and we will have on our hands the trouble of thirty years ago." Implicitly rejecting Welles's conclusions regarding the new government, Hull urged him to continue his "present and past policy of absolute neutrality towards each group and especially towards the group in power, keeping their confidence and goodwill as you have with each group in the past." It appeared that everything was "revolving around the army now." Hull was doubtful that "any group of leaders representing each faction" would be any more successful than Céspedes had been.[64]

Welles made no objection. He informed the political leaders that a landing would be "undesirable." It "would constitute intervention even though limited in scope and intention and would be considered as intervention by the Cuban people and by the world." He reported to Washington, however, "the sobering effect" of the publicized movements of warships toward Cuba and the unanimity with which Cuban leaders, including "even so radical a group as the ABC," requested that American forces be brought to the scene.[65]

Within a day Welles was again asking for consideration of military support to the opposition. He reported that Horacio Ferrer, recently the secretary of war, had told him that Céspedes and several members of his cabinet, with a group of eighty officers, were planning to take charge of the symbolically important Cabana fortress and to issue a proclamation which Céspedes was confident would precipitate the overthrow of the regime. Ferrer had asked whether the United States would be willing to use its forces to help a restored Céspedes government "in maintaining order." Welles argued that if the "recognized and legitimate" government could "make an effective demonstration of its intention to reestablish itself," it would be in the interest of the United States "to afford them immediate support." He outlined a "limited and restricted form of intervention" which would leave the Cuban regime in "full control of every branch of the Government." "Full intervention" was "to be avoided at all hazards."[66]

Welles acknowledged that even limited intervention would "incur the violent animosity of the extreme radical and communist groups" who would claim that our motives are "mercenary," but "we always have had and always will have the animosity of this group." He thought the Latin American countries would construe such assistance to the Cuban government "as well within the limits of the policy of the 'good neighbor' which we have done our utmost to demonstrate in our relations with the Cuban people during the past 5 months."[67] On the same day, however, the Mexican foreign minister, "in the interest of the solidarity of the American continent," informed the State Department that by its information at least four of the five members of the executive commission of the new Cuban government were not Communists "but persons of undoubted preparation, intellectual capacity and social responsibilities."[68]

Hull took Welles's message to the president, with the advice that he was "overinfluenced by local conditions in Cuba and misjudged the dangerous reaction that would follow throughout Latin America if we agreed to his request."[69] The reply, sent in less than four hours, gave the president's instruction, "after mature consideration," that there must be no departure from "strict neutrality."

We feel very strongly that any promise, implied or otherwise, relating to what the United States will do under any circumstances is impossible; that it would be regarded as a breach of neutrality, as favoring one faction out of many, as attempting to set up a government which would be regarded by the whole world, and especially throughout Latin America, as a creation and creature of the American Government. [Hull appended a word of support that was also an admonition:]. . . All of us appreciate the heavy load you are carrying and hope you may bear up well in order to get the best possible results in these trying circumstances.[70]

In response to this rejection, Welles reiterated his "considered judgment" that the government lacked both popular support and the means to maintain order. If it were not soon overturned by the conservative groups, he predicted, "it will be replaced by a soldier-workman [government] which will last until a concerted revolt of the majority takes place.'' He denied that his proposed action would make it appear that the Cuban government had been installed by the United States: ''We would not be 'favoring one faction out of many,' but lending friendly assistance at its request to a Cuban Government presided over by an impartial President and supported by every element of importance in the Republic.'' The ''prolonged military intervention'' that would become necessary if there should be a ''slide'' into ''complete anarchy,'' would indeed have ''disastrous effects in Latin America.'' At one point he touched the ''trigger of the Platt Amendment'' by suggesting that ''complete anarchy'' existed, as demonstrated by ''cumulative evidence from every province.'' But it was only a touch of the trigger. ''There is, of course,'' he concluded, ''no necessity for decision on this point now.''[71]

Welles's final initiative was to request authority to state that there would be no recognition of ''the revolutionary group at present in power in Havana.'' President Roosevelt, who joined the telephone conversation with Hull, authorized Welles only to say in effect ''that no question of recognition or non-recognition of the group now in power in Cuba had been considered by the American Government up to the present time.''[72] Roosevelt evidently set forth his views with emphasis, for two days later Welles was ''more than ever confident that . . . the only path for the United States to take is that which the President indicated to me on the telephone the other night, namely one of watchful expectancy.''[73]

Except for wavering under the pressure of immediate developments, from this time on Welles not only accepted, but eloquently expounded, the determination to avoid open intervention. On September 18 he found it a ''healthy sign'' that the political leaders realized that it was up to them to find a solution. It would be ''difficult to lift Cuba from the economic and financial prostrations towards which it is rapidly headed.'' A ''social revolution'' was underway, which it might not be possible to check. ''American properties and interests'' were being ''gravely prejudiced.'' Nevertheless:

All of these contingencies seem to me preferable to intervention. By intervention we not only would seriously jeopardize our continental interests but we also would once more give the Cuban people and particularly the Cuban leaders to understand that they did not have to assume the responsibility for their own patriotism or lack of vision, and that the United States Government stands always ready to repair the damage which they themselves cause their own country.[74]

Roosevelt and Hull were in agreement with this view. By warning that a ''watchful'' policy risked collapse and disorder, however, Welles managed subtly to nourish doubt, even while stressing rejection of intervention (and thus helping to overcome his recent apostasy).

On September 9 the five-member commission was replaced by a presidential government under one of the members of the commission, Dr. Grau San Martín, apparently in the belief that this would bring prompt recognition. Welles saw no significant shift; the government was still "solely representative of the student body and of extreme radical elements." But if the new regime could survive, attract popular support, and maintain public order, he thought the United States should consult the Latin American republics with a view toward recognition. Indefinite delay in recognition of a functioning government would make conditions "more thoroughly chaotic and anarchic." But he did not expect "the leaders of the large political parties" to accept a government "under the control of the enlisted men in the Army." In contrast to previous activity, he apparently did nothing to encourage opposition; when Ferrer approached him again, he said it was "absurd to imagine" that the United States would undertake a landing "at the request of 200 deposed Army officers" and "most decidedly refused" to rule out recognition.[75]

But Welles continued to be more militant than his superiors. Reporting that rumors of impending recognition were "causing both consternation and resentment," he suggested that the United States indicate that recognition would only be accorded to a government which

effectively represents the will of a majority of the people of the Republic. . . . is capable of maintaining order and of guaranteeing the protection of "life, property, and individual liberty" and . . . is competent to carry out the functions and obligations which are incumbent upon any stable government.[76]

In response, a statement was issued in the name of the president on September 11 in similar language but with a more positive emphasis; the United States was "prepared to welcome any Government" that would meet those conditions. "This has been the exact attitude of the United States from the beginning."[77] Roosevelt and Hull apparently believed that a hope of recognition might be an effective impetus to reform, while Welles assumed that the government had no chance to succeed unless it were recognized.[78]

Since nonrecognition was not avowedly designed to force a change of government, it could be justified as nonintervention. When the Mexican chargé d'affaires pressed Jefferson Caffery, the assistant secretary of state, to counter anti-American sentiments aroused by Cuban students in other Latin American countries by "some sort of public declaration . . . that you hope that Dr. Grau San Martín's government will be able to establish itself solidly," Caffery replied that such a statement "would be construed to mean that we have decided to support the *de facto* authorities and we would be attacked for it by all of the Cuban political leaders. We cannot commit ourselves that far yet."[79]

Welles portrayed a government "entirely under the domination of the student group" and incapable of maintaining order. He thought the United States could only "await developments." His role was to urge the opposition leaders to employ only "the force of public opinion." He thought he should remain in Cuba because, having the confidence of the political leaders, he might be able "to prevent sporadic and isolated outbreaks which would . . . merely complicate matters still further."[80]

A critical situation developed when the ousted officers, gathered at the hotel where Welles was staying, were surrounded and eventually attacked and defeated by Batista forces. Welles did not leave the hotel at once, lest he give an impression of personal fear and enhance the danger to Americans,[81] but interruption of utility services gave reason for evacuation before the attack took place. By this time several United States naval vessels were nearby. Roosevelt and Hull were careful to state that their purpose was to protect American citizens. Both Hull and Welles saw deterrent value in a ship actually in sight, but they wanted to avoid advantage to one side. During the fighting around the National Hotel, Welles argued against bringing the *Mississippi* into view, as this "would be regarded by the people in the government as . . . moral support to the officers and people opposed to the government." A short time later he suggested that the presence of American destroyers in Cuban ports was giving advantage to the government. Despite his concern over danger to American lives, he could "see no advantage" in a deployment that would "strengthen the position of the present government by assisting in preventing disturbances of public order."[82]

Expecting the government to collapse and convinced of its incapacity, Welles was not prepared to reward its clinging to power by changing his attitude toward recognition. It became increasingly evident that nonrecognition was more than a response to governmental incompetence. Without recognition the Grau regime lacked an essential factor of confidence without which it could not overcome the presumption of inadequacy. This caused a stalemate. "Intervention by inertia," in Grau's words, "intensifies the very ills it claims to pacify."[83]

Welles accepted Hull's conclusion that if the government should gain broader support "the maintenance of order question" as a condition for recognition could be waived, "because no government here will be able to maintain absolute order for some time to come."[84] He tried to relieve the impasse by meeting with the student directorate, with Grau, and finally with Batista, the man who held the key to control of Cuba. Grau insisted that his government was supported by an enormous majority and would gain general acceptance if the United States should grant recognition. Welles objected to the implication that recognition was something that could "be employed by him as a means of obtaining popular support." It would be an injustice to the Cuban people "to exert that power as a means of attempting to keep a minority group in control."[85]

Welles reported that Grau was distrustful of "the sergeants and soldiers" who had come to feel, "quite correctly, that the real control of the country is in their hands." Grau admitted that he had been "gravely mistaken" in believing that they "were so pure in mind and so devoted to the ideals of the students that they had no ulterior ambitions." Batista would not take orders and could not be removed. Grau thought he would try "to gain popular support for the coming elections among the laboring classes."[86] Batista needed the support of a legitimate government in order to give permanence to the forcible replacement of the officer corps.[87]

The older political leaders presented a united front, refusing to support Grau as president because they regarded him as a captive of the radical students. Concerning Batista, Welles found them more sanguine; they thought that once he saw that the government could not gain support and recognition, he could try to oust it, either working with the political parties or by taking power himself, with the student groups "eliminated by the Army." Those in contact with Batista were confident that a direct understanding with him "would avoid the danger of a military dictatorship."[88]

Welles talked with Batista on September 21. He found him "extremely responsible," anxious to reach a solution without "open hostility" from either side, and rigorously opposed to communism. He urged the president to support Batista's efforts by offering assistance to a provisional government. Anticipating the objection that this would favor one faction, he resumed his earlier theme that it would be "provisional and temporary" and would have "the confidence of all."[89] Hull objected that such a statement would enable "designing persons" to "set up the plea that this was an attempt to interfere."[90] Welles countered by describing the unpleasant and even "disastrous" alternatives. He wanted to avoid an impression that "due to fear of public opinion in Latin America" we would "countenance a complete disregard by the Cubans of any international or individual rights we may possess here." Hull's reply was curt; the president "said that thus far he has not felt justified in sending another message."[91]

After the fighting at the National Hotel demonstrated the competence of the new army leadership, Welles had a private talk with Batista. Batista gave assurances regarding treatment of the captured officers and promised to seize and expel "all foreign agitators" on the sugar plantations and to "imprison Cuban Communistic leaders." Welles said that he regarded him as "the only individual in Cuba today who represented authority" and urged him "to insist that an immediate fair and reasonable solution be found." All that stood in the way, Welles suggested, "was the unpatriotic and futile obstinancy of a small group of young men who should be studying at the university instead of playing politics and of a few individuals who had joined with them for selfish reasons."[92]

Welles's attitude went very far to place United States influence behind a claim to power that was based on control of the military, on condition that radicalism would be opposed.[93] Welles explained:

The situation as regards my relations with Batista is, of course, anomalous. I feel it necessary to make plain, however, that there does not exist at the present time in Cuba any authority whatever except himself and that in the event of further disturbances which may endanger the lives and properties of Americans or foreigners in the Republic it seems to be essential that this relationship be maintained.[94]

In a telephone conversation with Welles, after reading this despatch, Hull remarked, ''If that fellow could just use good judgment now and a little bit of self-assertiveness, he might be of great service to his country there.'' Welles replied, ''I think, quite frankly, it is the only hope.''[95] The hope was not without fruition. A decade later Welles referred to Batista as ''that extraordinarily brilliant and able figure.''[96]

When Hull brought this conversation to the attention of the president, Roosevelt threatened to undermine Welles's strategy by questioning the denial of recognition to Grau. Welles immediately pointed out that the success at the hotel should redound only to ''increased prestige for the Army as distinguished from the government.''[97] As Batista's strength grew, Welles saw that of Grau and the students as diminishing. We should ''give the Cuban people a further opportunity to settle their own problems without hindering that end through premature action.'' If, however, a change in government should ''result in popular support and restore confidence,'' he ''would most decidedly recommend immediate recognition without waiting until those customary objectives such as the complete maintenance of public order are attained.''[98] Thus, on the basis of presumed popular support, Welles was prepared to use recognition to help a government which Batista might be instrumental in establishing.

In his next meeting with Batista, Welles was encouraged to find him fully persuaded ''that the present regime was a complete failure and that a concentration government in which the political groups and the commercial interests of the country could have confidence was an absolute necessity.'' He also ''appreciated the fact that recognition by the United States was essential before any improvement in conditions here could be expected.'' Welles was gratified that a State Department release had ''counteracted the daily propaganda'' that the United States was on the verge of recognizing Grau.[99]

Yet the Grau government clung to power and resisted compromise, while Batista, concerned with the possible effects on his control of the army,[100] hesitated to risk a move against it. The impasse led Welles to argue that the time had come to ''decide upon a definite course in accordance with a permanent policy toward Cuba.'' The Céspedes government had fallen, Welles held, despite almost universal support, because of an army mutiny which ''was not political in its origin'' nor ''in any sense responsive to a social movement.'' Only at the last moment had the students, the ''radical professors,'' and ''other extreme radicals'' persuaded the soldiers to support a new government.[101] To ''recognize a government supported by a scant minority and only capable of maintaining itself through the present adherence of a disorganized and undisciplined Army'' would be sacrificing justice to expediency at cost both to our reputation and our interests:

We would incur exactly the same reproach which the Hoover administration incurred for not withdrawing recognition from Machado, namely, that . . . we are forcing upon the Cuban people a dictatorship against the will of the great majority of the people; we would incur the lasting hostility of the organized political parties who will not go to national elections held under this regime as well as of the professional and commercial classes who foresee ruin under this government; we would apparently favor the small anti-American as against the large pro-American groups; . . . there is no possible doubt that one revolutionary attempt after another will be made until the government is overthrown and in the meantime there will be no sugar crop and no permanent economic improvement; . . . we would postpone the time when national elections can be held and a permanent constitutional government be elected with which we can undertake the ratification of new treaty relations and which would itself be fitted to undertake those permanent social and economic reforms which alone can bring about real stability in Cuba.[102]

It was assumed that the "organized political parties" and "the professional and commercial classes" would sponsor needed reforms and that Batista and the army would be more reliable supporters of constitutional government than Machado and his predecessors had been.

Welles thought that the Platt Amendment made the United States responsible for determining whether a government had popular support. "Only because" of the right of intervention, "the United States would have been derelict in its obligations to the Cuban people themselves had it given official support to a de facto regime which, in its considered judgment, was not approved by the great majority of the Cuban people." After its abrogation, recognition should be "automatically accorded to any government as it comes to power."[103]

Welles and his successor, Caffery, were more concerned with the sources than with the volume of support for the Grau government. Caffery discounted "ignorant masses" which "in numbers . . . reach a very high figure," who were "misled by utopian promises."[104] But it would be a mistake to dismiss Welles's policy as a cynical attempt to promote minority rule in the name of freedom; it was not devoid of the naive idealism that equated free elections with desirable outcomes.

Welles was still mired in Cuba when the Inter-American Conference convened at Montevideo. He judged his "personal contacts and relationships" to be of such value that he could not leave while the situation was "precarious."[105] In mid-November, at his own request, Welles conferred with the president at Warm Springs, Georgia, to counter, once again, any inclination to accept the government. Roosevelt issued a statement, based on a draft by Welles which was only slightly softened by the State Department.[106] It amounted to a manifesto against the Grau regime. Premature recognition might obstruct "the free and untrammeled determination by the Cuban people of their own destinies." The United States could not play "the part of a good neighbor" until a provisional government with "popular support . . . shows evidence of genuine stability."[107]

Briefly back in Cuba, Welles plunged again into talks with those who held the frayed and twisted reins of power. He tried to link his proposals to a plan by Batista and the army for Grau to give way to Mendieta, but he found Grau evasive and concluded that he was immobilized between those "seeking to create a frankly communistic government" and those "solely in the government for the profits they can obtain.'' He thought that some of Grau's advisers were trying to delay until a coup might succeed in placing ''the extreme Left'' in power.[108] It seemed when Welles was about to leave that an agreement was in the making, but he had to depart in the face of an ''unexpected and complete collapse of negotiations'' on December 11, 1933.[109]

BATISTA

During the interval before the arrival of Caffery, the chargé d'affaires reported a meeting with Batista and three student leaders. The students wanted ''not only a change of leaders but a change of system,'' but they denied ''any sympathy for or tendency toward 'communism.' '' Both Batista and the students regarded the opposition leaders as ''front page photograph'' figures whose influence would rapidly diminish once the regime gained recognition.[110]

Like Welles, Caffery was convinced of the government's ''inefficiency, ineptitude and unpopularity with all the better classes'' and saw a threat to ''our manifold interests'' in its increasing reliance on ''radical and communistic elements.'' He was less optimistic regarding the chance for a consensus regime. He thought the government could be forced out only by armed intervention unless the army should turn against it. He deplored the opposition's reliance upon intervention and their refusal to believe that it would not take place.[111]

Caffery was better able than the more aloof Welles to gain the confidence of Batista.[112] It was not long, however, until Batista, apparently having concluded that his status and power would be more secure under a government that would not suffer the fatal handicap of nonrecognition,[113] decided to throw his support to Mendieta. When he asked what should be done for recognition, Caffery replied that he would ''lay down no specific terms; the matter of your government is a Cuban one and it is for you to decide what to do about it.''[114]

Just one day after a gloomy report that the opposition could not agree on a program, Caffery asked for authorization ''to recognize Mendieta in the Presidency.'' If this were not done, he warned, Batista would ''probably turn . . . to the left with definite disaster for all our interests here (or declare himself military dictator).''[115]

Coincident with the events in Cuba, which made it expedient to recognize a new government, the United States found reason in the noninterventionist emphasis of the Montevideo Conference to abandon nonrecognition.[116] Having withheld recognition from a functioning government on the ground that it did not represent the will of the people, the United States would now extend it to another government which had not yet been established and had not gained general support. All this would be done in response to the decision of a military leader and in fear of the consequences of not coming immediately to his support. Thus the prolonged attempt to promote freedom of choice and responsiveness to popular will in Cuba would end in an accommodative endorsement of traditional practices, compounded by acceptance of a new source of tyranny.

President Roosevelt was hesitant to toss aside the standards for recognition that Welles had rigorously insisted upon. He considered it "of course impossible to pledge recognition to any individual or group before certain conditions are an accomplished fact." Caffery responded rather wanly that "of course" this was "understood"; he had "made the suggestion regarding Mendieta in view of his well-known vacillating tendency and reluctance to assume responsibility."[117]

In the absence of "definite previous assurance from us which we cannot give," Caffery did not "recommend" to Batista that he "go ahead with Mendieta."[118] Instead, Batista deferred to opposition from the navy and the left and supported Carlos Hevia, who was secretary of agriculture in Grau's government. Grau turned over his office to Hevia on January 15, 1934, but Hevia had such opposition from both left and right that within two days Caffery was reporting that Batista had "decided to declare Mendieta president this afternoon." The move was delayed briefly while the navy was mollified and Mendieta persuaded, but on January 18, Mendieta was declared provisional president by "representatives of all the political groups."[119] Recognition came five days later. Welles, looking back, adjudged that the ascendancy of Mendieta "was unquestionably welcomed by an overwhelming majority of the people," but this was far from clear.[120]

The time had then come to relieve Cuban-American relations of the Platt Amendment. The text having been settled with "very little disagreement," an agreement was signed on May 29 and came into effect on June 9, abrogating any treaty basis for intervention.[121] At Caffery's insistence, and with Mendieta's consent, American warships were kept at Havana until September 1.[122]

Part IV
CONSEQUENCES AND RETURN ENGAGEMENTS

INTRODUCTION

The political history of the Caribbean countries in which the United States tried through its presence to promote free, competent, and stable government has subsequently been characterized by rapacious dictatorship, broken only by periods of more gentle corruption, and leading, in the case of Cuba, to an imposition of virtue as defined and demanded by a revolutionary totalitarianism that opened the land and people to weapons and influence from the Soviet Union.

The United States was not without responsibility for these outcomes, nor has it escaped their effects. Its acceptance of ruthless regimes that were residues of its historical presence, and that found refuge in the doctrine of nonintervention through which it tried to limit its responsibility while serving its convenience, was neither to its credit nor to its lasting advantage. Superficial judgment may plausibly hold that these outcomes exposed the reality of American purpose, but a more accurate conclusion sees them as signs of failure. Results were shaped by the interplay of choice and chance in politics rather than by American direction. Failure was the inevitable result of the inability of the United States to refrain from attempting the unattainable. Perverse consequences were accepted (although not with the reluctance and remorse which were merited) for want of an absolving alternative.

Issues of Caribbean intervention were seen in an altered setting after the coming to power of Fidel Castro in Cuba. The Cold War gave new plausibility to a security threat. Formalization of an Organization of American States had left the core commitment to nonintervention intact, but had left some room for common action to uphold security and to limit threats that might grow out of dictatorship.

While Batista had fought an increasingly desperate battle to stay in power, much as Machado had done a generation earlier, Cubans looked to the attitude of the United States for cues and prophecies. The State Department, rejecting the advice of those who thought that Castro was a menace, tried to avoid involvement by following rather than atttempting to deflect or direct the shift of power, but it could not be completely neutral. Maintaining normal relations with Batista signalized support, but cutting off arms aid, at a time when his strength was in rapid decline, helped his opponents. When a last-minute attempt was made to find an alternative to Castro, the State Department refused to make the commitment that would have been needed were such an attempt to have any chance of success. Recognition was quickly extended when Castro came to power.

In exaggerated and ironic fashion, Castro's accession and survival represented the achievement of an American objective in Cuba. A Cuban government at long last showed in the only conclusive way possible that it was not dependent on support from the United States—by openly defying this country. It did so, moreover, in the manner most calculated to arouse and to justify militant responses—by seeking and flaunting the aid of the Cold War antagonist.

The apparent dependence of Cuba upon the Soviet Union set up a security compulsion which was radically different from the assumptions that had permitted the emergence of a noninterventionist Caribbean policy. It also opened the door to counteraction by suggesting that intervention could be liberating. The Bay of Pigs attempt at sponsored invasion tested the notion that Castro's government was lacking in solid indigenous support. Perhaps fortunately, the plan was so bungled that Castro had great advantage. President Kennedy was strong and effective enough in his leadership to accept and absorb defeat. A prolonged struggle might have cost greater agony and led to deeper involvement by the United States without bringing about the demise of Castro, which would have been essential for success. Both on this occasion and in the missile crisis of the following year, the United States stopped short of direct confrontation with Cuba and avoided the incalculable consequences of engaging itself in a rupture and reconstitution of Cuban politics—although, according to later revelations, high levels of American authority attempted to have Castro removed by assassination.

In Haiti and the Dominican Republic excesses of personal rule opened prospects of growing radicalism and eventual chaos in which forces similar to or controlled by the revolutionary government of Cuba might gain power. Neither President Kennedy nor President Johnson was willing to risk the extension of Castro's influence. They were prepared to organize intervention under the aegis of the OAS or, if necessary, to undertake it unilaterally.

In Haiti the United States anticipated the collapse of Duvalier and seems to have been ready to intervene with force if chaos had followed, but "Papa Doc," having shrewdly interwoven his power with the fears and beliefs of the people, proved to be more resilient than expected.

With regard to the Dominican Republic, the United States, wanting to find a basis to organize inter-American opposition to Castro and hopeful of organizing a peaceful transition from the dictatorship of Trujillo, accepted an interventionary role through multilateral sanctions. After the dictator's assassination the United States mounted an open show of force to prevent a return to power by his family. It took a very active part in sustaining the provisional government and pressuring for a free election. Although relations with the elected government of Juan Bosch were impeded by Bosch's pride and suspicion and by some foot-dragging on the part of Americans who thought Bosch too radical, the overthrow of Bosch in September 1963 was a sharp setback for American hopes.

The outbreak of revolutionary violence in April 1965 put the future at hazard. President Johnson committed American forces to insure against a Communist seizure of power. This was only slightly different from the repudiated patterns of earlier years. The action was probably unnecessary and was initiated with devious concealment of its real purpose and in violation of established law and policy, but the intervention which it entailed was undertaken for defensive reasons, without a plan for lasting control or an illusion of permanent transformation. The United States maintained the assumption, although not always the scrupulous practice, of impartiality, while working (with token assistance from the Organization of American States) to discharge the task of reconstituting a Dominican government, which its intrusion had made necessary.

This breach of nonintervention brought no fundamental change in American attitudes. Belief that the United States could by forcible occupation eliminate the causes of instability and abuse in Caribbean countries had been superseded by the conviction that rigid adherence to nonintervention was consistent with the imperatives of American values and security. In cases of a Trujillo and a Duvalier, this doctrine was relaxed to permit action through which widespread disorder and uncertainty might be avoided, with the OAS serving to establish partial legitimacy. The Dominican Republic episode of 1965 showed that if a security threat or domestic political pressures became too strong, unilateral intervention was still possible, while also giving the United States a sharp reminder of the difficulty and frustration which it entailed. The constraints upon a great power limit both its ability to engage itself effectively in, and to remain completely aloof from, the politics of nearby states that are in political disorder.

13.
NICARAGUA

SOMOZA

In Nicaragua the emergence of the head of the guard, Anastasio Somoza, as a powerful and ambitious political figure subjected the State Department to the charge that nonintervention was simply a pretext for the acceptance of strongman rule.[1] The presumption that the United States was ultimately responsible for political outcomes in Nicaragua was so prevalent that the most explicit denials of interventionist intent were taken as proof that the United States desired the stronger force to prevail. Yet the State Department was far from pleased. The nonintervention policy of the U.S. held in check a strong impulse to resist Somoza's ascendancy.

President Sacasa confronted on the one hand a "tactless attitude" approaching insubordination on the part of Somoza and on the other a "threatening tone" and "lack of respect" from Sandino "which had resulted in the creation of a state within a state." On top of this, he faced the "open antagonism" of two former presidents, Generals Chamorro and Moncada. Sacasa told Minister Arthur Bliss Lane that he found the guard more menacing than Sandino. Strong feelings against Sandino prevailed within the guard, and there was an indiscipline which enabled Somoza to evade personal responsibility. Lane was told that members of the guard were "anxious to create a pretext in order to attack" the Sandino forces. Sandino came to Managua for talks with Sacasa but refused to give up his arms to the "unconstitutional" guard. On February 21, 1934, he was killed by a guard detachment.[2]

Although Somoza claimed at first, perhaps correctly, that the feeling against Sandino was so strong that "he could not prevent" the killing, it was not long before he admitted that the order had been his own.[3] Belief that the American minister had conspired in the deed became widespread and was given credence, ironically, by the efforts which he had made to avoid it. Lane had talked with Somoza frequently—twice on the day of the killing—trying to "persuade him not to do anything rash. . . . On four separate occasions," he reported, Somoza had promised that he "would take no action against Sandino without my consent." (The apparent implication that such consent might be forthcoming was doubtless a consequence of "not entirely fortunate phraseology.")[4]

Somoza was well aware of the advantage of it being believed that he had United States support. He is said to have told his officers that the American government wanted "the elimination of Sandino."[5] Several months later, when accepting responsibility for the killing, he openly claimed the backing of the minister.[6] He realized that it would be difficult for the United States to oppose him openly without entering again onto the interventionist path. He may have foreseen that the State Department would accept, and possibly even come tacitly to welcome, a dictatorship that would prevent political turbulence and thus remove inducements to intervention. He was content to move slowly and willing to affirm loyalty to Sacasa in order to avoid an open clash.

Lane wanted the State Department to combat any belief that the United States favored the guard by reaffirming "our policy of nonrecognition of non-constitutional governments." This policy was no longer firm, however. It was considered to be incompatible with strict nonintervention and had been abandoned for most of Latin America. The treaty of 1923 had kept it in place for Central America, pending the outcome of a scheduled conference. While the department permitted Lane to let Somoza know that the policy still prevailed, it balked at a public statement. If Somoza understood the American attitude, the department felt, its deterrent effect would not be lost.[7] But he may have understood it too well.

After Somoza publicly claimed support, the department did authorize the minister to deny "in the most categorical manner . . . rumors" that the U.S. was attempting "to influence political developments."[8] Lane could not, however, consistent with nonintervention, set forth in explicit terms the essential elements of United States policy: "that we do not support the political activities of the Guardia, that we do not regard the Guardia as a super-Government, and that the constitutionally constituted Government of Nicaragua is the normal channel through which we conduct our relations."[9]

The difficulty of defining an impartial stance was further demonstrated when the Nicaraguan foreign minister took the State Department's reticence regarding reorganization of the guard "as an approval of any action which the Government may take." Lane insisted that "silence should not be interpreted either as approval or disapproval." It meant "that the question . . . is one for Nicaragua to decide." He felt, however, that "Hands Off" should not be the only policy of a "Good Neighbor." If "a word from us" might help to maintain peace, our diplomatic representative should at least express his "personal views." He was doing all he could "to calm those persons whose ambitions and passions may lead them to commit acts which might have a disastrous effect on the well being of the country." Sumner Welles expressed the approval of the State Department.[10]

Unmistakable signs that Somoza was "determined to be the next President," in spite of his apparent ineligibility, increased the pressure for an American commitment. The foreign minister, who was himself ambitious for the presidency, asked Lane what the attitude of the United States would be should the next president "come into office illegally," while Somoza's wife sought "some good advice" in connection with her husband's future. Lane found it "disheartening, after all the efforts . . . to establish our intention of not interfering in Nicaraguan affairs . . . to learn that the general feeling among Nicaraguans is that Doctor Sacasa's successor . . . will be chosen by the United States." Anything he might say would be construed as either favoring or opposing Somoza's candidacy.[11] He could only suggest that recognition would be a question for later determination and urge Somoza not to resort to violence.[12] Welles commended his discretion and effectiveness. He had "aided materially in preventing the development of a situation of great danger to Nicaragua, which might likewise prejudice American interests."[13]

But all that Somoza needed to do in order to be regarded as the favorite of the United States was to avoid open censure. As Lane reported, the public did not forget that the guard which he commanded "was virtually created by the United States Government."[14] Political neutrality precluded the emphatic repudiation that would have been needed to overcome the presumption of American support.

When Somoza's brother-in-law and "political mentor" asked Lane whether it was true that he was working to separate Somoza from the guard, Lane replied that he "would not be a party" to such a proposal. To counter an apparent "feeling of relief," Lane added that nobody should "think that because of not using my influence against Somoza, I am favoring his political campaign." The reply, that it was well understood that the minister "could not be in favor of or against any candidate," conveyed a mood of complacency.[15]

During this time the State Department showed that it would accept an illegal government in Guatemala, where the dictator, Ubico, intended to remain in office. Hanna, the minister, who had previously been in Nicaragua, was rebuked for saying, after being instructed "to correct an impression" that the United States sympathized with Ubico's plan, that "he did not sympathize with it." He was tersely told that "this Government has no attitude, either of sympathy or lack of sympathy," toward such a movement.

Somoza made no serious attempt to conceal his purpose. He told Lane that he needed to place the guard "in control of important municipalities so that his interests in the 1936 elections would be protected," and when Lane blandly suggested that the role of the guard would be to insure fairness, he "laughingly replied that the guardia would do what he commanded." Somoza backed off from claiming State Department support when Lane threatened to issue "a statement which would react against him," but he told Lane "that he had determined to be the next President and that there was nobody in Nicaragua who could prevent it."[17]

Somoza's opponents were in a doubly weak position. Hoping to avoid violence, Lane advised Sacasa to seek accommodation. When asked about the attitude of the United States if Somoza "would not yield," Lane replied that "intervention is a thing of the past" and resort to force "would be tantamount to suicide of President and family and ruin of Nicaragua." The positions were epitomized in a colloquy which Lane summarized. The first speaker is a "person very close to the President."

Informant: In other words we are to do nothing. We are to allow the present fine situation (sarcastically) to continue. Somoza will be President and then the United States will be satisfied.

Myself: You misunderstand my Government's position. We are merely trying as a friend to prevent civil war and a Central American conflagration. We have no desire to intervene in Nicaraguan affairs. Nicaragua is perfectly free to take such administrative action as she wishes. Our hope, however, is that no action will be taken which will start bloodshed.[18]

When President Sacasa's brother asked for "advice," he was told that anything that an "official of the American Government might say would be capable of interpretation as intervention." To the suggestion that "silence at this time might also be interpreted as a kind of intervention, that is, an acquiescence in whatever might be done," the State Department spokesman replied that "it could only be thus interpreted by people in Nicaragua if their leaders tried to give it that interpretation, and that there was no justification for their doing so."[19] Two weeks later a request for "friendly moral assistance," brought no further response from Sumner Welles.[20]

If there was "less than a full meeting of minds" between the State Department and the legation, the difference was tactical.[21] The department's unwillingness to give advice had to do with the long-range and quintessentially political issue of control of the presidency. Lane's intention, unless otherwise instructed, to "endeavor personally to prevent any ill-advised action tending to disturb the peace of the country" had to do with moves aimed at avoiding disorder. The department did not disagree; it authorized Lane "to make appropriate expression" of its earnest hope "that nothing will occur to disturb the peace of Nicaragua."[22] The department never claimed to be neutral about order and disorder, to the ultimate advantage of Somoza, who controlled the only reliable instrument for maintaining order.

By the time that Somoza actually moved to take over the government the State Department had issued strict instructions to refrain from giving "informal advice" unless under specific direction.[23] This resulted from an unsuccessful attempt by the minister to El Salvador, Frank P. Corrigan, a medical doctor recently recruited to diplomacy, to persuade the department to counteract the "cynical attitude" that "nonintervention . . . gives dictatorship a free hand." Corrigan did his best to confront the department with a dilemma:

The powerful influence of our Missions . . . leads political elements in these countries, and the opposition as well, to expect either opposition or cooperation. . . . Failure of a Mission to use its influence constructively may become a sin of omission fully as grievous as the former sins of commission. . . . Liberal elements, some of whom have been formerly active critics of the United States and bitter opponents of intervention have indicated to me that the cooperation (by diplomatic means) of the United States is more than welcome when it seeks to retain progress, and prevent bloodshed and the establishment of autocratic regimes and actual setting up of dictatorships such as the Machado regime in Cuba and the Gómez dictatorship in Venezuela.[24]

Sumner Welles transmitted Corrigan's dispatch with the sympathetic comment that he (Welles) had "for some time, been unhappy because of my realization" of this situation. He suggested as an improved policy that while "governmental interference as such" would be improper, a minister might be permitted to exert "personal influence," if done "tactfully, quietly, and without publicity," on "matters in which the Central American Republics and ourselves, as well as, in a broad sense, all of the American Republics, have a legitimate interest."[25]

A memorandum prepared in the State Department suggested that "any general instruction" in this vein would be going too far. The response to Corrigan's initiative was, as Welles put it, "entirely negative." He wanted to avoid an "impression that this government is assuming a sterile police of aloofness." But with regard to the "serious political controversy" in Nicaragua he considered it particularly "undesirable to permit" the new minister "to get embroiled." Although the wording of the instruction included the phrase "constructive and effective friendship," it identified the "Good Neighbor policy" with abstention "from matters which are not directly of concern to us."[26] Thus what had begun as an attempt to mitigate any implicit encouragement to tyranny ended by affirming an attitude that would in practice reward a man who could seize and hold power through force.

It was decided at this time also that the United States would cease to adhere to the nonrecognition provision of the Treaty of 1923. (The policy of withholding recognition from governments which came to power by force had long since been abandoned with regard to the rest of Latin America.)[27] El Salvador and Costa Rica had denounced the treaty in 1932, and the United States had already shown that it would not adhere to it in regard to a state that was not formally a party, by extending recognition to the government of Martínez in El Salvador. This suggested that a dictator could qualify for recognition simply by denouncing the treaty. When Guatemala extended the term of its president, Honduras and Nicaragua recognized the action without protest and were followed by the United States, "in flagrant violation of the spirit of the 1923 Treaty." President Carías in Honduras was also planning to extend his term. For the United States to invoke the treaty "as a reason for denying recognition to any regime in Central America," under these conditions, the memorandum concluded, "would be arbitrary and capricious and would constitute 'meddling' of a flagrant kind."[28]

Somoza's move for power did not await the election of 1936. It became imminent when rioting broke out in Managua in February of that year. Sacasa was convinced that Somoza had instigated the trouble. Lane pointed out that "the trend of events" favored Somoza; he controlled the only force that could quell a riot and "certain elements of the mob" were asking him to "take over the Government at once." As dean of the diplomatic corps, Lane asked that order be maintained and was told that Somoza would not move against the government nor permit further mob influence.[29]

Lane was replaced early in 1936 by Boaz Long, whose experience with Central America had begun during the Wilson administration. The State Department was concerned to limit his participation in political discussions. After he reported a conference with Sacasa and Somoza, he was told that his presence at such meetings "might result in efforts to involve this Government in responsibilities arising out of decisions reached." Long replied with some petulance that he was "familiar with the Department's instructions" and would "be guided by the policy laid down."[30]

In May the Nicaraguan government approached the secretary of state directly. Asked whether he could say anything that might help "in avoiding a revolutionary outbreak or an uprising accompanied by force in connection with the coming election," Hull replied that he could not say "a single word" about " the domestic affairs of Nicaragua." The State Department also turned aside a suggestion by El Salvador to "lend Sacasa some aid," premised on "the view that sane Nicaraguan public opinion is with the Sacasa administration whereas the extremists and radicals are with Somoza." Welles did suggest "the possibility of rendering some assistance" under stringent conditions: "if the situation should become so critical as to threaten life and property, and if requested by all contending factions, . . . but only in company with a group of nations, and . . . even under these circumstances," the United States "would not take the initiative."[31]

An uprising on May 27 in Bluefields began the long-expected outbreak which would bring Somoza to power. In a memorandum to the United States, Mexico, and the other Central American countries, Sacasa pleaded for "a joint act of friendly cooperation": Somoza was working to establish "a military government or one subject to the pressure of militarism, in contempt of legitimate authority which the National Guard swore to defend. At any moment blood will probably be shed, anarchy will reign in the country and latent communism, favored by these events, will find a favorable field in which to develop."[32] The State Department refused to join the representatives of Great Britain, France, Mexico, El Salvador, and Honduras in an appeal to Somoza. Hull expressed disappointment "to see such a seriously threatened collapse of their political or governmental structure," but "knew of nothing more that could be said at the present time."[33] The State Department took the opportunity to chide governments, notably Chile and Peru, which had objected to Sacasa's approach to the United States, stating that they should have had more confidence in its noninterventionist resolve.[34]

Within a few days the president and vice president left Nicaragua. Somoza was clearly in charge. He told Long that he would "require our moral backing" and asked him to "intimate" whether to hold a constitutional convention to appoint a president or to schedule an election.[35] Both Long and the State Department replied that no opinion could be expressed. Recognition of the provisional government was extended routinely, by acknowledging a communication from the foreign minister.[36]

Several months later Welles received the deposed president. Sacasa described the situation as "very serious, holding no promise for law, order or public morality" and suggested fruitlessly that in establishing the guard the United States had assumed "a continuing responsibility for Nicaragua's welfare."[37] Some time later Sacasa and his former antagonists and fellow exiles, Díaz and Chamorro, joined without success in a plea for "the disinterested moral cooperation of the American Government in favor of the Nicaraguan people." They did not specify what this should entail.[38]

Somoza was elected president in December 1936, receiving over 98 percent of the votes. The minister suggested that a telegram of congratulation would promote "friendship toward us," but the State Department declined on the ground that it was "not customary" practice.[39] It also turned aside Somoza's attempt to claim a special relationship through "a defensive alliance" that would help him to oppose "pernicious doctrines" and to "annihilate drastically the germs of communism which are appearing."[40]

But while Somoza did not immediately gain the status of a favored and protected client, his power was secure as long as he could control the guard. A basic change had taken place in Nicaraguan politics. "Efficient and tenacious *caudillismo* based on Nicaragua's first modern, unified armed force had replaced inefficient *caudillismo* based on a divided armed force reflecting the anarchic two-party division of the old days."[41] The United States would not oppose Somoza if it might produce turmoil and entanglement. Any U.S. responsibility was expediently evaded by invoking nonintervention and recalling the failure of efforts to establish peaceful political competition. By 1939 Roosevelt was prepared to welcome Somoza with a parade. In 1947, when the State Department, influenced by Spruille Braden, tried briefly to promote democracy through the inter-American system, Somoza's removal of a newly elected president brought nonrecognition by the U.S. and the suggestion that he leave the country,[42] but the gesture was ineffective and was soon abandoned. Anastasio Somoza García was assassinated in 1956, but a durable dynasty had been created. Nicaragua presented itself as a staunch ally of the United States in contrast to the Cuba of Fidel Castro. In 1960 United States warships guarded Nicaragua against Cuban intervention. In 1965 Nicaragua joined the intervention that the United States initiated in the Dominican Republic. At least two ambassadors, Thomas E. Whelan (1951–1961) and Turner B. Shelton (1970–1975), were notorious as cronies of the Somozas. By 1975 more officers and enlisted men from Nicaragua than from any other country of Latin America had been trained by the United States.

Not until Somozan domination had lasted nearly forty-five years did a challenge arise which undermined and finally toppled the dynasty.[43] The political heirs of Sandino provided the daring and determination that enabled an opposite movement to gain broad participation. The incumbent Somoza, another Anastasio, was compelled to rely on the National Guard and on what remained to him of the actual and presumed support of the United States. Based on a premise that they were receiving outside aid from Cuba, the *sandinistas* were opposed by the United States. Increased military aid to Somoza contributed to a ruthless campaign of repression. In 1977 this aid was cut back, reflecting the Carter administration's concern for human rights and giving hope to moderates, but when fighting was stepped up, aid was expanded and repression became more devastating. In early 1978 the assassination of a highly respected editor, Pedro Joaquín Chamorro, galvanized such a broad national response that Cuba could no longer plausibly be scapegoated. Somozan rule was massively repudiated.

United States policy, inhibited by caution, by bureaucratic conflict, and by the influence of Somoza supporters in Congress, resisted this conclusion.[44] It tried to isolate the *sandinistas* by promoting concessions by Somoza to the moderates. This gave him hope that he could play for time and weakened the moderate component in the movement to overthrow him. When mediation failed, nonintervention provided a rationale for the United States to stop short of effective sanctions. But while the United States shunned the risk and responsibility of pressuring Somoza out of power, a *sandinista* offensive reached the edge of victory in June 1979. The United States failed utterly in last-ditch attempts to intervene through the Organization of American States and then, through renewed mediation, to arrange for maintaining the National Guard without Somoza. It was too late also to gain meaningful assurances from a provisional government that might limit *sandinista* ascendancy in a regime which came to power through military victory.

When Anastasio Somoza Debayle went into exile on July 17, 1979, Nicaragua was purged, as Cuba had been, of the lingering presumption that the United States bore ultimate responsibility for what its government might achieve or fail to achieve, and for what it might inflict on its people. The costs of drastic separation were offset in no small measure by the potential advantage of this release, both for the United States and for Nicaragua. There was reason to hope that the transition to a new relationship would be quicker and smoother than has been the case with Cuba.

14.
HAITI

The United States did not again become involved in the un-
steady progression of Haitian politics, although collapse of
governmental authority might have led to intervention either
by the OAS or by the United States. On one occasion American intervention
became an imminent probability, even before the Dominican landing of 1965.

Stenio Vincent gained a second term as president by overriding the constitution through resort to a plebiscite, but in 1941 he did not have the strength for a
repeat performance. Influenced by money from Trujillo, the Dominican dictator,
the assembly chose another member of the elite, Elie Lescot. Lescot collaborated
closely with the United States during the war and extended his term in 1944, but
was deposed by the guard in 1946, after Trujillo revealed his subventions. This
marked the first open political action by the American-created military force.
Military backing enabled Dumarsais Estimé to become president, the first non-
mulatto (although he had become one of the elite) to gain that office since the
occupation in 1915. There had begun to emerge a new awareness and appreciation of the African and rural components of Haitian culture and society and a
new assertiveness on the part of groups which had been passive and powerless.[1]
When the assembly refused to reelect him in 1950, Estimé stirred up riots, which
led the military force (called the army after 1949) again to assert itself. This
time, the commander, Paul Magloire, took the presidency, ostensibly through
popular election. Although Magloire was also black, expectations of social reform were not fulfilled. A presidency that began in a rare spirit of freedom and
determination ended in disillusionment and another coup by the army.[2]

After several months of disorder under interim presidents, the army arranged
an election in which it backed François Duvalier, a medical doctor and an
amateur ethnologist, who saw himself as the leader of black resurgence in the
tradition both of Estimé and of the victim of 1915, Guillaume Sam. Although the
ambassador was believed to prefer his opponent, Duvalier's election was not
displeasing to the State Department, which saw him as a moderate reformer
rather than the ruthless despot which he soon became.[3]

If, as is supposed, the army thought that it could control Duvalier, the result
was just the opposite. He built his own base of power. He astutely invited a
United States Marine mission to help train the army while he was destroying its

independence and effectiveness.[4] As the head of the military mission related, he "set out to wreck" the army and succeeded in rendering it "unfit for any purpose military or civil." "Ultimately, almost every American-trained man . . . was exiled or murdered."[5] Duvalier created his own uniformed security police, the *tonton macoutes* (amounting to "bogeyman" in Creole).[6] The *macoutes,* not without morale, discipline, and intelligence, was used without scruple to preserve the Duvalier regime in the name of "a kind of nationalist-negritude mystique."[7]

Duvalier incurred the disapproval of the United States, but managed to avoid overthrow, thanks in part to fear that, if pressed too hard, he might make a deal with Castro.[8] In 1962 the United States so badly needed the vote of Haiti against Cuba at the Punte del Este conference that it agreed to restore some of the economic aid that it had suspended in September 1961.[9] By the end of the year, however, economic aid was again almost eliminated.

Duvalier survived a time of crisis in 1963, when his term of office came to a close. War almost erupted with the Dominican Republic over a police invasion of the Dominican embassy. The United States helped to restrain President Bosch, but marines, ready for a landing, remained for three weeks just outside Haitian waters. Duvalier astutely made it appear that he was preparing to resign, thus leading the United States to hold back and tempting his opponents to expose themselves.[10] The ambassador was ready to join with some of his Latin American colleagues in setting up a temporary governing council and opposing any attempt by Duvalier's supporters to cling to power. American forces were to be landed if requested, for the avowed purpose of protecting the lives of Americans and others.[11] Jerome Slater concluded, on the basis of extensive interviewing, that the potential threat of communism in Haiti was "thought serious enough" in Washington to warrant "a collective effort to force at least a moderation of Duvalier's repression of the Haitian people and, optimally, get rid of Duvalier altogether."[12] However, an OAS committee investigating the complaint of the Dominican Republic did not produce the clear findings against Haiti that might have formed the basis for concerted action.[13] The United States is reported to have rejected a plan for invasion by exiles, but it may have been prepared to give support to an anti-Duvalier regime if one should have established itself on Haitian territory.[14]

The success of the resilient dictator in keeping power was contrary to the clear expectation and desire of the United States. In a largely subsistence economy, external pressure counted for little. Duvalier eliminated every cohesive group that might conspire against him. When the United States in effect acknowledged its impotence by resuming a "correct" relationship in 1964, it was at a cost to American prestige.[15] In that year Duvalier proclaimed himself president for life.

Despite continuing belief that intervention would be necessary when Duvalier should fall or die, nothing was accomplished, even after the Dominican intervention of 1965, to prepare for an exercise of responsibility by the OAS.[16] Nor was it clear how the United States would define the occasion for, or the objectives of, unilateral action, although there was little doubt that it would, if necessary, step in to prevent or rectify extreme chaos or subordination to Castro. Excesses of domestic tyranny did not provoke U.S. intervention, however, and Duvalier's political survival from 1963 until his death in 1971 demonstrated that the United States lacked the will or the folly to unseat him and to undertake once again to control and reform the political life of Haiti.

15.

CUBA

The government of Mendieta, "fighting for its life against the communistic elements," as Ambassador Caffery put it, was able to survive with the support of the army and by suspending constitutional guarantees. Although Cuba emerged from this period of imminent political and social revolution with the essential features of its government and society still intact, their foundations were gravely weakened. The price of their survival was also a source of continued jeopardy—the influence, as never before in Cuban history, of a military strong man. Caffery noted that "no Government, this or any other, could last a day, if opposed by Batista."[1] In June he reported that many Cubans of "so-called 'higher social classes,'" who had previously denounced Batista were openly saying that he should declare himself military dictator. "Of course," he had told them, "that is out of the question and impossible." But Caffery valued the army's role in suppressing strikes, as "the real force standing between a reasonable respect for property rights and chaos."[2]

The ambassador was reluctant to give up a tutelary role, but it was not "expedient" to see the president every day nor "to advise him on all matters political (for many obvious reasons)."[3] He was able to recall to Welles at a later time, however, that "on numberless occasions" he had "persuaded the military authorities to take steps and attitudes they did not want to take, and . . . not to take steps and attitudes which they desired to take," as well as having been "influential in patching up disagreements" between the president and Batista.[4]

Mendieta was bolstered by a reciprocal trade agreement with the United States in August 1934 and by an increased quota for Cuban sugar, but his political strength remained limited. Caffery referred to "the importance of his having a Cabinet that meets with some support among the public, a condition which his present Cabinet, of course, does not meet."[5]

The State Department used forthcoming elections as an occasion to explain its attitude under the new relationship. Referring to reports of favoritism, the department stated:

The consummation of the present Treaty of Relations has made it emphatically clear that this Government will not interfere directly or indirectly in the political concerns of the

Cuban people. It consequently neither favors nor opposes the participation in Cuba's national elections of any particular party or group. It does hope sincerely, however, because of the peculiarly close relationship existing between our two peoples that when national elections are held the result thereof may represent the effective will of the Cuban people, freely expressed.[6]

At the request of President Mendieta, a study of the problems and prospects of Cuba was conducted under auspices of the Foreign Policy Association by a group of eleven Americans, some of whom (Raymond Leslie Buell, Ernest Gruening, and Leland Hamilton Jenks) had criticized American policy. They found "widespread belief in Cuba that the American State Department attempts to make and unmake governments, and that the present disturbed situation is the outgrowth of a plan for provisional government which Washington induced the Cubans to accept." Many Cubans were fearful of continuing intervention. They concluded that "the interference of the United States in an internal revolutionary struggle" had contributed to disorder and the collapse of a "spirit of constructive patriotism."[7]

Mendieta resigned shortly before the presidential election of January 1936 to counter charges of partiality. On his invitation Harold W. Dodds worked out voting procedures, which were enacted into law. Miguel Mariano Gómez, a son of the second president, was the victor over former President Menocal.

Although Batista did not control the new president, he had a dominant influence in the Congress and worked steadily to build up the popularity and influence of the armed forces. A crisis developed in December 1936 over the veto of a bill to support a project of Batista's for a system of schools to be run by the army. Within the State Department the issue was seen as "larger . . . than control of rural education: namely, who is to have the balance of power in Cuba, the President or the Army."[8] Gómez's ambassador delivered a memorandum to President Roosevelt which predicted "military dictatorship" should Batista carry out a threat of removing the president by impeachment. In Havana Caffery was told that there could be no solution unless the United States would undertake "a 'moral' intervention." Roosevelt would go no farther, however, than to ask Caffery to point out that the exercise of a right to veto "was not considered in other countries to give grounds for the charge of infringement of legislative prerogatives." This Caffery had done already.[9] His attempts "personally and informally" to dissuade members of Congress and "to counsel moderation on the part of the military authorities" had no effect; indeed, they were not evident enough to persuade most Cubans that the American ambassador did not approve Batista's move.[10]

Gómez was impeached and removed, the vice president succeeding him. Caffery's successor, J. Butler Wright, undertook to put an end to the active advisory role that had been expected of American ambassadors.[11] Batista permitted the new president, Federico Laredo Brú, to serve out his term with a degree of independence. In a visit to Washington in 1938 the Cuban strong man improved his relationship with the American government and enhanced his prestige. He became an advocate and sponsor of progressive social and economic legislation. The impetus for reform, which had its origin in the revolutionary movement of 1933, culminated in the constitution of 1940. In general terms, which required legislative implementation, it guaranteed employment, extended social security, made reference to land reform "for reason of public utility or social interest," limited foreign land ownership, authorized expropriation of property, and promoted diversification of agriculture and industry "as sources of public wealth and collective benefit."[12] Reform stopped short, however, of a direct challenge to American predominance.

In 1940 Batista was elected president of Cuba in all proper form. The embassy took great care to take "no step which might indicate . . . any desire" regarding his candidacy. Although wanting to promote legislation to give effect to a debt settlement, Ambassador Messersmith refrained from "engaging in direct conversation on any subject with leaders of political opinion" because of the risk of "misinterpretation."[13] Soon after his inauguration Batista came under threat from the military, because in his new role he tried to bring it under civilian control. Messersmith conveyed to the Cuban Secretary of Defense the "great interest" of the United States in political stability.[14]

Batista made considerable show of cooperation with the United States in the Second World War. He resented the outspokenness of Ambassador Spruille Braden regarding corruption, but differences were patched up. Confident, apparently, in the strength of his support and the appeal of his program, Batista permitted the *Autentico* party, led by Grau San Martín, which had played a leading role in drafting the 1940 constitution, to mount a strong campaign in 1944 in support of the revolutionary goals of 1933. After his candidate was defeated, Batista retired to the United States, while Grau purged the army leadership of his supporters. In the election of 1948, the presidency passed smoothly to the designated candidate of the same party, Carlos Prío Socarrás. In 1949 a statement by the American ambassador seems to have been timed to counter the possible threat of a Grau coup.[15] Grau and Prío tragically squandered the chance for democratic reform in Cuba. While in doctrine they were of the left, their government became "a carnival of graft and irresponsibility."[16]

Batista, who had returned to Cuba after being elected a senator in 1948, announced his candidacy for president in elections scheduled for June 1, 1952. He ran a poor third in a public opinion poll but his popularity with the military enabled him to seize power. He made the preemptive move on March 10. During the years that followed, Batista was diverted from revolutionary or reformist goals in a grim and losing struggle for political survival. He became dependent on the economic support of the United States, on business and industry, and increasingly, in a deepening spiral of desperation, on arms and terror. The parallel with Machado was uncanny.

Batista's nemesis, Fidel Castro, came to prominence through a dramatic attack on the Moncada barracks on July 26, 1953, and through an impassioned courtroom speech. Given amnesty in 1955, he returned to Cuba on December 1, 1956, on the mission that resulted in the overthrow of Batista just two years and one month later.

NONCONTRAVENTION: CASTRO'S SUCCESS

Fidel Castro won control of Cuba by establishing the image of an idealist striving for national and humane values against a corrupt and ruthless group of racketeers who cared for nothing except profit and survival, and by goading Batista into accentuating the contrast through impotence and desperation. As late as April 1958, Castro had only 180 men actively fighting in the mountains, but the very smallness of his force enhanced the appeal of his cause. Batista, too long complacent, irrevocably lost the élan which had once been attached to his role as reformer. While Castro was helped by favorable publicity, particularly by Herbert Matthews of the *New York Times,* it was his own achievement and Batista's ineptitude that had decisive impact within Cuba. The impulse to reform had been frustrated or aborted so often and so cynically that the people were thirsty for heroic idealism that rejected past politics.

The government of the United States has been charged both with supporting Batista and with helping Castro to power. It did both, through its inescapable influence on Cuban affairs. Yet in broad intent official policy was consistent with the premises of nonintervention; while Batista held power, normal relations were maintained, but when it seemed that his government could not survive without outside support, the United States let Cubans know that it would not prevent either Batista's fall or Castro's success. Because it anticipated the outcome, the United States could plausibly be charged with having intended it. However, the U.S. decided only to refrain from an active opposition to Castro which would have entailed intensive and perhaps unmanageable involvement in Cuban politics. In so doing, State Department officials rejected or disregarded allegations that Castro was a dangerous radical who would bring communism to the Caribbean. Ambassadors Arthur Gardner and Earl E. T. Smith were bitterly opposed to Castro. Gardner later told Hugh Thomas that he had even suggested to Batista that the FBI or the CIA should arrange to assassinate him, but that Batista had replied, "No, no, we couldn't do that: we're Cubans."[17]

Once again, as in the time of Machado, the presence of a hated and tottering government made it exceedingly difficult for the United States to avoid actions and attitudes which could be seen as interventionist. Effusive friendship, such as that of Ambassador Gardner, who played canasta with the president several times a week and praised him in such public fashion that Batista was embarrassed, could only arouse bitter resentment from opponents and victims.[18] Smith, a wealthy financier and sportsman who replaced Gardner in 1957, arrived in Cuba proclaiming alliance "in the common fight against Communist subversion," although he intended to correct any impression that the United States endorsed dictatorship. Smith tried to get Batista to lift censorship and restore constitutional guarantees. He undertook to promote free and open elections "without intervening in any way in the internal affairs of Cuba."[19] Shortly after his arrival, he angered Batista by deploring "excessive police violence."[20] But Smith saw such menace in Castro that it became his principal preoccupation to keep him out of power. He was impressed with Batista's willingness to protect American lives and property, in return for arms aid, and "to have the Cuban delegation vote in accordance with the United States delegation" at the United Nations.[21] In the State Department, on the contrary, conviction that Batista would fall and the desire to avoid further entanglement overshadowed gratitude for his support or concern for the qualities of his probable successor.

Ambassador Smith began to explore the prospects for a national unity government as "the only way to salvage the situation."[22] Cuban leaders insisted upon a commitment of support, however, while the State Department refused to make a commitment such as that which Welles had made to the Céspedes government. William Wieland, director of the Office of Caribbean and Mexican Affairs, prepared a memorandum as early as January 1958 anticipating the early collapse of the government and recommending that the United States apply pressure to hasten it. According to Smith's account, the department justified its refusal to pay serious attention to any suggested plan that would exclude Castro on the ground of nonintervention.[23] Smith himself told a news conference—off the record, but it was soon known—that he thought the United States could never do business with Fidel Castro, while expressing hope that Cuba would hold acceptable elections and reaffirming adherence to the policy of nonintervention.[24]

In abandoning Batista, the United States would lend strength to Castro. If it should reject Castro at the same time, it would find itself in the role that Welles had occupied between Machado and Grau, with less hope of a favorable outcome. If, however, it did not cast loose from a sinking Batista, it would become the target for hatred and resistance. Supply of arms gave tangible content to the issue. Bombers, tanks, and armored cars supplied by the United States were used against the Cuban rebels.[25]

The United States tried "every means of persuasion" toward restoration of basic freedoms in Cuba, but Batista's desperation became such that constitutional guarantees were again suspended and censorship resumed on March 12, 1958.[26] Two days later the State Department held up a shipment of 1,950 Garand rifles that had been purchased by the Cuban government to replace 1903 models. The impact on the armed forces was very great.[27] The military mission was not withdrawn, however, and Ambassador Smith, still resisting any moves that might leave Cuba to Castro, told Batista that there had been no change in basic policy. The action had been taken only because of "the great criticism and pressure" from the press and members of Congress.[28] Three days later Castro called for "total war" and warned members of the armed forces to resign. With increasing frequency units surrendered or refused to fight. After June Batista found that "the active units could not win even a skirmish."[29]

The presidential election in November did nothing to relieve tension since it was controlled by Batista and denounced by Castro. Fraud was so blatant that even Smith finally concluded that Batista should be replaced. After the election Smith endorsed the view of American businessmen in Cuba that the United States "should promote and give full and actual support, including the shipment of arms, to a military-civilian junta," but there was no change in the department's view that such action would be unacceptable intervention.[30]

Under pressure from another source, however, the State Department and the CIA acquiesced in an "unofficial" approach which would suggest that Batista appoint a military junta and leave Cuba. This mission was advocated and conducted by William D. Pawley, formerly ambassador to Brazil, and an outspoken anti-Communist who had served on special assignment in the State Department at the time of the overthrow of Arbenz in Guatemala. Secretary of State Dulles was ill but was consulted by telephone. Pawley was not empowered to commit the United States. He could only say that he would "try to persuade the U.S. Government." He told Batista that five opposition figures had been "selected" and "approved" to form a caretaker government in "an effort to stop Fidel Castro from coming to power as a Communist," but Batista asked for more definite assurance that the plan had official United States support.[31]

On December 14, 1958, Ambassador Smith was instructed to make American policy clear to Batista. He told the Cuban foreign minister that the United States would "no longer support the present government" and that it believed "that the President is losing effective control."[32] Three days later, in a long talk with Batista, he reiterated that the United States would not "reinforce his position." He adhered unwillingly to instructions that withheld, as he put it later, "any prospect of appropriate United States backing for a solution which would have the genuine support of the people of his country." Batista told him that by refusing to intercede to stop the fighting, the United States was intervening on behalf of his opponents.[33]

Smith kept searching for a device that would provide an alternative. In the end he found Batista so anxious to frustrate Castro that "the United States was in a position to dictate terms."[34] But it would take a major commitment, including a supply of arms and a willingness to risk direct military action, to assure the survival of a government opposed to Castro. On the very night of Batista's departure, as 1959 began, Admiral Burke was urging that something be done to prevent Castro's taking power,[35] but the only possible means, open force, was not seriously considered by responsible leadership.

After power passed to Castro, the United States did not hesitate to extend recognition. Smith was soon relieved of his position, although there was a delay of several weeks in the arrival of his successor, Philip W. Bonsal, a career officer whose reputation signaled a desire for friendly relations.

THE WRENCH OF SEPARATION

Ambassador Bonsal, presumably reflecting opinions in the Department of State, thought that the strong middle class of Cuba, attached to constitutionalism, was far more likely to gain control than the Communists.[36] Fidel Castro had the determination, audacity, and charisma, however, to take hold on his own terms, drawing strength from the initial enthusiasm of the middle class, arousing sectors of the population that had remained outside of political life, and eventually repudiating democratic procedures in favor of Communist doctrine and methods. In so doing he wrenched Cuba from its dependent relationship with the United States.

Castro's course of action was not the preplanned execution of a Communist design, but it is not difficult, in retrospect, to see the almost inevitable logic of the succession of events through which radicalization took place and antagonism was focused upon the United States. It is hardly conceivable that a Cuban revolutionist, determined to build "a new nation and a new epoch," should not have seen his greatest challenge and opportunity in defiance of the United States, nor that the United States, with its fixation upon Communism, should not have played its expected role.[37] Austerity and repression were explained as necessary responses to foreign threat. Castro's rationale, cast in terms of doctrinal necessity, demonstrates the unlikelihood that a sharp break in Cuban-American relations could have been avoided:

One must realize that there are no solutions between capitalism and socialism. Those who try to find a third position are mistaken and suffer from utopian ideas and become the accomplices of imperialism. . . . To take money from the imperialists by threatening them with friendship with the Soviet Union . . . would have meant maintaining the *status quo* and respecting all the interests of imperialism. . . . There was no alternative: either revolution or betrayal! . . . We have chosen the only honest way . . . the way of anti-imperialist struggle, the way of socialist revolution.[38]

For more than a year the State Department tried for a friendly accommodation. Believing that the Cuban people were still "in a position to influence and to modify the direction of the Revolution," Ambassador Bonsal tried to persuade Castro that the United States would be a source of help.[39] When Castro visited the United States in April, however, there was no discussion of economic assistance. Explanations differ. Both the secretary of the treasury and the assistant secretary of state for inter-American affairs asked what aid was needed and received no reply. Perhaps Castro already knew, from the response of the International Monetary Fund to an earlier request and from comments by American officials, that any loan would carry a requirement for stabilization which would cripple his plans for reform.[40] During this visit, Vice-President Nixon talked with Castro and concluded that if he were not under Communist discipline, he was "incredibly naive about Communism" and that "we would have to treat and deal with him accordingly.'' However, ''the State Department line,'' as Nixon put it, continued to be one of ''trying to 'get along with' and 'understand' Castro.''[41]

Castro was less accessible after his visit to the United States, but Ambassador Bonsal maintained a conciliatory attitude. Agrarian reform, enacted in May, brought only the standard demand in American practice for ''prompt, adequate, and effective'' compensation.[42] Denunciation and prosecution of associates who warned against Communism suggested, however, that Castro would not resist Soviet influence. Sale of Cuban sugar to the Soviet Union, although not unusual, enhanced American nervousness. Yet, after a review of policy, the conciliatory approach and the commitment to nonintervention were reiterated in a White House statement in January 1960.[43]

It was not long, however, as denunciation of the United States continued and a trade deal arranged by a Soviet Politburo member, Anastas Mikoyan, demonstrated Castro's reliance upon the Soviet Union, until a hard line prevailed. By the end of March the United States decided to attempt the overthrow of Castro ''by all the means available . . . short of the open employment of American armed forces in Cuba.''[44] An offer to negotiate differences was rejected because it was thought that Castro could take advantage of such a reprieve.

The new policy made it easy for Castro to demonstrate the hostility of the United States as he carried out his avowed purpose of freeing Cuba from dependency. Following a mandate from Congress, the United States gave notice on May 26 that the technical assistance program would be terminated. In June, on a request of the secretary of the treasury, made without consultation with the State Department, American oil companies in Cuba rejected a demand that they process Soviet crude oil.[45] Castro responded by taking over the refineries and by initiating a general nationalization of private property. Meanwhile, Congress had authorized the administration to adjust the Cuban sugar quota. No attempt was made to apply gradual pressure.[46] In a sudden move on July 6, contrary to the ambassador's advice, further importation of Cuban sugar was in effect cut off, on the transparent pretext that Cuba had ceased to be a reliable supplier. Castro had been charging that the sugar quota enslaved Cuba to the United States. Preferential access to the American market was the major tangible feature of a relationship of economic dependence. In abandoning any attempt to make use of it to influence Cuban policies, the United States was saying that its opposition to the Castro government was basic and complete.

In October the administration announced an embargo on exports to Cuba, except for medical supplies and food. The formal break in diplomatic relations did not come until January 4, 1961, as one of the last acts of the Eisenhower presidency. It was precipitated by a demand that all but eleven of some three hundred members of the embassy staff be dismissed or sent out of the country within forty-eight hours.

Cuba was brought into Cold War politics in the summer of 1960, when the Soviet Union brought charges of American ''economic aggression'' and intervention and Nikita Khrushchev made threatening reference to ''rocket firepower'' in the event of an American attack on Cuba. The United States tried to persuade the Organization of American States to condemn Cuba's association with the Soviet Union and to vote sanctions, but at a conference in San José it was ''denied even symbolic support.''[47] ''Che'' Guevara hailed the Soviet purchase of Cuban sugar as a token of political support. In November Castro boasted that he had acquired arms from Czechoslovakia. Some of the arms were put on display in January.[48] Meanwhile, the United States intensified its preparations for an invasion of Cuba by Cubans opposed to Castro.

THE TESTING OF CONSTRAINT

Among the rationalizations for the plan that culminated in the fiasco at the Bay of Pigs, one of the most impelling was the belief that a landing in Cuba would give the Cuban people a chance to denounce or desert the Castro regime. It was difficult, in the emotional climate of that time, to doubt that they would do so. The operation would then be rendered morally valid by its liberating effect. Little attention was paid to the possibility that a mistaken anticipation of Cuban reactions might lead to its total failure.

The television debates between the presidential candidates of 1960, John F. Kennedy and Richard M. Nixon, dealt with Cuba in a way which suggested that opposition to a move against Castro was not to be taken seriously. Kennedy called bluntly for support to ''the non-Batista democratic anti-Castro forces in exile and in Cuba itself, who offer eventual hope of overthrowing Castro.'' Nixon expressed a different view, not because he disagreed, but because, as he explained later, ''the covert operation had to be protected at all costs'' (although the project was surely known to Castro long before it was launched). Nixon apparently did not believe that the plan would be damaged by an argument that it would violate international agreements and would cause the United States to ''lose all of our friends in Latin America.'' Nor did he hesitate to suggest that it ''would be an open invitation for Mr. Khrushchev . . . to come into Latin America and to engage us in what would be a civil war and possibly even worse than that.'' Doubtless he believed that success would make it possible to say afterwards of Castro, as he blandly did of Arbenz in Guatemala, that ''the people themselves . . . rose up and threw him out.''[49] Even so, his willingness to set forth arguments which he himself did not accept assumed that the American people could safely be told that a planned operation was immoral and inexpedient without destroying either its chance of success or the reputation of one who would make such an argument in such a circumstance.

The Bay of Pigs operation was a belated and rapid rerun of several features of earlier policy in the Caribbean: the belief that American activism would remove impediments to democracy, the failure to anticipate pressures for deeper and prolonged involvement, and the failure of high officials to give informed, objective, and sustained attention to the politics of a small country. In outcome it was also similar; the unwillingness of the United States to use its own forces in a direct attempt to overcome local resistance meant that the operation was abandoned when the too-confident assumptions upon which it was based were destroyed. In this instance failure was rapid and thorough.

In relations with leaders among Cuban exiles, the United States again experienced the contradictions and confusions of attempts to exert influence without accepting the onus and responsibility of illegitimate control. Contacts were first made by the CIA with a front of five centrist groups among the Cuban exiles. The leader of one of these withdrew in September 1960, complaining of "an incessant series of pressures and impositions,"[50] but those who remained accepted dependency upon the CIA and in so doing threw a burden upon the agency that it could not manage adequately in a political vacuum. Many of the exiles, as Meyer and Szulc put it, had a "Platt Amendment psychology." They "were seeking a colonial solution to a revolutionary problem," assuming that Washington knew best and that "American support assured the success of any venture."[51]

Among the exiles, of whom many had no vision of a new Cuba except the removal both of Batista-style and Castro-style repression, while others were nostalgic for old ways, there appeared some who were committed to what they conceived to be the liberating and reformist goals of a revolution that Castro had betrayed. In addition to there being a conflict over strategy between those who counted upon a revolution against Castro within Cuba and those training for an invasion, there was also a clash of political ideologies. Those planning the attack gave preference to men of the right and center, including former members of Batista's army, whom former revolutionists would not accept as comrades in arms.[52] With the control of post-Castro Cuba potentially at stake, Cuban leadership was subject to the unavowed and largely invisible manipulations of Americans. A plan was devised to bring into Cuba an apparatus of government that would supersede local resistance forces and place control in the hands of what Meyer and Szulc refer to as "unreconstructed anti-revolutionaries."[53]

In March 1961 under the Kennedy administration a new revolutionary council was formed, incorporating a People's Revolutionary Movement which had been established by Manuel Ray for the avowed purpose of redeeming the revolution.[54] The arrangement, forced upon the more conservative Cubans by a threat that the action would be called off,[55] called for "maximum priority to the aid of the combatants who are already inside Cuba" and denied any role to former supporters of Batista.[56] In a declaration on April 9, shaped largely by Professor John Plank of Harvard, the new council renounced counterrevolution and pledged to incorporate in the Constitution "some ideals of the people" that had been achieved after Castro's victory.[57] A similar position was taken in the White Paper which was written by Arthur Schlesinger, Jr. on instruction from President Kennedy.[58] None of this made much difference, however, in the activities of the CIA. The contradiction between actual preparations and expressed intentions was due in large measure to the secrecy of the operation, but in a broader sense it resulted from the dominance of Cold War stereotypes in bureaucratic politics.

Among the factors that inhibited critical judgment and good sense were belief that Soviet armament of Cuba would soon make Castro invulnerable and an awareness of how difficult it would be to accomplish and to explain disbandment of the ready force.[59]

Although the attack was fundamentally misconceived and therefore destined to fail, it was also misdirected in both geographical and political terms. Instead of being coordinated with an internal uprising, it was intended to "win by attrition rather than by rebellion" once a beachhead had been secured.[60] Among the attacking force there was a conviction, fostered by American organizers, that the United States would not accept failure.[61] Indeed, some of those who organized and approved the operation probably counted on this. It is difficult to reconcile otherwise the conclusions of the joint chiefs of staff—that success would depend either upon a sizable uprising within Cuba or substantial support from outside, but that the operation should proceed without assurance that either condition would be met.[62] President Kennedy, however, was explicit both in private and in public that there would be no direct American military involvement. In a press conference on April 12 Kennedy said: "There will not be, under any conditions, an intervention in Cuba by the United States armed forces. . . . The basic issue in Cuba . . . is between the Cubans themselves. I intend to see that we adhere to that principle. . . . " He tried twice, through personal emissaries, but apparently without success, to convince Miró Cardona, the head of the revolutionary council, that there would be no military support from the United States.[63]

The public pledge was a salutary defense against "step-by-step involvement"[64] which would pit the United States against Cuban nationalism. Draper's conclusion is convincing:

An invasion force that succeeded in overthrowing Castro without a demonstrative show of popular support could have ruled Cuba only in a state of perpetual civil war or as a thinly disguised American occupation. At best, it would have postponed another outbreak of *Fidelismo* for a few months or years. At worst, it could have made Cuba into another Algeria.[65]

One may only speculate as to whether President Kennedy's determination not to use American armed forces would have remained firm if a beachhead force of Cubans had been held under seige for any extended period or whether restraint would have prevailed if the United States had not faced possible consequences outside of Cuba, such as a Soviet move against Berlin.[66]

The unfolding of events revealed some of the pressures toward deeper involvement and abuse of power that are inherent in an attempt to achieve a major foreign policy objective by proxy. A plan which placed no reliance upon domestic uprising "excluded the Cuban people as untrustworthy allies."[67] Members of the revolutionary council were held under guard while pronouncements were issued in their name. Contrary to instruction, American frogmen were the first to reach the beach. Adlai E. Stevenson uttered blatant, though unwitting, false-hoods at the United Nations. The president, under great pressure, made one concession, authorizing air cover for a strike against the tanks that were dominating the beachhead fighting. This failed because of a mistake in timing. He refused to authorize a direct strike by carrier planes.

After the fiasco, in an eloquent address before the American Society of Newspaper Editors, Kennedy assessed "The Lesson of Cuba." The United States had held to a resolution not to intervene with its own armed forces because this "would have been contrary to our traditions and to our international obligations." But it would not "hesitate in meeting its primary obligations, which are to the security of our Nation," if it should "ever appear that the inter-American doctrine of nonintervention merely conceals or excuses a policy of nonaction." A "new and deeper struggle" was underway. "Subversion, infiltration, and a host of other tactics" were "picking off vulnerable areas one by one in situations which do not permit our own armed intervention. . . . We dare not fail to grasp the new concepts, the new tools, the new sense of urgency we will need."[67]

Like most "lessons" from failure, this was a source of exaggeration and rigidity, which led to further trouble. It was of doubtful relevance to what had happened in Cuba and implied that revolutionary change was to be identified with Communist threats to American security. Castro's coming to power was not the result of infiltration and subversion directed either from the Kremlin or from Peking, despite its outcome in a victory for communism. The sense of urgency with which the United States grasped for "new concepts" and "new tools" led to an attempt to combine new and traditional methods in an unwinnable war in Vietnam. Nervous doubt that means other than military intervention could be relied upon to prevent an extremist minority from gaining and consolidating control led in 1965 to direct use of American forces in the Dominican Republic.

In Cuba itself, however, when the issue was no longer revolutionary change, but Soviet arms, the criterion of national security did prevail in a crisis. When missiles were discovered in 1962, the ideological and emotional urge to destroy the Castro regime was subordinated to concern for Soviet power. Had the "quarantine" method not worked, however, an attack on Cuba probably could not have been avoided. At the height of the crisis, Kennedy asked the State Department to prepare "a crash program on civil government in Cuba to be established after the invasion and occupation of that country."[69] But the president not only rejected the advice of those who urged an attack but eventually accepted as part of the price of removal of Soviet missiles a promise that Cuba would not be invaded.

The pledge not to invade Cuba never became formally effective because Castro would not permit on-the-ground inspection. His rejection of terms that had been agreed upon by the Soviet Union ironically demonstrated that he was by no means a passive tool of Soviet designs. Indeed, identification with communism never has been permitted to jeopardize his personal control.[70]

It remains for time and events to reveal the terms of a rapprochement between Castro or post-Castro Cuba and the United States. If a renewed relationship should demonstrate that the long cycle of dependency has been outgrown, rather than merely interrupted, it will be due more to the achievement of a self-reliant vitality in Cuban politics than to any exercise of will or wisdom on the part of leadership in the United States. But it will owe something both to the values and to the practices of the political system within the Colossus of the North.

16.
THE DOMINICAN REPUBLIC

CAPTIVITY FROM WITHIN

Under Vásquez the Dominican Republic enjoyed a few years during which the presidency and the armed forces were kept from being immediate objects of political contention. There was no significant improvement, however, in the capacities of the Dominican political system. As Vásquez's health deteriorated and his term of office came to a close, factional rivalry again threatened to bring the armed forces into the political arena. What had changed was the nature and control of the organized force. Instead of being fragmented under local *caudillos*, it became the effective instrument of its commander. Rafael Trujillo rose rapidly in 1924. In quick succession, he was placed in command of the Northern Department, promoted to major, and then made lieutenant colonel and chief of staff. In June 1925 he reached the top, as colonel commandant. In 1927 his rank was elevated to brigadier general and the National Police became a brigade. The following year, its transformation into the National Army was completed. During these years, Trujillo's professions of loyalty to the elected president and his disavowal of personal political ambition relieved the fears of those who otherwise might have opposed his growing power to take over the country.

The old factionalism began to erupt again with a partially new cast in 1927, when Senator José Alfonseca gained political strength as leader of the former *horacistas*. Alfonseca incurred the hostility both of the adherents of Vice-President Velásquez, who had expected to be rewarded for supporting Vásquez, and of Trujillo. To avoid a divisive contest, with the likelihood of revolution, pressure was put upon Vásquez to extend his term to six years from the four prescribed by the constitution of 1924, on the ground that the election had actually taken place under the constitution of 1908. Alfonseca, angling to consolidate his position, eventually supported this plan and had the chance himself to become vice-president. The country "saw itself gagged and bound to the acceptance of some years more of the Vásquez regime, to be followed by Alfonseca, on account of a grossly unfair electoral law."[1]

The minister reported that Vásquez professed no strong personal desire to remain in office, but that it would take "strong official representations" to dissuade him. He advised against formal action, which might relieve the president of responsibility, but hoped that "the weight of this responsibility" could be "earnestly impressed" on the Dominican government. The department instructed him accordingly, but the presidential term was extended by a constituent assembly in 1927.[2] In conveying a combination of concern and detachment, the State Department was trying to free Dominican politics from fear or hope of American intervention. The suspicion remained, nevertheless, that formal abstention represented preference for the probable outcome. Velásquez suggested that if the United States objected to the "arbitrary infringement of the rights of the Dominican people," it should not interfere "if the Dominican people found it necessary . . . to take the remedy into their own hands." The department replied that it would view an attempt to overthrow the government "with the greatest regret," but that its attitude "would obviously depend upon the circumstances at that time."[3]

The United States was no longer the only force that could determine the outcome of political conflict in the Dominican Republic. While the State Department wanted stability, Trujillo could profit from disorder. It became increasingly evident in 1929 that the succession to Vásquez would not be peacefully resolved. In June the way was paved for his reelection by a constitutional convention, although the delicate condition of his health made it doubtful that this tactic could succeed. In November, while Vásquez was hospitalized in the United States, Alfonseca became acting president, and initiated a showdown with Trujillo. Fighting was averted when the American legation extracted assurances of restraint from both sides. In December, having learned that Trujillo was plotting a coup in case of the death of Vásquez, the minister told him that "any improper activities on his part would meet with the full opposition of the Legation." When Trujillo appeared sincere in repentance and in avowals of loyalty, the minister interceded on his behalf with Alfonseca.[4]

Trujillo had no intention of giving up his plans to take power.[5] On February 23, 1930, in a prearranged performance, the fortress at Santiago appeared to fall to civilian revolutionists and a motley column began a slow advance by auto from that northern city to the capital. A distraught Vásquez was buoyed up by the legation, while Trujillo maintained a pretense of loyalty that was convincing to the new minister.[6] When the president ordered the army to confront the advancing column, Trujillo, having removed the loyal officer in command of the intercepting force, let the column pass on the pretext that his troops had been outmaneuvered.[7] Once revolutionists entered the capital, it became apparent to the legation that in spite of "solemn assurances" Trujillo had "betrayed the Government."[8]

The minister gave notice that "under no circumstances" would he recommend recognition of a regime dominated by Trujillo.[9] Nevertheless, the takeover was completed when the feeble president was persuaded to resign (the vice-president having already done so), after appointing Trujillo's dupe, who was the nominal head of the revolt, Rafael Estrella Ureña, as minister of the interior. The minister reported that this was "most displeasing," but expressed the hope that no question of recognition would be raised, in view of the maintenance of legality and because it appeared that Estrella was "the only one who can reestablish peace."[10] This position was accepted in Washington.

Before the transfer of power had been completed, the State Department drafted a formal instruction aimed at avoiding direct involvement. Recalling the stable government of recent years, it hoped "that with good will on all sides the present opposing political parties will be able to work out a satisfactory basis for fair and free elections," but the minister was to refrain from raising any formal issues: "You are not authorized to suggest any United States participation in or even supervision of the elections. The last thing we want is to get in a situation where that would result."[11]

Within a month, Estrella admitted that he was dominated by Trujillo and would be unable to conduct a fair election. He asked the United States to oppose Trujillo's candidacy by making it publicly known that he would not be recognized. The State Department rejected any such statement. It did suggest that the minister give Trujillo "in a most friendly manner" his "personal advice" as to "the damage which he will do to the political development of the Dominican Republic" by persisting in his candidacy. It agreed with the minister that it was "most unfortunate that the head of the Army should use that position for his own political advancement" but considered it "most important" not to "impair . . . relations with him." It suggested that Trujillo's former commanding officer, Colonel Richard M. Cutts of the Marine Corps, might helpfully exercise his "great personal influence," but a meeting between the two did nothing to instill either caution or scruple.[12] Indeed, the tenor of Cutts's report suggests that his advice may have been more reassuring than admonishing to Trujillo.[13]

As expected, the election was no contest. Although the opposition leaders announced that they would not go to the polls, the number of votes for Trujillo was considerably in excess of the total number of eligible voters. Intimidation was so great before the election, the minister reported, that on election day "none was needed, and it would seem that none was practised."[14] The chargé d'affaires, John M. Cabot, urged the department to make known its intention to recognize Trujillo, in order to combat "propaganda maliciously circulated by the opposition." When the department agreed, he "immediately discussed with Trujillo the most appropriate use which could be made of the information" and, "both of us deeming it advisable," published the news at once.[15] The minister, Charles Curtis, who had observed Trujillo's triumph with genuine regret, attended the inauguration as the special representative of President Hoover.

The residue of a tutelary relationship persisted through the first years of the Trujillo regime in American supervision of finances and tariffs. After extended discussions, during which the Dominicans suggested that the Good Neighbor policy should override contractual obligations, the United States relinquished administration of customs in 1941. Under a new treaty, receipts and payments would go through a depository bank. Trujillo, temporarily out of office, represented his country at the exchange of ratifications, as ambassador extraordinary on special mission, during one of several visits to the United States.

The policy of nonintervention enabled Trujillo, with effusive expressions of his desire for friendly relations and considerable expenditure on lobbying and public relations, to gain remarkable immunity from censure by the United States. Although Sumner Welles argued for a more critical approach and tried to force Trujillo out of power after a massacre of several thousand Haitians in 1937,[16] Cordell Hull, the secretary of state, appealed to Trujillo as a "big, broadgauged man" to settle the Haitian trouble. Hull's approach prevailed as the Second World War preempted American concern.[17]

The end of the war brought a revulsion against dictatorship. With new men in responsible positions, Trujillo's exemption from American criticism lost strength. Ellis Briggs was appointed ambassador in 1944 and saw to it that his attitude toward Trujillo bore none of the servility and adulation that the dictator demanded of his own people.[18] Briggs urged the State Department to avoid any identification with Trujillo's dictatorship, despite his ability to "produce a whole series of headaches" in retaliation.[19] He objected to the willingness of American military personnel to curry favor with Trujillo and called on the department "to reassert its authority over the conduct of foreign relations" in the Caribbean area. This view was seconded within the department by John M. Cabot, who noted that Trujillo had always been one of "the Army leaders' fair-haired boys."[20] The mood to oppose Trujillo was further strengthened when Spruille Braden became assistant secretary of state, with Briggs as his principal assistant.[21] A request for arms was rejected on December 28, 1945, with brusque reference to violations of "democratic principles": "the lack of freedom of speech, freedom of the press, and freedom of assembly, as well as . . . the suppression of all political opposition and the existence of a one-party system."[22] By the middle of 1947, however, a managed election and the realization that Trujillo would buy arms elsewhere led the United States to revert to a policy of "cooperating with Trujillo in a correct but not excessively cordial manner."[23]

In the broader setting of the Caribbean region, however, Trujillo's achievement of stability was cast in doubt. In 1947, Dominican exiles, among whom was Juan Bosch, the organizer of the Dominican Revolutionary Party (PRD), gathered in Cuba for an expedition against Trujillo. The Cuban government at first lent active assistance, but after Trujillo began to invoke the peace-keeping procedures of the inter-American system it broke up the force,[24] probably at the instigation of the United States. This movement gave birth to the Caribbean Legion, which maintained bases first in Costa Rica and then in Guatemala, as threats both to Trujillo and to Somoza in Nicaragua. After a feeble attempt at a landing in the Dominican Republic was frustrated in 1949,[25] Secretary of State Dean Acheson condemned "plots and counterplots" in the Caribbean area as "repugnant to the entire fabric of the inter-American system."[26]

In 1953 Trujillo visited President Eisenhower and signed a military assistance treaty. Dominican-American relations were for several years disturbed by nothing more serious than the failure of the dictator's son to gain a diploma from the Command and General Staff College at Fort Leavenworth. But opposition to Trujillo never ceased to trouble Caribbean politics and became an issue in the United States Congress, spurred by the seizure and killing of Jesús de Galíndez of Columbia University. In March 1958 the United States put an end to the granting of new licenses for arms and munitions for the Dominican Republic, as it did for Batista in Cuba.

RELEASE

The coming to power of Fidel Castro in Cuba set into motion the events that led to Trujillo's demise. Castro gave open encouragement and support to a movement against the Dominican dictator. In June 1959 an abortive invasion took place. Trujillo's complaint to the Organization of American States was overshadowed by sentiment against his regime. At a meeting of consultation at Santiago, Venezuela and Cuba tried to organize diplomatic action against Trujillo. The United States, already anxious to avoid a spread of Castroism, praised nonintervention as "the traditional principle of the Americas."[27] A compromise was reached among the foreign ministers that accentuated concern for "the effective exercise of democracy" and set up a study of political tensions affecting peace. The implication was that nonintervention might not prevail if it should be determined that repressive dictatorship was a source of threat to peace.

Within a short time opposition to Castro brought a reversal of the significance of nonintervention for the United States. Instead of invoking it to block Castro's moves, the United States began to see it as an obstacle to moves against Castro. Meanwhile, for the first time, Trujillo encountered domestic opposition which he could not cow or kill; the church expressed sympathy for his victims. The study initiated at Santiago, in which the United States was influential,[28] found that repressive dictatorship was indeed a threat to peace because it gave rise to exile movements: "General sympathy with . . . democratic aspirations" bringing "moral support" to exiles would arouse or enhance international tensions.[29] This provided a rationale for action against Trujillo (or, potentially, against Castro) under the justifying cloak of collective security. A second report reached the specific conclusion that "international tensions in the Caribbean region have been aggravated by flagrant and widespread violations of human rights . . . in the Dominican Republic."[30]

Collective action against Trujillo was initiated at a meeting of consultation at San José in August 1960, in response to a complaint of Venezuela that Trujillo had tried to overthrow its government and assassinate its president. The United States wanted to postpone sanctions until inter-American machinery had been set up to monitor a transition. It advocated a special committee to supervise free elections,[31] reminiscent of the efforts of Woodrow Wilson.

The Latin American foreign ministers were unwilling to accept such a commitment, but they were less hesitant to embark on sanctions. Noncoercive measures—breach of diplomatic relations and cessation of arms shipments—were initiated, with the prospect of further action. Despite earlier qualms the United States was prepared to exert pressures for Trujillo's demise. Having already denied him arms, it broke off diplomatic relations. The administration overrode congressional objections to deprive Dominican sugar of the premium it had enjoyed. In December a committee of the OAS recommended an embargo on petroleum and related products and on trucks and spare parts. This was voted by the Council of the OAS in January 1961, by a bare majority, with strong support from the United States.

Meanwhile, within the government of the United States direct action was considered, aimed at the replacement of Trujillo by a regime which might offer better promise of stability. In April 1960 President Eisenhower approved a plan, if the situation should deteriorate further, to "take political action to remove Trujillo from the Dominican Republic as soon as a suitable successor regime can be induced to take over with assurance of U.S. political, economic, and—if necessary—military support."[32] Several special emissaries failed to persuade Trujillo to give up power. Ambassador Farland established close contact with Dominicans who were known to be planning to assassinate him. Transfer of rifles with telescopic sights was approved by Assistant Secretary of State Roy Rubottom and by the acting head of the CIA. Machine guns were later sent. Actual delivery of these weapons was never made, but a few small arms did reach the plotters' hands. Whether any were used is uncertain. After the Bay of Pigs, concern for the consequences of "a vacuum created by assassination" induced cautionary restraint. The National Security Council initiated "both emergency and long-range plans for anti-communist intervention in the Dominican Republic."[33]

On May 30, 1961, Rafael Trujillo was killed by a group of countrymen who had been both accomplices in his tyranny and victims of it. When repression was lifted, the statue of Cordell Hull "was one of the first to be pulled down."[34]

The dictator's demise did not cause immediate collapse of the government. A series of blunders led to the capture, torture, and death of most of the conspirators; only two remained in hiding. The president, Joaquín Balaguer, had come into office in August when Héctor Trujillo had resigned in an appeasing maneuver. Rafael Trujillo, Jr., known as "Ramfis," controlled the armed forces. His particular base of strength was a special force of tanks and infantry at San Isidro, just outside the capital.

The United States moved quickly to bring an OAS committee to the scene. Its avowed purpose was to determine whether the conditions giving rise to sanctions had ceased to exist. The Kennedy administration wanted the committee to remain in the country and exert continuous pressure for reforms which might head off a leftist takeover, but a majority was unwilling to go so far toward open intervention.[35] The committee did, however, call for continued observation and sanctions, "clearly implying that it would consider the existence of dictatorship in the Dominican Republic as per se a cause of continued collective action."[36]

President Kennedy sent John Bartlow Martin, a journalist and speechwriter, as an observer. Martin urged Kennedy not to seek stability at the risk of losing the people. He thought the United States should try "negotiating the Trujillos out if possible, and, if not, throwing them out." A high-level negotiator should be sent at once, with the fleet on the horizon to back him up. George McGhee, undersecretary of state, was then dispatched to Santo Domingo.[37]

It appeared, however, that the Kennedy administration might be content to extract concessions from Balaguer and "Ramfis." It proposed a partial lifting of sanctions with the evident purpose of enticing sugar interests—dominated by the Trujillo family—to press Balaguer for such liberalizing measures as would lead to reinstatement of the full premium.[38] This delicate game was cut short by moves on the part of the Trujillos that seemed to threaten the Balaguer government. Two of the surviving brothers returned from exile on November 15. On the following day, "Ramfis" left the country with his father's body on the family yacht. Two days later, fourteen American warships, including two carriers, were sent to patrol just outside Dominican waters, where they could easily be seen from shore. It was asserted "on the highest authority" that marines would have been landed if Balaguer had asked for them or if he had been ousted by a Trujillo coup.[39] The Trujillo brothers left the country on November 20.

This show of force, intended to promote liberalizing change and thus to head off leftist revolution, met hardly any objection either from Dominicans or from other countries of the hemisphere.[40] Rafael Trujillo and everything that he stood for had become so thoroughly unpopular that the action was viewed as an inter-American collective security measure despite its resemblance to "gunboat diplomacy."

RESTORATION, 1961–1962

With American naval vessels still nearby, active mediation was undertaken both by the chargé d'affaires, John C. Hill, and by an assistant secretary of state of Puerto Rican origin, Arturo Morales Carrión. They supported a group of traditional leaders, the Unión Cívica Nacional (UCN). Under pressure Balaguer agreed to the formation of a seven-man council. He remained as its nominal head for a short time, but after the new chief of the armed forces, General Rodríguez Echavarría, moved against the council in mid-January, Balaguer too was forced into exile. Rodríguez was overthrown after only two days in a military countercoup led by an emerging strong man, General Wessin y Wessin. The council was then reconstituted with Rafael Bonnelly as president. In all of them the American influence was strong.[41]

Juan Bosch, founder in exile of the PRD, a party that stood for radical reform and democratization in the vein of Figueres of Costa Rica and Betancourt of Venezuela, did not share the State Department's approval to the UCN. He saw its leadership as "natural adversaries," wanting "to distribute among themselves the financial legacy left by Trujillo." Balaguer, on the other hand, won some approval from Bosch in that he depended upon public support for political survival.[42] As Bosch saw it, the success of the UCN in ousting Balaguer, with support from the United States, frustrated the possibility of a "revolution from the top." He claimed that Balaguer had offered to turn the presidency over to him in preference to the UCN, but that he had insisted that his party would "accept power only from the people."[43]

After the departure of Balaguer the council of state was made up of four oligarchs, a monseñor, and the two surviving assassins of Trujillo. The United States took a determined role in helping it to survive and to prepare for elections. In March John Bartlow Martin was sent back as ambassador. Martin later recounted in vivid detail the trials and exploits of his mission, working first to conduct a free election and then to provide guidance and support to the faltering administration of the elected president, Juan Bosch.[44]

Martin saw his immediate task as similar to that which Sumner Welles had performed when he had prepared the way for withdrawal of the marines in 1922: "to keep the provisional government in office, help it hold elections, and help get the winner into the Palace alive."[45] In a tone reminiscent of Wilson, he claimed that the goal of free elections justified intervention:

We did it because we believed we were promoting the freedom of the Dominican people. We did it because we believed that freedom served our own interests. We had no wish to run their Republic. We wanted to create conditions in which no one else could run it—only the Dominican people.[46]

The priority that was given to preparing for elections rather than pressing for economic and social reform[47] was thoroughly in accord with the objectives of American policy a generation earlier.

Martin saw Bonnelly, the president of the council, at least once a week and when there was trouble several times a day.[48] On occasion he met with the council. He developed a friendly but guarded relationship with Antonio Imbert, one of the surviving killers of Trujillo, who could not relax his grip on power without jeopardizing his life. Contacts with the opposition were more limited. Although on his first visit he had thought that the Castroite fourteenth of June movement included moderates who should be cultivated, to his later regret he was persuaded by foreign service advisers not to talk with its leader.[49] He regretted also that he had not spent more time with university students and labor leaders.

Martin was willing to support the council "fully and publicly" until elections were held. With Bonnelly's approval he delivered a speech to the American Chamber of Commerce which would have been "so interventionist" as to be "unthinkable" in other Latin American countries.[50] The embassy "worked out a program" which it undertook "to sell" to members of the council. Martin arranged police-training for mob control and cooperated in deportation of "agitators." At the expense of a "bad conscience," he urged the regime to use harassing tactics such as those that he had seen used by the police in Chicago.[51] To forestall a military coup, President Kennedy authorized him to employ "the Loeb formula," devised for Peru, warning the military that it would be "extremely difficult to recognize and almost impossible to assist any regime which took power by force or threats of force."[52] The formula did not work in Peru but it may have had some effect in the Dominican Republic.

Martin had difficulty persuading his government to provide economic aid, but enough was given to make a sharp contrast with the Trujillo period: $70 million in 1962–63 as against $5 million from 1946 to 1961.[53] A sugar quota had to be legislated in Congress, where foreign policy was subordinated to producer interests, both domestic and foreign. Although congressional treatment of Dominican sugar aroused such strong resentment at one point that the council threatened in effect to go "on strike against the Alliance for Progress," the administration was able to salvage a substantial quota.[54]

Martin found "the oligarchy" not blindly reactionary. Realism and a sense of justice persuaded some of its members to accept and support change.[55] But there was no chance that the council would sponsor major land or tax reforms. The embassy staff tried to use aid as leverage, but their effort was "smothered" in turbulence or the necessities of political survival.[56] An agrarian reform bill was enacted after the key council member, Donald Reid Cabral, succumbed to the persuasion of Kennedy's press secretary, Pierre Salinger, but the chance to transfer the vast Trujillo holdings into the hands of small farmers was almost entirely thrown away.[57]

As the date for elections drew near, it became apparent that preparations were incomplete. Martin was deeply concerned. A premature election, he reasoned, would guarantee UCN victory without providing a basis of legitimacy. He pressed for delay, over the angry protest of Bosch, while serving notice on the military that the United States would support the council until elections should be held.[58] Privately his confidence ebbed as he reflected on how little there was to support democracy in the Dominican Republic—"no labor unions, no free civic associations, no men experienced in government (they were dead, in jail, or in exile), no money, no work, no going economy, no civil service, no democratic traditions, nothing."[59] His pessimism was deepened by belief that Juan Bosch could not be trusted and "would not do" for president. But he dismissed Imbert's suggestion that instead of trying to hold a democratic election between two inadequate candidates, the United States should simply pick the best man and "take him to the Presidency."[60]

Martin persuaded the candidates to agree to support the winner and to provide for the safety of Imbert and his co-conspirator, Amiami, lest they stage a coup in a desperate attempt to protect themselves.[61] When Bosch threatened to withdraw in the face of allegations from the clergy that he was a communist, Martin countered by reemphasizing the intention of the United States to "support" the victorious candidate. (He was rebuked by the State Department, which held that he should have promised only that the United States would "assist" the winner.)[62] Bosch, once persuaded that he had a fair chance, complimented Martin for having conducted an "intervention" which was not "odious." Bonnelly, however, was resentful at Martin's activity. "You make me feel I am no longer President," he told the ambassador, recalling the resignation of Jiménez when pressured by Americans in 1916.[63]

The election was tranquil and fair, to the satisfaction of a three-member OAS Technical Assistance Mission which prepared recommendations, most of which were followed, and brought in a group of jurists and scholars to hold a symposium on representative democracy as well as observing at the polls.[64]

RETROGRESSION, 1962-1963

Juan Bosch swept the election, having gained massive response from people who had never before been aroused to political activity, somewhat as another literary humanist, Louis Muñoz Marín, had done in Puerto Rico.[65] Unlike Muñoz, however, Bosch was unable to turn visions into reality through effective government and party organization. The obstacles were enormous. Perhaps no one could have succeeded. But Bosch went at his task in a spirit of fatalistic resignation and with a stubborn rejection of expediency that seemed almost to be seeking vindication through defeat. Martin thought he was "streaked with martyrdom."[66]

Martin did not have the close relationship with Bosch that he had had with the council, but he poured out energy in efforts at "counter attack" and "rescue."[67] Bosch was intent on self-reliance and Martin was sensitive enough not to press advice upon him, even while it seemed that precious opportunity was being lost by a "revolutionary . . . who enshrined Adam Smith" and seemed immobilized by principle.[68] On one occasion, Martin even wrote detailed notes for a speech through which Bosch would "assert leadership"—but Bosch had already prepared his own speech.[69] Bosch later paid warm tribute to Martin and to the AID director, Newell Williams, for having respected his "national pride" with "exemplary tact."[70]

The possibility that "Castro/Communists" might control Bosch or flourish under his regime was a matter of intense concern, both in itself and because their prominence would give impetus toward his overthrow by the right.[71] Martin worked assiduously to "drive wedges" between Bosch and the Communists. Bosch was unwilling to violate the law and the new democratic constitution in order to appease conservative critics who, he was convinced, were using the issue of communism as a means to oppose his program. Anticommunism was strong within the AID mission and the Military Assistance Advisory Group. CIA reports gave "rumors" linking Bosch with the Communists "a credibility far higher" than Martin thought they deserved. He felt, however, that strong concern was unavoidable, because "a Castro/Communist take-over was the one thing the U.S. government and the American people would not tolerate."[72]

The performance of the Bosch government was discouraging. New programs never seemed to get off the ground. Bosch made little use of the few educated and experienced Dominicans, due both to his emotional rejection of the elite and to their refusal to serve him. Martin found the presidential anteroom "full of bums and crooks, not revolutionaries."[73] He was able to draw in men from other Latin American countries through a group known as CIDES (Inter-American Center for Social Studies) under the leadership of a United States citizen of Rumanian birth, Sacha Volman. It was revealed later that some of the "various foundations" from which CIDES gained financial backing were fronts for the CIA.[74]

Martin tried to protect Bosch against the military by assuring the high command that communism was not an imminent threat and that the United States would "not permit another Castro in the Caribbean."[75] To his later regret, he did not, however, seek out "the emerging power," the fanatically anti-communist and "politically naive" General Wessin y Wessin, who controlled a special tank force at the San Isidro Air Base. He felt that such a move might have aroused too much suspicion.[76] But American policy neither ignored nor undercut the armed forces. While supporting Bosch, it "sought to take out reinsurance by simultaneously supporting the old military establishment."[77] Nonintervention had never ruled out close military relationships. Insofar as military commanders could be thought of as responsible caretakers, their capacity to intervene in their own societies could provide something close to a functional equivalent of the repudiated practice of international military intervention.[78]

In a memorandum which was never sent, Martin explored alternatives to continued support of Bosch: the United States might connive at his overthrow or give tacit consent to it, might attempt a "behind-the-scenes takeover," or try to persuade or pressure him to resign and go into exile. He found none of these desirable, but thought that "in dire necessity" the United States might work toward "either a covert power takeover or an overthrow." The former would entail "actually doing what we are always accused of doing"—"put our own people close to [Bosch] and through these people, run his government without his knowing it." The latter, he thought, would result in a civilian junta set up by the military, in which Donald Reid Cabral "might prove to be a key figure."[79]

Thus when Bosch was overthrown on September 25, 1963, Americans close to the Dominican scene were neither surprised nor uniformly dismayed. Some saw it as an inevitable and relatively favorable outcome to a situation that had become hopeless. Bosch seems to have been resigned to his overthrow. It had clearly been the formal policy of the United States, set forth in an instruction from the State Department, to support the elected president. But it was not clear what could be done in a crunch. Martin thought that our influence then would depend "on our willingness to bring the fleet to the horizon. But it was one thing to bring the fleet to eject the Trujillos, quite another to stop an anti-Bosch *coup*."[80]

Bosch's attempt to remove Wessin from his command precipitated the *golpe*. Martin reflected later that he should have moved more vigorously to prevent "a few" Americans who "worked actively to overthrow [Bosch], or at least encouraged the Dominican golpistas," "from undermining the policy of the United States government."[81] Unlike the ambassador, the American military had close ties with Wessin; there is no evidence that it was used to dissuade him from moving against Bosch. Some of the attachés greeted the coup with delight.[82]

Almost at the last moment, Bosch asked Martin to have a carrier on alert, but when Martin asked him whether he wanted marines to land his reply was negative.[83] In desperation Martin went so far as to prepare for himself a fake instruction to show the Dominican military, stating, in words earlier suggested by President Kennedy, that any regime that might come to power as a result of Bosch's overthrow would have great difficulty in gaining recognition.[84] The State Department put an end to such efforts, presumably with Kennedy's approval, by cabling that it saw little that could be done to save Bosch. The United States would not intervene militarily unless this should be necessary to prevent a Communist takeover.[85]

An oligarchic triumvirate was placed in power. Martin asked to be recalled. The State Department softened the gesture, but agreed to withhold recognition. Martin did not, however, recommend the restoration of Bosch. "What kind of a democracy is it," he asked, "that can be kept in the Palace only by a foreign fleet in the harbors?" Bosch would have agreed, with a deep pride and an edge of resentment. But Martin went further; he told President Kennedy that the United States should not work toward the restoration of Bosch "because he isn't a President."[86]

The State Department issued a cautionary statement which related to Honduras as well as the Dominican Republic: "recent military *coups*" had left "no opportunity for effective collaboration by the United States under the Alliance for Progress or for normalization of diplomatic relations."[87] President Kennedy tried to use a rumor of imminent armed resistance to press the triumvirate for a face-saving compromise that would preserve a thread of constitutionality, but the new rulers were strong enough to react with indignation, charging "intervention" in a formal complaint to the OAS. The State Department felt it could do nothing but deny any interventionist intent.[88]

There ensued a protracted but steady retreat. Before long, it appeared that further delay in recognition might play into the hands of "Castro/Communists." The act of recognition, made by Lyndon B. Johnson on December 12, was precipitated by the false rumor of a countercoup. The usurpers had so firmly established themselves that the United States shifted its interest and concern toward the survival of the new regime.[89]

Within a short time Donald Reid Cabral replaced one of the original triumvirs and emerged as the dominant figure, ruling with firmness and without brutality, although lacking the legitimacy of either constitutional origin or popular approval. The new ambassador, W. Tapley Bennett, a career officer, kept himself aloof in a style that contrasted to Martin's "excessive and counter productive" involvement.[90] Martin speculated later that this detachment contributed to "the circumstances that compelled President Johnson" to send troops in 1965: "Political non-involvement in such a country is likely to lead to military intervention."[91]

REVERSION AND RECOVERY, 1965–1966

Opposition to Reid's government occupied a broad spectrum of political positions.[92] Groups of the left, including those which the American embassy called "Castro/Communists," wanted to bring back Bosch. The PRD refused, however, to enter into a pact of political alliance.[93] More potent supporters of Bosch were to be found within the armed forces, including some who had been trained in the Canal Zone. The embassy seems largely to have overlooked them.[94] Reid's opponents in the military also included adherents of Balaguer and others who had served Trujillo; they wanted to form a junta to hold new elections.[95]

A move against Reid was triggered prematurely on Saturday, April 24, 1965, when he tried to cancel the commissions of officers who were plotting against him. His overthrow was proclaimed on the radio by a leader of Bosch's PRD. The announcement was false, but it aroused public excitement. Reid found little or no support from the police and the armed forces. "Rebels" or "constitutionalists" were soon able to retake the radio, arrest Reid (although he was soon permitted to escape) and proclaim as provisional president a PRD leader, José Molina Ureña, who had presided over the Chamber of Deputies while Bosch was president. A large supply of arms brought into Santo Domingo by officers sympathetic to Bosch quickly found its way into the hands of the people.

No one doubted that the attitude of the United States would be of critical importance. Its role might have been minimized if it could have supported a government that could claim legitimacy, but Reid was too weak (he made a desperate appeal for support just before he resigned) and the PRD, which asked for a "U.S. presence" when it assumed power, was thoroughly distrusted.[96] Not recognizing Bosch's strength within the military, American officials believed that a junta pledged to hold elections could readily gain acceptance.[97]

When the emergence of a Boschist government became a real possibility, American influence swung strongly against it. The State Department instructed the chargé d'affaires to encourage formation of a provisional government.[98] The embassy, in a judgment which in all probability was shared in Washington, concluded that "Bosch's return . . . is against U.S. interests in view of extremists in the coup and Communist advocacy."[99] The military attachés urged the Dominican commanders to do "everything possible . . . to prevent a Communist takeover."[100] There is no conclusive evidence as to whether their instigation was decisive. With Wessin the only notable exception, the key generals had decided not to fight, but when it seemed likely that Molina Ureña would be sworn in as provisional president, Wessin undertook "an escalation of violence unprecedented in Dominican history," the strafing of the National Palace.[101] Instead of a simple coup attempt that could be managed by the military, the Dominican crisis was becoming a civil war. The chargé d'affaires recommended a "strong diplomatic initiative" toward a provisional junta which would include the "rebel" military leadership, but the State Department was unwilling to extend its political involvement.[102]

When Ambassador Bennett returned from the United States on the fourth day of the outbreak, Tuesday, April 27, it seemed that the conservative elements had gained the upper hand and that the United States, "having chosen sides without expecting to participate," could avoid open commitment.[103] Deserted by most of his military officers, who had gone to the American embassy in pursuit of a cease-fire, Molina Ureña himself appeared there, only to find that Bennett refused to mediate.[104] But the pro-Bosch movement unexpectedly survived this rejection. While Molina Ureña gave up the struggle, others resumed it, most notably Lieutenant Colonel Francisco Caamaño Deñó, holding positions in the city.

Within a few hours, in an unexpected reversal of fortunes, it was the anti-Bosch military that was asking for rescue. Ambassador Bennett requested authorization to give fifty walkie-talkies to the forces of General Wessin. His cable posed a stark issue:

I regret that we may have to impose a military solution to a political problem. . . . While leftist propaganda will fuzz this up as a fight between the military and the people, the issue is really between those who want a Castro-type solution and those who oppose it.

I don't want to overdramatize, but if we deny the communications equipment, and if the opposition to the leftists lose heart, we may be asking in the near future for a landing of Marines to protect U.S. interests and for other purposes. What does Washington prefer?[105]

On the same day, Wednesday, April 28, a military junta was formed, "at the instance of the C.I.A.," according to Senator Joseph Clark.[106] Although the principal power behind it was General Wessin, he was not a member. It was headed by a little-known air force officer, Colonel Pedro Benoit. Although the

United States did not extend formal recognition to this group (its claim was extremely tenuous), it did respond to requests for assistance as if it were the government. The junta asked for twelve hundred American marines "to restore peace" and followed this with a formal request for "unlimited and immediate military assistance." Bennett himself recommended a marine landing, mentioning danger to the lives of Americans. President Johnson quickly decided to send forces. In a follow-up cable Bennett asked that serious thought be given to "armed intervention which goes beyond the mere protection of Americans" in the interest of preventing "another Cuba." In order to tidy up the basis for landing, Bennett was instructed to ask the junta chief to put in writing a rationale that had been omitted from his earlier written request: that he considered American lives to be in danger and that he could not protect them properly.[107] Only on this premise could the use of American forces be justified in the face of inter-American treaties. The requested statement reached the embassy some hours after the marines had landed.[108]

It is clear, whether or not the belief that American lives were in jeopardy was genuine, that, in Slater's words, "the primary, indeed the overwhelming factor in the U.S. decision to intervene was the belief in both the embassy and the State Department that the apparently imminent constitutionalist victory would pose an unacceptable risk of a communist takeover."[109] Attempts to cling to the rationale of protection opened a credibility chasm that the American press thoroughly exposed. Within a few days the broader objective was acknowledged with the explanation that a shift in "rebel" leadership had made it necessary to forestall Communist control.[110] But this was soon undermined when it appeared that a major part of the "evidence" was false.

Single-minded refusal to accept any risk of a Communist takeover precluded objective assessment of the degree of risk. On the day after the first troops were landed, as reported by Martin,

Secretaries Rusk and McNamara and others asked Ambassador Bennett by telephone if he agreed with their view that a rebel victory would probably lead to a pro-Communist government. Bennett did, adding that the rebels might install Bosch but probably would quickly discard him. They asked if direct military action was necessary to prevent the installation of a pro-Communist government and to protect American lives. Bennett said this seemed likely because of the weakness of the San Isidro Generals. The Administration leaders in Washington told Bennett he should not hesitate to recommend whatever action he thought was needed.[111]

President Johnson, confronting this assessment, resolved that he would not "sit here with my hands tied and let Castro take that Island." He added (in words more of irony than of persuasive force, it turned out): "What can we do in Vietnam if we can't clean up the Dominican Republic?"[112]

If it was difficult to demonstrate that Communists had gained control of the movement, it was impossible to prove that they would not do so. They did play an active role in organizing the street fighting.[113] The exaggerated atrocity stories given currency by the ambassador were probably indicative not so much of bad faith as of the desire, indeed the need, to believe and to propagate whatever would justify military commitment. Inconsistent statements by Johnson, Secretary of State Rusk, and others, as to whether the Communists actually had taken over or merely threatened to do so, had no significant bearing on actual decisions, because the United States was reacting to the possibility of a takeover. To suggest that the communist menace was intentionally exaggerated as an excuse for opposition to Bosch is to reverse the actual priority; Abraham Lowenthal is persuasive in concluding that Bosch was not the primary object of American hostility.[114]

The United States thrust itself, in effect, into the position of arbiter or architect of legitimacy which its Latin American policy had tried to avoid. But this was not its direct intent, and it stopped short of open acknowledgment of this role. Under Secretary of State Thomas C. Mann claimed that the United States refrained from recognizing the Benoit junta "because this would have amounted to taking sides in the internal struggle" and "would have been inconsistent with the principles that govern the inter-American system."[115] He used the same reasoning in a later speech to explain why the United States failed to support restoration of the constitutional government:

Latin Americans do not want a paternalistic United States deciding what particular political faction should rule their countries. . . . This explains why, in the case of the Dominican Republic, we refrained during the first days of violence from "supporting" the outgoing government or "supporting" either of the factions contending for power.[116]

If "support" of a particular "faction" is interventionist, active opposition to the adherents of a freely-elected president must be no less so. In deciding to prevent the success of the constitutionalists, the United States undoubtedly did peremptorily interject itself into Dominican politics. Yet in this episode, as in earlier Caribbean involvements, the United States was constrained by goals and values which required that an act of intervention be justified as a contribution toward nonintervention. Moreover, while stability through dictatorial or military control might be an accepted outcome, the goals actively promoted through intervention placed emphasis on democratic procedures.

Slater's conclusion is strongly supported by evidence and by circumstance:

. . . the Johnson administration was not only committed to the reestablishment of democratic government through genuinely free elections in the near future, but also intended to use the opportunity to begin gradually to reform and restructure the Dominican military establishment, the main bulwark of the status quo.[117]

The attempt at political reconstruction had to confront on one hand the strand of legitimacy represented by Bosch and the constitutionalists and on the other hand the military forces that controlled most of the country, with their links to military and intelligence components of the United States government and their asserted role as the bulwark against communism.

Although Bosch had been ignored by the Johnson administration before the revolt, he soon became a center of attention. Three respected Latin American liberals, Figueres of Costa Rica, Betancourt of Venezuela, and Muñoz of Puerto Rico, were brought together at the White House on April 29 and asked to go to Santo Domingo in a mediating role. Figueres initiated a telephone consultation with Bosch in Puerto Rico. The three men posed stiff conditions, but it was apparently opposition from conservative OAS members, particularly Brazil, rather than United States rigidity that caused the project to be abandoned.[118]

Martin saw Bosch on May 3. Although Bosch had planned to return to the Dominican Republic, he had no means of doing so while the fighting was going on.[119] Now he was dependent on the United States. What transpired between Martin and Bosch with regard to his return remains somewhat unclear.[120] Bosch received the impression that the United States did not want him back. He did not press hard, probably from pride and the desire to have his position as president confirmed beforehand.[121]

President Johnson did not write off the PRD, despite these setbacks. He told Martin to pursue the possibility of accepting Molina Ureña and asked him to assure Bosch "that our purpose is to protect lives and have a progressive liberal government there and have elections."[122] Abe Fortas, Johnson's close advisor, suggested a statement in which Bosch would recognize and denounce the Communist danger while accepting American forces as needed to preserve order. Instead, Bosch denounced the occupation as a return to the pattern of 1916 and urged resistance to "a foreign military government." [123] His attitude was succinctly set forth in an article which appeared shortly afterward:

The hour for the Dominican People's maturity had arrived: it had proved that with its blood; it was not now possible to govern the Dominican Republic from Washington by means of docile Dominicans. Either this new country born in the April Revolution would be governed directly by the American military or it would be left to govern itself.[124]

As soon as Martin arrived back in Santo Domingo, he turned his efforts toward establishing a "third force." In apparent disregard of his instructions, he approached "Tony" Imbert with an offer of full support and quick recognition.[125] Imbert described himself, with a show of reluctance, as the only man strong enough to force out the generals of the junta and to form a new government which could gain broad support.[126] Martin worked feverishly to put together a Government of National Reconstruction under Imbert, then tried to arrange negotiations between Imbert and Caamaño. His efforts, interrupted by outbreaks of fighting, were superseded by a high-level mission from Washington under McGeorge Bundy, which renewed the attempt to devise a "Boschist formula."

Bundy's mission grew out of negotiations in which Figueres and Fortas, among others, tried to reach an understanding with Bosch on "constitutional government, without Communism and without Trujilloism."[127] Apparently it was agreed that a suitable candidate would be Antonio Guzmán, a wealthy planter, formerly Bosch's minister of agriculture.[128] The Guzmán plan hardly got off the ground, however. Imbert and the military leaders put up expected resistance. It was by no means certain that Guzmán could gain "rebel" support. Bundy's visit resulted in the posing of conditions that Guzmán was unwilling to meet, entailing deportation of Communists and of three constitutionalist leaders, along with Wessin.[129] The failure of this approach signalized a resurgence of doctrinaire anti-communism in Washington, expressed particularly by Under Secretary of State Thomas Mann. Objection to the Guzmán plan exploited the mystique of nonintervention; a memorandum was drawn up for President Johnson criticizing the attempt of Sumner Welles to "impose a government" on Cuba in 1933.[130] A false story alleging financial impropriety also undermined Guzmán's support.

By this time OAS action had transformed the United States troops, with token additions from Brazil, Costa Rica, Honduras, Nicaragua and Paraguay, into an inter-American force, commanded by a Brazilian general, with an American as deputy. Following the departures of Martin and Bundy, mediation efforts were also brought nominally under the OAS, through a three-man team dominated by Ellsworth Bunker, the chairman of the OAS Council. This group succeeded, after three months, in setting up a provisional government under Héctor García-Godoy, a "progressive, independent, and effective" figure,[131] once foreign minister under Bosch. This was more acceptable to the constitutionalists than to the rightist military leadership.[132] After an early attack by Imbert, the OAS contingents kept the Dominican military under restraint.[133] Imbert was pressured to resign by depriving him of United States financial support. Wessin was placed aboard a plane for Miami, where he had been appointed consul general. Balaguer was permitted to return from exile in July, after having been contacted indirectly by the State Department.[134] Bosch came back in September. A clash within the military in December led García-Godoy to order the exile or resignation of leaders of both factions. Bunker at first opposed any action against the rightist chiefs of staff, but when they moved into open revolt, he came down firmly on the side of the government. He refused, however, to support any measure that might threaten to eliminate the military establishment, because the United States was unwilling to risk the removal of a safeguard against communism.[135]

Balaguer and Bosch confronted each other in a relatively peaceful election on June 1, 1966, from which Balaguer emerged the decisive victor. While a facile interpretation of this outcome could represent it as the culmination of a plan by the United States to frustrate Bosch, and indeed American advocacy of an election had been encouraged by poll results showing the strength of Balaguer, the United States had been prepared to accept a Bosch victory and for some time considered this likely.[136] American policymakers were not willing to countenance dealing with communists or the crippling of the Dominican military, but they were confident that Bosch would comply with both requirements.[137] The vote for Balaguer was cast in part out of weariness and fear of new turmoil, to which the presence of American forces, police harassment of supporters of Bosch, and a timid and hesitant campaign by Bosch contributed.[138]

The peace force remained for three months, to enable the new government to gain secure control. It left behind a country still in jeopardy, its political life dominated by "civilian and military cliques," Balaguer's ascendancy only moderating "the politics of chaos."[139] Elections in 1970 and 1974 were boycotted by the opposition. Tactics of terror against the left aroused cries of neo-Trujilloism and charges that the CIA was directing the repression of any movement that it could not control. When an indigenous political capacity that might relieve the United States of implication in Dominican affairs did not develop, it remained for American policymakers to set prudent limits to their involvement.

In the presidential election of 1978, Antonio Guzmán of the PRD stayed in the race and received a substantial majority over Balaguer. Amidst rumors of a military coup, the United States made known its desire for a fair count and the installation of the victor. The efforts of a new ambassador, Robert Yost, were reinforced, it was reported, by visiting spokesmen from the Pentagon who told their military counterparts that there was no reason to hope for American support in reversing the outcome.[140]

NOTES

1 CUBA

1. Margaret Leech, *In the Days of McKinley* (New York, 1959), 188; Philip C. Jessup, *Elihu Root*, 2 vols. (New York, 1938), 1: 285.

2. Horatio S. Rubens, *Liberty: The Story of Cuba* (New York, 1932), 341–42.; Elmer Ellis, *Henry Moore Teller: Defender of the West* (Caldwell, Idaho, 1941), 312, 312 n; David F. Healy, *The United States in Cuba, 1898–1902* (Madison, Wis., 1963), 85.

3. *Papers Relating to Foreign Relations of the United States*, 1898, lxvi–vii. (This series, published by the Department of State, will be cited hereafter as *Foreign Relations* or *FR*.)

4. Ibid., 1899, xxviii–ix.

5. Albert G. Robinson, *Cuba and the Intervention* (New York, 1905), 109.

6. Roosevelt to Lodge, July 21, 1899, quoted in Healy, *US in Cuba,* 102.

7. Hermann Hagedorn, *Leonard Wood* (New York, 1931), 1: 259.

8. Speech at Williamstown, Mass., June 25, 1902, reported in *Boston Transcript;* Hagedorn Papers, Library of Congress, Washington, D.C.; Hagedorn, *Wood,* 1: 261.

9. Healy, *US in Cuba,* 116–17, 124–25.

10. Testimony at Senate hearings, 1903, quoted in Jessup, *Root,* 1: 286–87.

11. Root to Willard Bartlett, December 31, 1899, quoted in Jessup, *Root,* 1: 232.

12. Civil Report of General Leonard Wood for 1902, [Baltimore, 1903] Part I, 271.

13. Rubens to Root, December 13, 1899, Elihu Root Papers, Library of Congress, Washington, D.C. (hereafter cited as RP).

14. Wood to Root, January 13, February 6, February 23, 1900, RP.

15. Root to Wood, June 30, 1900, RP.

16. Wood to Root, February 23, 1900, RP.

17. Wood to Root, January 19, 1900, RP.

18. Wood to Root, September 26, 1900, RP.

19. Wood to Root, December 23, 1900, RP.

20. Wood to Root, January 19, 1901, RP.

21. Wood to Root, February 27, 1901, RP. Emphasis in original.

22. Wood to Root, January 19, 1901, RP.

23. Robert Bacon and James Brown Scott, eds., *The Military and Colonial Policy of the United States: Addresses and Reports by Elihu Root* (Cambridge, 1916), 172–74.

24. Robinson, *Cuba,* 208. Emphasis added by Robinson.

25. Rubens to Root, August 24, 1900. RP.

26. Rubens to Root, September 3, 1900, RP.

27. *Civil Report, 1900,* 2, quoted in James H. Hitchman, *Leonard Wood and Cuban Independence 1898–1902* (The Hague, 1971), 100.

28. Root to Hay, January 11, 1900, RP.

29. Senator Foraker, *Congressional Record,* 56th Cong., 2d sess., February 27, 1901, 34: 3151.

30. Leland Hamilton Jenks, *Our Cuban Colony* (New York, 1928), 74. For a recent interpretation giving emphasis to Root's concern for national security, *see* Lejeune Cummins, "The Formulation of the 'Platt' Amendment," *The Americas* 23 (April 1967): 370–89.

31. Jessup, *Root,* 1: 314–15; Root to Wood, January 9, 1901. RP. Quoted in Jessup, *Root,* 1: 309.

32. Root to Wood, January 9, January 19, 1901, RP.

33. Root to Wood, January 9, 1901, RP.

34. Wood to Root, February 27, 1901, RP.

35. Root to Albert Shaw, February 23, 1901, RP.

36. Root to Wood, February 9, 1901, RP. Jessup, *Root,* 1: 311–12. The convention is well discussed in Hitchman, *Wood,* 94–114.

37. Root to Albert Shaw, February 23, 1901, RP.

38. *U.S. Statutes at Large* 31, 2: 895–96.

39. Root to Wood, March 2, 1901, RP.

40. Jessup, *Root,* 1: 317.

41. Ibid., 320.

42. Rubens to Root, March 5, 1901, RP.

43. As given in Cuban sources, quoted in Jenks, *Cuban Colony,* 82. For these discussions, *see* Hitchman, *Wood,* 150–55.

44. Jessup, *Root,* 1: 320.

45. Charles E. Chapman, *A History of the Cuban Republic* (New York, 1927), 130–31; Russell H. Fitzgibbon, *Cuba and the United States, 1900–1935* (Menasha, Wis., 1935), 72.

46. Chapman, *Cuban Republic,* 144–46.

47. Ibid., 169–75.

48. Ibid., 180.

49. Ibid., 190.

50. *FR,* 1906, 463. For an excellent discussion of the revolt and the occupation, Allan Reed Millett, *The Politics of Intervention: The Military Occupation of Cuba, 1906–1909* (Columbus, Ohio, 1968).

51. *FR,* 1906, 466.

52. "Report of William H. Taft, Secretary of War, and Robert Bacon, Assistant Secretary of State . . . ," Appendix E, Report of the Secretary of War, *House Documents* 2, 59th Cong., 2d sess., 444 (hereafter cited as "Report of Taft").

53. Ibid., 444–45.

54. Ibid., 483.

55. Ibid., 446. In *FR,* 1906, 476, the text is somewhat different; the word "secrecy" is omitted.

56. "Report of Taft," 446.

57. *FR,* 1906, 478–79.

58. Millett, *Politics,* 80, 89–90, 109, 111.

59. "Report of Taft," 492.

60. Ibid., 491.

61. Ibid., 492.

62. Ibid., 448.

63. Ibid., 470.

64. Ibid., 457–58.

65. Ibid., 471.

66. Ibid., 473.

67. Ibid., 474.

68. James Brown Scott, *Robert Bacon: Life and Letters* (New York, 1923), 117.

69. "Report of Taft," 475.

70. Ibid., 476–77.

71. Ibid., 478.

72. Ibid., 479.

73. Ibid., 481.

74. Ibid., 480–81.

75. Ibid., 482.

76. Quoted in Chapman, *Cuban Republic,* 215.

77. Enrique José Varena, quoted in ibid., 216.

78. Scott, *Bacon,* 118.

79. Jackson to Knox, May 4, 1910, State Department Decimal File, 837.00/380 (further citations from this file will be by numbers only).

80. "Annual Report of Charles E. Magoon, Provisional Governor of Cuba, to the Secretary of War, 1907," *Senate Document 155,* 60th Cong., 1st sess., 8 (hereafter cited as "Report, 1907").

81. Ibid., 20.

82. "Message from the President of the United States transmitting a communication from the acting Secretary of War . . . ," *Senate Document 80,* 61st Cong., 1st sess., 20.

83. Jenks, *Cuban Colony,* 100.

84. "Report of Taft," 485–86.

85. Annual Message to Congress, December 3, 1906, quoted in Millett, *Politics,* 145.

86. Millett, *Politics,* summarized at 214.

87. Ibid., 149–50.

88. Letter of October 21, 1921, to Henry P. Fletcher, quoted in Robert F. Smith, *The United States and Cuba: Business and Diplomacy, 1917–1960* (New York, 1960), 25.

89. "Report, 1907," 17, 28–29.

90. Millett, *Politics,* 182.

91. "Report, 1907," 32.

92. Letter of April 16, 1908, quoted in Millett, *Politics,* 249–50.

93. Millett, *Politics,* 150–51, 158.

94. "Report, 1907," 17.

95. David A. Lockmiller, *Magoon in Cuba: A History of the Second Intervention, 1906–1909* (Chapel Hill, N.C. 1938), 80; Millett, *Politics,* 160–61.

96. Luis E. Aguilar, *Cuba 1933: Prologue to Revolution* (Ithaca, 1972), 28–29.

97. Millett, *Politics,* 215.

2 NICARAGUA

1. Mario Rodríguez, *Central America* (Englewood Cliffs, N.J., 1965), 73–74.

2. Philip C. Jessup, *Elihu Root*, 2 vols. (New York, 1938), 1: 501.

3. Dana G. Munro, *Intervention and Dollar Diplomacy in the Caribbean, 1900–1921* (Princeton, N.J., 1964), 148–49.

4. Ibid., 150; Jessup, *Root,* 1: 508.

5. Jessup, *Root,* 1: 505.

6. Ibid.

7. *Foreign Relations of the United States,* 1907, 2: 688 (hereafter cited as *FR*).

8. Ibid., 672.

9. Ibid., 695–98.

10. Charles L. Stansifer, "Application of the Tobar Doctrine to Central America," *The Americas* 23 (January 1967): 254–55.

11. Munro, *Intervention,* 156; Jessup, *Root,* 1: 510–11.

12. Huntington Wilson, "The Relation of Government to Foreign Investment," *The Annals* 68 (November 1916): 300–7.

13. Munro, *Intervention,* 164.

14. Stansifer, "Application," 256.

15. J. Fred Rippy, *The Caribbean Danger Zone* (New York, 1940), 168–77. Rippy provides an excellent brief account of the establishment of the Nicaraguan protectorate.

16. Ibid., 174; Walter V. Scholes and Marie V. Scholes, *The Foreign Policies of the Taft Administration* (Columbia, Missouri, 1970), 51.

17. Charles A. Beard, *The Idea of National Interest* (New York, 1934), 172–73; Samuel Flagg Bemis, *The Latin American Policy of the United States* (New York, 1943), 162.

18. *FR,* 1908, 457–70; Rippy, *Caribbean,* 171.

19. Munro, *Intervention,* 174.

20. *FR,* 1909, 452.

21. *Congressional Record,* 68th Cong., 2d sess., 1556.

22. Moffat to Knox, May 25, 1911, 817.00/1608.

23. Memorandum "read to the Secretary by HW [Huntington Wilson] at a conference on July 10, 1911," 817.51/168.

24. Munro, *Intervention,* 175.

25. *FR,* 1909, 449–50; Scholes and Scholes, *Foreign Policies,* 52–53.

26. Munro, *Intervention,* 176–77.

27. *FR,* 1909, 455–56.

28. Munro, *Intervention,* 178.

29. *FR,* 1909, xviii.

30. Munro, *Intervention,* 180.

31. Ibid., 186.

32. Ibid., 181–82.

33. *FR,* 1910, 747. A complaint by Madriz to Taft appears at 751–52.

34. Lowell Thomas, *Old Gimlet Eye: The Adventures of Smedley D. Butler as Told to Lowell Thomas* (New York, 1933), 127–28.

35. *New York Times,* June 1, 2, 6, 1910.

36. Moffat to Knox, June 12, 1910, State Department Numerical Case 6369/1053.

37. Munro, *Intervention,* 186.

38. *FR,* 1910, 765.

39. Memorandum, June 10, 1911, 817.51/168.

40. *FR,* 1911, 648.

41. Ibid., 766.

42. Dana G. Munro, *The Five Republics of Central America* (New York, 1918), 232–33.

43. *FR*. 1911, 662.

44. Ibid., 627.

45. Isaac J. Cox, *Nicaragua and the United States, 1909–1927* (Boston, 1927), 713.

46. *FR*, 1911, 655–56.

47. Moffat to Knox, May 25, 1911, 817.00/1608.

48. Memorandum by F. M. Huntington Wilson, July 10, 1911, 817.51/168.

49. *FR*, 1911, 657–60.

50. Ibid., 660–61.

51. Memorandum initialed GTW (Weitzel), June 24, 1911, 817.00/1687.

52. Memorandum, July 10, 1911.

53. *FR*, 1911, 662.

54. Ibid., 666.

55. Munro, *Intervention*, 192.

56. *FR*, 1911, 666–68.

57. Ibid., 670–71.

58. *FR*, 1912, 1013.

59. Ibid., 995–96.

60. Ibid., 994.

61. Ibid., 997.

62. Ibid., 1020.

63. Munro, *Intervention*, 204.

64. Ibid., 194–47, 202.

65. *FR*, 1912, 1115.

66. Ibid., 1112–13.

67. Ibid., 1122.

68. William Bayard Hale, "With the Knox Mission in Central America" *World's Work* 24 (June 1912): 186.

69. *FR*, 1912, 993.

70. Ibid., 1118–19.

71. Quoted by Senator Borah, *Congressional Record,* 69th Cong., 2d sess., 1557.

72. *FR*, 1912, 1025–26.

73. Ibid., 1027.

74. George T. Weitzel in *Congressional Record,* 69th Cong., 2d sess., 3114.

75. *FR*, 1912, 1032.

76. Wilson to Taft, August 30, 1912, 817.00/1940a.

77. *FR*, 1912, 1043–44.

78. Wilson to Taft, September 23, 1912, 817.00/2003B.

79. Thomas, *Gimlet Eye,* 151.

80. *FR*, 1912. 1055, 1068.

81. Ibid., 1061.

82. Ibid., 1069.

83. Munro, *Intervention*, 216.

84. Memorandum by J. Butler Wright, October 27, 1912. 817.00/2118.

85. *FR*, 1912, 1063–64. J. Butler Wright asserted baldly in 1916 that Chamorro had withdrawn "at the suggestion of the American Legation." 817.00/2435$^{1}/_{2}$.

86. Weitzel to Knox, October 9, 1912, 817.00/2081.

87. Weitzel to Knox, October 25, 1912, 817.00/2122.

88. Munro, *Intervention*, 211; Munro, *Five Republics*, 245. Emphasis added by author.

89. Weitzel to Knox, October 9, 1912.

90. Ibid. Emphasis in original.

91. Munro, *Intervention*, 212–14.

92. *FR*, 1913, 1035.

93. Ibid., 7.

94. Munro, *Intervention*, 271.

95. Ray Stannard Baker, *Woodrow Wilson: Life and Letters, President, 1913–14*, 8 vols. (London, 1932), 4: 438.

96. Douglas to Bryan, June 9, 1913. 817.812/38.

97. Munro, *Intervention*, 389; *FR*, 1913, 1040–42.

98. Munro, *Intervention*, 390.

99. Selig Adler, "Bryan and Wilsonian Caribbean Penetration," *Hispanic American Historical Review* 20 (May 1940), 210–11.

100. *FR, The Lansing Papers*, 1914–1920, 2: 466.

101. Arthur S. Link, *Wilson: The Struggle for Neutrality, 1914–1915* (Princeton, 1960), 338; Adler, "Bryan," 214.

102. Quoted in Link, *Wilson*, 336.

103. Munro, *Intervention*, 391; Adler, "Bryan," 214.

104. Link, *Wilson*, 337; Baker, *Life and Letters*, 4: 433.

105. Baker, *Life and Letters*, 4: 433–34.

106. Munro, *Intervention*, 392–97.

107. Baker, *Life and Letters*, 4: 440.

108. Senator Borah, quoted in Link, *Wilson*, 339.

109. Letter of January 7, 1915 in *Congressional Record*, 69th Cong., 2d sess., 1557. *See also* Jessup, *Root*, 252–53.

110. Ibid.

111. *FR*, 1914, 181–84; *FR*, 1915, 264–66.

112. *FR*, 1913, 1025.

113. Quoted in Link, *Wilson*, 344.

114. Memorandum by Weitzel, January 9, 1917, 817.51/914.

115. Harold Norman Denny, *Dollars for Bullets* (New York, 1929), 165–66; George W. Baker, Jr., "The Wilson Administration and Nicaragua, 1913–1921," *The Americas* 22 (April 1966): 363–70.

116. Munro, *Intervention*, 415.

3 THE DOMINICAN REPUBLIC

1. Otto Schoenrich, *Santo Domingo: A Country with a Future* (New York, 1918), 322–23.

2. John Bassett Moore in *Foreign Relations of the United States*, 1905, 344 (hereafter cited as *FR*).

3. Sumner Welles, *Naboth's Vineyard: The Dominican Republic, 1844–1924*, 2 vols. (New York, 1928), 2: 515, 559.

4. Ibid., 528–29, 533–34.

5. For a summary of Dominican politics by the minister, Thomas C. Dawson, *see FR*, 1905, 382–89. For a chronology, *see FR*, 1906, 572–600.

6. Welles, *Vineyard*, 2: 561.

7. Ibid., 604.

8. Ibid., 606–7.

9. J. Fred Rippy, "The Initiation of the Customs Receivership in the Dominican Republic,"*Hispanic American Historical Review* 17 (November 1937): 444.

10. Dana G. Munro, *Intervention and Dollar Diplomacy in the Caribbean, 1900–1921* (Princeton, 1964), 94–95.

11. Rippy, "Initiation," 445.

12. Munro, *Intervention*, 88–89.

13. Memorandum presumably by Francis B. Loomis, assistant secretary of state, in *The Independent* 16 (March 3, 1904): 467; Rippy, "Initiation," 422; Munro, *Intervention*, 90.

14. Jacob H. Hollander, "The Financial Difficulties of Santo Domingo," *The Annals* 30 (July 1907): 94.

15. Schoenrich, *Santo Domingo*, 328.

16. Munro, *Intervention*, 91–92.

17. Letter of February 23, 1904, quoted ibid.

18. Quoted in Rippy, "Initiation," 443.

19. Letter of April 4, 1904, quoted in Munro, *Intervention*, 92.

20. Quoted in Rippy, "Initiation," 450.

21. *FR*, 1904, 266.

22. Welles, *Vineyard*, 2: 620–21.

23. Quoted in Munro, *Intervention*, 98.

24. Ibid., 98–99.

25. *FR*, 1904, xli.

26. *FR*, 1905, 398.

27. Quoted in Rippy, "Initiation," 447.

28. *FR*, 1905, 299.

29. Ibid., 324.

30. Ibid., 339–42.

31. Ibid., 379.

32. Welles, *Vineyard*, 2: 631.

33. Quoted in Munro, *Intervention*, 106; Howard C. Hill, *Roosevelt and the Caribbean* (Chicago, 1927), 164.

34. *FR*, 1905, 408.

35. *FR*, 1906, 540–41.

36. Philip C. Jessup, *Elihu Root*, 2 vols. (New York, 1938), 1: 546; Munro, *Intervention*, 120.

37. *FR*, 1906, 552.

38. Ibid., 562.

39. Quoted in Munro, *Intervention*, 118.

40. *FR*, 1907, 1: 309.

41. Munro, *Intervention*, 123.

42. Jessup, *Root*, 1: 549.

43. Welles, *Vineyard*, 2: 640, 647.

44. *FR*, 1911, 171.

45. Welles, *Vineyard*, 2: 681.

46. *FR*, 1912, 389, 1091.

47. *Ibid.*, 344.

48. Welles, *Vineyard*, 2: 690.

49. *FR*, 1912, 346.

50. Welles, *Vineyard*, 2: 693.

51. *FR*, 1912, 336-63.

52. Quoted in Munro, *Intervention*, 263.

53. McIntyre to Walcutt, October 8, 9, 1912, 839.00/760; McIntyre-Doyle report, November 18, 1912, 839.00/775, 10-11.

54. Welles, *Vineyard*, 2: 697-98.

55. Ibid., 700-1.

56. *FR*, 1912, 378.

57. *FR*, 1913, 419-20.

58. Arthur S. Link, *Wilson: the Struggle for Neutrality, 1914-1915* (Princeton, 1960), 549.

59. Munro, *Intervention*, 276.

60. Welles, *Vineyard*, 2: 711-12; Munro, *Intervention*, 275.

61. *FR*, 1913, 425.

62. Memorandum of September 4, 1913, and Bryan to Tumulty, 839.00/872.

63. Charles W. Hathaway to Bryan, October 6, 1913, 839.00/943.

64. *FR*, 1913, 426-27.

65. Ibid., 432-33.

66. Hathaway to Bryan, October 31, 1913, 839.00/957.

67. Sullivan to Bryan, October 31, 1913, 839.00/961.

68. *FR*, 1913, 436.

69. Ibid., 438; Memorandum by Long, December 4, 1913, 839.00/1005; Russell to Lansing, October 29, 1915, 839.00/1776.

70. *FR*, 1913, 440.

71. Ibid., 441-42.

72. Ray Stannard Baker, *Woodrow Wilson: Life and Letters, President, 1913-14*, 8 vols. (London, 1932), 4: 444; *FR*, 1913, 443-44.

73. *FR*, 1913, 451-52.

74. Munro, *Intervention*, 282; *FR*, 1914, 201 (the quote), 219.

75. *FR*, 1914, 205.

76. Hathaway to Bryan, November 13, 1913, 839.00/968.

77. *FR*, 1914, 206.

78. Ibid., 209-10.

79. Ibid., 213.

80. Ibid., 215.

81. Ibid., 218, 220-21.

82. Ibid., 222-25.

83. Ibid., 226-27.

84. Ibid., 242.

85. Latin American Division memorandum, May 28, 1914, 839.00/1520.

86. *FR*, 1914, 234.

87. Munro, *Intervention*, 291.
88. Link, *Wilson*, 512.
89. *FR*, 1914, 247–48.
90. Link, *Wilson*, 515.
91. Ibid., 514.
92. Munro, *Intervention*, 293.
93. *FR*, 1914, 250.
94. Welles, *Vineyard*, 2: 744.
95. FR, 1914, 257–58.
96. Link, *Wilson*, 516.
97. *FR*, 1915, 287.
98. Ibid., 279–80, 284.
99. Ibid., 297–99.
100. Ibid., 292.
101. Ibid., 290.
102. Ibid., 284.
103. Ibid., 292–93.
104. Ibid., 287.
105. Melvin M. Knight, *The Americans in Santo Domingo* (New York, 1928), 64.
106. Munro, *Intervention*, 302.
107. Knight, *Americans*, 68–69.
108. *FR*, 1915, 321–23.
109. Russell to Lansing, October 29, 1915, 839.00/1776.
110. Munro, *Intervention*, 303; *FR*, 1915, 331, 333–34.
111. Russell to Lansing, October 29, 1915.
112. *FR*, 1915, 339.
113. Munro, *Intervention*, 305.
114. Lansing to Wilson, November 25, 1915, 839.00/1776.
115. Munro, *Intervention*, 304.
116. Link, *Wilson*, 543.
117. Welles, *Vineyard*, 2:764.
118. Ibid., 766–67.
119. *FR*, 1916, 223.
120. Welles, *Vineyard*, 2: 769–70.
121. *FR*, 1916, 225.
122. Munro, *Intervention*, 306–7.
123. *FR*, 1916, 227; Welles, *Vineyard*, 2: 773.
124. Knight, *Americans*, 72.
125. *FR*, 1916, 227–30.
126. Latin American Division memorandum, June 3, 1916, 839.00/1897.
127. Lansing to Russell, June 3, 1916, 839.00/1847.
128. Russell to Lansing, June 4, 1916, 839.00/1851.
129. *FR*, 1916, 230–31.
130. Welles, *Vineyard*, 2: 776.
131. Russell to Lansing, August 8, 1916, 839.00/1913.
132. *FR*, 1916, 233.
133. Ibid., 252.

134. Ibid., 234; Knight, *Americans,* 76.

135. *FR,* 1916, 235.

136. Welles, *Vineyard,* 2: 782.

137. Knight, *Americans,* 77.

138. Welles, *Vineyard* 2: 788–89.

139. *FR,* 1916, 237, 254.

140. Ibid., 240.

141. Munro, *Intervention,* 311, 314.

142. Link, *Wilson,* 547.

143. October 27, 1916, 839.00/1941.

144. *FR,* 1916, 241–42.

145. Ibid., 247–49.

4 HAITI

1. Ludwell Lee Montague, *Haiti and the United States, 1714–1938* (Durham, N.C., 1940), 101–2, 148–51. *See also* Rayford L. Logan, *The Diplomatic Relations of the United States with Haiti, 1776–1891* (Chapel Hill, N.C. 1941).

2. Philip C. Jessup, *Elihu Root,* 2 vols. (New York, 1938), 1: 554.

3. Ibid., 555.

4. *Foreign Relations of the United States,* 1908, 435, 439 (hereafter cited as *FR*).

5. Dana G. Munro, *Intervention and Dollar Diplomacy in the Caribbean, 1900–1921* (Princeton, 1964), 245–55.

6. Quoted ibid., 251.

7. Ibid., 253; Hans Schmidt, *The United States Occupation of Haiti, 1915–1934* (New Brunswick, N.J., 1971), 39.

8. Munro, *Intervention,* 332.

9. Montague, *Haiti,* 18–19.

10. Antenor Firmin, quoted in H. P. Davis, *Black Democracy* (revised ed., New York, 1936), 244.

11. Montague, *Haiti,* 251.

12. *FR,* 1916, 312–13; Munro, *Intervention,* 326–27, 330.

13. Arthur S. Link, *Wilson: The Struggle for Neutrality, 1914–1915* (Princeton, 1960), 517.

14. Ibid., 518–19.

15. Memorandum for Bryan, February 3, 1914, 838.00/894.

16. Smith to Bryan, February 16, 1914, 838.00/857.

17. Link, *Wilson,* 520.

18. Munro, *Intervention,* 335.

19. Link, *Wilson,* 521–22.

20. Memoranda for Bryan, May 13, 14, 1914, 838.00/1667, 8.

21. *FR,* 1914, 346.

22. Munro, *Intervention,* 337–38; Link, *Wilson,* 522–23.

23. Munro, *Intervention,* 341.

24. Link, *Wilson,* 524.

25. U.S., Congress, Senate, *Hearings before a Select Committee on Haiti and Santo Domingo,* 67th Cong., 1st sess., 1921, pt. 1, 338 (hereafter cited as *Hearings*).

26. FR, 1914, 354–55.

27. Munro, *Intervention*, 342.

28. *FR,* 1914, 357–58.

29. Ibid., 359.

30. Ibid., 363–64, 367.

31. Ibid., 367, 376.

32. Ibid., 370–71.

33. Ibid., 372. *See also FR,* 1915, 500.

34. *FR,* 1916, 312.

35. *FR,* 1915, 462–63, 466.

36. *Hearings,* 290, 293.

37. Link, *Wilson,* 528.

38. *FR,* 1915, 464.

39. Ibid., 464, 466.

40. Link, *Wilson,* 529; Munro, *Intervention,* 347.

41. *FR,* 1915, 273.

42. Bryan to Sullivan, April 1, 1915, 838.00/1154.

43. Link, *Wilson,* 530–31.

44. Quoted in Selig Adler, "Bryan and Wilsonian Caribbean Penetration," *Hispanic American Historical Review* 20 (May, 1940): 225.

45. Link, *Wilson,* 531.

46. Ibid., 531–32.

47. *Hearings,* 306–7; *FR,* 1916, 317. A detailed account by the chargé d'affaires appears in *FR,* 1916, 313–17. See also Robert Debs Heinl, Jr. and Nancy Gordon Heinl, *Written in Blood: The Story of the Haitian People, 1492–1971* (Boston, 1978), 398–400.

48. *Hearings,* 307; FR, 1915, 475.

49. *Hearings,* 308–9; *FR,* 1915, 477–78. For detail on Caperton's activities, *see* David Healy, *Gunboat Diplomacy in the Wilson Era: The U.S. Navy in Haiti, 1915–1916* (Madison, Wis., 1976), Heinl and Heinl, *Written,* 400–14.

50. Healy, *Gunboat Diplomacy,* 55–57.

51. *Hearings,* 312; *FR,* 1915, 478.

52. Link, *Wilson,* 535, 535 n.

53. Welles to Hughes, April 17, 1922, 838.00/2006.

54. *FR, The Lansing Papers, 1914–1920,* 2: 164.

55. 838.00/1418; Link, *Wilson,* 536; Munro, *Intervention,* 353.

56. Lansing to Cone Johnson, August 10, 1915, 838.00/1418.

57. Memorandum by Boaz W. Long, August 5, 1915, 838.00/1426.

58. Undated memorandum, Latin American Division, apparently written in the summer of 1915. Initials appear to be BWL [Boaz W. Long], 838.00/1391.

59. *Hearings,* 313.

60. *FR,* 1915, 478–79.

61. *Hearings,* 315.

62. *FR,* 1915, 479.

63. *Hearings,* 316, 320.

64. Healy, *Gunboat Diplomacy,* 112.

65. *Hearings,* 321.

66. Ibid., 319; *see also* Healy, *Gunboat Diplomacy,* 99–100.

67. *Hearings*, 362.
68. Ibid., 317.
69. Munro, *Intervention*, 356.
70. *FR*, 1916, 319.
71. Montague, *Haiti*, 214.
72. *FR*, 1915, 431–33.
73. Ibid., 437.
74. Ibid., 436–38.
75. Ibid., 439; *Hearings*, 336.
76. *Hearings*, 333–35. This portion of the instruction is omitted in *FR*, 1915, 508–9.
77. Healy, *Gunboat Diplomacy*, 140.
78. *Hearings*, 369, 634.
79. Munro, *Intervention*, 359; *Hearings*, 347; *FR*, 1915, 484.
80. *Hearings*, 349–50; *FR*, 1915, 486.
81. *FR*, 1915, 442.
82. *Hearings*, 353.
83. Ibid., 387.
84. *FR*, 1915, 447.
85. *Hearings*, 381–82.
86. *FR*, 1915, 443.
87. Ibid., 445.
88. Ibid., 451, 455.
89. Ibid., 452.
90. Healy, *Gunboat Diplomacy*, 172–73.
91. *FR*, 1915, 457–58; *Hearings*, 394.
92. *Hearings*, 395.
93. Montague, *Haiti*, 223–24.

5 CUBA

1. Elting E. Morison, ed., *The Letters of Theodore Roosevelt*, 8 vols. (Cambridge, 1953), 6: 1137–38.
2. Knox to Jackson, May 11, 1910, 837.00/380.
3. Huntington Wilson to Taft, March 9, 1912, 837.00/777a.
4. Jackson to Knox, April 22, 1911, 837.00/473.
5. Jackson to Knox, May 10, 1911, 837.00/474.
6. Dana G. Munro, *Intervention and Dollar Diplomacy in the Caribbean, 1900–1921* (Princeton, 1964), 482.
7. *Foreign Relations of the United States*, 1912, 240–41 (hereafter cited as *FR*).
8. Ibid., 247.
9. Ibid., 248–50.
10. Ibid., 258–59.
11. Gonzales to Bryan, November 3, 1914, 837.00/1012.
12. Louis A. Pérez, Jr., *Intervention, Revolution, and Politics in Cuba, 1913–1921* (Pittsburgh, 1978), 12.
13. Ibid., 8–9, 13, 15.
14. Wright to Lansing, May 3, 1916, 837.00/1784.

15. Pérez, *Intervention,* 18.
16. Munro, *Intervention,* 490.
17. *FR,* 1917, 350, 352.
18. Pérez, *Intervention,* 23–29.
19. *FR,* 1919, 2: 7.
20. *FR,* 1917, 355–56.
21. Pérez, *Intervention,* 37–39; *FR,* 1917, 358.
22. Pérez, *Intervention,* 48–61.
23. *FR,* 1917, 374, 382.
24. Ibid., 377.
25. Pérez, *Intervention,* 77–80.
26. Ibid., 90.
27. Memorandum, June 25, 1919 and Phillips to Sen. Nugent, July 19, 1919, 837.00/1562.
28. *FR,* 1919, 2: 1, 80.
29. Leland Hamilton Jenks, *Our Cuban Colony* (New York, 1928), 186.
30. *FR,* 1919, 2: 5, 7–8.
31. Johnson to Polk, June 12, 1919, 837.51/339.
32. *FR,* 1919, 2: 42.
33. Ibid., 14–15.
34. Ibid., 74–75.
35. Ibid., 20, 56.
36. Ibid., 22.
37. Ibid., 78–79.
38. Ibid., 81–84.
39. Pérez, *Intervention,* 111–12.
40. Munro, *Intervention,* 508; Johnson to Polk, June 12, 1919.
41. JCD [James Clement Dunn] to Rowe, January 8, 1920, 837.00/1611. *FR,* 1920, 2:2.
42. Pérez, *Intervention,* 112–13, 137–38.
43. *FR,* 1920, 2: 4, 7.
44. Ibid., 9–10.
45. Ibid., 13–14.
46. Ibid., 18. Emphasis in original.
47. Munro, *Intervention,* 511, 513–14.
48. Memorandum, August 27, 1920, 837.00/1764.
49. Pérez, *Intervention,* 122–25.
50. Louis A. Pérez, Jr., *Army Politics in Cuba, 1898–1958* (Pittsburgh, 1976), 36–43.
51. *FR,* 1920, 2: 31–32.
52. Pérez, *Intervention,* 125–26.
53. Munro, *Intervention,* 517.
54. *FR,* 1920, 2: 40–41.
55. *World's Work* 41 (Spring 1922): 530–31.
56. *FR,* 1921, 1: 673.
57. *The Cabinet Diaries of Josephus Daniels* (Lincoln, Neb., 1963), 585.
58. *FR,* 1921, 1: 673, 683.

59. Ibid., 675.

60. Robert F. Smith, *The United States and Cuba: Business and Diplomacy, 1917–1960* (New York, 1960), 87; Dana G. Munro, *The United States and the Caribbean Republics, 1921–1933* (Princeton, 1974), 19–21.

61. *FR,* 1921, 1: 676–77.

62. Ibid., 681.

63. Ibid., 688.

64. Ibid., 690.

65. Ibid., 690, 692; 1922, 1: 1008.

66. *FR,* 1921, 1: 705–6, 714.

67. Ibid., 730.

68. Ibid., 708, 710.

69. Ibid., 704.

70. Jules Robert Benjamin, *The United States and Cuba: Hegemony and Dependent Development, 1880–1934* (Pittsburgh, 1977), 26–27.

71. *FR,* 1921, 1: 728–29.

72. Ibid., 743, 745.

73. Ibid., 772.

74. *FR,* 1922, 1: 1008, 1027.

75. Ibid., 1023; Munro, *Caribbean Republics,* 29.

76. *FR,* 1922, 1: 1020, 1024.

77. Memorandum No. 7, Crowder to Zayas, April 1922, 837.51/756.

78. Harry F. Guggenheim, *The United States and Cuba* (New York, 1934), 157.

79. *FR,* 1922, 1: 1025–27.

80. Ibid., 1031.

81. Quoted in Russell H. Fitzgibbon, *Cuba and the United States, 1900–1935* (Menasha, Wis., 1935), 177.

82. Charles E. Chapman, *A History of the Cuban Republic* (New York, 1927), 437; FR, 1922, 1: 1036–37, 1042.

83. *FR,* 1923, 1: 838–39.

84. Ibid., 842.

85. Munro, *Caribbean Republics,* 35.

86. *FR,* 1923, 1: 845–46.

87. Ibid., 847–48.

88. White to Phillips, October 3, 1923, 837.00/2373.

89. White to Grew, November 7, 1924, quoted in Smith, *US and Cuba,* 102.

90. Quoted in David A. Lockmiller, *Enoch H. Crowder: Soldier, Lawyer, and Statesman* (Columbia, Missouri, 1955), 244.

91. Chapman, *History,* 479.

92. Ibid., 483–89.

93. Francis White to Crowder, November 15, 1924, quoted in Lockmiller, *Crowder,* 246.

94. Quoted in Fitzgibbon, *Cuba and the US,* 185.

95. Pérez, *Army Politics,* 60–61.

96. *FR,* 1927, 2: 521–22.

97. Ibid., 527–28.

98. Luis E. Aguilar, *Cuba 1933: Prologue to Revolution* (Ithaca, 1972), 61, 66.

99. Smith, *US and Cuba,* 116; Bryce Wood, *The Making of the Good Neighbor Policy* (New York, 1961), 51; Crowder to Kellogg, April 16, 1927, 837.00/2646.

100. Memorandum, Scotten to Morgan, April 25, 1927, 837.00/2646.

101. *FR,* 1927, 2: 519.

102. Curtis to Kellogg, November 6, 1928, 839.00/2717.

103. Undated memorandum by Laurence Duggan, about December 1935, quoted in Wood, *Making,* 51.

104. *FR,* 1928, 2: 653–54.

105. *FR,* 1929, 2: 895–96.

106. JRC [J. Reuben Clark] memorandum for the secretary of state, April 1929, 837.00/2749.

107. Smith, *US and Cuba,* 134–35.

108. Benjamin, *US and Cuba,* 68; Guggenheim to Stimson, May 28, 1930, 837.00/2808.

109. Guggenheim, *US and Cuba,* 181–84.

110. *FR,* 1930, 2: 649–51.

111. Ibid., 657.

112. Guggenheim, *US and Cuba,* 231.

113. *FR,* 1930, 2: 663–65.

114. Munro, *Caribbean Republics,* 357.

115. *FR,* 1930, 2: 668.

116. Ibid., 670–71.

117. Ibid., 682–83.

118. *FR,* 1931, 2: 45.

119. Metzger to Stimson, February 5, 1931, 837.00/2989; February 20, 1931, 837.00/2990; March 26, 1931, 837.00/3016½.

120. *FR,* 1931, 2: 52–54.

121. Munro, *Caribbean Republics,* 363.

122. *FR,* 1931, 2: 61–63.

123. Ibid., 68.

124. Munro, *Caribbean Republics,* 365.

125. *New York Times,* August 15, 1931, 7.

126. *FR,* 1931, 2: 69.

127. Ibid , 71.

128. Guggenheim, *US and Cuba,* 232.

129. *FR,* 1931, 2: 70.

130. Ibid., 71–73.

131. Ibid., 73–75.

132. Ibid., 75–76.

133. Quoted in Smith, *US and Cuba,* 130.

134. R. Hart Phillips, *Cuba: Island of Paradox* (New York, 1959), 7.

135. *FR,* 1932, 5: 533–38.

136. Ibid., 542–43.

137. Ibid., 544–47.

138. Wood, *Making,* 57.

139. Memorandum by Francis White, October 27, 1932, 837.00/3382.

140. Ibid., January 25, 1933, 837.00/3431.

141. *FR*, 1933, 5: 555, 557.

142. Ibid., 562.

143. Ibid., 571–73.

144. Guggenheim, *US and Cuba*, 236–38; Smith, *US and Cuba*, 132.

145. Benjamin, *US and Cuba*, 86.

6 NICARAGUA

1. Dana G. Munro, *Intervention and Dollar Diplomacy in the Caribbean, 1900–1921* (Princeton, 1964), 406–7.

2. Wicker to Lansing, February 29, 1916, 817.00/2440.

3. Munro, *Intervention*, 407.

4. Jefferson to Lee, April 27, 1916, 817.00/2545.

5. Munro, *Intervention*, 408.

6. Wright memorandum, January 14, 1916, 817.00/2439. Discussed in George W. Baker, Jr., "The Wilson Administration and Nicaragua, 1913–1921," *The Americas* 22 (April 1966): 357–59.

7. Wright memorandum, February 28, 1916, 817.00/2435½; Munro, *Intervention*, 409–10.

8. Latin American Division memorandum, December 15, 1915, 817.00/2538.

9. Wilson to Lansing, April 2, 1916, 817.00/2444½.

10. Munro, *Intervention*, 410–11.

11. Jefferson to Department, October 16, 1916, 817.00/2526.

12. Munro, *Intervention*, 413.

13. Long to Lansing, November 11, 1916, 817.00/2525.

14. Report of Major Jesse I. Miller, 817.00/2760, 17.

15. Memorandum, Commander, Division 2, Pacific Fleet, March 20, 1918, 817.00/2583.

16. *Foreign Relations of the United States*, 1920, 3: 292 (hereafter cited as *FR*).

17. Munro, *Intervention*, 418. Munro was presumably one of the officers referred to. His account is based on recollection. See also Dana G. Munro, *The United States and the Caribbean Republics, 1921–1933* (Princeton, 1974), 161.

18. *FR*, 1920, 3: 294–96.

19. Ibid., 296.

20. Memorandum, Dominian to Welles, August 6, 1920, 817.00/2668.

21. Welles to the undersecretary, August 9, 1920, 817.00/2675.

22. *FR*, 1920, 3: 298–305.

23. Report of Major Jesse I. Miller, 817.00/2760, 148–49; Munro, *Intervention*, 422.

24. Davis to Tumulty, January 21, 1921, 817.00/2755.

25. *FR*, 1920, 3: 307.

26. Munro, *Caribbean Republics*, 163–64.

27. *FR*, 1923, 2: 606–7.

28. Mario Rodríguez, *Central America* (Englewood Cliffs, N.J., 1965), 123.

29. *FR*, 1921, 1: 161; Munro, *Caribbean Republics*, 119–21.

30. Munro, *Caribbean Republics*, 122.

31. Charles L. Stansifer, "Application of the Tobar Doctrine to Central America," *The Americas* 23 (January 1967): 262; Munro, *Caribbean Republics,* 125.

32. Marvin Goldwert, *The Constabulary in the Dominican Republic and Nicaragua* (Gainesville, Fla., 1962), 24.

33. *FR,* 1923, 2: 606-7.

34. Munro, *Caribbean Republics,* 168-70; Virginia L. Greer, "State Department Policy in Regard to the Nicaraguan Election of 1924," *Hispanic American Historical Review* 34 (November 1954): 457-58.

35. *FR,* 1924, 2: 506-7; Greer, "State Department Policy," 459-60.

36. Harold W. Dodds, "The United States and Nicaragua," *The Annals* 132 (July 1927): 138.

37. *FR,* 1924, 2: 509.

38. Ibid., 492; Munro, *Caribbean Republics,* 176.

39. Dodds, "United States and Nicaragua," 138.

40. Munro, *Caribbean Republics,* 178; Greer, "State Department Policy," 462.

41. *FR,* 1924, 2: 503.

42. Munro, *Caribbean Republics,* 180.

43. *FR,* 1925, 2: 619.

44. Ibid., 623.

45. Ibid., 627.

46. Ibid., 624-25.

47. Ibid., 629.

48. Ibid., 632.

49. Ibid., 634-35.

50. Greer, "State Department Policy," 465.

51. Calvin B. Carter, "Kentucky Feud in Nicaragua," *World's Work* 54 (July 1927): 317.

52. Harold Norman Denny, *Dollars for Bullets* (New York, 1929), 204-5.

53. Munro, *Caribbean Republics,* 188; Carter, "Kentucky Feud," 318, for a somewhat different account.

54. *FR,* 1925, 2: 638.

55. Carleton Beals, "Chamorro, the Strong Man of Nicaragua," *The Nation* 126 (April 18, 1928): 431.

56. Denny, *Dollars,* 209, 214.

57. Carter, "Kentucky Feud," 319; Richard Millett, *Guardians of the Dynasty* (Maryknoll, N.Y., 1977), 47; Goldwert, *Constabulary,* 27.

58. *FR,* 1925, 2: 641.

59. Ibid., 645.

60. Ibid., 643.

61. Ibid., 645.

62. Ibid., 644.

63. L. Ethan Ellis, *Frank B. Kellogg and American Foreign Relations, 1925-1929* (New Brunswick, N.J., 1961), 63.

64. Ibid., 255 n.

65. *FR,* 1926, 2: 780-81.

66. Eberhardt to Kellogg, March 8, 1926, 817.00/3511.

67. Eberhardt to Kellogg, April 26, 1926, 817.00/3570.

68. Dennis to Kellogg, June 9, 1926, 817.00/3611.

69. Kellogg to Dennis, June 12, 1926, 817.00/3616.

70. Dennis to Kellogg, June 17, 1926, 817.00/3665.

71. Dennis to Kellogg, June 10, 1926, 817.00/3617; 817.00/3637.

72. Dennis to Kellogg, June 26, 1926, 817.00/3682.

73. Dennis to Kellogg, July 10, 1926, 817.00/3688.

74. Grew to Lewis S. Gannett, June 26, 1926, 817.00/3651.

75. Dennis to Kellogg, June 25, 1926, 817.00/3649.

76. Denny, *Dollars,* 223; *FR,* 1926, 2: 787.

77. *FR,* 1926, 2: 789-91.

78. Munro, *Caribbean Republics,* 201-2.

79. *FR,* 1926, 2: 797, 800.

80. Munro, *Caribbean Republics,* 205-6; *FR,* 1926, 2: 800.

81. *FR,* 1926, 2: 804-5.

82. Lawrence Dennis, "Revolution, Recognition, and Intervention," *Foreign Affairs* 9 (January 1931): 213.

83. *The Nation* 132 (December 1, 1926): 547.

84. Ellis, *Kellogg,* 69. Henry L. Stimson claimed that Díaz "was not a part of the Chamorro conspiracy." *American Policy in Nicaragua* (New York, 1927), 30.

85. *FR,* 1926, 2: 804.

86. Ibid., 805-6.

87. Eberhardt to Kellogg, January 6, 1927, 817.00/4510.

88. *FR,* 1926, 2: 807.

89. Ibid., 808-9.

90. Dennis to Kellogg, November 1, 1926, 817.00/3763.

91. Lawrence Dennis, "What Price Good Neighbor?" *American Mercury* 45 (October 1938): 153, 158.

92. *FR,* 1926, 2: 809-10.

93. Ibid., 810-11.

94. Denny, *Dollars,* 243; *Congressional Record,* 69th Cong., 2d sess., 1646.

95. *FR,* 1926, 2: 812-13.

96. Ellis, *Kellogg,* 70.

97. Denny, *Dollars,* 264-65.

98. *FR,* 1926, 2: 819-20; Munro, *Caribbean Republics,* 212-13.

99. *FR,* 1926, 2: 822.

100. *FR,* 1927, 3: 285-86.

101. Ibid., 297-98.

102. Munro, *Caribbean Republics,* 216.

103. Quoted in Millett, *Guardians,* 52.

104. *Congressional Record,* 69th Cong., 2d sess., 1644-49.

105. *FR,* 1927, 3: 298.

106. Denny, *Dollars,* 273-75.

107. *FR,* 1927, 3: 305-6.

108. Ibid., 309.

109. Ibid., 311.

110. Denny, *Dollars,* 272.

111. Ibid., 279.

112. Quoted ibid., 288.

113. *FR*, 1927, 3: 472–75.

114. Ibid., 476–78.

115. Carroll Binder, "On the Nicaraguan Front," *New Republic* 16 (March 16, 1927), 88.

7 THE DOMINICAN REPUBLIC

1. Dana G. Munro, *Intervention and Dollar Diplomacy in the Caribbean, 1900–1921* (Princeton, 1964), 315–16.

2. *Foreign Relations of the United States*, 1917, 711 (hereafter cited as *FR*).

3. Melvin M. Knight, *The Americans in Santo Domingo* (New York, 1928), 89; Sumner Welles, *Naboth's Vineyard: The Dominican Republic, 1844–1924*, 2 vols. (New York, 1928), 2: 789.

4. *FR*, 1918, 387.

5. Welles, *Vineyard*, 2: 801 (the quote), 819, 827; Munro, *Intervention*, 320.

6. *FR*, 1919, 2: 157–61.

7. *FR*, 1920, 2: 134, 144.

8. *Hearings before a Select Committee on Haiti and Santo Domingo, United States Senate, 67th Cong., 1st sess. . . .* (Washington, 1921), 1: 94.

9. *FR*, 1917, 712.

10. Welles, *Vineyard*, 2: 804–10.

11. Quoted ibid., 820.

12. Ibid., 802, 818–19.

13. *FR*, 1919, 2: 100.

14. Ibid., 142, 144.

15. Welles, *Vineyard*, 2: 809.

16. Latin America Division memorandum, January 27, 1919, 839.00/2114.

17. *FR*, 1919, 2: 106–7, 113–16, 129.

18. Ibid., 121.

19. Ibid., 134.

20. Welles, *Vineyard*, 2: 822.

21. *FR*, 1919, 2: 136.

22. Memorandum, Judge Otto Schoenrich, December 11, 1919, 839.00/2247.

23. *FR*, 1919, 2: 139.

24. Welles, *Vineyard*, 2: 826.

25. Ibid., 827, 830; Munro, *Intervention*, 322–23.

26. *FR*, 1920, 2: 160.

27. Ibid., 163, 165.

28. Ibid., 171–73.

29. Ibid., 136. Daniel M. Smith, "Bainbridge Colby and the Good Neighbor Policy, 1920–1921," *Mississippi Valley Historical Review* 50 (June 1963): 59, 64. For an account of this period placing emphasis on public opinion, *see* Joseph Robert Juárez, "United States Withdrawal from Santo Domingo," *Hispanic American Historical Review* 42 (May 1962): 152–90.

30. *FR*, 1920, 2: 145, 148.

31. *FR*, 1921, 2: 829, 832.

8 HAITI

1. Proclamation of the treaty by the president of the United States, *Foreign Relations of the United States*, 1916, 328 (hereafter cited as *FR*).

2. U.S., Congress, Senate, *Hearings before a Select Committee on Haiti and Santo Domingo*, 67th Cong., 1st sess., 1921, pt. 1: 392 (hereafter cited as *Hearings*).

3. Ibid., 692.

4. *FR*, 1916, 355.

5. *FR*, 1919. 2: 333–34.

6. *Hearings*, 18.

7. Ibid., 115, 120.

8. Ibid., 89.

9. Dana G. Munro, *Intervention and Dollar Diplomacy in the Caribbean, 1900–1921* (Princeton, 1964), 365.

10. Colonel Cole in *Hearings*, 712.

11. *FR*, 1919, 2: 305–6.

12. *FR*, 1916, 320.

13. *Hearings*, 415.

14. Ibid., 720.

15. *FR*, 1920, 2: 804.

16. *Hearings*, 415.

17. Ibid., 24.

18. Ibid., 420.

19. Ibid., 23.

20. Ibid., 25.

21. *FR*, 1917, 802.

22. *Hearings*, 689.

23. Ibid., 690–91.

24. Ibid., 693.

25. Ibid., 696.

26. Ibid., 697.

27. Ibid., 698–99, 720.

28. Ibid., 701–2.

29. Munro, *Intervention*, 369; *Hearings*, 702–3.

30. *Hearings*, 536–37; Lowell Thomas, *Old Gimlet Eye: The Adventures of Smedley D. Butler as Told to Lowell Thomas* (New York, 1933), 213–17.

31. Thomas, *Gimlet Eye*, 218–22.

32. *Hearings*, 718.

33. H. P. Davis, *Black Democracy* (rev. ed., New York, 1936), 209–10.

34. Latin American Division memorandum (F. Mayer), January 3, 1921, 838.011/69.

35. Lansing to Blanchard, February 7, 1918, 838.011/42b.

36. *Hearings*, 566.

37. Blanchard to Lansing, May 29, 1918, 838.011/57.

38. Report of June 17, 1918, 838.00/64.

39. Latin American Division memorandum, June 21, 1918, 838.002/70; Mayer to Woolsey, August 7, 1918, 838.002/73.

40. *FR*, 1919, 2: 311.

41. Ibid., 312–26, quote at 316.

42. Ibid., 330.

43. Ibid., 331.

44. *FR*, 1915, 493–95; *Hearings*, 398.

45. James H. McCrocklin, *Garde d'Haiti, 1915–1934* (Annapolis, Md., 1956), 125. The quote is from Munro, *Intervention*, 372.

46. *FR*, 1919, II, 351–52.

47. Ibid., 337, 339.

48. *Hearings*, 600.

49. *FR*, 1919, 2: 304; 1920, 2: 761, 807.

50. *FR*, 1920, 2: 760.

51. Ibid., 771; Blanchard to Colby, August 20, 1920, 838.51/948.

52. *FR*, 1920, 2: 772, 775.

53. Memorandum, Office of Foreign Trade Adviser, August 11, 1920, 838.00/1666.

54. *FR*, 1920, 2: 785.

55. Ibid., 796.

56. Ibid., 799.

57. Ibid., 805–6.

58. Ibid., 811.

59. Munro, *Intervention*, 384.

60. Knapp to Colby, January 15, 1921, 838.00/1742.

61. *New York Times*, Aug. 31, 1920.

62. *FR*, 1921, 2: 193.

63. Ibid., 200.

64. Dana G. Munro, *The United States and the Caribbean Republics, 1921–1933* (Princeton, 1974), 76–77.

65. *FR*, 1921, 2: 201.

66. Hughes to Harding, September 3, 1921, 838.00/1788.

67. *FR*, 1921, 2: 202.

68. *Senate Report 794*, 67th Cong., 2d sess., 23.

69. Ibid., 23–24.

70. *Congressional Record*, 67th Cong., 2d sess., 8941.

71. Ibid., 8949.

72. Ibid., 8974.

73. Munro to Hughes, April 28, 1922, 838.00/1872.

74. The words quoted appear in *FR*, 1929, 3: 210. *See also* Arthur C. Millspaugh, *Haiti under American Control, 1915–1930* (Boston, 1931), 102.

75. Munro, *Caribbean Republics*, 84–85.

76. Memorandum by Russell, October 1, 1921, 838.00/1842.

77. *FR*, 1922, 2: 466.

78. Ibid., 465; *FR*, 1921, 2: 188.

79. *Annual Report of the High Commissioner*, 1926, quoted in Millspaugh, *Haiti*, 114.

80. Millspaugh, *Haiti*, 111. The quoted words are from *Annual Report of the High Commissioner*, 1928.

81. Raymond Leslie Buell, *The American Occupation of Haiti* (New York, 1929), 361; *Hearings*, 87, 571–72.

82. *FR*, 1922, 2: 465.

83. Arthur C. Millspaugh, "Our Haitian Problem," *Foreign Affairs* 7 (July 1929): 564.

84. Ludwell Lee Montague, *Haiti and the United States, 1714–1938* (Durham, N.C., 1940), 260 n.

85. Rayford L. Logan, quoted in Buell, *American Occupation,* 364.

86. Memorandum, Mayer to Stabler, July 19, 1918, 838.00/D25/5; Paul H. Douglas, "The American Occupation of Haiti," *Political Science Quarterly* 42 (June 1927): 86–87; Munro, *Caribbean Republics,* 86–87.

87. Robert Debs Heinl, Jr. and Nancy Gordon Heinl, *Written in Blood: The Story of the Haitian People, 1492–1971* (Boston, 1978), 476 n.

88. *FR,* 1922, 2: 469.

89. Millspaugh, *Haiti,* 107.

90. Munro, *Caribbean Republics,* 107.

91. *FR,* 1925, 2: 298, 303–4; Munro, *Caribbean Republics,* 108.

92. *FR,* 1925, 2: 307–8.

93. Douglas, "American Occupation," 257–58; Montague, *Haiti and the US,* 241.

94. *FR,* 1927, 3: 52.

95. Munro, *Caribbean Republics,* 113–14; *FR,* 1927, 3: 62–63.

96. Millspaugh, *Haiti,* 236–37.

97. *FR,* 1929, 3: 167–68.

98. Ibid., 172.

99. Munro, *Caribbean Republics,* 311.

100. Millspaugh, *Haiti,* 176.

9 THE DOMINICAN REPUBLIC

1. Dana G. Munro, *The United States and the Caribbean Republics, 1921–1933* (Princeton, 1974), 46.

2. *Foreign Relations of the United States,* 1920, 2: 835–37 (hereafter cited as *FR*).

3. Ibid., 838; Sumner Welles, *Naboth's Vineyard* (New York, 1928), 2: 849–50.

4. *FR,* 1921, 1: 839.

5. Ibid., 843.

6. Welles, *Vineyard,* 2: 851; Munro, *Caribbean Republics,* 48.

7. Welles, *Vineyard,* 2: 852.

8. *FR,* 1932, 2: 14–17.

9. Ibid., 13–14, 17.

10. Ibid., 18–19.

11. Welles, *Vineyard,* 2: 855.

12. *FR,* 1922, 2: 26; Welles, *Vineyard,* 2: 855–56.

13. *FR,* 1922, 2: 26–27; Munro, *Caribbean Republics,* 56.

14. *FR,* 1922, 2: 33–35.

15. Ibid., 38–39.

16. Welles, *Vineyard,* 2: 860–61.

17. *FR,* 1922, 2: 41, 45.

18. Ibid., 64–65, 68.

19. Welles, *Vineyard,* 2: 873, 878; *FR,* 1922, 2: 68.

20. Welles, *Vineyard,* 2: 884.

21. *FR*, 1923, 1: 894–95.
22. Ibid., 903.
23. Ibid., 906.
24. Ibid., 909–12.
25. *FR*, 1924, 1: 619–20.
26. Ibid., 621.
27. Ibid., 622; Welles, *Vineyard*, 2: 893.
28. Welles, *Vineyard*, 2: 895.
29. *FR*, 1924, 1: 626.
30. Welles, *Vineyard*, 2: 912.
31. Ibid., 810.
32. Ibid., 849.
33. *FR*, 1922, 1: 46.
34. *FR*, 1924, 1: 618.
35. Munro, *Caribbean Republics*, 65.
36. *FR*, 1922, 1: 646, 649.
37. Ibid., 679.

10 NICARAGUA

1. Henry L. Stimson, *American Policy in Nicaragua* (New York, 1927), 42.
2. L. Ethan Ellis, *Frank B. Kellogg and American Foreign Relations, 1925–1929* (New Brunswick, N.J., 1961), 73.
3. Richard Millett, *Guardians of the Dynasty* (Maryknoll, N.Y., 1977), 54.
4. Ibid.; *Foreign Relations of the United States*, 1927, 3: 321–22 (hereafter cited as *FR*).
5. *FR*, 1927, 3: 324.
6. Ibid., 325.
7. Stimson, *American Policy*, 69.
8. Harold Norman Denny, *Dollars for Bullets* (New York, 1929), 295.
9. Stimson, *American Policy*, 75.
10. Moncada to Huntington Wilson, November 21, 1916, 817.00/2155.
11. *FR*, 1927, 3: 316; Denny, *Dollars*, 292.
12. *FR*, 1927, 3: 327.
13. Ibid., 329.
14. Ibid., 330.
15. Joseph O. Baylen, "Sandino: Patriot or Bandit?" *Hispanic American Historical Review* 31 (August 1951): 398. *See also* Neill Macaulay, *The Sandino Affair* (Chicago, 1967).
16. *FR*, 1927, 3: 332, 335–41; Stimson, *American Policy*, 65–67.
17. Stimson, *American Policy*, 76.
18. Henry L. Stimson and McGeorge Bundy, *On Active Service in Peace and War* (New York, 1948), 114; *FR*, 1927, 3: 337.
19. Quoted in Richard N. Current, *Secretary Stimson: a Study in Statecraft* (New Brunswick, N.J., 1954), 95 n.
20. *FR*, 1927, 3: 331.
21. Stimson and Bundy, *Active Service*, 114.

22. Foreign Policy Association, *Information Service* 3 (January 20, 1928): 345–46.

23. Quoted in Elting E. Morison, *Turmoil and Tradition: A Study of the Life and Times of Henry L. Stimson* (Boston, 1960), 276.

24. *FR*, 1927, 3: 348.

25. Ibid., 339.

26. Stimson, *American Policy*, 60.

27. *FR*, 1927, 3: 348.

28. *FR*, 1928, 3: 430.

29. Letters of June 24 and September 23, 1927, quoted in William Kammann, "A Search for Stability: United States Diplomacy toward Nicaragua, 1925–1933," dissertation at Indiana University, 1962 (microfilm), 147 n.

30. *FR*, 1927, 3: 364; Dana G. Munro, *The United States and the Caribbean Republics, 1921–1933* (Princeton, 1974), 238. Munro provides a detailed account of efforts to maintain neutrality in a free election in which he was a central figure, 230–54.

31. *FR*, 1927, 3: 358, 367–68.

32. *New York Times*, October 26, 1927.

33. *FR*, 1927, 3: 373–74, 378.

34. Ibid., 375.

35. Ibid., 384–85.

36. Ibid., 397–98.

37. *FR*, 1928, 3: 450.

38. Ibid., 418–20.

39. Lawrence Dennis, "Revolution, Recognition, and Intervention," *Foreign Affairs* 9 (January 1931): 215.

40. *FR*, 1928, 3: 534.

41. Ibid., 525–26, 538–39.

42. Ibid., 536–37, 539.

43. Ellis, *Kellogg*, 84; *New York Times*, November 24, 1928.

44. *FR*, 1928, 3: 487.

45. Ibid., 489, 500–1.

46. Denny, *Dollars*, 376; H. W. Dodds, "American Supervision of the Nicaraguan Election," *Foreign Affairs* 7 (April 1929): 493, for the quote.

47. Denny, *Dollars*, 372–73.

48. Dodds, "Supervision," 488–96.

49. *FR*, 1928, 3: 515.

50. Ibid., 500, 511–12.

51. Department of State, *The United States and Nicaragua*, Latin American Series, no. 6, 92.

52. Denny, *Dollars*, 311; Stimson and Bundy, *Active Service*, 115.

53. Quoted in Denny, *Dollars*, 325.

54. *FR*, 1927, 3: 441–42.

55. Ibid., 444, 450.

56. Denny, *Dollars*, 323.

57. *FR*, 1928, 3: 588; Munro, *Caribbean Republics*, 252–53.

58. *FR*, 1927, 3: 437; Millett, *Guardians*, 70.

59. Marvin Goldwert, *The Constabulary in the Dominican Republic and Nicaragua* (Gainesville, Fla., 1962), 32–35.

60. *FR*, 1929, 3: 567.

61. Millett, *Guardians*, 109.

62. Ibid., 113–16.

63. *FR*, 1929, 3: 569.

64. Ibid., 575.

65. *FR*, 1930, 3: 677.

66. Ibid., 691.

67. Stimson and Bundy, *Active Service*, 183.

68. *FR*, 1930, 3: 677, 675.

69. Ibid., 684–85.

70. Ibid., 678.

71. Ibid., 686, 691.

72. *FR*, 1931, 2, 841–44.

73. Ibid., 808; Willard L. Beaulac, *Career Ambassador* (New York, 1951), 125.

74. *FR*, 1931, 2: 812.

75. Quoted in Stimson and Bundy, *Active Service*, 182.

76. Stimson to Coolidge, April 29, 1931, 817.00/7111A.

77. *FR*, 1932, 5: 854–56.

78. Ibid., 867–69.

79. Goldwert, *Constabulary*, 43. *See also* Millett, *Guardians*, 130.

80. *FR*, 1932, 5: 876–77.

81. Bryce Wood, *The Making of the Good Neighbor Policy* (New York, 1961), 138; Millett, *Guardians*, 135.

82. *FR*, 1929, 3: 605.

83. Raymond Leslie Buell, "Reconstruction in Nicaragua," Foreign Policy Association, *Information Service* 6 (December 24, 1930): 390.

84. *FR*, 1929, 3: 646; Munro, *Caribbean Republics*, 264–65.

85. *FR*, 1929, 3: 650.

86. *FR*, 1930, 3: 705.

87. Hanna to White, December 4, 1930, 817.00/6956.

88. *FR*, 1930, 3: 708.

89. 817.00/Woodward Election Commission/231 (Report of the Commission).

90. Beaulac to Stimson, December 24, 1931, 817.00/7282; White memorandum, December 31, 1931, 817.00/7286; Stimson Memorandum, January 11, 1932, 817.00/7292.

91. Beaulac to Stimson, January 30, 1932; Stimson to Beaulac, February 3, 1932. 817.00/7316.

92. *FR*, 1932, 5: 768–69.

93. Ibid., 779–80.

94. Ibid., 784.

95. Ibid., 789, 792; Dana G. Munro, "The Establishment of Peace in Nicaragua," *Foreign Affairs* 11 (July 1933): 701–2.

96. *FR*, 1932, 5: 796, 803–4; Commission report, cited.

97. Hanna to White, September 9, 1932, 817.00/7549.

98. *FR*, 1932, 5: 828.

99. Ibid., 832.

100. Ibid., 833–34, 839.

101. Ibid., 846, 837; Munro, "Establishment," 704.

102. Munro, "Establishment," 705.
103. *FR,* 1936, 5: 844.
104. *FR,* 1933, 5: 849.
105. Ibid., 850–51; 1934, 5: 542.

11 HAITI

1. *Foreign Relations of the United States,* 1929, 3: 180 (hereafter cited as *FR*).
2. Ibid., 182.
3. Ibid., 184 (the quote), 187–88.
4. Ibid., 191.
5. Ibid., 189.
6. Ibid., 193.
7. Ibid., 195; *Annual Report of the High Commissioner,* 1929 (Washington, 1930), 10.
8. *FR,* 1929, 3: 204–5.
9. Henry Prather Fletcher, "Quo Vadis, Haiti," *Foreign Affairs* 8 (July 1930): 533.
10. *FR,* 1930, 3: 217.
11. Fletcher, "Quo Vadis," 543.
12. *FR,* 1930, 3: 212–13.
13. Walter Johnson, *William Allen White's America* (New York, 1947), 417–19.
14. Ibid., 420, quoted from a letter to his son.
15. *FR,* 1930, 3: 225.
16. Ibid., 235.
17. Ibid., 227.
18. FR, 1930, 3: 198–99, 204.
19. Dana G. Munro, *The United States and the Caribbean Republics, 1921–1933* (Princeton, 1974), 315–16.
20. Ibid., 316.
21. *FR,* 1930, 3: 213–14, 238.
22. Ibid., 206.
23. Ibid., 248.
24. Memorandum of conversation with Colonel Cutts, May 7, 1930, 830.00/2813.
25. Department of State, *Press Releases,* no. 53, October 4, 1930, 225.
26. Munro, *Caribbean Republics,* 318.
27. *FR,* 1930, 3: 255.
28. Ibid., 257–58. Stimson noted that Munro thought it "vitally important that we should not leave Haiti." Diary entry, October 1, 1930 quoted in Wilfred Hardy Callcott, *The Western Hemisphere: Its Influence on United States Policies to the End of World War II* (Austin, Texas, 1968), 262 n.
29. *FR,* 1930, 3: 263–66, 271.
30. *FR,* 1931, 2: 424.
31. *FR,* 1932, 5: 630–31.
32. *FR,* 1931, 2: 427, 477.
33. Ibid., 427–33, 438–39; Munro, *Caribbean Republics,* 326–27.
34. *FR,* 1931, 2: 512.
35. Ibid., 522.

36. *FR*, 1932, 5: 639-40.

37. Ibid., 671.

38. Munro, *Caribbean Republics*, 339.

39. Raymond Leslie Buell, "The Caribbean Situation: Cuba and Haiti," *Foreign Policy Reports* 9 (June 21, 1933): 91; Ludwell Lee Montague, *Haiti and the United States* (Durham, N.C., 1940), 274.

40. *FR*, 1932, 5: 686-87.

41. Ibid., 683, 689, 692.

42. *FR*, 1933, 5: 699-700.

43. Ibid., 707-8; 711-12.

44. Ibid., 736.

45. Ibid., 745.

46. Ibid., 707.

47. Ibid., 737-38.

48. Ibid., 754.

49. Ibid., 764-65.

50. Ibid., 786, 771; 1934, 5: 344; 1935, 4: 725.

51. Ibid., 1935, 4: 725.

52. Ibid., 704.

53. Ibid., 707, 715.

54. Ibid., 718.

55. Montague, *Haiti*, 276.

12 CUBA

1. Franklin D. Roosevelt, "Our Foreign Policy: A Democratic View," *Foreign Affairs* 6 (July, 1928): 585, quoted in Jules Robert Benjamin, *The United States and Cuba: Hegemony and Dependent Development* (Pittsburgh, 1977), 78.

2. Quoted in Bryce Wood, *The Making of the Good Neighbor Policy* (New York, 1961), 60-61.

3. Benjamin, *US and Cuba*, 78.

4. Norman H. Davis, "Wanted: A Consistent Latin American Policy," *Foreign Affairs* 9 (July 1931): 549.

5. Ibid., 554.

6. Ibid., 558.

7. *Foreign Relations of the United States*, 1933, 5: 280, 282 (hereafter cited as *FR*).

8. Ibid., 283-85.

9. Sumner Welles, *The Time for Decision* (New York, 1944), 195.

10. *FR*, 1933, 5: 285-86.

11. Edgar B. Nixon, ed., *Franklin D. Roosevelt and Foreign Affairs*, 3 vols. (Cambridge, 1969), 1: 140-41. Welles's goals and methods are well discussed in Benjamin, *US and Cuba*, 93-95.

12. *FR*, 1933, 5: 288-89.

13. Ibid., 290.

14. Ibid., 297-98.

15. Ibid., 299.

16. Ibid., 303, 305.

17. Ibid., 311.

18. Ibid., 323-25.

19. Ibid., 329.

20. Ibid., 330; Hugh Thomas, *Cuba: The Pursuit of Freedom* (New York, 1971), 613.

21. *FR*, 1933, 5: 331-32.

22. Ibid., 333-35.

23. Benjamin, *US and Cuba*, 101.

24. *FR*, 1933, 5: 336.

25. Ibid., 337.

26. Ibid., 348.

27. Wood, *Making*, 63.

28. *FR*, 1933, 5: 340.

29. Ibid., 347.

30. Ibid., 342. Emphasis added by author.

31. Ibid., 339-40.

32. Ibid., 341-42.

33. Ibid., 343-44.

34. Benjamin, *US and Cuba*, 106.

35. Ibid., 352-53.

36. Ibid., 354.

37. Ibid., 357.

38. Irwin F. Gellman, *Roosevelt and Batista: Good Neighbor Diplomacy in Cuba, 1933-1945* (Albuquerque, N.M., 1973), 31; Welles, *Time*, 196; Benjamin, *US and Cuba*, 224-25.

39. Louis A. Pérez, Jr., *Army Politics in Cuba, 1898-1958* (Pittsburgh, 1976), 72-75.

40. *FR*, 1933, 5: 288.

41. Ibid., 359; Benjamin, *US and Cuba*, 109-10, 226.

42. R. Hart Phillips, *Cuba: Island of Paradox* (New York, 1959), 38-39.

43. *FR*, 1933, 5: 359; Wood, *Making*, 67.

44. *FR*, 1933, 5: 359.

45. Benjamin, *US and Cuba*, 111.

46. *FR*, 1933, 5: 366-67; Pérez, *Army Politics*, 80.

47. *FR*, 1933, 5: 364-67.

48. Ibid., 377-78.

49. Phillips, *Cuba*, 50.

50. Pérez, *Army Politics*, 80.

51. Phillips, *Cuba*, 53.

52. *FR*, 1933, 5: 367-68.

53. Ibid., 370.

54. Pérez, *Army Politics*, 82-83; Luis E. Aguilar, *Cuba 1933: Prologue to Revolution* (Ithaca, N.Y., 1972), 156, 161.

55. Fulgencio Batista, *Cuba Betrayed* (New York, 1962), 196-97.

56. *FR*, 1933, 5: 380.

57. Phillips, *Cuba*, 90-91.

58. *FR*, 1933, 5: 383. For Welles's attitude, *see also* Aguilar, *Cuba 1933*, 200-10.

59. *FR*, 1933, 5: 384; Wood, *Making*, 71.

60. *FR*, 1933, 5: 380.

61. Ibid., 385, 387–88.

62. Ibid., 387.

63. *The Memoirs of Cordell Hull*, 2 vols. (New York, 1948), 1: 314.

64. *FR*, 1933, 5: 389–90.

65. Ibid., 391–92.

66. Ibid., 396–98.

67. Ibid., 398.

68. Ibid., 394. For an account that emphasizes the noninterventionist views of Josephus Daniels, ambassador to Mexico, *see* E. David Cronon, "Interpreting the Good Neighbor Policy," *Hispanic American Historical Review* 39 (November 1959): 538–67.

69. *Memoirs*, 1: 315.

70. *FR*, 1933, 5: 402.

71. Ibid., 406–7; Wood, *Making*, 74. Wood's interpretation is different; it holds that Welles "probably intentionally pulled the trigger of the Platt Amendment by this usage, but the old blunderbuss did not go off, for Hull had changed the magic words."

72. *FR*, 1933, 5: 410.

73. Ibid., 417; Wood, *Making*, 75.

74. *FR*, 1933, 5: 447–48.

75. Ibid., 417–18.

76. Ibid., 423.

77. Ibid., 424.

78. Wood, *Making*, 82–83.

79. *FR*, 1933, 5: 430–31.

80. Ibid., 426, 428.

81. Ibid., 427.

82. Wood, *Making*, 77–80.

83. Quoted in ibid., 90.

84. *FR*, 1933, 5: 439–40.

85. Ibid., 440, 444.

86. Ibid., 445.

87. Pérez, *Army Politics*, 98.

88. *FR*, 1933, 5: 446–47.

89. Ibid., 451–52, 455.

90. Memorandum of telephone conversation, September 22, 1933, 837.00/39.

91. *FR*, 1933, 5: 457–59.

92. Ibid., 469–72.

93. Wood, *Making*, 89.

94. *FR*, 1933, 5: 472.

95. Memorandum of telephone conversation, October 5, 1933, 837.00/4173.

96. Welles, *Time*, 197.

97. *FR*, 1933, 5: 472–73.

98. Ibid., 474.

99. Ibid., 477, 482.

100. Benjamin, *US and Cuba*, 162–63.

101. *FR*, 1933, 5: 487–88.

102. Ibid., 490.

103. Welles, *Time*, 198–99.

104. Wood, *Making,* 85, 91; *FR,* 1934, 5: 95.

105. *FR,* 1933, 5: 515.

106. Benjamin, *US and Cuba,* 165.

107. *FR,* 1933, 5: 525.

108. Ibid., 535–36.

109. Ibid., 539.

110. Ibid., 541–42.

111. *FR,* 1934, 5: 95–96.

112. Benjamin, *US and Cuba,* 168.

113. Wood, *Making,* 100–2.

114. *FR,* 1934, 5: 97.

115. Ibid., 98.

116. Gellman, *Roosevelt and Batista,* 100–1.

117. *FR,* 1934, 5: 100.

118. Ibid., 101.

119. Ibid., 103–5.

120. Welles, *Time,* 199.

121. The quotes are from a letter of Sumner Welles, March 1, 1948, ibid., 185. For treaty text, *see* ibid., 182–83.

122. Gellman, *Roosevelt and Batista,* 110.

13 NICARAGUA

1. Bryce Wood, *The Making of the Good Neighbor Policy* (New York, 1961), 136–41. Richard Millett, *Guardians of the Dynasty* (Maryknoll, N.Y., 1977), 182–85.

2. *Foreign Relations of the United States,* 1934, 5: 527–28 (hereafter cited as *FR*).

3. Millett, *Guardians,* 160.

4. *FR,* 1934, 5: 535; Wood, *Making,* 141.

5. Neill Macaulay, *The Sandino Affair* (Chicago, 1967), 253.

6. *FR,* 1934, 5: 556.

7. Ibid., 535–39.

8. Ibid., 557.

9. Ibid., 562.

10. Ibid., 549–54.

11. *FR,* 1935, 4: 843, 845.

12. Ibid., 847–49, 851–53.

13. Ibid., 855.

14. Ibid., 869.

15. Ibid., 860.

16. Ibid., 631, 634.

17. Ibid., 865–66.

18. Ibid., 872–74.

19. Ibid., 877–78.

20. Ibid., 884.

21. Wood, *Making,* 144.

22. *FR,* 1935, 4: 873–74.

23. *FR,* 1936, 5: 135.

24. Ibid., 126–27.

25. Ibid., 127–28.

26. Ibid., 129–31, 135–36.

27. Lawrence Dennis, "Revolution, Recognition, and Intervention," *Foreign Affairs* 9 (January 1931): 204–9.

28. *FR,* 1936, 5: 136–48.

29. Ibid., 815–16.

30. Ibid., 817–19.

31. Ibid., 819–22.

32. Ibid., 826.

33. Ibid., 828–30.

34. Ibid., 835–38.

35. Ibid., 839.

36. Ibid., 841–42.

37. Ibid., 843.

38. Ibid., 844–47. The quote is at 847.

39. Ibid., 848–49.

40. Ibid., 852.

41. Marvin Goldwert, *The Constabulary in the Dominican Republic and Nicaragua* (Gainesville, Fla., 1962), 46.

42. *FR,* 1947, 8: 854, 871–72. The quote is at 872.

43. Paul E. Sigmund and Mary Speck, "Virtue's Reward: the United States and Somoza, 1933–1978," in *Latin America: Hearings before the Subcommittee on Western Hemisphere Affairs of the Committee on Foreign Relations,* 95th Cong., 2d sess., 1979, 204–18.

44. William M. LeoGrande, "The Revolution in Nicaragua: Another Cuba?" *Foreign Affairs* 58 (Fall 1979): 28–50.

14 HAITI

1. Sidney W. Mintz, "Introduction to the Second Edition," in James G. Leyburn, *The Haitian People* (New Haven, 1966), xii; Robert I. Rotberg, *Haiti: The Politics of Squalor* (Boston, 1971), 158–61, 171–75. For detail on Haitian politics *see also* Robert Debs Heinl, Jr. and Nancy Gordon Heinl, *Written in Blood: The Story of the Haitian People, 1492–1971* (Boston, 1978), 398–400.

2. Rotberg, *Haiti,* 179–86.

3. Mintz, "Introduction," xv; Robert Debs Heinl, Jr., "Are We Ready to Intervene in Haiti?" *The Reporter* 34 (June 2, 1966), 11: 27.

4. Mintz, "Introduction," xix.

5. Heinl, "Are We Ready?" 28.

6. Rotberg, *Haiti,* 215–16.

7. Mintz, "Introduction," xix.

8. John Bartlow Martin, *Overtaken by Events: The Dominican Crisis from the Fall of Trujillo to the Civil War* (Garden City, N.Y., 1966), 392. For details on Duvalier, *see* Rotberg, *Haiti,* 197–257.

9. Arthur M. Schlesinger, Jr., *A Thousand Days: John F. Kennedy in the White House* (Boston, 1965), 782; J. Lloyd Mecham, *A Survey of United States–Latin American Relations* (Boston, 1965), 279.

10. Heinl, "Are We Ready?" 27.

11. Martin, *Overtaken*, 444; Jerome Slater, *The OAS and United States Foreign Policy* (Columbus, Ohio, 1967), 231.

12. Slater, *OAS*, 221.

13. Ibid., 224–26.

14. Ibid., 232, 237 n.

15. *New York Times*, December 3, 1964.

16. Heinl, "Are We Ready?" 28; *New York Times*, November 20, 1966.

15 CUBA

1. Caffery to Hull, April 2, 1934, 837.00/4964, quoted in Bryce Wood, *The Making of the Good Neighbor Policy* (New York, 1961), 387.

2. Caffery to Hull, June 25, 1934, 837.00/5146; Louis A. Pérez, Jr., *Army Politics in Cuba, 1898–1958* (Pittsburgh, 1976), 102.

3. Caffery to Hull, April 9, 1934, 837.00/4982.

4. Caffery to Hull (for Welles), December 18, 1936, 837.00/7761.

5. Caffery to Hull, October 11, 1934, 837.00/5577, quoted in Wood, *Making*, 108.

6. *Foreign Relations of the United States*, 1935, 4, 476 (hereafter cited as *FR*).

7. *Problems of the New Cuba. Report of the Commission on Cuban Affairs* (New York, 1935), 496–97.

8. Latin American Division Memorandum, December 19, 1936, 837.00/7759.

9. Wood, *Making*, 114.

10. Caffery to Hull, December 16, 1936, 837.00/7759; Philip W. Bonsal, *Cuba, Castro, and the United States* (Pittsburgh, 1971), 274, 301.

11. Irwin F. Gellman, *Roosevelt and Batista: Good Neighbor Diplomacy in Cuba, 1933–1945* (Albuquerque, N. Mex., 1973), 163.

12. Ramon Eduardo Ruiz, *Cuba: The Making of a Revolution* (Amherst, Mass., 1968), 104–5; on the constitution of 1940 *see also* William Appleman Williams, *The United States, Cuba, and Castro* (New York, 1962), 62–66.

13. *FR*, 1940, 5: 742, 749.

14. Pérez, *Army Politics*, 119–20.

15. Gellman, *Roosevelt and Batista*, 210–11, 219–20.

16. John Edwin Fagg, *Cuba, Haiti, and the Dominican Republic* (Englewood Cliffs, N.J., 1965), 88.

17. Hugh Thomas, *Cuba: The Pursuit of Freedom* (New York, 1971), 947.

18. Earl E. T. Smith, *The Fourth Floor: An Account of the Castro Communist Revolution* (New York, 1962), 20; R. Hart Phillips, *Cuba: Island of Paradox* (New York, 1959), 324–25.

19. U.S., Congress, Senate, *Communist Threat to the United States through the Caribbean. Hearings before the Subcommittee to Investigate the Administration of the Internal Security Act and Other Internal Security Laws of the Committee on the Judiciary*, 86th Cong., 2d sess., 1960, pt. 9: 689, 693.

20. Smith, *Fourth Floor*, 21.

21. Ibid., 54–55.

22. Ibid., 66.

23. Ibid., 58–59, 71.

24. Ibid., 60.

25. Thomas, *Cuba*, 964.

26. Smith, *Fourth Floor*, 88.

27. Ibid., 48, 107; Pérez, *Army Politics*, 160–61.

28. Smith, *Fourth Floor*, 85; Cole Blasier, "The Elimination of United States Influence," Carmelo Mesa-Largo, ed. *Revolutionary Change in Cuba*, (Pittsburgh, 1971), 47.

29. Fulgencio Batista, *Cuba Betrayed* (New York, 1962), 42–43, 95.

30. Thomas, *Cuba*, 1014; Smith, *Fourth Floor*, 162.

31. *Hearings*, pt. 10, 739; Williams, *US, Cuba, and Castro*, 33–34.

32. Smith, *Fourth Floor*, 170.

33. Ibid., 173–74.

34. Ibid., 183.

35. Thomas, *Cuba*, 1025–26.

36. Philip W. Bonsal, *Cuba, Castro, and the United States* (Pittsburgh, 1971), 39.

37. Williams, *US, Cuba, and Castro*, 29; Thomas, *Cuba*, 1058–60.

38. Speech of December 1, 1961, quoted in Boris Goldenberg, *The Cuban Revolution and Latin America* (New York, 1965), 182.

39. Bonsal, *Cuba, Castro, and the US*, 39–42.

40. Theodore Draper, *Castro's Revolution: Myths and Realities* (New York, 1962), 158–67; Williams, *US, Cuba, and Castro*, 98–100.

41. Richard M. Nixon, *Six Crises* (Garden City, N.Y., 1962), 351–52.

42. Bonsal, *Cuba, Castro, and the US*, 72–76; for a contrasting interpretation, Williams, *US, Cuba, and Castro*, 127–29.

43. *Department of State Bulletin* 42 (February 15, 1960): 238; Bonsal, *Cuba, Castro, and the US*, 121–123.

44. Bonsal, *Cuba, Castro, and the US*, 135; United States policies are well analyzed in Cole Blasier, *The Hovering Giant: U.S. Responses to Revolutionary Change in Latin America* (Pittsburgh, 1976), 189–200.

45. Bonsal, *Cuba, Castro, and the US*, 149–50.

46. Karl E. Meyer and Tad Szulc, *The Cuban Invasion: The Chronicle of a Disaster* (New York, 1962), 63–62; Bonsal, *Cuba, Castro, and the US*, 151.

47. Jerome Slater, *The OAS and United States Foreign Policy* (Columbus, Ohio, 1967), 142–49. The quoted words are at 149.

48. Draper, *Castro's Revolution*, 82.

49. Nixon, *Six Crises*, 355; extensive quotations in Meyer and Szulc, *Cuban Invasion* 68–70. With regard to Guatemala, President Eisenhower is said to have remarked: "I'm prepared to take any steps to see that it succeeds. For if it succeeds it's the people of Guatemala throwing off the yoke of communism. If it fails, the Flag of the United States has failed." Quoted in Slater, *OAS*, 131.

50. Draper, *Castro's Revolution*, 71.

51. Meyer and Szulc, *Cuban Invasion*, 59.

52. Draper, *Castro's Revolution*, 94–95; Meyer and Szulc, *Cuban Invasion*, 92–94; Arthur M. Schlesinger, Jr., *A Thousand Days: John F. Kennedy in the White House* (Boston, 1965), 230–31.

53. Meyer and Szulc, *Cuban Invasion*, 95.

54. Ibid., 106.

55. Schlesinger, *Thousand Days*, 244.

56. Printed in Draper, *Castro's Revolution*, 92.

57. Schlesinger, *Thousand Days,* 261; Draper, *Castro's Revolution,* 92.

58. Schlesinger, *Thousand Days,* 244.

59. Ibid., 242.

60. Ibid., 247. *See also* Thomas, *Cuba,* 1302.

61. Detailed account of the viewpoint of the invading force is given in Haynes Johnson et al., *The Bay of Pigs: The Leaders' Story of Brigade 2506* (New York, 1964).

62. Schlesinger, *Thousand Days,* 238–39.

63. Ibid., 262, 264–65.

64. Ibid., 262.

65. Draper, *Castro's Revolution,* 102. *See also* Bonsal, *Cuba, Castro, and the US,* 185.

66. As implied by Schlesinger, *Thousand Days,* 287.

67. Meyer and Szulc, *Cuban Invasion,* 124.

68. *Department of State Bulletin* 44 (May 8, 1961): 659–60.

69. Robert F. Kennedy, *Thirteen Days: A Memoir of the Cuban Missile Crisis* (New York, 1969), 85.

70. Andrés Suárez, *Cuba: Castro and Communism, 1959–1966* (Cambridge, Mass., 1967), in foreword by Ernst Halperin, x–xi; Thomas, *Cuba,* Epilogue.

16 THE DOMINICAN REPUBLIC

1. *Foreign Relations of the United States,* 1930, 2: 716 (hereafter cited as *FR*).

2. Ibid., 1927, 2: 546–48.

3. Ibid., 552–54.

4. Robert D. Crassweller, *Trujillo: The Life and Times of a Caribbean Dictator* (New York, 1966), 59–60.

5. Ibid., 61–62.

6. *FR,* 1930, 2: 700.

7. Crassweller, *Trujillo,* 65–66.

8. *FR,* 1930, 2: 704.

9. Ibid., 714–15.

10. Ibid., 708 (the quotes), 717.

11. Ibid., 704.

12. Ibid., 718–19.

13. Crassweller, *Trujillo,* 68.

14. *FR,* 1930, 2: 723.

15. Ibid., 725–26. For Stimson's apparent acceptance of Trujillo, *see* diary entries quoted in Wilfred Hardy Callcott, *The Western Hemisphere: Its Influence on American Policies to the End of World War II* (Austin, Texas, 1968), 264.

16. Ellis O. Briggs, *Farewell to Foggy Bottom: Recollections of a Career Diplomat* (New York, 1964), 221.

17. Crassweller, *Trujillo,* 157–58, 213–14.

18. Briggs, *Farewell,* 221–25.

19. *FR,* 1944, 7: 1018. *See also FR,* 1945, 9: 981–82.

20. Ibid., 1022–23, 1025.

21. Crassweller, *Trujillo,* 214–15; *FR,* 1946, 11: 809–15.

22. *FR,* 1945, 9: 994.

23. Crassweller, *Trujillo,* 216; *FR,* 1947, 8: 635–48. For an analysis of United States policy, *see* G. Pope Atkins and Laman C. Wilson, *The United States and the Trujillo Regime* (New Brunswick, N.J., 1972).

24. Crassweller, *Trujillo,* 237–39; R. Hart Phillips, *Cuba: Island of Paradox* (New York, 1959), 242.

25. Crassweller, *Trujillo,* 241.

26. Jerome Slater, *The OAS and United States Foreign Policy* (Columbus, Ohio, 1967), 79.

27. Ibid., 94.

28. John C. Dreier, *The Organization of American States and the Hemisphere Crisis* (New York, 1962), 98.

29. Quoted in Slater, *OAS,* 186–87.

30. Ibid., 189.

31. Ibid., 191.

32. "Alleged Assassination Plots Involving Foreign Leaders," *Senate Report 465,* 94th Cong., 1st sess. (Washington, 1975), 192.

33. Ibid., 206, 209. Information on "The United States and the Assassination of Trujillo" is conveniently summarized in Piero Gleijeses, *The Dominican Crisis: the 1965 Constitutionalist Revolt and American Intervention* (Baltimore, 1978), Appendix I, 303–7.

34. John Bartlow Martin, *Overtaken by Events: The Dominican Crisis from the Fall of Trujillo to the Civil War* (New York, 1966), 46.

35. Slater, *OAS,* 195–96.

36. Ibid., 198.

37. Martin, *Overtaken,* 64–83. The quote is at 82.

38. Slater, *OAS,* 198–99.

39. Tad Szulc in the *New York Times,* November 20, 1961, for the quoted words. *See also* Tad Szulc, *Dominican Diary* (New York, 1965), 181–82; Dan Kurzman, *Santo Domingo: Revolt of the Damned* (New York, 1965), 53.

40. Slater, *OAS,* 205.

41. *New York Times,* January 20, 1962. For an elaboration on the role of the United States, *see* Abraham F. Lowenthal, "Foreign Aid as a Political Instrument: the Case of the Dominican Republic," in John D. Montgomery and Arthur Smithies, eds., *Public Policy* (Cambridge, Mass., 1965), 14: 145–46.

42. Juan Bosch, *The Unfinished Experiment: Democracy in the Dominican Republic* (New York, 1965), 6, 17–18.

43. Ibid., 20, 46–47.

44. Martin, *Overtaken. See also* Lowenthal, "Foreign Aid," 147–49.

45. Martin, *Overtaken,* 30.

46. Ibid., 713.

47. Amitai Etzioni, "Intervention for Progress in the Dominican Republic," in John D. Montgomery and Albert O. Hirschman, eds., *Public Policy* (Cambridge, Mass., 1968), 17: 304.

48. Martin, *Overtaken,* 88.

49. Ibid., 72, 131, 721.

50. Ibid., 93, 119.

51. Ibid., 92, 99–100.

52. Ibid., 122, 126.

53. Ibid., 48.

54. Ibid., 163, 171–72.

55. Howard J. Wiarda, *The Dominican Republic: Nation in Transition* (New York, 1969), 204–5.

56. Martin, *Overtaken*, 97.

57. Ibid., 114, 134.

58. Ibid., 156–61, 180, 192–96.

59. Ibid., 196.

60. Ibid., 210, 229–30.

61. Ibid., 209.

62. Ibid., 292.

63. Ibid., 226, 230.

64. Henry Wells, "The OAS and the Dominican Elections," *Orbis* 7 (Summer 1963): 150–63.

65. The comparison is made by Bosch himself. *Unfinished*, 82.

66. Martin, *Overtaken*, 344.

67. Ibid., 347, 479. *See also* Lowenthal, "Foreign Aid," 150.

68. Martin, *Overtaken*, 351, 369. A similar estimate of Bosch appears in Kurzman, *Santo Domingo*, 78–84.

69. Martin, *Overtaken*, 510.

70. Bosch, *Unfinished*, 162, 164.

71. Martin, *Overtaken*, 357–58, 486–87, 562–63.

72. Ibid., 389, 451, 457–58.

73. Ibid., 363, 369.

74. Bosch, *Unfinished*, 167–78; Ruth Sheriff, "Liberals in Wonderland," *Commonweal* 86 (May 5, 1967): 198–203.

75. Martin, *Overtaken*, 559.

76. Ibid., 485, 492, 722.

77. Etzioni, "Intervention," 303; Theodore Draper, *The Dominican Revolt: A Case Study in American Policy* (New York, 1968), 7.

78. William Everett Kane, *Civil Strife in Latin America: A Legal History of U.S. Involvement* (Baltimore, 1972), 185–86.

79. Martin, *Overtaken*, 521–22.

80. Ibid., 545–46.

81. Ibid., 722.

82. Kurzman, *Santo Domingo*, 103.

83. Martin, *Overtaken*, 565.

84. Ibid., 566.

85. Ibid., 570.

86. Ibid., 594, 601.

87. Quoted ibid., 601–2.

88. Ibid., 605–57.

89. Ibid., 630–31.

90. Abraham F. Lowenthal, *The Dominican Intervention* (Cambridge, Mass., 1972), 155.

91. Martin, *Overtaken*, 709.

92. Gleijeses, *Dominican Crisis,* 119–24.

93. Martin, *Overtaken,* 643; Lowenthal, *Intervention,* 40, 56; José A. Moreno, *Barrios in Arms: Revolution in Santo Domingo* (Pittsburgh, 1970), 115–17.

94. Martin, *Overtaken,* 664; Lowenthal, *Intervention,* 52–53, 55–56.

95. Jerome Slater, *Intervention and Negotiation: The United States and the Dominican Revolution* (New York, 1970), 20–27; Moreno, *Barrios,* 26.

96. Senator J. William Fulbright in *Congressional Record,* 89th Cong., 1st sess., September 15, 1965, 23856.

97. Lowenthal, *Intervention,* 71, 80.

98. Slater, *Intervention,* 24, 24 n.; Theodore Draper, "The Dominican Intervention Reconsidered," *Political Science Quarterly* 86 (March 1971) 6–9.

99. Cable of April 25, 1965, quoted in Draper, *Dominican Revolt,* 60–61.

100. Slater, *Intervention,* 26.

101. Lowenthal, *Intervention,* 77.

102. Ibid., 85.

103. Ibid., 80.

104. Gleijeses, *Dominican Crisis,* 242–43; Martin, *Overtaken,* 653–54.

105. As given in Szulc, *Diary,* 54. Phrasing differs slightly in the portion in Gleijeses, *Dominican Crisis,* 253.

106. *Congressional Record,* 89th Cong., 1st sess., September 17, 1965, 24242.

107. Martin, *Overtaken,* 656–57.

108. Lowenthal, *Intervention,* 104.

109. Slater, *Intervention,* 31; Lowenthal, *Intervention,* 137–38.

110. Martin considers that the claim of neutrality should have been dropped at an early stage. *Overtaken,* 707.

111. Ibid., 695.

112. Ibid., 661.

113. Bryant Wedge, "The Case Study of Student Political Violence: Brazil, 1964, and Dominican Republic, 1965," *World Politics* 21 (January 1969): 187, 187 n.; Slater, *Intervention,* 35–38; Moreno, *Barrios.*

114. Lowenthal, *Intervention,* 140–42.

115. Interview by Max Frankel, *New York Times,* May 9, 1965.

116. *Department of State Bulletin* 53 (November 8, 1965): 730–38, quote at 731.

117. Slater, *Intervention,* 48.

118. Ibid., 67–69.

119. Gleijeses, *Dominican Crisis,* 399.

120. Martin, *Overtaken,* 677.

121. Juan Bosch, "A Tale of Two Nations," *New Leader* 18 (June 21, 1965) 13: 2, 7; Draper, *Dominican Revolt,* 154–56; Martin, *Overtaken,* 679.

122. Martin, *Overtaken,* 678.

123. Ibid., 679.

124. Bosch, "Two Nations," 5.

125. Slater, *Intervention,* 63–64.

126. Martin, *Overtaken,* 681.

127. Ibid., 695; Draper, *Dominican Revolt,* 176.

128. Szulc, *Diary,* 215.

129. Slater, *Intervention,* 90–93.

130. Szulc, *Diary,* 255, 262–63, 286–87.

131. Jerome Slater, ''The Limits of Legitimization in International Organization: The Organization of American States and the Dominican Crisis,'' *International Organization* 23 (Winter 1969): 60–66.

132. Slater, *Intervention,* 134.

133. Ibid., 115–19.

134. Kurzman, *Santo Domingo,* 295.

135. Slater, *Intervention,* 144–62.

136. Ibid., 49, 163–67.

137. Ibid., 170–71.

138. Gleijeses, *Dominican Crisis,* 281.

139. Abraham Lowenthal, ''The Dominican Republic: The Politics of Chaos,'' in Arpad von Lazar and Robert R. Kaufman, eds., *Reform and Revolution: Readings in Latin American Politics* (Boston, 1959), 40. *See also* Robert D. Crassweller, *The Caribbean Community: Changing Societies and U.S. Policy* (New York, 1972), 76–81.

140. *Latin American Political Report* 12 (May 26, 1978): 158; ibid. (June 30, 1978): 199.

BIBLIOGRAPHY

GENERAL

Documents and Manuscripts

Congressional Record.
Department of State Archives.
Department of State *Bulletin.*
Department of State *Press Releases.*
Elihu Root Papers, Library of Congress, Washington, D.C.
Foreign Relations of the United States.
Hearings before a Select Committee of Haiti and Santo Domingo, United States Senate,,
    Sixty-Seventh Congress, First Session.... (Washington, D.C.: Government Print-
    ing Office, 1921).

Books

Baker, Ray Stannard. *Woodrow Wilson: Life and Letters.* 8 vols. Vol. 4, *President,*
    1913–14. London: Heinemann, 1932.
Bemis, Samuel Flagg. *The Latin American Policy of the United States.* New York:
    Harcourt, Brace, 1943.
Blasier, Cole. *The Hovering Giant: U.S. Responses to Revolutionary Change in Latin*
    America. Pittsburgh: University of Pittsburgh Press, 1976.
Callcott, Wilfred Hardy. *The Western Hemisphere: Its Influence on American Policies to*
    the End of World War II. Austin, Texas: University of Texas Press, 1968.
Crassweller, Robert D. *The Caribbean Community: Changing Societies and U.S. Policy.*
    New York: Praeger, 1972.
Daniels, Josephus. *The Cabinet Diaries of Josephus Daniels.* Lincoln, Neb.: University
    of Nebraska Press, 1963.
Ellis, L. Ethan. *Frank B. Kellogg and American Foreign Relations, 1925–1929.* New
    Brunswick, N.J.: Rutgers University Press, 1961.
Fagg, John Edwin. *Cuba, Haiti, and the Dominican Republic.* Englewood Cliffs, N.J.:
    Prentice-Hall, 1965.
Gellman, Irwin F. *Good Neighbor Diplomacy: United States Policies and Latin America,*
    1933–1945. Baltimore: Johns Hopkins, 1979.
Goldwert, Marvin. *The Constabulary in the Dominican Republic and Nicaragua.* Gaines-
    ville, Fla.: University of Florida Press, 1962.

Hill, Howard C. *Roosevelt and the Caribbean.* Chicago: University of Chicago Press, 1927.

Jessup, Philip C. *Elihu Root.* 2 vols. New York: Dodd, Mead, 1938.

Kane, William Everett. *Civil Strife in Latin America: A Legal History of U.S. Involvement.* Baltimore: Johns Hopkins, 1972.

Link, Arthur S. *Wilson: The Struggle for Neutrality, 1914–1915.* Princeton, N.J.: Princeton University Press, 1960.

Martin, John Bartlow. *U.S. Policy in the Caribbean.* Boulder, Colo.: University of Colorado Press, 1978.

Mecham, J. Lloyd. *A Survey of United States–Latin American Relations.* Boston: Houghton Mifflin, 1965.

Munro, Dana G. *Intervention and Dollar Diplomacy in the Caribbean, 1900–1921.* Princeton, N.J.: Princeton University Press, 1964.

————. *The United States and the Caribbean Area.* Boston: World Peace Foundation, 1934.

————. *The United States and the Caribbean Republics, 1921–1933.* Princeton: N.J.: Princeton University Press, 1974.

Perkins, Dexter. *The United States and the Caribbean.* Cambridge, Mass.: Harvard University Press, 1966.

Rippy, J. Fred. *The Caribbean Danger Zone.* New York: Putnam's, 1940.

Ronning, C. Neale. *Law and Politics in Inter-American Diplomacy.* New York: Wiley, 1963.

Schlesinger, Arthur M., Jr. *A Thousand Days: John F. Kennedy in the White House.* Boston: Houghton Mifflin, 1965.

Scholes, Walter V. and Marie V. Scholes. *The Foreign Policies of the Taft Administration.* Columbia, Mo: University of Missouri Press, 1970.

Slater, Jerome. *The OAS and United States Foreign Policy.* Columbus, Ohio: Ohio State University Press, 1967.

Thomas, Lowell. *Old Gimlet Eye: The Adventures of Smedley D. Butler as Told to Lowell Thomas.* New York: Farrar & Rinehart, 1933.

Tulchin, Joseph S. *The Aftermath of War: World War I and U.S. Policy toward Latin America.* New York: New York University Press, 1971.

Welles, Sumner. *The Time for Decision.* New York: Harper, 1944.

Wood, Bryce. *The Making of the Good Neighbor Policy.* New York: Columbia University Press, 1961.

Articles and Newspapers

Abrams, Richard M. "United States Intervention Abroad: The First Quarter Century." *American Historical Review* 59 (February 1979): 72–102.

Adler, Selig. "Bryan and Wilsonian Caribbean Penetration." *Hispanic American Historical Review* 20 (May 1940): 199–226.

Davis, Norman H. "Wanted: A Consistent Latin American Policy." *Foreign Affairs* 9 (July 1931): 547–68.

Plank, John. "The Caribbean: Intervention, When and How." *Foreign Affairs* 44 (October 1965): 37–48.

Smith, Daniel M. "Bainbridge Colby and the Good Neighbor Policy, 1920–1921." *Mississippi Valley Historical Review* 50 (June 1963): 56–78.

Wilson, Huntington. "The Relation of Government to Foreign Investment." *The Annals* 68 (November 1916): 298–311.

Wright, Theodore P., Jr. "Free Elections in the Latin American Policy of the United States." *Political Science Quarterly* 74 (March 1959): 89–112.

CUBA

Documents

Civil Report of General Leonard Wood for 1902. Baltimore: Government Printing Office, 1903.

Problems of the New Cuba: Report of the Commission on Cuban Affairs. New York: Foreign Policy Association, 1935.

"Report of William H. Taft, Secretary of War, and Robert Bacon, Assistant Secretary of State. . . ." Appendix E, Report of the Secretary of War. *House Document 2,* 59th Cong., 2d sess.

Books

Aguilar, Luis E. *Cuba 1933: Prologue to Revolution.* Ithaca, N.Y.: Cornell University Press, 1972.

Bacon, Robert, and James Brown Scott. *The Military and Colonial Policy of the United States: Addresses and Reports by Elihu Root.* Cambridge, Mass.: Harvard University Press, 1916.

Batista, Fulgencio. *Cuba Betrayed.* New York: Vantage, 1962.

Benjamin, Jules Robert. *The United States and Cuba: Hegemony and Dependent Development, 1880–1934.* Pittsburgh: University of Pittsburgh Press, 1977.

Blasier, Cole. "The Elimination of United States Influence." In *Revolutionary Change in Cuba* edited by Carmelo Mesa-Largo. Pittsburgh: University of Pittsburgh Press, 1971.

Bonsal, Philip W. *Cuba, Castro, and the United States.* Pittsburgh: University of Pittsburgh Press, 1971.

Chapman, Charles E. *A History of the Cuban Republic.* New York: Macmillan, 1927.

Domínguez, Jorge I. *Cuba: Order and Revolution.* Cambridge, Mass.: Harvard University Press, 1978.

Draper, Theodore. *Castro's Revolution: Myths and Realities.* New York: Praeger, 1962.

Fitzgibbon, Russell H. *Cuba and the United States, 1900–1935.* Menasha, Wis.: George Banta, 1935.

Gellman, Irwin F. *Roosevelt and Batista: Good Neighbor Diplomacy in Cuba, 1933–1945.* Albuquerque, N. Mex.: University of New Mexico Press, 1973.

Guggenheim, Harry F. *The United States and Cuba.* New York: Macmillan, 1934.

Hitchman, James H. *Leonard Wood and Cuban Independence, 1898–1902.* The Hague, Holland: Nijhoff, 1971.

Jenks, Leland Hamilton. *Our Cuban Colony.* New York: Vanguard, 1928.

Johnson, Haynes et al. *The Bay of Pigs: The Leaders' Story of Brigade 2506*. New York: Norton, 1964.

Healy, David F. *The United States in Cuba, 1898–1902*. Madison, Wis.: University of Wisconsin Press, 1963.

Lockmiller, David A. *Enoch H. Crowder: Soldier, Lawyer, and Statesman*. Columbia, Missouri: University of Missouri Press, 1955.

————. *Magoon in Cuba: A History of the Second Intervention, 1906–1909*. Chapel Hill, N.C.: University of North Carolina Press, 1938.

Meyer, Karl E. and Tad Szulc. *The Cuban Invasion: the Chronicle of a Disaster*. New York: Praeger, 1962.

Millett, Allan Reid. *The Politics of Intervention: The Military Occupation of Cuba, 1906–1909*. (Columbus, Ohio: Ohio State University Press, 1968.

Pérez, Louis A., Jr. *Army Politics in Cuba, 1898–1958*. Pittsburgh: University of Pittsburgh Press, 1976.

————. *Intervention, Revolution, and Politics in Cuba, 1913–1921*. Pittsburgh: University of Pittsburgh Press, 1978.

Phillips, R. Hart. *Cuba: Island of Paradox*. New York: McDowell, Obolensky, ca. 1959.

Rubens, Horatio S. *Liberty: The Story of Cuba*. New York: Brewer, Warren, Putnam, 1932.

Smith, Earl E. T. *The Fourth Floor: An Account of the Castro Communist Revolution*. New York: Random House, 1962.

Smith, Robert F. *The United States and Cuba: Business and Diplomacy, 1917–1960*. New York: Bookman Associates, 1960.

Thomas, Hugh. *Cuba: The Pursuit of Freedom*. New York: Harper & Row, 1971.

Williams, William Appleman. *The United States, Cuba, and Castro*. New York: Monthly Review, 1962.

Wyden, Peter. *Bay of Pigs: The Untold Story*. New York: Simon and Schuster, 1979.

Articles

Cronon, E. David. "Interpreting the Good Neighbor Policy: The Cuban Crisis of 1933." *Hispanic American Historical Review* 39 (November 1959): 538–67.

Cummins, Lejeune. "The Formulation of the 'Platt' Amendment." *The Americas* 23 (April 1967): 370–89.

Stokes, William S. "The 'Cuban Revolution' and the Presidential Elections of 1948." *Hispanic American Historical Review* 31 (February 1951): 37–79.

Wright, Theodore P., Jr. "United States Electoral Intervention in Cuba." *Inter-American Economic Affairs* 13 (Winter 1959): 50–71.

NICARAGUA

Books

Beaulac, Willard L. *Career Ambassador*. New York: Macmillan, 1951.

Cox, Isaac J. *Nicaragua and the United States, 1909–1927*. Boston: World Peace Foundation, 1927.

Denny, Harold Norman. *Dollars for Bullets*. New York: L. MacVeagh, 1929.

Kammann, William. *A Search for Stability: United States Diplomacy toward Nicaragua, 1925-1933*. South Bend, Ind.: University of Notre Dame Press, 1968.

Macaulay, Neill. *The Sandino Affair*. Chicago: Quadrangle Books, 1967.

Millett, Richard. *Guardians of the Dynasty*. Maryknoll, N.Y.: Orbis, 1977.

Munro, Dana G. *The Five Republics of Central America*. New York: Oxford University Press, 1918.

Rodríguez, Mario. *Central America*. Englewood Cliffs, N.J.: Prentice-Hall, 1965.

Stimson, Henry L. *American Policy in Nicaragua*. New York: Scribner's, 1927.

_____ and McGeorge Bundy. *On Active Service in Peace and War*. New York: Harper, 1948.

Articles

Baker, George W. Jr. "The Wilson Administration and Nicaragua, 1913-1921." *The Americas* 22 (April 1966): 339-76.

Baylen, Joseph O. "Sandino: Patriot or Bandit?" *Hispanic American Historical Review* 31 (August 1951): 394-419.

Binder, Carroll. "On the Nicaraguan Front." *New Republic* 56 (March 16, 1927): 87-90.

Buell, Raymond Leslie. "Reconstruction in Nicaragua." Foreign Policy Association, *Information Service 6* (December 24, 1930): 385-402.

Carter, Calvin B. "Kentucky Feud in Nicaragua." *World's Work* 54 (July 1927): 312-21.

Dennis, Lawrence. "Revolution, Recognition, and Intervention." *Foreign Affairs* 9 (January 1931): 204-21.

_____. "What Price Good Neighbor?" *American Mercury* 45 (October 1938): 150-58.

Dodds, H. W. "American Supervision of the Nicaraguan Election." *Foreign Affairs* 7 (April 1929): 488-96.

_____. "The United States and Nicaragua." *The Annals* 132 (July 1927): 134-41.

Greer, Virginia L. "State Department Policy in Regard to the Nicaraguan Election of 1924." *Hispanic American Historical Review* 34 (November 1954): 445-67.

Hale, William Bayard. "With the Knox Mission in Central America." *World's Work* 24 (June 1912): 179-93.

LeoGrande, William M. "The Revolution in Nicaragua: Another Cuba?" *Foreign Affairs* 58 (Fall 1979): 28-50.

Munro, Dana G. "The Establishment of Peace in Nicaragua." *Foreign Affairs* 11 (July 1933): 696-705.

Sigmund, Paul E. and Mary Speck. "Virtue's Reward: The United States and Somoza, 1933-1978." In *Latin America: Hearings before the Subcommittee on Western Hemisphere Affairs of the Committee on Foreign Relations, 95th Cong., 2d sess.* . . . (Washington, D.C.: Government Printing Office, 1979): 204-18.

Charles L. Stansifer. "Application of the Tobar Doctrine to Central America." *The Americas* 23 (January 1967): 251-72.

THE DOMINICAN REPUBLIC

Books

Atkins, G. Pope and Laman C. Wilson. *The United States and the Trujillo Regime*. New Brunswick, N.J.: Rutgers University Press, 1972.

Bosch, Juan. *The Unfinished Experiment: Democracy in the Dominican Republic.* New York: Praeger, 1965.

Briggs, Ellis O. *Farewell to Foggy Bottom: Recollections of a Career Diplomat.* New York: McKay, 1964.

Crassweller, Robert D. *Trujillo: The Life and Times of a Caribbean Dictator.* New York: Macmillan, 1966.

The Center for Strategic Studies. *Dominican Action 1965: Intervention or Cooperation?* Special Report Series: No. 2. Washington, D.C.: Georgetown University, 1966.

Draper, Theodore. *The Dominican Revolt: A Case Study in American Policy.* New York: Commentary, 1968.

Gleijeses, Piero. *The Dominican Crisis: The 1965 Constitutionalist Revolt and American Intervention.* Baltimore: Johns Hopkins, 1978.

Guitiérrez, Carlos Maria. *The Dominican Republic: Revolution and Repression.* New York: Monthly Review, 1972.

Knight, Melvin M. *The Americans in Santo Domingo.* New York: Vanguard, 1928.

Kurzman, Dan. *Santo Domingo: Revolt of the Damned.* New York: Putnam's, 1965.

Lowenthal, Abraham F. *The Dominican Intervention.* Cambridge, Mass.: Harvard University Press, 1972.

Martin, John Bartlow. *Overtaken by Events: The Dominican Crisis from the Fall of Trujillo to the Civil War.* New York: Doubleday, 1966.

Moreno, José A. *Barrios in Arms: Revolution in Santo Domingo.* Pittsburgh: University of Pittsburgh Press, 1970.

Schoenrich, Otto. *Santo Domingo: A Country with a Future.* New York: Macmillan, 1918.

Slater, Jerome. *Intervention and Negotiation: The United States and the Dominican Revolution.* New York: Harper & Row, 1970.

Szulc, Tad. *Dominican Diary.* New York: Dial Press, 1965.

Welles, Sumner. *Naboth's Vineyard: The Dominican Republic, 1844-1925.* 2 vols. New York: Payson & Clarke, 1928.

Wiarda, Howard J. *The Dominican Republic: Nation in Transition* New York: Praeger, 1969.

Articles

Bosch, Juan. "A Tale of Two Nations." *New Leader* 48 (June 21, 1965) 13: 3-7.

Draper, Theodore. "The Dominican Intervention Reconsidered." *Political Science Quarterly* 86 (May 1971): 1-36.

Etzioni, Amitai. "Intervention for Progress in the Dominican Republic." In *Public Policy* XVII, edited by John D. Montgomery and Albert O. Hirschman, 299-306. Cambridge, Mass: Harvard University Press, 1968.

Ferguson, Yale H. "The Dominican Intervention of 1965: Recent Interpretations." *International Organization* 27 (Autumn 1973): 517-48.

Juárez, Joseph Robert. "United States Withdrawal from the Dominican Republic." *Hispanic American Historical Review* 42 (May 1962): 152-90.

Lowenthal, Abraham. "Foreign Aid as a Political Instrument: The Case of the Dominican Republic." In *Public Policy* xiv, edited by John D. Montgomery and Arthur Smithies, 141-60. Cambridge, Mass.: Harvard University Press, 1965.

Rippy, J. Fred. "The Initiation of the Customs Receivership in the Dominican Republic." *Hispanic American Historical Review* 17 (November 1937): 419–57.

Sheriff, Ruth. "Liberals in Wonderland." *Commonweal* 86 (May 5, 1967): 198–203.

Slater, Jerome. "The Limits of Legitimization in International Organizations: The Organization of American States and the Dominican Crisis." *International Organization* 23 (Winter 1969): 48–72.

Wedge, Bryant. "The Case Study of Student Political Violence: Brazil, 1964, and Dominican Republic, 1965." *World Politics* 21 (January 1969): 183–206.

Wells, Henry. "The OAS and the Dominican Elections." *Orbis* 7 (Summer 1963): 150–63.

HAITI

Books

Buell, Raymond Leslie. *The American Occupation of Haiti.* New York: Foreign Policy Association, 1929.

Davis, H. P. *Black Democracy: The Story of Haiti.* New York: Dodge, 1936.

Healy, David. *Gunboat Diplomacy in the Wilson Era: The U.S. Navy in Haiti, 1915–1916.* Madison, Wis.: University of Wisconsin Press, 1976.

Heinl, Robert Debs, Jr. and Nancy Gordon Heinl. *Written in Blood: The Story of the Haitian People, 1492–1971.* Boston: Houghton Mifflin, 1978.

Johnson, Walter. *William Allan White's America.* New York: Holt, 1947.

Leyburn, James G. *The Haitian People.* New Haven, Conn.: Yale University Press, 1966.

Logan, Rayford L. *The Diplomatic Relations of the United States with Haiti, 1776–1891.* Chapel Hill, N.C.: University of North Carolina Press, 1941.

McCrocklin, James H. *Garde d'Haiti.* Annapolis, Md.: U.S. Naval Institute, 1956.

Millspaugh, Arthur C. *Haiti under American Control, 1915–1930.* Boston: World Peace Foundation, 1931.

Montague, Ludwell Lee. *Haiti and the United States, 1714–1938.* Durham, N.C.: Duke University Press, 1940.

Nicholls, David. *From Dessalines to Duvalier: Race, Colour, and National Independence in Haiti.* Cambridge, England: Cambridge University Press, 1979.

Rotberg, Robert I. *Haiti: The Politics of Squalor.* Boston: Houghton Mifflin, 1971.

Schmidt, Hans. *The United States Occupation of Haiti, 1915–1934.* New Brunswick, N.J.: Rutgers University Press, 1971.

Articles

Buell, Raymond Leslie. "The Caribbean Situation: Cuba and Haiti." *Foreign Policy Reports* 9 (July 1933): 82–92.

Douglas, Paul H. "The American Occupation of Haiti." *Political Science Quarterly* 42 (June 1927): 228–58; (September 1929): 368–96.

Fletcher, Henry Prather. "Quo Vadis, Haiti." *Foreign Affairs* 8 (July 1930): 533–48.

Heinl, Robert Debs. "Are We Ready to Intervene in Haiti?" *The Reporter* 34 (June 2, 1966) 11: 26–28.

Millspaugh, Arthur C. "Our Haitian Problem." *Foreign Affairs* 7 (July 1929): 556–70.

INDEX

About the Author

WHITNEY T. PERKINS is Professor of Political Science at Brown University. He is the author of *Denial of Empire: The United States and Its Dependencies*, and has contributed articles to such journals as *International Organization* and *Polity*.